Temporal Representation and Inference

Cognitive Science Series

Collections

1. Reasoning and Discourse Processes *T. Myers, K. Brown and B. McGonigle (eds), 1986*
2. New Directions in Semantics *E. Le Pore (ed.), 1987*
3. Language Perception and Production: Relationships between listening, speaking, reading and writing *A. Allport, D. G. MacKay, W. Prinz and E. Scheerer (eds), 1987*

Monographs

Agreement and Anaphora *P. Bosch, 1983*
Temporal Representation and Inference *B. Richards, I. Bethke, J. van der Does and J. Oberlander, 1989*

Temporal Representation and Inference

BARRY RICHARDS

Imperial College, London

INGE BETHKE

Centre for Cognitive Science, Edinburgh

JAAP VAN DER DOES

Department of Philosophy, Amsterdam

JON OBERLANDER

Centre for Cognitive Science, Edinburgh

ACADEMIC PRESS

Harcourt Brace Jovanovich, Publishers

London San Diego New York Berkeley Boston

Sydney Tokyo Toronto

ACADEMIC PRESS LIMITED
24/28 Oval Road,
LONDON NW1 7DX

U.S. Edition Published by

ACADEMIC PRESS INC.
San Diego, CA 92101

British Library Cataloguing in Publication Data
Richards, Barry, *1942–*
Temporal representation and inference. (Cognitive science series)
1. Natural language. Syntax. Logic
I. Title II. Series
415

ISBN 0-12-587770-6

Printed in Great Britain by St Edmundsbury Press Limited, Bury St Edmunds, Suffolk

Authors*

Barry Richards *University of London, Imperial College of Science, Technology and Medicine, Department of Computing, 180 Queen's Gate, London SW7 2BZ, England*

Inge Bethke *University of Edinburgh, Centre for Cognitive Science, 2 Buccleuch Place, Edinburgh EH8 9LW, Scotland*

Jaap van der Does *University of Amsterdam, Department of Philosophy, Nieuwe Doelenstraat 15, 1012 CP Amsterdam, The Netherlands*

Jon Oberlander *University of Edinburgh, Centre for Cognitive Science, 2 Buccleuch Place, Edinburgh EH8 9LW, Scotland*

* The list is in alphabetical order, except for the leading author.

Contents

Part Two: Formal Aspects

Notation

NOTATION	DESCRIPTION
$\models^-$	falsifies
$\models$	logical consequence
$\sqsubseteq$	partial order
$\vdash$	provable
$\models^+$	verifies
$\uparrow$	superinterval operator
$\downarrow$	subinterval operator
A	actual
A_V	referential operator
AF	atomic formulas
C_S	individual constants of sort s
F	Priorean future tense
F	formulas
$FUN_{\mathbf{s}}$	function symbols of sort **s**
$FUT_{(v,t)}$	future tense
$FUT_{(i)}$	future tense
G-operator	
$IB_\lambda(i)$	intervals before i (modulo λ)
$IA_\lambda(i)$	intervals after i (modulo λ)
$ISUB_\lambda(i)$	subintervals of i (modulo λ)
$ISUP_\lambda(i)$	superintervals of i (modulo λ)
K	day before
L	day after
L_{iq}	non-logical constants
$\Lambda_{\mathbf{p},<}$	sentence defining order < on partition **p**

$\mathbf{M}?\varphi$	φ undefined in $\mathbf{M}$
N	now
N_t	now
P	Priorean past tense
$PAST_{(v,w)}$	past tense
$PAST_{(i)}$	past tense
$PRES_{(v,w)}$	present tense
$PRES_{(i)}$	present tense
$REL_{\mathbf{s}}$	relation symbols of sort **s**
S	the set of sorts
$T^+(\mathbf{M})$	sentences verified in $\mathbf{M}$
$T^+(\mathbf{M},g)$	formulas verified in $\mathbf{M}$ under g
$T^-(\mathbf{M})$	sentences falsified in $\mathbf{M}$
$T^-(\mathbf{M},g)$	formulas falsified in $\mathbf{M}$ under g
$T^?(\mathbf{M})$	sentences undefined in $\mathbf{M}$
$T^?(\mathbf{M},g)$	formulas undefined in $\mathbf{M}$ under g
T_s	terms of sort s
T	tomorrow
T_t	tomorrow
VAR_s	variables of sort s
Y	yesterday
Y_t	yesterday
$Y[X_1,\ldots,X_n]$	set application as a notational device

Introduction

This book presents a new perspective on temporal representation and inference.[1] It gathers together a selection of papers on the temporal system IQ, which is an interval-based framework of a somewhat distinctive sort. IQ was originally designed to treat temporal phenomena in natural language, but its special technical resources have since been independently studied and applied in other areas, in particular, to temporal databases and certain aspects of meta-level programming.

The IQ perspective is based on the premise that indexical reference is central to the interpretation of temporal expressions in natural language. This assumption is rendered explicitly in IQ where there is a special relation between indexicality and temporal quantification, hence the name 'IQ'. The particular technical formulation makes it possible to treat a wide variety of temporal phenomena, among them the tenses (*past*, *present* and *future*), frequency adverbs (*always* and *exactly twice*), indexicals (*now* and *tomorrow*) and dates (*on 31st August 1988*). IQ is unusual, if not unique, in having the capacity to treat the interaction of these different kinds of expressions. When they occur in the same sentence, IQ can capture their semantic connections, thereby revealing insights which would not otherwise emerge.

Of the distinctive features of IQ the treatment of tenses is perhaps the most fundamental. The tenses of IQ are similar to Priorean tenses in that they involve quantification over time; but they are non-Priorean in that they also invoke reference to time. The form of such reference is essentially indexical, and its import is not unlike the indexicals of Kaplan (1977). It is interesting

1 The research reported in part II of this book was supported by a grant from SERC (Alvey), 'A Pure Logic Language: Foundations and Theoretical Aspects', GR/D59335.

that Kaplan does not analyze tense as in IQ; his account is purely Priorean. The difference has rather 'dramatic' consequences, some of which we shall discuss.

While IQ is an interval based theory, it takes a somewhat non-standard approach to certain semantic matters. In IQ an individual will be said to have a property for an interval only if that individual has the property for all its subintervals. Such a view is said to be homogeneous, in contrast to the heterogeneous position of Cresswell (1977) and Dowty (1979). They contend that an individual can have a property for an interval even though it does not have the property for all its subintervals. We shall not debate the competing metaphysical claims of these views, nor their relative technical strengths. Indeed we shall not directly compare them at all. Our aim is rather to explore comparison a useful exercise. This is taken up in Lascarides (1988) where the two views are compared with respect to certain puzzles about the progressive. From this study it would appear that homogeneity may be more than a distinctive aspect of IQ; it may be an essential feature of the formal semantics.

The original version of IQ was presented in 1984 at a conference on the work of Donald Davidson.[2] Since then, its assumptions and ramifications have gradually been explored, reflecting two distinct but related aspects of enquiry. The first has been directed towards the semantics of natural language, where the aim has been to extend the coverage of the theory and probe its philosophical foundations. The second has been concerned with more technical issues and their relation to logic programming. Here the horizons are just beginning to open up. The application of IQ to temporal databases suggests a method of approaching the semantics of some meta-level predicates in PROLOG. Some meta-predicates can, it seems, be regarded as modal operators. For such cases IQ offers a new perspective on the relation between modal databases and reasoning. It allows reasoning from modal databases to be approached in an efficient way through its model theory.

---

2 This appeared in Richards (1986) and is here reprinted with some modifications as Chapter 1. The permission of Basil Blackwell is gratefully acknowledged

Whatever the results of these and other applications, however, IQ would seem to be a rich and stable environment in which to seek logical results. This emerges in the later chapters and in Blackburn (1989), which presents a number of new theorems and conjectures.

To provide an overview of the book we now outline the main themes of each of the chapters, except for Chapter 1. There are two reasons for reprinting it here. First, it is the paper from which the others spring; each one develops an aspect of the system first adumbrated there. Second, there are several aspects of the system which are not further explored in this volume; an awareness of some of these may help to illuminate the significance of those aspects which are explored. The reader may, in any case, wish to have a more comprehensive picture of IQ than is provided elsewhere in the book. It should be noted, finally, that the chapters appear in the order in which they were written.

Chapter 2. Indexicals: Bound and Unbound

The temporal indexicals traditionally studied by logicians tend to occur in sentences such as (i). But there are other sentences such as (ii) in which they appear to serve a different function:

(i) It will soon be the case that all that is *now* beautiful is faded.

(ii) Max always said that he would be rich *tomorrow*.

There are two interpretations of (ii); in the first, there is a specific date—the day after the day on which (ii) is uttered—which Max is reported to have looked forward to; in the second (the preferred reading), Max always looked forward to the day after the day of *his* speaking. These two types of indexicals we call *unbound* and *bound*.

Unbound temporal indexicals are taken to be similar to tenses in invoking reference to speech time. In contrast, bound indexicals do not refer to speech time; they are bound to some other linguistic referring expression. The basic aim of the chapter is to show that these two kinds of indexicals can be systematically related. By using IQ's parameters in the representation of unbound indexicals, the bound indexicals can be 'derived' from them by applying the deparametrizing G-operator.

In showing how to represent the indexical in (ii), we develop an account of indirect speech reports in IQ. There is an interesting contrast between sentence (ii) and the following sentence:

(iii) Max always said that he will be rich tomorrow.

Whereas (ii) has two readings, (iii) has only one, and it is just the non-preferred reading of (ii). We will argue that the *will* of the subordinate clause in (iii) is still related to speech time in a way the *would* of (ii) is not, and go on to explore ways of representing this in a minimally altered IQ. The solution arrived at is an alternative to the one developed more thoroughly in Chapter 4, and can be fruitfully compared with it.

Chapter 3. Two Theories of Indexicals

There are two different, though related, approaches to temporal indexicality. One is represented in Kaplan (1979), and the other in the system IQ. To explore the difference, we contrast our approach with Kaplan's Logic of Demonstratives. For the sake of comparison, both approaches may be cast as 'double-indexing' theories, following Kamp (1971).

For Kaplan, a formula containing a tense or indexical will be evaluated with respect to a pair consisting of a context index and a circumstance index. The former is, minimally, a pair of the world and time of the context of speech; the latter is a pair of the world and time of the circumstances of evaluation. Even in the case of formulae containing indexicals, there need be no relationship whatsoever between these two indices. In contrast, if we construe IQ as evaluating its formulae with respect to context-circumstance pairs, the truth value of a formula will depend on a certain relation holding between the two indices. In other words, IQ really only uses a single index, and the range of circumstances relevant to truth is completely determined by the context index.

Looking at the propositions denoted by the formulae of the respective systems, the *effect* of this difference can be made clear. Given an indexical utterance, the systems will assign it rather different propositions. In both cases, the proposition will be a function from circumstances to truth values. In LD, the proposition may go to true at *many* circumstances. In IQ, the proposition will go to true at only *one* circumstance, at most, and that will be the one which stands in the appropriate relation to the context of speech. We express this as follows: a proposition which happens to go to true at every circumstance is *eternal*. LD's temporal operators leave eternal propositions eternal; IQ's operators turn eternal propositions into non-eternal ones. So we call LD's operators *eternity-preserving* and IQ's *eternity-disturbing*.

We go on to suggest that natural language tense disturbs eternity, rather than preserves it. We show how IQ's disturbing view of indexicality captures the oddity of sentences such as (i), for which there is no occasion of utterance at which they can be true.

(i) The Prime Minister will leave Britain yesterday.

We show that an eternity-preserving view of indexicality cannot explain (i)'s oddity in the same way.

Chapter 4. Subordinate Tenses

From the point of view of natural language one of the more interesting aspects of IQ is the perspective it offers on subordinate tenses. We shall consider two kinds of subordinate tenses, viz. those in relative clauses of subject noun-phrases, as in

(i) Someone who *ate* an apple will regret it.

and those in oblique contexts, such as

(ii) Adam will say that someone *ate* an apple.

The semantic relation between the past and future tenses in these two sentences seems clear enough. In (i) the tenses are independent; neither has scope over the other. And in (ii) the future tense in the main clause has scope over the past tense in the subordinate clause. The question is whether these relations are maintained for all pairs of tenses. It is arguable that the tenses in this sentence do not have the same relation as those in (i):

(iii) Someone who ate an apple would regret it.

Here *would* is naturally interpreted as falling within the scope of *ate*. Since (i) and (iii) share the same basic structure, one wonders how the difference can be explained. A similar question arises in the case of (ii). Consider this sentence.

(iv) Adam said that someone will eat an apple.

Here the tenses can only be interpreted as independent, neither having scope over the other. Again one wonders how this can be accounted for, given the subordinate relation of the tenses in (ii).

IQ yields an answer to such questions in its analysis of tense; IQ tenses have a structure which can be used to explain scope relations which are beyond the reach of other theories. Unfortunately, there seem to be cases which IQ cannot explain, even though it can capture their semantic content. In fact, the phenomena seem so complex as to defy any general structural account. This presents a non-trivial challenge to natural language processing systems which approach semantics via syntax. In the circumstance, IQ may help to indicate why some people believe that semantics has a certain autonomy.

Chapter 5. Temporal Connection

Examples of temporal connection have been considered by many who are interested in natural language understanding systems. But curiously, the examples almost never involved temporal quantifiers, such as in the following case.

(i) Harry had a headache five times last week.
Twice he took some aspirin and it went away.

One reading of this discourse is given by the paraphrase, of the five times Harry had a headache last week he took aspirin twice and his heachache went away. We shall attempt to explain how this interpretation arises from the logical forms of the sentences involved. The key, as we see it, lies in a certain 'context sensitivity' of the temporal quantifiers, a feature which we shall characterize formally. Although our proposals are speculative, they serve to indicate the complexity of the problem under investigation. They may even be seen to highlight the richness of the IQ framework, which may be unique in having something to say about such phenomena.

Chapter 6. The Temporal Logic IQ

In Chapter 1 we sketched a formal system which offers a new and integrated perspective on a wide range of temporal phenomena. The main concern there was the logical form of temporal statements, i.e. their logical form in the system IQ. Here the focus turns to IQ itself, specifically on defining a suitable logic. We provide a precise formalization of IQ, thereby distinguishing the set of valid formulas. The semantics is an extension of Kleene's strong three-valued logic for predicate logic, and the valid formulas are defined as those which can never be false. As we mentioned above, the tense operators in IQ are not strictly Priorean. They are indexed in a way that involves reference to time. The Priorean tenses, however, can be 'recovered' in IQ with the help of a special operator called G. This functions to bind the indices of IQ tenses. In Chapter 9 it is shown how to use G to define the Priorean tenses. Here we pin down the semantic status of G by proving a 'Skolemization' theorem for it; it is shown that G can be eliminated from IQ without loss of expressiveness. This is not to imply that G ought to be eliminated; it plays a useful rôle in IQ, one that is not evident in the Skolem theory.

Chapter 7. Temporal Databases: An IQ Approach

The main issue in this chapter is how temporal databases are to be structured and queried. One might reasonably ask, for example, whether temporal databases should contain tensed statements. We suggest that tenses can serve no useful function in storing information but they can be very useful in retrieving it. Kowalski and Sergot, in contrast, find tenses wholly redundant; this at least is the upshot of their Event Calculus, where tenses are analyzed away. In the Event Calculus temporal information is represented in terms of an ontology of events and states; intervals of time are derived entities and are unavailable for reference. This is not the case in our approach, called IQ-Prolog, where intervals are explicitly represented in just the way they are in IQ itself. Indeed, IQ-Prolog will be shown to approximate the expressive power of the Horn clause fragment of IQ. In proving this we shall reveal that the temporal meta-predicates of IQ-Prolog can be interpreted as modal operators. This would suggest, we speculate, a general strategy for dealing with meta-predicates, although we do not pursue the idea further.

Chapter 8. On IQ^{int} and Related Systems

In the system IQ intervals are defined from points. But to facilitate the comparison of our work with that of Kowalski and Sergot, and Allen and Hayes, it is worth studying an interval-based variant of IQ, viz. IQ^{int}. In this chapter we provide such a system and give an axiom system which is sound and complete with respect to its semantics. The completeness proof will make use of a notion of logical consequence which, although defined with respect to a partial environment, coincides with classical consequence. We also prove soundness and completeness results for extensions similar to those of IQ^E defined in Chapter 7. This chapter can also be viewed as an introduction to the way downward closed sets (Hintikka sets) are used in a partial setting.

Chapter 9. Indexed Operators and Completeness

IQ's origins lie in the semantics of natural language where rich and expressive formal systems are commonly used. From a logical point of view, however, it is useful to focus on the propositional part of IQ, if only to clarifying IQ's essential properties.

This chapter begins with a description of the syntax and semantics of IQ^π. Stricly speaking, IQ^π is not IQ's propositional fragment but rather a bimodal extension thereof. In this extension we eliminate some asymmetries between the syntax and semantics of the original formulation. The semantics of IQ is based on interval structures which carry two relations, viz. 'is before' and 'is a subinterval of'. In IQ's syntax, however, there are operators which quantify over the former, but none which quantify over the latter. To remove this limitation we add two operators $\uparrow$ and $\downarrow$ which function like the familiar F and P except for the fact that they quantify over the subinterval relation instead of the relation 'is before'. That these operators are not indexed points to another minor deviation from the original approach. As well as the Priorean F and P and the already mentioned $\uparrow$ and $\downarrow$, we use only one indexed operator, viz. A_V. We shall show that IQ^π is powerful enough to define IQ's original indexed tense operators, and also to define all the 'simple', non-quantificational operators defined in Chapter 1.

In Chapter 7 the relation between IQ and its implementation in PROLOG, viz. IQ-Prolog, is given via an intermediate language IQ^E. In section 2 we argue that in this process the distinctive feature of IQ's operators is lost. This discussion is followed by a program which directly implements IQ into PROLOG. A procedural completeness result is given stating that the procedures used are correct and complete with respect to their intended meaning.

We begin the final section with a discussion of the notion of logical consequence used. Next we note and remove another asymmetry between IQ's syntax and semantics. The original languages only allowed constants, parameters and variables as interval terms. But such structureless terms cannot syntactically capture the fact that intervals in a model are characterized by means of their endpoints. Once we have remedied this limitation, we shall prove a completeness result as regards IQ^π-models which are induced by a finite total order.

BARRY RICHARDS
INGE BETHKE
JAAP VAN DER DOES
JON OBERLANDER

Acknowledgements

This book would have been very different had we not had the benifit of lenghty discussions with members of the Tense and Discourse Workshop at the Centre for Cognitive Science and with many other colleagues. In particular we would like to express our gratitude to: Johan van Benthem, Patrick Blackburn, Kit Fine, Dov Gabbay, Dick de Jongh, Ewan Klein,

Marcus Kracht, Alex Lascarides, David McCarty, Marc Moens, Dana Scott, Mark Steedman, Lesley Stirling, Frank Veltman, Jan de Vuyst and Henk Zeevat.

The book was printed from a camera-ready manuscript prepared by van der Does and Oberlander using the equipment of the Centre for Cognitive Science in Edinburgh.

Part One

Natural Language and Logical Form

1

Tenses, Temporal Quantifiers and Semantic Innocence

BARRY RICHARDS

Introduction

How does temporal reference relate to the semantics of tense and temporal quantification? Broadly speaking, there are two perspectives one can adopt, a Russellian one and a Priorean one. The Russellian view is that temporal reference is an essential feature of the meaning of both tenses and temporal quantifiers. They involve explicit reference to time and this is crucial to understanding their semantic import. In contrast the Priorean view is that temporal reference is irrelevant to the semantics of tenses and temporal quantifiers. While their meaning can be defined over time segments, they invoke no explicit reference to them.

It is natural to wonder which view more accurately reflects the facts of language, but one may suspect that neither can be uniformly satisfactory. The Russellian account seems more appropriate to tenses while the Priorean account appears better suited to temporal quantifiers. Tensed sentences are typically sensitive to the time of utterance in that they may be true on one occasion and false on another. This shift in truth value can, plausibly, be traced to a shift in time reference. As the Russellian view would have it, utterances of a tensed sentence involve reference to the time of speech, and what is past, present or future is determined relative to that time. Since different utterances invoke different speech times, the truth value of a sentence may vary from time to time. But when sentences are modified by temporal quantifiers, e.g. *always*, *twice* or *never*, the time of speech seems less relevant. What is always, twice or never the case is, apparently, to be judged from a perspective which surveys the whole of time rather than one which is located in it. In the circumstance a Priorean formulation is the more appropriate.

Despite the convenience of eclecticism, there is a disposition to hope that one of the approaches may emerge as uniformly satisfactory. The 'shape' which a generally adequate theory might take has been the subject of much speculation, but the results to date have been less than conclusive. Since no comprehensively suitable proposal has yet to be identified, it seems not inappropriate to consider another alternative. We shall sketch an approach which, though innovative in some technical and philosophical respects, is essentially Russellian in spirit. We shall take temporal reference to be the key to a general explanation of the semantics of both tenses and temporal quantifiers.

Among the more fundamental aspects of the theory is the distinction between tensed and untensed sentences. When one utters a tensed sentence, one is understood to refer deictically to the time of utterance and thus to say something about that time. In contrast an utterance of an untensed sentence is taken to have no special connection to the time of speech. No reference to speech time occurs when one utters an untensed sentence, unless the sentence contains some appropriate adverb, and thus an untensed utterance does not generally say anything about the occasion of utterance.

Russell is not the only one to regard tensed utterances to be about the time of speech. Reichenbach has a similar view, but he envisages a somewhat more elaborate system of reference. He suggests that tensed assertions involve reference not only to speech time but also to what he calls event time and reference time. It has been noted that his tripartite system of temporal reference may make it difficult, if not impossible, to treat tenses as sentential operators.[1] Since we intend to treat tenses in just this way, i.e. as sentential operators, it should be said that nowhere do we resort to Reichenbach's notions of event time and reference time. Although we often invoke reference to time, we never appeal to his special concepts of reference time and event time.

While speech time plays an essential rôle in the analysis of tense, we take it to be irrelevant to the treatment of temporal quantifiers, i.e. of such expressions as *always*, *sometimes* and *never*. This is not to say, however, that reference to time is generally irrelevant. Temporal quantifiers are understood to invoke temporal reference just as tenses do, but reference is not always or even typically to speech time. The interval referred to may be any one at all. Its semantic rôle is to restrict the range of temporal quantification; that is, temporal quantifiers range over an interval fixed referentially at the time of utterance. This referential aspect of temporal quantifiers figures significantly in their interaction with temporal connectives, in particular with *when*, *before* and *after*.

Among our more philosophical concerns will be certain issues revolving around two familiar Davidsonian themes, viz. logical form and semantic innocence. The logical form of tensed sentences has been difficult to characterize, especially in relation to other temporal devices such as adverbs, quantifiers and connectives. We shall argue that if tenses are characterized in a Russellian way, i.e. in the manner we suggest, a fully comprehensive account of temporal phenomena can be constructed. One of the consequences of our proposal is that semantic innocence is not a property of sentences. Sentences which occur in subordinate position do not have the same semantic rôle that they have as main clauses. This is an important fact of language which can be explained if the rôle of tenses is appropriately specified.

---

1 See Dowty (1979).

§1 Untensed Sentences

Let us start by considering untensed sentences. Linguists may debate whether there are any such sentences, but it cannot be denied that English contains a range of putative candidates, particularly in subordinate position. One might note, for example, the following instances.

(1) It was important that Max exercise regularly.

(2) The doctor recommended that Max run daily.

Prima facie one seems justified in supposing that the two sentences in subordinate position, viz.

(3) Max exercise regularly

(4) Max run daily

are both untensed. For one thing there is no apparent syntactic marking for tense, and for another this fact seems to be semantically important. Note the following variant of (1) where the subordinate sentence is tensed as past.

(5) It was important that Max exercised regularly.

Clearly (5) implies that Max did exercise regularly, but no similar implication attaches to (1) which is consistent with the assertion,

(6) But he never did.

The difference between (1) and (5) is naturally attributed to tense, although it may equally be associated with mood. The subordinate sentence in (5) is in the indicative mood while the subordinate sentence in (1) is in the subjunctive mood. It is interesting to note that the subjunctive mood in English seems to coincide with the absence of tense. In the case of (2) the subordinate sentence can only be read 'subjunctively', and significantly it can never be tensed, as one can see by replacing *run* with *ran*.

(7) *The doctor recommended that Kim ran.

There is, in effect, no factive reading of *recommended that* as there is of *was important that*. One is tempted to conjecture that subordinate sentences in *that* contexts can be read factively only if they are tensed; when they are untensed, they must be read counterfactually.

It may be suggested that English is not a sure guide to universal syntax. When (1) and (2) are translated into other languages, the subordinate sentences are typically marked for tense, even though their status is counterfactual. There is a sense, nevertheless, in which such counterfactual sentences are 'semantically' untensed. Later we shall indicate just what sense this is, at which point it may emerge that English is not entirely misleading to drop tense.

Since we shall use untensed sentences as a basis for analyzing tensed sentences, we must address the difficult problem of how they are to be semantically characterized, a problem which has worried many philosophers and logicians. It does not seem appropriate to regard untensed sentences as having a truth value, since there is no occasion on which it would be correct to say that they are true or false. Utterances of sentences such as (3) and (4) are not assertions about what is purportedly true and hence, they cannot be rightly seen as bearing truth value. In this respect their status can only be seen as independent of truth. From the perspective of formal semantics this is awkward, for it suggests that the concept of truth cannot be invoked to analyze sentences like (3) and (4). Although truth may yield a natural account of sentences that can bear truth value, many doubt that it can be applied to other kinds of sentence.

Despite such skepticism, it is arguable that truth can still be invoked to characterize the semantic content of untensed sentences. It is helpful to recall the 'speech act' view of declarative and nondeclarative sentences. According to this theory, both types of sentence express propositions, the only difference being that declaratives assert them and nondeclaratives do not. For example, these two sentences are said to express the same proposition.

(8) Max exercises regularly.

(9) Max, exercise regularly!

Significantly the proposition is taken to be the one expressed by the untensed sentence,

(3) Max exercise regularly.

While (8) is understood to assert this proposition (with respect to the present), (9) is held to command it (with reference to the future).

Bearing in mind the status of (3), viz. that it never bears a truth value relative to an utterance, one might legitimately use truth values to characterize the proposition expressed by (3), provided there is no implication that (3) ever has a truth value *simpliciter*. Let us suppose then that propositions take the form of functions from moments of time to truth values. In the case of (3) the proposition expressed picks out those moments of time at which Max has the property of exercising regularly. This is not to say that an utterance of (3) is tantamount to asserting, or even implying, that the given proposition is true at the moment of utterance. Although the proposition may well be true at this particular time, the utterance neither says nor implicates that it is. In effect (3) does not take on truth values relative to utterances. While it expresses a proposition, it does so in what we shall call a value-free way. This is characteristic of all simple untensed sentences, which never invoke any moment as a moment of evaluation. Although the propositions expressed are represented as functions from moments to truth values, no moment has the status of being the intended moment of evaluation.

Evaluation is invoked through the medium of tense, e.g. the present tense as in (8). To utter (8) is to invoke the time of speech as the intended interval of evaluation; it is tantamount to asserting that the proposition expressed by (3) is true for this, and only this particular interval. As a result, (8) is appropriately regarded as bearing a truth value relative to the time of speech. We shall say that it is value-specific for that interval. This is in marked contrast to (3), no utterance of which identifies any interval as the intended interval of evaluation. What particular interval the truth value of (3) is relative to is not something which an utterance of (3) can raise by itself. Only through tense does this arise.[2]

If (3) is seen to result from (8) by 'factoring' present tense, it is natural to view the mood of (8) as associated with its tense. Since introducing present tense into (3) must then be sufficient to realize (8), the mood of (8), viz. the indicative mood, seems a parasitic phenomenon; it requires no characterization independent of tense. In effect there is no component of (8), other than the present tense, which corresponds to what has been called the speech act device, here the device associated with assertion. Tense is what makes (8) assertable. Significantly (8) is not taken to express the same proposition as (3). While (8) always asserts something about the time of utterance, viz. that (3) is true there, (3) itself never expresses this proposition. The proposition expressed by (3) is, as it were, value-free while the one expressed by (8) is value-specific.

The contrast between value-specific and value-free propositions will play a central rôle both in the characterization of tense and in the analysis of sentential subordination. Sentences which occur in subordinate position typically express value-free propositions, as in the following example.

---

2 Below it will emerge that propositions are defined to be partial functions from the set of interval-world pairs to the set $\{true, false\}$. In this connection the terms *value-free* and *value-specific* may be thought to mean respectively 'everywhere undefined' and 'constant for the values in its domain'. Neither is intended. The *value-free* propositions are those functions which carry no restriction on their graph; that is for each interval-world pair for which the proposition is defined, it is 'free' to have either *true* or *false* as its value. For *value-specific* propositions, on the other hand, the value *true* is specific in the sense that such propositions will be true for at most one interval-world pair.

(10) It is my wish that God save the Queen.

For me to utter (10) is of course to express a wish relative to the time of utterance, viz. that God save the Queen. However, it is not a wish merely about the present moment, for I plainly intend to invoke God's good offices for some indefinite period in the future. In fact there is a sense in which my wish might be seen to be omnitemporal; it is a wish that the proposition expressed by the subordinate sentence

(11) God save the Queen

evaluate to true for any moment of time, at least for all future moments. So understood, the proposition expressed by (11) must be regarded as value-free, i.e. as not involving any moment in particular. How this interpretation can be technically realized will subsequently become clear.

Let us now turn to the task of characterizing the content of those sentences which are assumed to be both moodless and tenseless. We propose to treat propositions as functions from intervals of time to truth values. Intervals may be of any length as long as they are continuous, with points of time being just minimal intervals. The need to have intervals in a temporal theory is sometimes justified on metaphysical grounds. It is argued that some things are true for intervals but not for all the points in those intervals, for example the process of taking a walk. This might be true for an interval even though the interval is punctuated with periods of rest.[3] Such considerations, however, do not figure among our reasons for regarding intervals as the fundamental notion. Intervals are needed as objects of reference and quantification, i.e. as required by tenses and other temporal devices. In effect intervals are invoked for semantic rather than metaphysical reasons.

3 This does not seem to be a particularly compelling argument for intervals. For an extended discussion, see Richards (1982) where it is argued that processes like walking must be homogeneous, i.e. true for all the points in any interval of walking.

Much has recently been made of Vendler's classification of verbs according to whether they express activities, accomplishments, achievements or states.[4] Doubtless there are important semantic differences, of which some may be relevant to formal semantics. One thinks of the adverb *in an hour* which occurs with verbs expressing achievements and accomplishments but not normally with those expressing activities or states.[5] We shall not, however, be concerned with such matters in this paper and thus need not seek to characterize the relevant factors.[6] Moreover, we shall not attempt to account for certain semantic anomalies, e.g. the incommensurability between achievement verbs and durational adverbs.

(12) *Sandy arrived for 10 minutes.

Some would be disposed to require that a fully adequate semantic theory should explain why (12) is anomalous and the following is not.

(13) Sandy walked for 10 minutes.

We shall set such problems aside and treat all verbs as having a common semantic structure. Although this may seem linguistically shortsighted, our general concern is with semantic structure that abstracts from 'lexical' differences.

The envisaged semantic theory will be defined over a quasi-formal language supplemented with certain propositional operators. The syntax of this language is based on a categorial analysis of a fragment of English and is extended to include certain resources from quantified modal logic. The resulting compromise between formality and informality is intended to allow for ease of comprehension while maintaining a certain rigour.

Although we shall focus on those aspects of semantics relating to temporal structures, it will also be necessary to invoke possible worlds. A model for

4 See Vendler (1967).
5 See Dowty (1979), p. 54.
6 For this see Lascarides (1988).

our quasi-formal language is based on a point structure (T, earlier-than) where T is a nonempty set of time points strictly ordered by the earlier-than relation. Let I be the set of convex intervals constructed from T; that is, let i be a member of I only if for any points p and q in i all the points between p and q are also in i. A model is then a quintuple (D, W, I, < , f) such that

(14) (i) D, W and I are nonempty disjoint sets to be understood respectively as the set of possible objects, possible worlds and intervals of time;

(ii) The relation < is the partial ordering of I induced by the earlier than relation; that is, for intervals i and j, i < j iff all the moments in i are earlier than all the moments in j;

(iii) and f is a function that assigns a suitable intension to each nonlogical constant of the language.

Since we do not propose to pin down any particular logic, there is no need here to restrict the definition of a model to any specific temporal structure. Our strategy is to investigate certain issues relating to logical form which do not immediately require a general definition of logical consequence. Once these issues are clarified we can then seek to define an appropriate consequence relation.

We must, however, specify the range of admissible intensions, for which we invoke two special conditions. The possible extensions of constants are as one would expect. The extension of a name is an individual in D unless the name is a temporal one, in which case its extension is an interval in I. The extension of an n-ary relation is a subset of n-tuples from D^n. The intension denoted by a constant is then a function with domain (W × I), the cartesian product of W and I, which satisfies the following conditions.

(14) (iv) If b is a name and f(b)(w,i) is an entity d of D, then for all subintervals j of i f(b)(w,j) is also d.

(v) If r is an n-ary relation and f(r)(w,i) is a subset of D^n, then for all subintervals j of i f(r)(w,j) includes f(r)(w,i).

The point of (iv) and (v) is basically to ensure that if an atomic sentence is true at a world for an interval it will be true at that world for all subintervals of the given interval.

It will be noted that (iv) and (v) admit the possibility of defining intensions which are partial functions, since there is no requirement that intensions be defined for all intervals. This possibility emerges independently of whether intensions are defined for all moments of time, i.e. for the smallest intervals. With a view to speculating about the general nature of temporal quantification, we allow f to assign partial functions; but we assume that all such functions are still defined for each moment of time. That is, we adopt the following condition on the definition of f.

(14) (vi) If c is a nonlogical constant and i a moment of time in I, f(c)(w,i) must be defined.

This reflects our view that at points our language is bivalent, a thesis we discuss in detail in Richards (1982). Apart from conditions (iv)-(vi) f is free to assign any appropriate intension to a nonlogical constant.

Given the admissibility of partial functions, we must specify their import for the intensions of sentences. Suppose that a sentence (relative to a world) is not true for every subinterval of a given interval. Is it to be taken as false or undefined for that interval? Although it would be convenient (and possible) to adopt the former view, an interesting distinction emerges if the latter is chosen. It will arise from our formalization that the intension of an untensed sentence is usually a partial function but the intension of a tensed sentence (and other types of sentence involving temporal quantification) can be interpreted as giving rise to a total function. Such an interpretation yields a significant difference between tensed and untensed sentences, one that will become clearer below.

The definition of truth, given just below, will be seen to yield the following homogeneity property for untensed atomic sentences.

(15) An untensed atomic sentence is true at an index (w,i) only if for all subintervals j of i the sentence is true at (w,j).

It should be stressed that homogeneity is not a general restriction on the truth definition; rather it is a property which typically (though not always) emerges from it. With this clarification we specify the initial clauses of the truth definition, taking A and B to be any sentences of the language, and **M** any model.

(16) (i) An atomic sentence consisting of an n-ary relation R_n and n terms $a_1,\ldots,a_n$ is true in **M** at (w,i) if the sequence $f(a_1)(w,i),\ldots,f(a_n)(w,i)$ belongs to $f(R_n)(w,i)$; it is false at(w,i) if the given sequence does not so belong; and otherwise it is undefined.

(ii) (A *and* B) is true in **M** at (w,i) if both A and B are true in **M** at (w,i); it is false at (w,i) if either A or B is false at (w,i); and otherwise it is undefined.

(iii) (A *or* B) is true in **M** at (w,i) if either A or B is true in **M** at (w,i); it is false at (w,i) if both A and B are false at (w,i); and otherwise it is undefined.

(iv) *Not* (A) is true in **M** at (w,i) if A is false in **M** at (w,i); it is false at (w,i) if A is true at (w,i); and otherwise it is undefined.[7]

Before giving the clauses for the quantifiers, we should note that there is a choice as to the range of quantification. Consider a sentence of the form,

(17) *Every* x (A).

---

7 These clauses conform to Kleene's strong three-valued logic, as do the following clauses for the quantifiers.

Given a model, (17) may be treated in at least two different ways. Relative to an index (w,i) it can be interpreted as asserting that every object in the domain of the model has the property A at (w,i). Here the quantifier is understood to range over the whole of the domain. Alternatively the quantifier can be interpreted as ranging only over those objects in the domain which exist at the index (w,i). In this case (17) will be read as saying that each of the entities in this set has the distinguished property at (w,i). From the point of view of natural language the 'restricted' reading of the quantifier may seem more suitable. Typical quantifier phrases, such as *every swimmer*, seem paradigm instances of restricted quantification. It is arguable, nevertheless, that *every* itself should be treated as an unrestricted quantifier. This is how we define it.

Let A(b/x) be the sentence which results from A by replacing all the free occurrences of x by a name b which does not already occur in A. Let M^b be a model which is like **M** except possibly for what the function f assigns to b. The standard quantifiers *every* and *some* are then defined as follows.

(16) (v) *Every* x (A) is true in **M** at (w,i) if A(b/x) is true at (w,i) for every $\mathbf{M}^b$; it is false at (w,i) if A(b/x) is false at (w,i) for some $\mathbf{M}^b$; and otherwise it is undefined.

(vi) *Some* x (A) is true in **M** at (w,i) if A(b/x) is true at (w,i) for some $\mathbf{M}^b$; it is false at (w,i) if A(b/x) is false at (w,i) for every $\mathbf{M}^b$; and otherwise it is undefined.

Quantified sentences may be undefined at an index because they contain a predicate or a name that is undefined at that index.

We can now illustrate how the given semantics may be appropriate for untensed moodless sentences like,

(18) Hilary swim.

Relative to a model, (18) will express a proposition represented by a possibly partial function. This proposition will be determined by the intensions of

Hilary and *swim* and will be indifferent as to the intended interval of evaluation. Not only does (18) not contain devices for explicit reference to intervals, but its analysis at the level of logical form does not presuppose any such reference. In effect the proposition is characterized in a value-free way: there is not, nor can there be, an intended interval of evaluation. This is just what distinguishes an untensed moodless sentence.

§2 Tensed Sentences

From the beginning we have supposed that tensed sentences are in a certain sense context sensitive; that is, they express a determinate proposition only relative to an occasion of utterance. Thus the present tense sentence,

(19) Hilary swims

does not in itself express any particular proposition; only relative to an utterance does it say anything definite. What it says relative to an utterance is essentially that the proposition expressed by (18) is true at the designated time. Obviously the proposition expressed by (18) must be different that the proposition expressed by an utterance of (19). The latter is about a specific interval of time while the former is not so.

The source of the difference lies in the deictic nature of tense. Tenses involve deictic reference to speech time, and it is this semantic fact which explains why (18) and (19) diverge in the propositions they can express. Since (19) is tensed, an utterance of it involves reference to the time of utterance and thus says something about it: it says, as we have noted, that the proposition expressed by (18) is true at that interval. Since (18) is not tensed, no utterance of it can invoke reference to the interval of utterance, and for that reason it can only express a proposition different than (19).[8]

To reflect the referential aspect of tense we shall give the tense operators a complex syntactic structure. The present tense, for example, is represented as $\text{PRES}_{(v,t)}$ with v and t read as deictic parameters ranging over worlds and intervals. These parameters are to be seen as acquiring their values relative to the context of utterance. A certain latitude will be allowed in the possible assignments to t in that they need not be strictly confined to the intervals of utterance. While the value of t must always have a final segment representing the interval of utterance, it may extend back into the past, indeed indefinitely far back. Such an assignment, i.e. where the value of t extends beyond the interval of utterance, is sometimes called the 'extended now'.

While reference to time seems a natural ingredient of tense, one may wonder about the reference to possible worlds. Possible worlds do not seem to have any special relation to tense, i.e. as distinct from their relation to other kinds of expressions. It is arguable, nevertheless, that the value-specific character of tensed utterances involves more than just time. When one utters a tensed sentence, it is not only speech time which is fixed but also the intended 'location', normally the actual world. When one utters (19), for example, one usually intends to say something that is true at the time of speech in the actual world. While reference to the actual world does not obviously arise from

8 Some have argued that (18) and (19) are not to be seen as differing in this way. The propositions they express do not diverge at the point of utterance, since they always express the same proposition. Where (18) and (19) differ is in respect of a certain conversational convention. There is a general convention that when one utters a tensed sentence, one offers the proposition expressed as being true for the interval of utterance. When one utters (19), one commits oneself by convention to the claim that the proposition expressed by (19) (and also by (18)) is true at the time of speech. One does not actually assert this to be so, either by referring to the given time or in any other way. If one did, the proposition expressed by (19) would then be different from the proposition expressed by (18), which it is said not to be. Hence one can only be taken to implicate the intended state of affairs in some indirect sort of way. By eschewing reference to speech time such a view coincides with the Priorean perspective. While it may seem appropriate here to venture a counterargument, we prefer to let the counterargument emerge as a 'byproduct' of developing our Russellian alternative. If the the theory is seen to explain a wide variety of complex phenomena, no further argument may be needed.

tense, it also does not obviously arise from any other device. In the circumstance it is not unreasonable to regard tense as involving deictic reference to worlds. This at least allows a certain economy of analysis and may even lead to an unexpected insight, a matter we shall subsequently consider.

As for the syntactic rôle of $\text{PRES}_{(v,t)}$, we propose to treat it as a sentential operator but for reasons that emerge below, we do not allow it to iterate without restriction. We let $\text{PRES}_{(v,t)}$ apply only to those sentences which are defined as context free. Roughly speaking, a context-free sentence is one that does not contain any occurrences of the deictic parameters ranging over worlds and intervals.[9] On the assumption that A is a context-free sentence, the semantic content of the present-tense operator is specified as follows. Let g_c be a (possibly partial) function which assigns values to the 'deictic' parameters v and t relative to a context c.

(20) $\text{PRES}_{(v,t)}$A is true in a model **M** at a world-interval index (w,i) if $w = g_c(v)$ and $i = g_c(t)$ and A is true in **M** at (w,i); it is false in **M** if either $w \neq g_c(v)$ or $i \neq g_c(t)$ or A is false in **M** at (w,i); and otherwise it is undefined.

It should be noted that (20) is actually a definition schema in that it gives rise to different intensions for different assignments to v and t.

By way of example let us consider the logical form of (19). Since (18) is a paradigm instance of a context-free sentence, (19) can be analyzed in this way.

(21) $\text{PRES}_{(v,t)}$(Hilary swim)

Relative to an utterance, v and t acquire specific values, which for convenience may be referred to as V and T. With respect to and T (19) is construed basically as expressing the proposition that the proposition

9 For a precise definition see page 18.

expressed by (18) is true at (V,T). When formally characterized in terms of (21), this proposition is the intension which takes at most one world-interval pair to true, viz. the pair(V,T). From definition (20) it can be immediately seen that this intension will be true at (V,T) only if the intension denoted by (18) is true at (V,T); otherwise it will be either false or undefined. Since the intension denoted by (21) is, as it were, value specific for (V,T), it captures the special character of an utterance of a tensed sentence.

Some would argue, however, that (20) leads to counterintuitive consequences. Suppose that the two context-free sentences,

(18) Hilary swim

(22) Kim walk

are both true in a model at (V,T). Then (20) would imply that

(23) PRES(V,T)(Hilary swim)

(24) PRES(V,T)(Kim walk)

denote the same intension in that model. In effect cotemporal utterances of

(19) Hilary swims

(25) Kim walks

would express the same proposition and hence convey the same information.

Although the intensions would be the same, there is a clear sense in which the utterances would still convey different information. For the occasion (V,T) (19) will convey the information that the proposition expressed by

(18) Hilary swim

is true at (V,T), while for the same occasion (25) would intimate that the proposition expressed by

(22) Kim walk

is true at (V,T). Since the intensions denoted by (18) and (22) typically differ in a given model, the information content of (19) and (25) is not usually the same for cotemporal utterances. The difference in information content becomes relevant in statements of propositional attitude. How this is to be accommodated technically will be considered in some detail below. For the moment let it suffice to emphasize the main point. Although (19) and (25) may denote the same intension relative to (V,T), they will do so with respect to different intensions, viz. the ones expressed by (18) and (22). These intensions account for the difference in information content and have special relevance in contexts of propositional attitude.

Let us now formalize the notion of a context-free sentence. We first define the concept of a context-sensitive sentence. All tense operators are assumed to have a common form which can be represented as $Q_{(v,t)}$, with Q having PRES, PAST and FUT as substitution instances. Let A and B be sentences, and let (v,t) be a specific pair of world-interval parameters.

(26) A is said to be *context-sensitive* if it has the form $Q_{(v,t)}B$ or if it contains a subformula of this form.[10]

We take B to be a subformula of A if it is one of its main clauses, for example, if A is of the form B *or* C, but not if B is a subordinate clause of A such as in *Sandy said that B*. We then say that

(27) A is *context-free* if each occurrence of a tense operator in a subformula is of the form $Q_{(v',t')}$ where v' and t' are variables.

As we indicated above, (27) will be invoked to restrict the iteration of tenses.

10 It is important to appreciate that the context-sensitive parameters, viz. v and t, serve to identify the intended index of evaluation. Their rôle is actually fixed in the semantic clauses for the tense operators, which follow immediately. While v and t receive their assignments from context, they are not the only parameters that do so. They are, however, the only parameters to be styled as context-sensitive according to (26).

The need to restrict iteration becomes evident in the definitions of the past and future tenses. Though they have a certain familiar form, the definitions are not entirely standard, mainly because of the rôle of the deictic parameters. Let A be any context-free sentence; then,

(28) $PAST_{(v,t)}A$ is true in a model **M** at (w,i) if $w = g_c(v)$, $i = g_c(t)$ and there is an interval $j < i$ such that A is true in **M** at (w,j); it is false at (w,i) if either $w \neq g_c(v)$ or $i \neq g_c(t)$ or there is no $j < i$ such that A is true at (w,j); (and otherwise it is undefined).

(29) $FUT_{(v,t)}A$ is true in **M** at (w,i) if $w = g_c(v)$, $i = g_c(t)$ and there is an interval j such that $i < j$ and A is true in **M** at (w,j); it is false at (w,i) if either $w \neq g_c(v)$ or $i \neq g_c(t)$ or there is no j such that $i < j$ and A is true at (w,j); (and otherwise it is undefined).[11]

Since tense operators are intended to apply only to context-free sentences, the following formula is not syntactically well-formed.

(30) $PAST_{(v,t)}[PAST_{(v,t)}A]$

That (30) is also not semantically coherent can be readily appreciated. According to definition (28), (30) would be true in a model at (w,i) if $w = g_c(v)$, $i = g_c(t)$ and there is a $j < i$ such that $PAST_{(v,t)}A$ is true at (w,j); and this obtains only if $j = g_c(t)$ and there is a $k < j$ such that A is true at (w,k). But obviously no j can satisfy these conditions since it cannot satisfy both $j = g_c(t)$ and $j < g_c(t)$.[12]

Since the parameters v and t obviously occupy referential positions, it is natural to envisage the possibility of binding into these positions. Replacing v and t by variables (for the purpose of binding) gives rise to context-free

---

[11] For fixed values of v and t (28) and (29) can be read as determining total functions, hence the reason for the parentheses around the final clause. Where there may be a third possibility, we shall put the 'undefined' clause in parentheses.

[12] It can be shown that semantics alone is enough to pick out the coherent sentences. (For details see Chapter 9.) One may nevertheless find the syntactic restrictions used here semantically revealing.

sentences; that is, if all the occurrences of v and t are replaced by variables, the resulting sentence is by definition context free. With a view to creating a particular kind of context-free sentence we introduce a new operator whose rôle is to bind only into those positions where v and t can occur. Let v' and t' be variables ranging over worlds and intervals respectively. Where A is any sentence, either context-free or context-sensitive,

(31) Gv'[A] and Gt'[A] are also sentences.

In the first sentence G binds all the free occurrences of v' in A, and in the second it binds all the free occurrences of t'. For sentences of the form Gv'[Gt'[A]] we adopt the abbreviation Gv't'[A]. To minimize the complexity of the definition of G, we supplement our quasi-formal language with the following convention: given a world-interval index (w,i), let w* be a name of w and i* a name of i, and let A[w*/v',i*/t'] be the formula which results from A by replacing all free occurrences of v' by w* and all free occurrences of t' by i*. Now for any context-free sentence A, we say that

(32) Gv't'[A] is true in a model **M** at (w,i) if A[w*/v',i*/t'] is true in **M** at (w,i); it is false at (w,i) if A[w*/v',i*/t'] is false at (w,i); and otherwise it is undefined.

The intension of Gv't'[A] will typically be a partial function, unless A contains tense operators.

Let us illustrate the rôle of G by considering the following instance of tense iteration, where A is assumed to be context-free.

(33) $\mathrm{PAST}_{(v,t)}\mathrm{G}v't'[\mathrm{PAST}_{(v',t')}A]$

Unlike (30), (33) has a coherent interpretation, since it expresses a definite proposition in every model. To be precise, (33) will be true in a model at (w,i) if $w = g_c(v)$, $i = g_c(t)$ and there is a $j < i$ such that $\mathrm{G}v't'[\mathrm{PAST}_{(v',t')}A]$ is true at (w,j); and this formula will be true at (w,j) if $\mathrm{PAST}_{(w^*,j^*)}A$ is true at (w,j), which obtains if there is a $k < j$ such that A is true at (w,k). If (33) is to be true in a model, there must be distinct intervals i, j and k which satisfy the indicated conditions, one of them being that $k < j < i$. Plainly there are models in which these conditions are met. As for the import of (33), it is tempting to think that it may represent the pluperfect, which is sometimes taken to be a tense. Although it may be possible to characterize the pluperfect as a compound of two past tenses, i.e. as given in (33), it can also be analyzed as a compound of past tense and perfective aspect. Below we offer an account of perfective aspect and illustrate the analysis.

To exemplify our approach to tense iteration let us characterize the difference between these two sentences.[13]

(34) A prince was invested who would be king.

(35) A prince was invested who will be king.

Clearly (34) and (35) do not mean the same thing, and this can be traced to the different roles of the future tense in the subordinate clauses. In (35) the future tense is to be evaluated relative to the time of utterance: (35) will be true relative to an occasion of utterance only if there is some future time at which a prince invested in the past will be king. In contrast the future tense of (34) is to be evaluated relative to the past tense in the main clause: (34) will be true relative to an utterance only if there is some time in the past at which a prince was invested such that relative to it there is some future time at which he is king.

To capture the difference in truth conditions we invoke the operator G and render the logical form of (34) as follows.

(36) *Some* x [PAST(v,t)[[Prince(x) *and* x be invested] *and* Gv't'[FUT(v',t')(x be king)]]]

---

13 For an alternative treatment see Kamp (1971).

It can be easily seen that (36) renders the intended sense of (34). Relative to a model and an index (w,i), (36) will be true if there is some b in the model such that

(37) $PAST_{(v,t)}$[[Prince(b) *and* b be invested] *and* Gv't'[$FUT_{(v',t')}$(b be king)]]

is true at (w,i). This will obtain only if $w = g_c(v)$, $i = g_c(t)$ and there is some $j < i$ such that

(38) [[Prince(b) *and* b be invested] *and* Gv't'[$FUT_{(v',t')}$(b be king)]]

is true at (w,j). Obviously this will hold just in case both the conjuncts hold at (w,j), i.e. if and only if these two formulas are true at (w,j).

(39) [Prince(b) *and* b be invested]

(40) Gv't'[$FUT_{(v',t')}$(b be king)]

Since (40) will be true at (w,j) only if

(41) $FUT_{(w^*,j^*)}$(b be king)

is true at (w,j), it is plain that the future-tense operator is evaluated relative to (w,j). In effect (41) will be true at (w,j) if there is some k such that $j < k$ and

(42) b be king

is true at (w,k). At this point it should be evident that (36) is an appropriate characterization of the logical form of (34), at least as far as the tenses are concerned.

It is easy to see, moreover, how (36) can be adjusted to capture the intended meaning of (35) where both tenses are to be interpreted relative to speech time. Since neither tense has scope over the other, (35) should be analyzed as follows.

(43) *Some* x [$PAST_{(v,t)}$(Prince(x) *and* x be invested) *and* $FUT_{(v,t)}$(x be king)]

Now (43) will be true in a model at an index (w,i) only if there is some b such that

(44) $PAST_{(v,t)}$(Prince(b) *and* b be invested) *and* $FUT_{(v,t)}$(b be king)

is true at (w,i). Since both occurrences of v and t in (44) will be instantiated to the same world and interval, viz. to $g_c(v)$ and $g_c(t)$ respectively, the past and future operators will be evaluated relative to the same world-interval pair. In effect (44) will be true only if there is some interval j earlier than the time of speech such that

(45) Prince(b) *and* b be invested

is true at (w,j), and also some interval k later than speech time such that

(46) b be king

is true at (w,k). Plainly these are the truth conditions of the desired reading of (35).

§3 Tenses and Temporal Adverbials

3.1 The Semantics of Temporal Reference

Tenses are not the only devices which involve reference to time; other examples are adverbials such as *at 9.0*, *before 1493*, *on 1st April '89*, and *yesterday*. We shall treat these adverbials like tenses, i.e. as sentential operators. It has been argued, however, that they function rather differently, finding their proper rôle only in the context of tense. In effect time adverbs occupy an argument position created by tense and their rôle is to specify the time of the event.[14] This would suggest that where there is no tense there can be no time adverbs, a situation which is plainly not the case. Note the subordinate clause in the sentence,

(47) The secretary requests that Sandy phone at 9.0.

Clearly *at 9.0* is not to be taken as specifying the time of the secretary's requesting. It is rather associated with the untensed verb *phone*, or as we see it, with the untensed sentence *Sandy phone*. How it is so associated remains to be specified.

At 9.0 might be read intuitively as referring to the time at which the proposition expressed by *Sandy phone* is to be considered; it invites one to consider this proposition with respect to the interval 9.0. This idea can be rendered technically by introducing a sentential operator corresponding to *at 9.0* and defining it as follows. Where A is a context-free sentence,

(48) AT 9.0 (A) is true in a model **M** at (w,i) if i = 9.0 and and A is true in **M** at (w,i); it is false at (w,i) if i ≠ 9.0 or A is false at (w,i); and otherwise it is undefined.

It will be observed that if *9.0* is read 'specifically', i.e. as referring to a definite interval on a definite day, the proposition denoted will be value specific in respect of time. That is, it can evaluate to true at only one interval, viz. the one referred to by *9.0*. This is not to imply that the proposition will also be value specific with respect to a particular world. There may be many worlds for which the intension evaluates to true.

By way of example let us consider the logical form of the subordinate clause in sentence (47), viz.

(49) Sandy phone at 9.0.

---

14 See Tichy (1980).

Its logical structure will be represented by this quasi-formal formula.

(50) AT 9.0 (Sandy phone)

The proposition expressed by (50), i.e. the intension it denotes, will be taken as the object of the relation *requests*, at least on one natural analysis. It is significant, therefore, that this intension does not necessarily coincide with the one denoted by the formula,

(51) AT 9.0 (Sandy arrive).

Although both intensions will be value specific with respect to 9.0, they will not generally be true at the same possible worlds. Hence, the propositions expressed by (47) and

(52) The secretary suggests that Sandy arrive at 9.0

will be appropriately distinct.[15]

In this connection we should note that (49) and its present-tense 'derivative',

(53) Sandy phones at 9.0

will be characterized as expressing different propositions.[16] Since the latter involves tense, it will be value specific for both world and time. This would lead one to ask whether the difference between (49) and (53) will be reflected in a difference between (47) and,

(54) The secretary requests that Sandy phones at 9.0.

---

15 Here we see the reason for introducing possible worlds into the model theory.

16 There is a natural disposition to read (53) either as saying something about the future, viz. about what Sandy will do at 9.0, or as saying something about Sandy's current habits, i.e. his habit of phoning at 9.0. But (53) may also be read as identifying a current event, although perhaps less naturally.

We shall consider the matter below.

There is a certain 'efficiency' in definition (48) in that it allows for an ambiguity in the use of *9.0*. It might be used, as we have noted, to refer to a definite time on a definite day; but it might also be used to indicate a definite time *simpliciter*, i.e. without regard to any particular day. The latter usage will not by itself engender a value-specific proposition; that is, the intension denoted by

(55) AT 9.0 (A)

may be true at a number of intervals, provided each one has the property of being a '9.0 o'clock' interval. The interpretation of (48) will of course depend upon how *9.0* is used in the definiens, whether with respect to a particular day or not.

Adverbs of temporal reference will generally be treated in a manner similar to *at 9.0*, i.e. in regard to their logical form. For example, the clauses defining *before 1493* and on *1st April '89* are as follows, with A understood as a context-free sentence.

(56) BEFORE 1493 (A) is true in a model **M** at (w,i) if i is earlier than 1493 and A is true in **M** at (w,i); it is false at (w,i) if i is not earlier than 1493 or A is false at (w,i); and otherwise it is undefined.

(57) ON 1st April '89 (A) is true in **M** at (w,i) if i is a subinterval of 1st April '89 and A is true in **M** at (w,i); it is false at (w,i) if either i is not a subinterval of 1st April '89 or A is false at (w,i); and otherwise it is undefined.

It may be helpful to illustrate (56) with respect to a tensed sentence, e.g.

(58) Columbus crossed the Atlantic before 1493.

The logical form of (58) must be represented as (59) since *before 1493* can apply only to a context-free sentence.

(59) $PAST_{(v,t)}$[BEFORE 1493 (Columbus cross the Atlantic)]

On the given definitions (59) will be true at (w,i) if $w = g_c(v)$, $i = g_c(t)$ and there is a $j < i$ such that

(60) BEFORE 1493 (Columbus cross the Atlantic)

is true at (w,j); (60) will be true at (w,j) if j is earlier than 1493 and

(61) Columbus cross the Atlantic

is true at (w,j).[17]

3.2 Temporal Reference and Negation

The analysis of (58) is a paradigmatic treatment of the connection between tense and adverbs of temporal reference, i.e. we conjecture that tense always has scope over temporal adverbials. Note, in particular, that the analysis invokes no reference to any specific value of j at which (61) is given to be true. The rôle of *before 1493* is to indicate that the verifying value of j, whatever it may be, falls before 1493. No further specification is given. Those who would approach (58) from a Reichenbachian perspective would, in contrast, be disposed to look for a precise reference, viz. to the time of the event type distinguished by (61). What they would assume is that (58) invokes a reference to some particular interval before 1493. This assumption, however, is not immediately obvious. Not only does (58) not contain a

---

[17] It is instructive to note that the truth conditions of the sentence

(i) Jon will walk before 14:00

with logical form

(ii) $FUT_{(v,t)}$[BEFORE 14:00(Jon walk)]

can be paraphrased as

(iii) Jon will walk in between speakers time and 14:00

which is as it should be.

suitable referring phrase, it is not easy to add one without anomaly, which can be seen from this sentence.

(62) *Columbus crossed the Atlantic before 1493 in 1492.

Clearly one of the two adverbs must go, in this case the so-called locating adverb *in 1492*. It seems to have no proper rôle to play in the analysis of (58). Since our theory implies as much, it can be seen not to make use of the Reichenbachian notion of reference time.

It also does not invoke the Reichenbachian concept of event time, as can be seen from the treatment of negative sentences like

(63) Columbus did not cross the Atlantic before 1492.

Intuitively there is no event which is being referred to here, nor any particular time at which (as opposed to during which) it is alleged not to have occurred. Our theory respects this intuition by rendering the logical form of (63) as follows.

(64) *Not* [$PAST_{(v,t)}$[BEFORE 1492 (Columbus cross the Atlantic)]]

The import of the analysis can be summarized by the paraphrase,

(67) Columbus never crossed the Atlantic before 1492.[18]

Some may find this somewhat odd since *not* does not generally mean *never*. Still there seems no denying that (63) and (67) coincide in import.

---

[18] (64) will be true at (w,i) if

(65) $PAST_{(v,t)}$[BEFORE 1492 (Columbus cross the Atlantic)]

is false at (w,i). On the assumption that $w = g_c(v)$ and $i = g_c(t)$, (65) is false at (w,i) only if there is no $j < i$ such that

(66) BEFORE 1492 (Columbus cross the Atlantic)

is true at (w,j). This holds (given the analogue of definition (56)) only if there is no such j earlier than 1492 for which

(61) Columbus cross the Atlantic

is true, i.e. at (w,j).

Let us consider another example, one that happens to invoke the nonspecific use of *9.0*.

(68) Mandy did not phone before 9.0 on 1st April '89.

The logical structure of (68) is represented in the following way.

(69) *Not* [PAST$_{(v,t)}$[ON 1st April '89 [BEFORE 9.0 (Mandy phone)]]]

On this analysis (68) emerges as equivalent to the paraphrase

(74) Mandy never phoned before 9.0 on 1st April '89.[19]

Though (74) may be linguistically awkward, it does seem to capture the truth conditions of (68). What Mandy never did before a certain date she did not do before that time, and vice versa.

But there are, it must be said, certain problematic cases, in particular negative sentences which contain no time adverbials, as in the following sentence.

(75) Mandy did not phone.

On the assumption that (75) is similar in structure to (68), its logical form will be

(76) *Not* [PAST$_{(v,t)}$(Mandy phone)]

---

19 (69) will be true at (w,i) if

(70) PAST$_{(v,t)}$[ON 1st April '89 [BEFORE 9.0 (Mandy phone)]]

is false at (w,i). On the assumption that $w = g_c(v)$ and $i = g_c(t)$, (70) is false at (w,i) if there is no $j < i$ such that

(71) ON 1st April '89 [BEFORE 9.0 (Mandy phone)]

is true at (w,j), which itself holds if for no $j < i$ is j a subinterval of 1st April '89 and

(72) BEFORE 9.0 (Mandy phone)

true at (w,j); and finally this obtains if there is no such j falling before 9.0 such that

(73) Mandy phone

is true at (w,j).

and thus it will be equivalent to the paraphrase

(77) Mandy never phoned.

But (77) is not an obvious paraphrase of (75); at least it is not obvious that (77) and (75) coincide on truth conditions. When one utters (75), one typically intends to say something about some specific time in the past, viz. that Mandy did not phone *then*. No similar specificity seems to be involved in an utterance of (77); one does not purport to assert anything about Mandy's phoning at any particular time in the past. Since there is no explicit reference to past time in (76), it is insufficient as an analysis of (75), although it may be adequate for (77). To make (76) suitable for (75) it seems necessary to add some sort of referential parameter.

One natural idea is to interpret such a parameter as identifying a past time at which the event, viz. Mandy's phoning, is purported not to have occurred. This suggestion, which seems similar to Reichenbach's proposal, is not only plausible but predicts that any utterance of (75) 'requires' a certain completion, either by context or explicitly. To express something definite there must be an indication of when the event is claimed to have happened. This could be given by context and thus be implicit in the utterance; it could be understood that the envisaged past time is, say, 9.0 on 1st April '89. On the other hand it could be specified explicitly by continuing the utterance with the phrase *at 9.0 on 1st April '89*. Though somewhat pedantic, the following sentence is complete in the intended sense.

(78) Mandy did not phone at 9.0 on 1st April '89.

One might be led to conjecture, therefore, that the logical form of (75) is perhaps similar to that of (78), with the 'underlying' structure being something like this.

(79) *Not* [PAST$_{(v,t)}$[AT u (Mandy phone)]]

Here u is to be taken as an interval parameter which receives its values from context. From an intuitive point of view (79) may be seen to offer an adequate analysis of (75). It may also be seen to 'underlie' (78) whose analysis is arguably as follows.

(80) *Not* [PAST$_{(v,t)}$[AT 9.0 [ON 1st April '89 (Mandy phone)]]]

Intuition notwithstanding, there are grounds for supposing that (79) cannot constitute the correct analysis of (75), even though the import of uttering (75) may occasionally suggest as much.

Note that (75) can be made explicitly complete (in the intended sense) in ways other than exemplified in (78).

(81) Mandy did not phone after March '89

(82) Mandy did not phone before Easter '89

(83) Mandy did not phone during 1989

These sentences are entirely explicit and independent of contextual factors. Indeed, if one attempts to add any further specification, e.g. *at 9.0 on 1st April '89*, the effect will be uniformly anomalous. This suggests that (79) cannot generally be the analysis of (75); if it were, it would have to figure in the analyses of (81)-(83) in the way exemplified in the putative analysis of (78), i.e. as in (80). The incompleteness of (75) does not in general arise from a need to specify a particular past time at which Mandy's phoning is supposed not to have happened; it rather arises from the need to indicate an interval during which it supposedly did not happen. Once this is understood, one might reasonably claim that (81)-(83) are equivalent in truth conditions to (84)-(86) respectively.

(84) Mandy never phoned after March '89.

(85) Mandy never phoned before Easter '89.

(86) Mandy never phoned during 1989.

But what then is the logical form of (75) and how is it related to the logical forms of (81)-(83)?

At this point we would question the 'intuitive' assumption about (75), viz. that it is semantically incomplete. It has been supposed that if (75) is to express a definite proposition it must be supplemented by a reference to some past interval. This can be achieved implicitly at the time of utterance or it can be realized explicitly by adding a suitable referring phrase. But is there always a need for such referential supplementation? Consider the following sentence which is very similar to (75).

(87) Wittgenstein did not die in Vienna.

What proposition (87) expresses does not depend upon any reference to a past time, either implicit or explicit; there is no need to indicate any specific time in the past in order to fix the proposition expressed by (87). In fact any attempt to add such a reference will give rise to a proposition different from the one expressed by (87) *simpliciter*. For example, no utterance of (87) will be equivalent in import to an utterance of

(88) Wittgenstein did not die in Vienna at 9.0 on 1st April '49.

To assert that Wittgenstein did not die in Vienna is not to say anything about any specific time in the past. It is rather to say something about the whole of the past, viz. that nowhere in it did Wittgenstein die in Vienna. In effect the truth conditions of (87) coincide with those of

(89) Wittgenstein never died in Vienna.

Hence the logical form (87) should be represented as follows.

(90) *Not* [PAST$_{(v,t)}$(Wittgenstein die in Vienna)]]

As far as time reference is concerned, there is no further structure to be uncovered.

Since (75) is similar in surface form to (87), it should presumably be represented as having a similar logical form. That is, the logical structure of

(75) Mandy did not phone

should be the following.

(91) *Not* [PAST$_{(v,t)}$(Mandy phone)]

But as we have noted, this would imply that (75) means

(77) Mandy never phoned.

Although there may be occasions on which (75) does mean (77), this is not generally or even typically the case. Usually there is a specific time in the past which is at issue, one that is implicitly determined by context. It is thus natural to look for a term in the analysis of (75) whose referent will be fixed contextually. But this is not the only option, nor one that is easy to sustain in light of (87). We would conjecture that utterances of (75) are actually elliptical when they do not coincide in meaning with (77). This is not to say that (75) is syntactically elliptical; it cannot be because it sometimes means (77). But when an utterance of (75) is not equivalent to (77), the utterance is strictly speaking incomplete or, as we would say, elliptical; it is in need of some further specification which could be given by a deictic expression. For example an utterance of (75) might be equivalent to,

(92) Mandy did not phone then

where the deictic *then* is interpreted as referring to a specific past interval. One might say that this utterance of (75) is 'contextually' elliptical for (92). The relevant analysis is thus the logical form of (92) which is the following.

(93) *Not* [PAST$_{(v,t)}$(Mandy phone then)]

Below we shall indicate how temporal adverbs like *then* are to be treated but in the meantime it is enough to say that the analysis will entail that (92) is equivalent in truth conditions to

(94) Mandy never phoned then.

While (94) may be stylistically strange, it nevertheless expresses a coherent proposition.

3.3 Temporal Indexicals

Having resorted to paraphrases in which *not* and *never* seem to have the same import, we should emphasize that they will not in general be characterized as meaning the same thing. Before defining *never* and other temporal quantifiers, let us first consider temporal adverbs like *yesterday* and *then*. Both of these are paradigmatically contextual in that their interpretations are given relative to the occasion of utterance. It should be noted, nevertheless, that they acquire these interpretations under somewhat different constraints. In the case of *then* the interpretation may depend partly upon the intentions of the speaker; which time he is talking about is to some degree a matter of which time he intends to talk about. No similar choice is possible with respect to *yesterday*. If a speaker utters a sentence containing *yesterday* on Wednesday, then he must be talking about Tuesday, whatever his intentions at the time of utterance.

There is another difference between *then* and *yesterday* which becomes apparent in the interpretations of these two sentences.

(95) Sammy arrived then.

(96) Sammy arrived yesterday.

The proposition expressed by (95) is that Sammy arrived at a particular time, viz. then; it was at that time that his arriving is claimed to have occurred. In contrast the proposition expressed by (96) is that Sammy arrived sometime during a certain day, viz. yesterday; his arriving is said to have occurred, not at that time, but somewhere in it. To reflect this difference between *then* and *yesterday* at the level of logical form, we shall invoke an ambiguity which is exemplified in the way we described the contrast: *then* and *yesterday* can be referring expressions as well as temporal adverbs. From a logical point of view the adverb *then* can be analyzed in terms of the prepositional phrase *at then*, where *then* is the object of the preposition *at*. The adverb *yesterday* may be similarly analyzed, although the choice of preposition is perhaps not uniquely determined. It could be *during* or *within* or *on*. In view of the definition of *on*, which was formulated above, it seems reasonable to render the content of the adverb *yesterday* in terms of the prepositional phrase *on yesterday* where *yesterday* is a referring expression. Although the chosen analysans is in neither case linguistically equivalent to its analysandum, i.e. not strictly intersubstitutable *salve congruitate*, it does nevertheless give a fair rendering of semantic content. As a result we shall represent the logical status of *then* and *yesterday* in terms of their 'prepositional' analyses which will be treated as sentential operators. Let A be any context-free sentence.

(97) AT then (A) is true in a model **M** at (w,i) if i = then and A is true at (w,i); it is false at (w,i) if i ≠ then or A is false at (w,i); and otherwise it is undefined.

(98) ON yesterday (A) is true in a model **M** at (w,i) if i is a subinterval of yesterday and A is true in **M** at (w,i); it is false at (w,i) if i is not a subinterval of yesterday or A is false at (w,i); and otherwise it is undefined.

As in the case of the other definitions, (97) and (98) are definition schemas since the occurrences of the terms *then* and *yesterday* in the definiens admit of alternative interpretations. It should be noted that time adverbs differ in one important respect from tenses: while the latter involve quantification over intervals, the former do not.

With these definitions in hand, we now consider the logical forms of (95) and (96), which will be represented as follows.

(99) PAST(v,t)[AT then (Sammy arrive)]

(100) PAST(v,t)[ON yesterday (Sammy arrive)]

For the sake of illustration it is enough to unpack (100). This formula will be true at (w,i) if $w = g_c(v)$, $i = g_c(t)$ and there is a $j < i$ such that

(101) ON yesterday (Sammy arrive)

is true at (w,j); this will obtain if j is a subinterval of yesterday and

(102) Sammy arrive

is true at (w,j). The analysis here is tantamount to taking (95) to be true if Sammy arrived sometime yesterday, i.e. sometime within yesterday.

3.4 Perfective Aspect

Turning to perfective aspect, let us first distinguish it from tense. Note that perfective sentences can apparently be unmarked for tense. Consider the complement sentence in this example.

(103) It is important that Ben have finished by the time Hilary comes back.

Here the verb phrase *have finished* cannot properly be construed as involving past tense. If any tense is involved, it must surely be the present tense since the import of (103) can arguably be paraphrased by replacing *have finished* with *finishes*. It is interesting to note, however, that in this position *finishes* does not invoke any reference to speech time, unlike the main verb *is*. Since reference to speech time is taken to be an essential feature of tense, it is reasonable to suspect that the morphology of *finishes* is not a sure guide to its semantic rôle in complement position. In the circumstance it seems appropriate to envisage a 'tenseless' analysis of *have finished*. We propose that *have* in conjunction with the morpheme *-ed* should be understood as marking perfective aspect and be treated as a sentential operator. In our quasi-formal language it is convenient to represent this operator as HAVE.

Before we define it, note that perfective aspect is normally taken to have something to do with perspective. It is widely thought that perfective aspect invokes reference to a time from which a certain event is to be viewed. This interval, the interval of perspective, is regarded as constituting a time within which the event is supposed to have occurred. When understood in this way, the interval is sometimes called the 'extended-now', which may suggest that perfective aspect is essentially related to speech time. We do not see perfective aspect as having any special relation to speech time, but it does invoke what we call an interval of perspective.

To render the idea of perspective we introduce the concept of an anchored interval. Where i and j are intervals, we say that

(104) i is anchored to j if j is a final segment of i.

Intuitively i is to be thought of as a perspective relative to j. The operator HAVE is then defined as follows, with A being any context-free sentence.

(105) HAVE (A) is true in a model **M** at (w,i) if there is an interval j which is anchored to i such that for some subinterval k of j A is true in **M** at (w,k); it is false at (w,i) if there is no j anchored to i such that for some subinterval k of j A is true at (w,k); (and otherwise it is undefined).

Since (105) makes no provision for speech time, it effectively distinguishes perfective aspect from tense. To illustrate the definition, it is useful to consider aspect together with tense, say in the form of the pluperfect.

(106) Ben had finished before 9.0.

The logical structure of (106) is to be analyzed as follows.

(107) PAST$_{(v,t)}$[BEFORE 9.0 [HAVE (Ben finish)]]

Working through the definitions again, (107) will be true at (w,i), provided $w = g_c(v)$ and $i = g_c(t)$, if there is a $j < i$ such that

(108) BEFORE 9.0 [HAVE (Ben finish)]

is true at (w,j); (108) will be true at (w,j) if j is earlier than 9.0 and

(109) HAVE (Ben finish)

is true at (w,j). Now this obtains if there is a k anchored to j such that for some subinterval l of k

(110) Ben finish

is true at (w,l). What is interesting here is that no unique perspective is identified from which to view the proposition expressed by (110). Only the range of admissible values of k and j is restricted, viz. to those intervals which precede 9.0. Thus the perspective fixed by k and j will be a variable one.[20]

Where the perspective is less variable is in the present perfect, as in this sentence.

(111) Ben has finished.

The logical rendering of (111) is,

(112) PRES$_{(v,t)}$[HAVE (Ben finish)]

---

20 Below we shall consider the interaction of perfective aspect and temporal quantifiers like *exactly twice*. Tichy (1985) has argued that an interval approach to the semantics of temporal expressions, such we as we propose, may not yield a satisfactory characterization.

which will be true at (w,i), given that w = $g_c(v)$ and i = $g_c(t)$, if

(109) HAVE (Ben finish)

is true at (w,i). And this holds if there is a j anchored to i such that for some subinterval k of j

(110) Ben finish

is true at (w,k). Since j is anchored to i, which here is speech time, the interval of perspective, viz. j, has one of its ends fixed. The other end, however, is variable, which reflects a certain indefiniteness in the perspective. This, we would venture, is just as it should be, i.e. as intuition would have it.

§4 Temporal Quantifiers and Connectives

4.1 Quantifiers and the Connective *When*

Temporal quantifiers, such as *always*, *never* and *exactly twice*, are treated in conformity with the 'standard' structure of temporal modifiers; that is, they are characterized as sentential operators applying only to context-free sentences. With a view to motivating the envisaged analysis, which is similar to that of the tense operators, let us examine the following sentence.

(113) Scott always dined at home.

It is clear (113) cannot naturally be interpreted as an unrestricted assertion, i.e. as saying that for the whole of past time Scott had the property of dining at home. It must rather be understood as a statement restricted to some intended interval; only of this period is it asserted that he always dined at home.[21] Depending upon context the intended period might be the one in which Scott lived in Edinburgh, or the one in which he lived at Abbotsford, or perhaps some entirely different interval. Which interval is intended on a given occasion of utterance is a pragmatic matter. But the rôle it plays in determining the proposition expressed is a semantic matter, i.e. of the semantic structure of (113). Here there is a question. Is the intended interval to be seen as the referent of some deictic expression revealed at the level of logical form? Or is it to be seen as identified in some non-referential way, say by a 'suppressed' *when* clause?

Let us consider a situation which evokes both possibilities. Suppose that one wanted to make an assertion about Scott's dining habits during the period when he lived at Abbotsford. If the context is sufficient to identify this as the intended interval, one might utter (113) with the intention of asserting that Scott always dined at home during that time. If, on the other hand, the relevant interval is not clear from context, one might opt to be more explicit by uttering this sentence.

(114) When he lived at Abbotsford, Scott always dined at home.

There may be some uncertainty as to whether (114) expresses the same proposition as (113), but there can be no doubt that the propositions are closely related, close enough to make them on occasion 'pragmatically' equivalent.

What does (114) tell us about the analysis of (113)? Suppose that (113) is represented as containing a deictic expression at the level of logical form; (114) will then share this structure. A 'deictic' analysis seems very plausible when (113) stands alone, but it raises an awkward question in the context of (114). The *when* clause in (114) is naturally regarded as specifying the interval over which *always* quantifiers. If the deictic in the main clause also serves this end, one of the devices must be redundant. Given that the deictic

---

21 Plainly it is a dispositional property that is relevant here.

is part of the logical form of (113), the *when* clause must be superfluous. While it might be useful for emphasis or clarification, it can have no essential semantic rôle, a result which would seem to misrepresent (114).

Intuitively (114) needs no deictic reference to specify the interval over which *always* quantifiers. The *when* clause is by itself sufficient. This suggests that there should be no deictic in the analysis of (113). Such an analysis would, however, leave it unclear how (113) identifies the intended interval of quantification when it stands alone. It seems there must be a deictic in the analysis here. But where is the deictic to be located? And how does it allow the *when* clause in (114) to be semantically relevant?

Since the deictic is to identify the interval over which the quantifier *always* ranges, it is natural to locate it as part of the quantifier itself. Accordingly we take *always* to be a complex sentential operator of the form ALWAYS_r, where r is a parameter whose values are intervals assigned from context. Like all temporal operators, ALWAYS_r applies only to context-free sentences, and thus (113) has the following logical form.[22]

(115) $\text{PAST}_{(v,t)}[\text{ALWAYS}_r(\text{Scott dine at home})]$

Before defining ALWAYS_r, let us first consider (114). One is inclined to think that the rôle of *when* clause is to fix the interval over which *always* quantifies. Although this intuition is not without substance, it is somewhat misleading since it tends to obscure the fact that the *when* clause has another independent semantic rôle. To reveal this rôle it is necessary to 'factor' tense from the sentences conjoined by *when*. In sentences like (114) the tenses of the conjoined sentences are not independent of each other; they are related by what is sometimes called sequence of tense, which is to say that the sentences must be in the same tense. The two sentences must also be evaluated conjointly, i.e. relative to the same speech time, and as such, they are in a

---

22 It should be noted that the occurrence of the parameter r in

(i) $\text{ALWAYS}_r(\text{Scott dine at home})$

does not make (i) context-sensitive in the technical sense, i.e. according to definition (26).

sense semantically bound.[23] We can capture this relationship by 'factoring' past tense from the two constituents and representing it as a operator over the resulting compound, i.e. over the following sentence in which *when* is a conjunction.

(116) Scott dine at home *when* he live at Abbotsford.

The logical form of (114) can now be analyzed in at least two different ways.

(117) PAST(v,t)[ALWAYS$_{r}$(Scott dine at home *when* he live at Abbotsford)]

(118) PAST(v,t)[ALWAYS$_{r}$(Scott dine at home) *when* he live at Abbotsford]

These may be seen to correspond to two possible interpretations of (114).

Suppose that Scott had several different periods of residence at Abbotsford, and suppose that one wishes to say something about just one of these periods. One could utter (114) with the intention of saying that that for every subinterval of that period Scott had the property of dining at home. Clearly it is the dispositional property one would have in mind here, since this can be true of Scott even at times when he is not actually in the process of dining at home.[24] This reading of (114) may be associated with (118), where *always* occurs within the scope of *when*.

The other reading of (114) emerges from the following paraphrase.

(119) Whenever Scott lived at Abbotsford, he dined at home.

Usually one would utter (119) with the intention of attributing to Scott the property of dining at home through each of the intervals during which he was resident at Abbotsford. One can also realize this intention by uttering (114).

---

23 The following sentence is not really a counterexample.

(ii) When he leaves, Max will be happy

From a semantic point of view the *when* clause is plainly about the future which agrees with the future tense in the main clause. This will be reflected at the level of logical form.

24 Dispositional properties are typically involved in sentences like (114). In fact the attribution of non-dispositional properties seems to be the special case

Here the appropriate analysis seems to be (117), where *always* has scope over *when*. To vindicate these claims we must first define ALWAYS_r and *when*.

To this end we introduce the concept of a cover for an interval. The underlying idea is to partition an interval into subintervals so as to consider what is true in them. A cover is a partition roughly defined as follows.

(120) A set of intervals P is a *cover* for an interval i if the elements of P are mutually distinct (non-overlapping) subintervals of i whose 'sum' is identical to i.[25]

The special significance of a cover will not emerge until we define the conjunction *when*. In the meantime it may seem to have a redundant rôle in the definition of ALWAYS_r. As usual A is assumed to be a context-free sentence.

(121) ALWAYS_r(A) is true in a model **M** at (w,i) if $i = g_c(r)$ and there is a cover P of $g_c(r)$ such that for each p in P, A is true in **M** at (w,p); it is false at (w,i) if $i \neq g_c(r)$ or there is no such cover; (and otherwise it is undefined).

We illustrate (121) by unpacking (115), given the analysis of (113).

(115) $\text{PAST}_{(v,t)}[\text{ALWAYS}_r$(Scott dine at home)].

This formula is true at (w,i), provided $w = g_c(v)$ and $i = g_c(t)$, if there is a $j < i$ such that

(122) ALWAYS_r(Scott dine at home)

25 Intuitively the 'sum' of P is given by the idea that if all the elements of P are matched with their place in i, the result is exactly i. It should also be noted that a cover may consist of both closed and open intervals; this will be the case for any cover of a real interval.

is true at (w,j), which holds if j = $g_c(r)$ and there is a cover P of $g_c(r)$ such that for each p in P

(123) Scott dine at home

is true at (w,p). Note that if there is a cover for $g_c(r)$ which verifies (123), (123) will be true for all the points in r (and vice versa). If (123) is true at (w,p), the homogeneity condition implies that it is true for every subinterval of p, including all singleton points.

As for the connective *when*, there is a temptation to think that it just means cotemporal with, but it is easy to see that this is not in general the case. Consider these two sentences.

(124) When Jocelyn received a letter, she wrote a reply.

(125) When Jocelyn went on holiday, she notified the police.

Clearly (124) will be true if Jocelyn wrote a reply to each letter she received, even though the reply was written sometime after the time of receipt. Since one typically replies only to those letters one has received (although not always so), the event in the *when* clause precedes the event in the main clause. In the case of (125), however, there is a perfectly acceptable interpretation where the event in the *when* clause is taken to come after the event in the main clause. If Jocelyn notified the police before she went on holiday, say to protect her house from burglary, (125) is surely true.

To accommodate these readings, as well as the preferred interpretation of (114), we shall distinguish two senses of *when*, the case sense and the cotemporal sense. The former is intended to account for both (124) and (125) while the latter is invoked to explain (114). The case sense of *when* is formulated in the following definition, where A and B are any context-free sentences.

(126) (A *when* B) is is true in a model **M** at (w,i) if there is a unique subinterval j of i such that B is true at (w,j) and at least one subinterval k of i such

that A is true at (w,k); it is false at (w,i) if there are no j and k of i which satisfy the indicated conditions; (and otherwise it is undefined).

The requirement that an interval uniquely satisfy certain conditions is a relative notion which we define roughly in this way. Assuming an account of what it is for an interval to satisfy a set of conditions S, we say that

(127) An interval j uniquely satisfies S with respect to i if j is a subinterval of i which satisfies S, and for any subinterval k of i if k satisfies S, k is a subinterval of j.[26]

There are at least two features of the case account of *when*, (as defined in (126)), that should be stressed. First the temporal order of subintervals j and k is undetermined; it does not matter what the order of precedence is, nor indeed whether they overlap. Second (A *when* B) is not equivalent to (B *when* A). To see this it is enough to assume for some interval i that j uniquely satisfies B with respect to i and that there are two subintervals k of i which satisfy A. By (126) (A *when* B) is true at i, but (B *when* A) is not.

The case sense of *when* is actually the more basic one since the cotemporal sense can be derived from it by adding the requirement that the subinterval j be a subinterval of k or, as we shall say, that k subsume j. One may wonder why k should subsume j and not be identical to it, given that the point is to capture cotemporality. If the relation between j and k were one of identity, then (A *when* B) would imply (B *when* A), and this seems almost as counterintuitive on the cotemporal reading as it is on the case reading. The stipulation that k subsume j blocks this entailment. For the sake of completeness we give the 'cotemporal' definition below.

(128) (A *when* B) is true in a model **M** at (w,i) if there is a unique subinterval j of i such that B is true at (w,j) and a subinterval k of i such that k subsumes j and A is true at (w,k); it is false in **M** at (w,i) if there are no j

26 In other words, for i j is maximal with respect to S.

and k which satisfy the indicated conditions; (and otherwise it is undefined).

It is this definition we shall use in considering the two interpretations of (114), i.e. the readings associated with (117) and (118).

To begin with, it may be helpful to examine (114) without the quantifier *always*, that is, to consider this sentence first.

(129) When he lived at Abbotsford, Scott dined at home.

The logical form of (129) is as follows.

(130) $PAST_{(v,t)}$(Scott dine at home *when* he live at Abbotsford)

Now (130) will be true at (w,i) if $w = g_c(v)$, $i = g_c(t)$ and there is a $j < i$ such that

(116) Scott dine at home *when* he live at Abbotsford

is true at (w,j). This will hold if there is a unique subinterval k of j such that

(131) He live at Abbotsford

is true at (w,k), and a subinterval l of j such that l subsumes k and

(123) Scott dine at home

is true at (w,l). It should be noted that while the value of k may be the whole of the period during which Scott lived at Abbotsford, it need not be so. What matters is that there is some part of that period during which Scott dined at home. If there is such a part, it is (modulo j) an appropriate value of k, and of course also of l.

Let us now turn back to (114), in particular to the reading putatively represented by (118).

(118) $PAST_{(v,t)}$[$ALWAYS_r$(Scott dine at home) *when* he live at Abbotsford)]

On the familiar pattern, (118) will be true at (w,i) if $w = g_c(v)$, $i = g_c(t)$ and there is a $j < i$ such that

(132) $ALWAYS_r$(Scott dine at home) *when* he live at Abbotsford

is true at (w,j). Since $ALWAYS_r$ falls within the scope of *when*, (132) will be true at (w,j) if there is a unique subinterval k of j such that

(131) He live at Abbotsford

is true at (w,k) and there is a subinterval l of j such that l subsumes k and

(122) $ALWAYS_r$(Scott dine at home)

is true at (w,l). Here the contextually determined referent of r becomes significant; (122) will be true at (w,l) if $l = g_c(r)$ and there is a cover P of $g_c(r)$ such that for each p in P

(123) Scott dine at home

is true at (w,p). This is just to say that (123) must be true throughout $g_c(r)$ since there will be an appropriate cover if and only if this is true.

The rôle of $g_c(r)$ is semantically pivotal since it picks out the interval of temporal quantification. The *when* clause, in contrast, has no semantic status in determining the past interval referred to; this is fixed solely by the reference of r. Nevertheless, the *when* clause may help to identify the interval of reference, since (118) will be true only if $g_c(r)$ is an interval for which Scott lived at Abbotsford. If one intends to tell the truth in uttering (118), one must intend to refer to a past interval satisfying this condition. But of course one may not want to tell the truth, or may unintentionally say something false.

There is, however, a 'wrinkle' which deserves comment. Suppose that $g_c(r)$ is only part of some period in which Scott lived at Abbotsford. Suppose that during that subinterval Scott always dined at home but that for some other subinterval of the period he did not do so. Now if one utters (114) intending to refer only to the former subinterval, one would be represented by (118) as saying something true. But can (114) be uttered felicitously in such a situation? We would say that it can if the context is right. Imagine a situation in which one is in a discussion about Scott's daily habits, say, during the period in which he was writing Waverley. Suppose that one wishes to say of some part of that period that he had the habit of dining at home. If that subinterval is contained as a part of an interval during which Scott resided at Abbotsford, one might locate the intended subinterval for one's audience by uttering (114): the combination of the *when* clause and the context might serve to identify subinterval referred to. One's assertion would then be restricted to just that part of the time during which Scott lived at Abbotsford. Although it seems possible to use (114) in this way, it is plainly not the typical case: one normally utters (114) with the intention of referring to the whole of an interval for which Scott lived at Abbotsford. Nevertheless, there is no semantic requirement to do so.

Here we turn to the second interpretation of (114), i.e. the one associated with (117).

(117) PAST(v,t)[ALWAYS_r(Scott dine at home *when* he live at Abbotsford)]

Recall that (117) will be true at (w,i) if w = g_c(v), i = g_c(t) and there is some j < i such that

(133) ALWAYS_r(Scott dine at home *when* he live at Abbotsford)

is true at (w,j). In contrast to (132), ALWAYS_r has scope over *when* in (133). Thus (133) will be true at (w,j) if j = g_c(r) and there is a cover P of g_c(r) such that for each p in P

(116) Scott dine at home *when* he live at Abbotsford

is true at (w,p). And (116) is true at (w,p) if there is a unique subinterval k of p such that

(131) He live at Abbotsford

is true at (w,k) and a subinterval l of p subsuming k such that

(123) Scott dine at home

is true at (w,l). What this means is that for each interval p of the cover there must be a unique instance of Scott's living at Abbotsford throughout which he had the habit of dining at home. If there is a cover of $g_c(r)$ meeting these conditions, then (117) is true. Note that the contextual assignment to r, i.e. $g_c(r)$ may be some stretch of past time in which there are several distinct periods when Scott resided at Abbotsford. According to (117), (114) asserts that he dined at home during each such period.

It is important to stress that $g_c(r)$ need not embrace all the intervals during which Scott was resident at Abbotsford. One might utter (114), or alternatively this sentence

(119) Whenever he lived at Abbotsford, Scott dined at home

without intending to make an assertion about all the periods in which Scott lived at Abbotsford. One might intend to refer to a stretch of time which includes only some subset of these periods. In the event one's assertion would be restricted to this interval.[27] The restriction here is similar to that noted above in connection with (118).

At this point one may begin to wonder whether the relative scopes of *always* and *when* are sufficient to distinguish the different readings of (114).

---

[27] The following sentence offers a clear example of this.

(i) When he travelled by bus, Franky always took a flask of gin.

Plainly *always* is not naturally read as quantifying over all the cases of Franky's travelling by bus. What he did as a child is irrelevant. But what he did during some interval of his adult life may well be topical, depending upon the context and the intentions of the speaker.

The fact is that any assignment to r for which (118) is true is one for which (117) is also true. Although the converse does not hold, one is tempted to think that this does not by itself explain the real ambiguity in (114). It lies, we conjecture, in the conjunction *when*, which has two meanings, viz. a case sense and the cotemporal sense. On the case reading (114) has (117) as its logical form, while on the cotemporal reading (118) is the appropriate logical form. We must leave a more detailed discussion of this hypothesis to another time. But before we leave the semantics of *when*, it might be useful to examine a sentence where the case reading is unmistakable.

(134) When she went away, Jocelyn always phoned the police.

On the above conjecture (134) has the following logical form.

(135) PAST(v,t)[$ALWAYS_r$(Jocelyn phone the police *when* she go away)]

The case interpretation of *when* allows any ordering between the intervals of Jocelyn's going away and her phoning the police: the former might precede the latter, or succeed it, or overlap it to some degree. In effect (135) expresses the proposition that for some designated past interval r there is at least one case of Jocelyn's phoning the police for each case of her going away.[28]

---

[28] To see that this is in fact the proposition expressed, note that (135) is true at (w,i) only if there is some $j < i$ such that

(136) $ALWAYS_r$(Jocelyn phone the police *when* she go away)

is true at (w,j); and (136) is true at (w,j) if $j = g_c(r)$ and there is a cover P of $g_c(r)$ such that for each p in P

(137) Jocelyn phone the police *when* she go away

is true at (w,p). Here the case definition (126) of *when*, applies: according to (126), (137) is true at (w,p) if there is a unique subinterval k of p such that

(138) She go away

is true at (w,k) and at least one subinterval l of p such that

(139) Jocelyn phone the police

is true at (w,l).

4.2 The Quantifier *Exactly Twice*

Let us now suppose that Jocelyn had habit of phoning the police more than once for each occasion of her going away. Perhaps she was never confident that the initial call was recorded and hence always phoned a second time to be sure. We might then assert the following.

(140) When she went away, Jocelyn always phoned the police exactly twice.

The quantifier *exactly twice* will be treated very similar to *always*; it will be represented as involving a deictic parameter and as quantifying over a cover. The definition goes as follows, with *exactly twice* represented as TWICE!_r.

(141) $\text{TWICE!}_r(A)$ is true in a model **M** at (w,i) if $i = g_c(r)$ and there is a cover P of $g_c(r)$ such that for exactly two elements p_1 and p_2 in P A is true at (w,p_1) and (w,p_2) and for any other cover Q of $g_c(r)$ and element q of Q if A is true at (w,q) then q is a subinterval of either p_1 or p_2; it is false at (w,i) if $i \neq g_c(r)$ or there is no cover P satisfying the indicated conditions; (and otherwise it is undefined).

To capture the logical form of (140) one must bear in mind that each of the temporal quantifiers has its own deictic parameter. It is clear, moreover, that the parameters are not to be given the same assignment since there is a significant scope relation; that is, *exactly twice* must be read as occurring within the scope of *always*. In effect the deictic parameter of *exactly twice* must be interpreted relative to the elements over which *always* quantifies.
We have seen a analogous situation with regard to the scoping of tenses, i.e. in respect of tense iteration. To represent tense iteration on our approach it is necessary to invoke the quantifier G, and this is just what is required in the case of (140). Its logical form is thus given by the following formula.[29]

---

29 Note that r' is a variable rather than a parameter.

(142) $\text{PAST}_{(v,t)}[\text{ALWAYS}_r[\text{Gr}'[\text{TWICE!}_{r'}$(Jocelyn phone the police) *when* she go away]]]

Let us run through the truth conditions: (142) is true at (w,i) only if there is a $j < i$ such that

(143) $\text{ALWAYS}_r[\text{Gr}'[\text{TWICE!}_r$(Jocelyn phone the police) *when* she go away]]

is true at (w,j); and this obtains if $j = g_c(r)$ and there is a cover P of $g_c(r)$ such that for each p in P

(144) $\text{Gr}'[\text{TWICE!}_r$(Jocelyn phone the police) *when* she go away]

is true at (w,p). Since G has widest scope here, (144) is true at (w,p) if

(145) TWICE!_{p*}(Jocelyn phone the police) *when* she go away

is true at (w,p), which holds if there is a unique subinterval k of p such that

(138) She go away

is true at (w,k), and at least one subinterval l of p such that $l = p$ and there is a cover Q of p for which there are exactly two subintervals m and n of p where

(139) Jocelyn phone the police

is true at (w,m) and (w,n). What all this amounts to can be summarized as follows: (142) is true at i (modulo w) if there is some past interval j where each case of Jocelyn's going away is matched with exactly two cases of her phoning the police. This is just what (140) was taken to mean.[30]

---

30 Tichy (1985) has suggested that an interval semantics will find it difficult, if not impossible, to provide an adequate analysis of temporal quantifiers like *exactly twice* while at the same time giving an appropriate rendering of both perfective aspect and adverbials like *yesterday*. It is worth noting, therefore, that the following two sentences seem to be adequately characterized within the present framework.

4.3 The Quantifier *Never*

Finally we turn to the quantifier *never*. It was noted earlier that sentences involving the connective *not* can sometimes be paraphrased using *never*. In fact there is an inclination to conjecture that they may actually be so close in meaning as to make the difference semantically uninteresting. With a view to pursuing this, let us define *never*. Where A is any context-free sentence,

(146) NEVER_r(A) is true in a model **M** at (w,i) if i = g_c(r) and there is no cover P of g_c(r) such that for some p in P A is true in **M** at (w,p); it is false at (w,i) if i ≠ g_c(r) or there is a cover P of g_c(r) such that for some p in P A is true at (w,p); (and otherwise it is undefined).

By way of illustration consider the sentence,

(147) Sally never stayed at the Savoy when she went to London

whose logical form is represented in the following way.

(148) $\mathrm{PAST}_{(v,t)}$[NEVER_r(Sally stay at the Savoy *when* she go to London)]

On this reading (148) will be true only if there are no cases in g_c(r) where Sally went to London and stayed at the Savoy.[31]

(i) Jocelyn has visited London exactly twice.

(ii) Jocelyn went to London exactly twice yesterday.

The logical forms of (i) and (ii) are given respectively by these formulas.

(iii) $\mathrm{PRES}_{(v,t)}$[HAVE [$\mathrm{TWICE!}_r$(Jocelyn visit London)]]

(iv) $\mathrm{PAST}_{(v,t)}$[$\mathrm{TWICE!}_r$[ON yesterday (Jocelyn go to London)]]

To see that (iii) and (iv) result in the intended truth conditions it is essential to appreciate that the value of the parameter is determined contextually in both cases. Its value is g_c(r) and is fixed, as it were, from the beginning, i.e. before the operators are 'peeled off'. In (iv) the intended value of r is yesterday. With the help of lambda abstraction any ambiguity could be removed. Since the verification is straightforward, we shall leave the proof to the reader.

31 This formula will be true at (w,i) only if there is a j < i such that

(149) NEVER_r(Sally stay at the Savoy *when* she go to London)

is true at (w,j), which will hold if j = g_c(r) and there is no cover P of g_c(r) such that for some p in P

(150) Sally stay at the Savoy *when* she go to London

Although there is undoubtedly a difference between *never* and *not*, it is interesting to consider the sentence which results from (147) by replacing *never* by *not*.

(153) Sally did not stay at the Savoy *when* she went to London.

Significantly (153) can be used in either of two ways. It can be uttered with the intention of making an assertion about Sally's habit when she went to London, in which case its logical form would be rendered in this way.

(154) *Not* [PAST(v,t)(Sally stay at the Savoy *when* she go to London)]

The import of (154) is equivalent to (148) if the assignment to r is the whole of the past relative to the time of speech. On the other hand, (153) can also be used with the intention of making an assertion about some particular occasion on which Sally went to London. To render the resulting proposition in terms of *not* it is necessary to invoke a 'suppressed' time reference, which (as above) is represented by the time adverbial *at then*. The desired formula is the following.

(155) PAST(v,t)[*Not* [AT then (Sally stay at the Savoy)] *when* she go to London)]]

In (155) *when* has wider scope relative to both *not* and AT then.

An alternative way of characterizing the same proposition can be formulated in terms of NEVER_r, viz. in this way.

(156) PAST(v,t)[NEVER_r(Sally stay at the Savoy) *when* she go to London]

---

is true at (w,p). On the case reading of *when* this obtains if there is no unique subinterval k of p such that

(151) She go to London

is true at (w,k), or any subinterval l of p such that

(152) Sally stay the Savoy

is true at (w,l).

Here *when* has scope over NEVER_r. Given that $g_c(r)$ coincides with some period in which Sally went to London, (156) says that Sally never stayed at the Savoy during that period. This is just what (155) says if the referent of *then* meets the conditions on $g_c(r)$. In fact when the referent of *then* is identical to $g_c(r)$, (155) and (156) are equivalent.

This is not to say of course that one can always substitute *never* for *not*. It does suggest, however, that where propositions are represented in terms of both negation and time reference they can always be re-characterized in terms of NEVER_r. This may not be linguistically significant, but it is of some semantic importance.

Although we have only examined one temporal connective, viz. *when*, it should be clear how we would treat other cases, in particular *before* and *after*. The definition of *after* is straightforward since its meaning is strictly temporal in character. In the case of *before*, however, the situation is different. While it has a temporal sense, it also has a modal sense, which emerges in this sentence.

(157) Max stopped the car before he hit the tree.

Since (157) implies that Max did not hit the tree, it is clear that *before* does not have the same factive import that *after* does. That is, the sentence

(158) Max stopped the car after he hit the tree

can only be interpreted as implying that Max hit the tree. The question then is how to formulate the modal sense of *before*. It is not inconceivable that *before* may have only a modal sense. For those 'special' cases where it has factive import, the reasons may be non-logical: it may be due to lexical features, or contextual factors, or perhaps something entirely different. In any case there is an issue here which we must leave for another time.

§5 Oblique Contexts and the Subjunctive

Davidson has suggested that the logical form of sentences of indirect discourse, e.g.

(159) Galileo said that the earth moves

should be understood in terms of two sentences which are related paratactically, in this case the sentences

(160) Galileo said that.

and

(161) The earth moves.

The expression *that* in (160) has the status of a demonstrative pronoun which in utterances of (159) is used to refer to the utterance of (161). Since (161) occurs as part of (159) it is not itself asserted. What is asserted is (160), with the utterance of (161) serving to identify what Galileo said. One who utters (161) as part of (159) represents himself as being a samesayer with Galileo. That is, Galileo is given to have uttered some sentence in his language, Italian or Latin, whose purport is the same as one's own utterance of (161).
Let us suppose that sameness of purport consists in expressing the same proposition.[32] The question then is what proposition does (160) attribute to Galileo. On our Russellian theory an utterance of (161), when it stands as an independent sentence, expresses a value-specific proposition, i.e. one which is true at most of the time of utterance. Since the past tense in this context engenders reference to speech time, the utterance amounts to an assertion about that time and must be true of it if it is to be true at all. When (161)

[32] Although Davidson eschews reference to propositions, it is useful here to set this aside.

stands as part of (159), however, its utterance will have a rather different relation to the time of speech. Plainly there can be no reference to the present speech time if the utterance is to express the same proposition which was expressed by Galileo. Since Galileo will have referred to his speech time, one can be a samesayer with him only if one refers to that time. If one does so refer in uttering (161), it may seem that one would express the same proposition as he did. This must of course be a value-specific proposition, at least according to our theory.

But can such a proposition be a suitable relatum for the relation of saying? To be more precise, can the occurrence of *said* in the utterance of

(160) Galileo said that.

be interpreted as a relation between Galileo and some value-specific proposition? To see that it cannot be one need only consider another contingent sentence, say

(162) The moon has craters

and suppose that it happens to be uttered with respect to the same speech time as (161). Given that both utterances are true of this time, they will express the same value-specific proposition (modulo a common reference to possible world). In fact there are just two such propositions possible here, one that evaluates to true only for the interval of utterance and the other that evaluates to false for all intervals. If one takes all the utterances uttered simultaneously with Galileo's utterance (regardless of who may have done the uttering), all the true utterances will express one value-specific proposition and all the false ones the another. Hence any relation Galileo sustains to one true utterance he also sustains to the others, and similarly for any false utterance. Clearly value-specific propositions are not appropriate relata for saying, since they cannot discriminate among the different things that may be said. The same is obviously true in the case of all propositional attitudes.

From the viewpoint of our theory it is significant that oblique contexts, such as the one formed by *Galileo said that*, do not allow contained sentences to be asserted. No utterance of (159) can give rise to an assertion of (161). Davidson's analysis of (159) does not explain why this is so. Since he represents (161) as having the status of an independent sentence which is related paratactically to (160), he portrays it as having an occurrence suitable for assertion. The fact that the occurrence is plainly otherwise is a fact that stands against his analysis. If one amends the analysis by supposing that (160) and (161) are connected more than paratactically, it seems possible to explain why (161) is not assertable. On the assumption that (161) occurs as a genuine contained formula in (159), one can say that in such contexts there can be no appropriate reference, i.e. of the sort that occurs when (161) is uttered as a main clause. Assertion requires reference to the actual world and to speech time and thus, it is natural to trace the unassertability of (161) to the impossibility of appropriate reference. Where there cannot be reference to both the actual world and the time of utterance, there can be no assertion. The point to note is that if there were such reference in uttering (161), it would express a value-specific proposition, which is something we have just seen to be unacceptable in the context.

How then is (161) to be represented when it occurs as part of (159)? The answer is foreshadowed in the treatment of the tense operators. As such operators can apply only to context-free formulas, so (161) will require a context-free rendering when it occurs in an oblique position. Given that the subordinate verb *moves* falls within the scope of the main verb *said*, (161) must be characterized as follows.

(163) $Gv',t'[PRES_{(v',t')}(\text{the earth move})]$

Recall that (163) expresses a value-free proposition which may be true at indices other than the index of utterance. Note moreover that the 'context-free' rendering of (162), viz.

(164) Gv',t'[PRES(v',t')(the moon have craters)]

expresses a different value-free proposition. Even if (163) and (164) both happen to be true at the time of utterance, they will not always be true together and hence do not express the same proposition. Since this is the sort of propositional discrimination required for oblique contexts, it is natural to think that value-free propositions are proper objects for the attitudes.[33]

At this point it seems not unreasonable to abandon Davidson's approach to (159). Indeed it now seems right to analyze (159) in the obvious way, with (161) taken as a genuine subordinate clause. While *said*, or rather *say*, is to be interpreted as a relation, *that* is not a referring term but a propositional operator which creates a name; the result of applying *that* to a formula is a name which refers to the proposition expressed by that formula. Thus the logical form of (159) is represented as follows.

(165) PAST(v,t)[Galileo say that [Gv',t'[PRES(v',t')(the earth move)]]

Here *that* applies to the formula (163) to name the value-free proposition expressed by (163). It should be noted that both occurrences of the tense operators apply to context-free formulas, i.e. to formulas which contain no occurrences of the parameters v and t.[34]

On this approach to indirect discourse it emerges that sentences are not semantically innocent, even though their subcomponents may be. An utterance of the sentence,

(161) The earth moves

expresses a different kind of proposition depending upon the linguistic context in which the sentence occurs. It expresses a value-specific proposition

---

33 Unfortunately value-free propositions are not 'fine-grained' enough to yield a general solution to the problem of logical omniscience. Nevertheless, they represent a step in the right direction and serve our immediate objectives.

34 See definitions (26) and (27).

if the sentence stands as a main clause, but when it is embedded in an oblique context, as in (159), it expresses a value-free proposition. This would suggest a rather paradoxical situation: it seems impossible to report what someone said through indirect discourse. The 'feeling' of paradox seems most tangible in this sentence.

(166) The moon has craters and I say that the moon has craters.

Anyone who utters (166) cannot, it seems, be a samesayer with himself, since his two utterances of

(162) The moon has craters

will express different propositions.

The paradox, however, is more apparent than real. There is an inclination to suppose that the proposition one expresses in uttering (162) must be what one says. After all there is a long philosophical tradition which holds just that. Nevertheless, it is still possible to draw a distinction between what one says and the proposition expressed. Since the concept of a proposition is a technical term, it can be defined as one chooses. We choose to define it in a way which implies that it cannot always be identified with what is said. On our analysis one who utters (162) expresses a value-specific proposition whose status is closely related to the truth value of the utterance. If the utterance is true for the index of utterance, it expresses one of the two possible value-specific propositions for that index, viz. the one which is true for that index alone. If the utterance is false, it expresses the universally false value-specific proposition, i.e. the proposition which is false for all indices. The content of one's utterance is plainly not given by either of these propositions.

We take its content to be given by the value-free proposition expressed by the following formula.

(164) $Gv',t'[PRES_{(v',t')}(\text{the moon have craters})]$

What one says in uttering (162) is distinguished, not by its truth value, but by its content, and this is discriminated by (164). Hence if one wishes to report what one says in such an utterance, one must invoke the value-free proposition expressed by (164). If one wishes to report that what one says is true, one must refer to the index of utterance. This requires an explicit reference, which is not found in (159).

Certain tense phenomena lend support to the view that oblique contexts are not semantically innocent. The 'relational' import of tenses in oblique contexts is not always the same as their import in main clauses. Take this sentence.

(167) Someone will say that Bush was a great President.

If one were to utter (167) today (17th May 1986), one would naturally intend the complement sentence,

(168) Bush was a great President

to be understood as saying something about the future relative to some later time in the future. One would at least not wish to be taken as saying something about the past relative to the present time, not unless there were some misapprehension. Note that the future time relative to which (168) is to be interpreted is indeterminate; it is just some time in the future. If one wishes to make the time definite, say 17th May 2000, one could modify (167) as follows.

(169) Someone will say on 17th May 2000 that Bush was a great President.

It is important to appreciate that the indicated future time cannot be fixed from within the subordinate position itself, i.e. in this way.

(170) Someone will say that Bush was a great President on 17th May 2000.

In fact there is no way of modifying the contained occurrence of (168) to refer to the time relative to which it is to be considered. When (168) stands as a main clause, however, there is no avoiding such a reference since it must be the time of speech. This strongly suggests that (168) does not occur innocently in (167).

In this connection it may be mentioned that the tenses in (167) should not be seen as iterated. Since the future tense occurs in the main clause and the past tense in the complement clause, the two cannot be rendered at the level of logical form as a 'prenex' prefix to any formula. The relation between the tenses is not really a matter of logical scope but of the linguistic contexts within which the tenses occur. The tense of the subordinate sentence is a significant constituent of the relatum of the main verb and thus, its relation to the tense of the main verb is not strictly a relation of iteration.

We are now able to speculate about what is semantically characteristic of subjunctive sentences, e.g. of occurrences like (168) in (167). Subjunctive sentences may sometimes be marked for tense but they are never sensitive to the time of speech, as indicative sentences are. In this respect they are uniformly untensed. Accordingly the logical form of a subjunctive sentence never has occurrences of the context parameters v and t and hence always expresses a value-free proposition.

2

Indexicals: Bound and Unbound

JON OBERLANDER

> *I just want to mention—en passant—that all treatments of* now *and* then *by philosophers and logicians are hopelessly inadequate for the description of the behaviour of these words in natural language.*
>
> [Kamp and Rohrer 1983: 264]

Introduction

The purpose of this chapter is to provide a treatment of temporal indexicals which *is* adequate for the description of two distinct patterns of behaviour which such expressions can exhibit. If this can be done, then Kamp and Rohrer's claim will have been overtaken by events. The two types of occurrence will be called *unbound* and *bound* for reasons which will become apparent. The treatment which we give will be a formal semantics based on IQ. It will be demonstrated that IQ can capture both bound and unbound indexicals by treating them as *parametric* expressions in the language of IQ, and using the substitutional G-operator to derive the former from the latter.

The plan of action is as follows: first, we shall introduce unbound indexicals, which have been dealt with in considerable detail by Kaplan (1977). The fact that Kaplan's analysis was devoted solely to unbound indexicals is presumably one of the reasons Kamp and Rohrer would deem it 'hopelessly' inadequate; we turn then to examples of bound indexicals from discourse, which they would take to falsify a Kaplan-style analysis. Next we turn to examples of bound indexicals from single sentences, in order to demonstrate that bound indexicals are not simply a discourse-level phenomenon. Finally, the greater part of the chapter assumes some familiarity with the IQ framework, and shows how it can capture both indexicals bound and unbound.

§1 Indexicals Unbound

(1a), (2) and (3) are examples of unbound indexicals:

(1a) It was predicted last week that the earthquake would occur.

(1b) It was predicted last week that the earthquake would occur now.

(2) It will soon be the case that all that is now beautiful is faded.

(3) It is possible that in Pakistan, in five years, only those who are actually here now will be envied.

The difference between (1a) and (1b) lies in the addition of *now*. The examples, which are adapted from Kamp (1971), demonstrate that *now* can play a genuine semantic rôle. An utterance of (1b) is more specific than an utterance of (1a); (1a) could be true where (1b) is not, if for instance the prediction reported was merely that an earthquake would occur within the next year or so. For our purposes, however, it is only necessary to note that if (1b) is uttered on t_1, what is supposed to have been predicted is that the earthquake would occur at t_1. One way to express this is to say that *now* refers to the time of speech; even if one doesn't accept that *now* is a referring expression, one can agree that what was predicted to occur in (1a) is predicted to occur at the time of speech in (1b).

As with (1b), so with (2). Although it is in the scope of the English language expression *It will soon be the case that* which corresponds to an intensional operator, *now* drags the contained sentence back to the time of the utterance of (2). Indeed, *now* must ensure that the beautiful things we are talking about in (2) are those which are beautiful at the time of speech. If it did not, (2) would be trivially false, for an utterance would have to be interpreted as saying that things were both beautiful and faded at the same time, which is not generally held to be possible.

We are concerned in this chapter with temporal indexicals such as *now*, *today*, *tomorrow* and so on, but (3) illustrates that other kinds of indexical expression such as *here* remain unaffected by linguistic contexts traditionally regarded as intensional. What is common to these examples is the occurrence of indexicals which refer back (or whatever) to the extralinguistic context of the utterance in which they occur. They are unaffected by arbitrarily complex linguistic contexts. In the words of David Kaplan:

> [N]o operator can control the character of the indexicals within its scope, because they will simply leap out of its scope to the front of the operator.
>
> [Kaplan 1977: 32]

To the extent that such indexicals always leap out of the scope of operators, the indexicals remain *unbound*. It should be noted, of course, that this term is merely a metaphorical description of their behaviour; the semantic account is still to follow in sections 3 and 4.

Now, unbound indexicals have been studied before, and Kaplan's (1977) is something of a *locus classicus*. He there calls them directly referential terms, and they are the only kinds of indexical he envisages. The quote above comes from a section where he argues against the possibility of any other type of occurrence. For the record, here is Kaplan's theory of indexicals (Kaplan (1977: 10)):

Principle-1: The referent of a pure indexical depends on the context, and the referent of a demonstrative depends on the associated demonstration.

Principle-2: Indexicals, pure indexicals and demonstratives alike, are directly referential.

A directly referential term is a strict form of rigid designator, which has no descriptive element at all (there are some descriptions which are, so to speak, accidentally rigid). Two things are worth noting: first, in the formal development of his theory, Kaplan (1979) renders indexicals as sentential operators rather than as singular terms; secondly, it is this kind of account which Kamp and Rohrer take to fly in the face of evidence about the behaviour of indexicals in natural language.

§2 Indexicals Bound

What other kind of indexical behaviour is there? In this section, we shall first survey the evidence from discourse which Kamp and Rohrer (1983) and Dry (1979) amongst others have used to undermine confidence in existing analyses. We will then go on to give a number of examples of similar behaviour of indexicals within single sentences.

2.1 Discourse Indexicals

Consider the following examples, of which (4) to (6) are translated and emended versions of examples Kamp and Rohrer give:

(4) Last Thursday, the House discussed the privatisation of the BBC. First A gave the government's point of view. He was immediately attacked by B.

Then, C, D and E spoke in turn. Finally, at 2am, Mr Hurd rose to the dispatch box...

(5a) At that time, there were no more than twenty-five MPs present.

(5b) There were now no more than twenty-five MPs present.

(6) ...Rieux got up, his face now in shadow.

(7) The Prime Minister authorised the aid package. The team was now ready to take the initiative.

(8) She was a plain, motherly kind of woman, who had worked hard in her youth, and now thought herself entitled to the occasional holiday of a tea-visit...

(5a) and (5b) are both possible continuations of (4); the difference between them undoubtedly lies in the fact that *now* makes (5b) seem more immediate than the *at that time* of (5a). Indeed, one could say that (5a) adopts a detached mode of reporting, whereas (5b) adopts an involved one. As with almost all these examples, it is hard to resist the temptation to say that the difference between an indexical term and a non-indexical equivalent (as in (5a)) lies in the realm of stylistic variation. However, even if this is so, the important semantic fact is that the *now* in (5b) does not refer back to the time of utterance of (4) as a whole. So too with the other examples: whatever *now* is doing, it is not functioning as one of Kaplan's directly referential terms; the indexical is not unbound. Indeed, where a temporal indexical no longer bears its usual intimate relation to features of the extralinguistic context of utterance, we shall call that indexical *bound.*

It should be noted that in a complex (and real) example such as (8), which is cited by Dry (1979), and comes from Jane Austen's *Emma*, *now* refers not to narrator's time, but to a time within the narrative; so it cannot be thought of as working off the narrator's 'speech time'. Like the other examples of indexicals in discourses above, it is bound. This might lead one to think that the binding of indexicals is effected by some mechanism which operates only at the level of discourse. The examples in the next section indicate that such a conclusion would be premature.

2.2 More Bound Indexicals

Bound indexicals can occur in single sentences:

(9) Never put off until tomorrow what you can do today.

(10) Tomorrow never comes.

(11) Max always said that he would be rich tomorrow.

(12) The reptiles have been told to confine their remarks to tomorrow's weather.

If a theory can deal with such single-sentence examples (the last of which comes from *Private Eye*), then there is no need to invoke special discourse mechanisms to explain them. The claim of this chapter is that IQ can represent single sentence indexicals, either bound or unbound, without using a new mechanism. To deal with multi-sentence examples, such as those from section 2.1, we would need to invoke some notion of temporal connexion such as that pursued in Chapter 5. What does IQ do with temporal indexicals, and how?

§3 Unbound Indexicals in IQ

We claim that it is possible to represent both unbound and bound indexicals in IQ. In order to represent either adequately, we will have to change the representation of the former so as to properly represent the features they do and do not share with IQ's tenses. Once this has been done, we will go on to examine two examples of unbound indexicals, one of which seems to present a problem for the representation we adopt. Then, in section 4, we will demonstrate how to represent a bound indexical like that in (11). The representation adopted will depend to some extent on our analysis of indirect speech reports, and so section 4 will contain a discussion of these which is quite independent from that pursued in Chapter 4. First, then, let's look at the original IQ representation for indexicals.

3.1 Richards' Treatment of Indexicals

In Chapter 1, Richards provides semantic clauses for two indexical expressions: *yesterday* and *then*. Each is treated as a noun, which together with a preposition forms a sentential operator. Where A is a context-free sentence, (13) and (14) give Richards' definitions.

(13) ON yesterday (A) is true in a model **M** at (w,i) if i is a subinterval of yesterday and A is true in **M** at (w,i); it is false at (w,i) if i is not a subinterval of yesterday or A is false at (w,i); and otherwise it is undefined.

(14) AT then (A) is true in a model **M** at (w,i) if i = then and A is true at (w,i); it is false at (w,i) if i ≠ then or A is false at (w,i); and otherwise it is undefined.

Richards admits that these clauses are in fact definition schemas, because the indexicals admit of alternative interpretations. Presumably, this must be read as a claim that indexicals are context-sensitive, and that the referent of an indexical varies, depending on the context of use. To illustrate the behaviour of indexicals in the system, it is only necessary to unpack the truth-conditions for (16), the representation of (15).

(15) Donald arrived in London yesterday

(16) $PAST_{(v,t)}$[ON yesterday (Donald arrive in London)]

(16) is true in model **M** at (w,i) if w = $g_c(v)$ and i = $g_c(t)$ and there is a j earlier than i such that (17) is true at (w,j).

(17) ON yesterday (Donald arrive in London)

According to (13), (17) is true at (w,j) if j is subinterval of yesterday and (18) is true at (w,j).

(18) Donald arrive in London

Clearly, there is an unreduced indexicality in the truth-conditions; it must be this that Richards is adverting to when he admits multiple interpretations for *yesterday*. The problems attached to this representation of indexicals will be addressed in the next section.

3.2 Problems with Richards' Treatment

Richards' representation of temporal indexicals runs into problems in two major areas. First, it cannot adequately represent unbound indexicals. Secondly, it cannot represent bound indexicals at all. We shall deal with each of these points in turn.

Unbound indexicals are, in Kaplan's terms, both context-sensitive and directly referential. Kaplan isolated the two properties of indexicals which give rise to their unique behaviour, but failed to unify them. An essential aspect of our approach to unbound indexicals is that their behaviour can be explained by treating the indexical as a parametric expression in IQ. Both the directly referential and context-sensitive properties are possessed by parameteric expressions. More about parametric expressions below; suffice it for the moment that the tenses of IQ are parametric, and that indexicals are like them in some relevant respects.

As far as their representation is concerned, parametric expressions must be systematically distinguished from ordinary expressions, both referential and quantificational. Section 3.1 indicated the representation Richards gives to indexicals such as *yesterday*. It is significant that the schema he offers differs hardly at all from the representation he gives dates such as *1st April 1985:*

(19) ON 1st April 1985 (A) is true in **M** at (w,i) if i is a subinterval of 1st April 1985 and A is true in **M** at (w,i); it is false at (w,i) if either i is not a subinterval of 1st April 1985 or A is false at (w,i); and otherwise it is undefined.

There is no distinction between this representation and that for the indexical given in section 3.1. The syntactic forms of the expressions are exactly the same. The truth clauses are exactly the same. Thus the existing representation does not distinguish parametric temporal expressions from other temporal expressions. Kaplan would regard this as a fundamental error, since it is a central contention of Kaplan (1977) that indexicals are logical words, and may in this respect be suitably contrasted with dates. In Richards' defence, it might be argued that he does maintain a distinction between dates and indexicals; namely, indexicals contain an unreduced indexical expression in their semantic clauses. This is indeed the case, but it is not a cause for celebration. On the one hand, the unreduced indexical does allow the indexical expression to be re-used again and again, with a different referent each time. On the other hand, trouble arises when an attempt is made to deal with utterances of sentences such as (20).

(20) ?John ate his breakfast tomorrow

The trouble with (20) is that there is mismatch between the interval specified by the tense and the interval specified by the indexical. For this reason, it would be desirable if the semantic structure of (20) were ill-formed, so that (20) was inexpressible using the original resources of IQ. (21) is the representation which Richards would assign to (20).

(21) $PAST_{(v,t)}$ [ON tomorrow (John eat his breakfast)]

(21) is true in model **M** at (w,i) if w = g_c(v) and i = g_c(t) and there is a j earlier than i such that (22) is true at (w,j).

(22) ON tomorrow (John eat his breakfast)

(22) is true at (w,j) if j is a subinterval of tomorrow and (23) is true at (w,j).

(23) John eat his breakfast

(23) is true at (w,j) if John eats his breakfast at that time. As it stands, the semantics of *tomorrow* leaves (21) well-formed. The only constraints on j, the interval at which (23) is true, are that it be before speech time, and that it be a subinterval of tomorrow. The fact that tomorrow cannot be *before* speech time is not registered by the semantics: it is a matter of world knowledge or pragmatics. So (20) is not semantically ill-formed, just pragmatically inadvisable. The blame for this lies with the unreduced indexical in Richards' representation of *tomorrow*. Nothing relates it to speech time, beyond the fact that the utterance and its evaluation via the semantic clauses are supposed to occur simultaneously, and the evaluator (or language comprehender) is supposed to know that his or her tomorrow is therefore the same as the tomorrow of the speaker of the utterance. If, for instance, the velocity of communication is low, the wrong truth conditions will result. So, although it distinguishes indexicals from dates, the unreduced indexical does so by moving an apparently semantic matter out of the domain of semantics.

The unreduced indexical is unsatisfactory, then, and must be reduced. The means of reduction is at hand, and with it comes the possibility of systematically separating the indexicals from the dates. If an indexical is given a parameter in its representation, and that parameter is evaluated by the function g_c, troublesome instances of *tomorrow* are excluded semantically. The choice of parameter made in section 3.3 allows this, and we return to (20) in section 3.5.

It was stated that the Richards representation runs into problems over both unbound and bound indexicals. We have seen why it has difficulties with unbound indexicals; its problem with bound indexicals arises because there is no way of representing indexicals as anything other than referring expressions which occur with prepositions to form sentential operators. In other words, the bound cases cannot be represented at all. One way of treating bound indexicals is to assume that they have some sort of variable within their form, which is available for binding. Richards allows no such structure in unbound indexicals, and as a result, there is no structure available to allow the formation of expressions which could represent bound indexicals. By contrast, the proposal below will introduce enough structure to permit the formation of expressions representing bound indexicals. In fact, of course, the parametric representation of indexicals introduces not a variable, but a parameter. However, if there is an operator which includes parameters in its domain, then bound indexicals may be represented. There is indeed such an operator: G.

3.3 The Formal Apparatus

The previous section suggested that we might adopt a representation of the indexical which gives it a parameter in its logical form. This for two reasons: first, it will allow the context-sensitive and directly referential nature of indexicals to be properly portrayed; secondly, it will allow bound indexicals to be represented, using the metamathematical substitution operator G to bind the parameters, thereby defeating direct reference (or parametricity). G replaces a linguistic expression with another linguistic expression formed by naming an entity from the domain. In this section, we will consider what kind of parameter indexicals should receive, and what consequences such a choice will have for the theory. As far as parameter-binding goes, that topic will be tackled in section 4, where the choice made in this section will ultimately be vindicated.

In the system given in Chapter 1, there are two types of temporal parameter, labelled ‘t’ and ‘r’. The former appear as part of the tense operators, the latter as part of temporal quantifiers. Assuming that we wish to represent indexicals without introducing a new type, a choice must be made between r and t.

3.3.1 The Parameter r

Is the parameter for indexicals r? Although r is only used in the original IQ system for temporal quantifiers, there is no reason why there should not be singular deictic temporal expressions, with the parameter r attached. According to Richards, v and t are ‘the only parameters to be styled as context-sensitive’.[1] From this, it would be natural to argue in the following way.

First, a sentence containing an instance of the parameter t would be context-sensitive, and therefore unsuitable material for a tense operator (or indeed, any temporal operator), because the operators are defined as taking context-free sentences as their domain. Secondly, indexicals must occur inside tensed sentences; therefore indexicals cannot invoke the parameter t. So, the only alternative is that indexicals are represented with the parameter r attached in their form.

However, such a conclusion cannot be correct, because it misconstrues the point of distinguishing r from t. t is the parameter which the function g_c takes to speech time. In other words, its value is assigned from context, and that value is the time of the utterance. Uttering a tensed sentence, a speaker has no choice over the value of $g_c(t)$. By contrast, r is the parameter which g_c can take to any deictically appropriate interval. The value is indeed assigned from context, but need have no relation to speech time whatsoever. The difference is that in this case, the speaker has a choice about the value of $g_c(r)$. In this

1 Footnote 7 in Chapter 1. Note that Richards' use of the term does not coincide with Kaplan's.

respect, r resembles Kaplan's true demonstratives rather than his pure indexicals. For two reasons, r must be the wrong parameter for indexicals, and t the right one: first, indexical expressions such as *yesterday*, *now* and *next year* have referents which are necessarily related to speech time; secondly, a speaker has no choice about their reference. Thus, we must consider in more detail what happens if we use the parameter t.

3.3.2 The Parameter t

If the parameter is t, then *yesterday* would be represented as yesterday_t with the truth clause in (24).

(24) ON yesterday_t (A) is true in a model **M** at (w,i) if i is a subinterval of the day before the day of $g_c(t)$ and A is true in **M** at (w,i); it is false at (w,i) if i is not a subinterval of the day before $g_c(t)$ or A is false at (w,i); and otherwise it is undefined.

To see that this representation gives the correct truth-conditions for a sentence, consider an utterance of the sentence (25), which is represented by (26).

(25) Sue phoned yesterday

(26) $\text{PAST}_{(v,t)}$ [ON yesterday_t (Sue phone)]

(26) is true in model **M** at (w,i) if w = $g_c(v)$ and i = $g_c(t)$ and there is a j earlier than i such (27) is true at (w,j). Note that, as usual, the speech time i is the value of $g_c(t)$.

(27) ON yesterday_t (Sue phone)

(27) is true at (w,j) if j is a subinterval of the day before the day of $g_c(t)$, and (28) is true at (w,j).

(28) Sue phone

So, (25) is true if Sue phoned at some time on the day before the day of the utterance of (25). This is just as it should be. However, recalling the argument in the previous section, it might be claimed that (26) cannot be the correct representation for (25), because (26) is actually semantically ill-formed. If the presence of the parameter t makes a sentence context-sensitive, then the past tense operator cannot apply to (27) to give (26). If the representation of *yesterday* is correct, we must alter the sentence to which the tense applies in order that it is context-free. Using G to deparametrize the t attached to *yesterday* the resulting representation for (25) is (29):

(29) $PAST_{(v,t)}$ [Gt'[ON $yesterday_{t'}$ (Sue phone)]]

This would be true at (w,i) if w = $g_c(v)$ and i = $g_c(t)$, as before, and there was a j earlier than i such that (30) was true at (w,j).

(30) Gt'[ON $yesterday_{t'}$ (Sue phone)]

(30) is true at (w,j) if (31) is true at (w,j).

(31) ON $yesterday_{j*}$ (Sue phone)

(31) is true at (w,j) if j is a subinterval of the day before the day of $g_c(j^*)$ and (28) is true at (w,j). But this is impossible, since $g_c(j^*)$ is simply j; thus (31) would be true if j is a subinterval of the day before the day of j, which cannot be. Deparametrizing t so that a tense operator can apply to a sentence containing an indexical will not do. And even if it could, it would defeat the whole point of parametrization, which was to portray the parametric nature of unbound indexicals while using G to capture bound indexicals; if unbound indexicals are not parametric, and if we have to use G before we even treat bound indexicals, we have failed badly.

3.3.3 Parameters and Context-Sensitivity

All is not lost. It is possible to retain the representation for *yesterday* suggested above, and maintain (26) as the representation for (25) if a little more attention is paid to the notion of context-sensitivity alluded to above. It was stated that v and t are the only context-sensitive parameters. This is, however, a slightly sloppy way of speaking. By definition, for a sentence A,

> A is said to be context-sensitive if it has the form $Q_{(v,t)}B$ or contains a subformula of this form. [Chapter 1, 20]

Sure enough, v and t do appear in context-sensitive formulae; however, a sentence is only context-sensitive if it actually contains a formula of the form $Q_{(v,t)}$, where Q ranges over {PAST, PRES, FUT}. That is, a sentence is technically context-sensitive only if has an undeparametrized tense in it. An occurrence of t is not enough; it is not enough even if we allow *yesterday* to be reconstructed as ON yesterday$_{(\{\},t)}$, so that a sentence containing *yesterday* contains a subformula of the form $Q_{(v,t)}$. It is not enough, because a sentence is context-sensitive *only* if the Q in the subformula in question is one of PAST, PRES or FUT. Once the full implications of the definition of context-sensitivity are recognised, it becomes clear that (27) is context-free after all, so that the tense operator can apply to it without impediment. Of course, it also becomes clear that 'context-sensitive' is a slightly misleading term, since it cannot really apply to terms which gain their referents relative to a context of utterance. It only applies to those terms (the tenses) which, as it were, force the evaluation of the sentence in their scope. Tenses are evaluation inducing, in that once one has been encountered, a sentence is pegged to an interval relative to which it must be evaluated. It is no coincidence that it is value-specific propositions (i.e. truths or falsehoods) that are expressed with tensed sentences, and value-free propositions (the content of the former) that are expressed in tenseless sentences. Nor is it any surprise that there can be no more than one undeparametrized tense in a sentence: after all, the sentence cannot be evaluated twice.

3.4 The New Representation

From the discussion in section 3.3, it seems as though the right parameter for almost all temporal indexicals is t; and this necessitates a more rigorous conception of context-sensitivity. The choice of parameter allows us to systematically distinguish indexicals from dates: the former are related to speech time, the latter are not. Schematically, the situation is as follows. (32a) shows the general form of AT with dates, (32b), the form of AT with indexicals; (33a) shows the form of ON with dates and (33b) the form of ON with indexicals; (34a) and (34b) show the form of BEFORE with dates and indexicals respectively. Where d is a schema for dates, and x_t a schema for indexicals,

(32a) AT d (A) is true in **M** at (w,i) if i = d and A is true in **M** at (w,i); it is false at (w,i) if either i ≠ d or A is false at (w,i); and otherwise it is undefined.

(32b) AT x_t (A) is true in **M** at (w,i) if i = the x relative to $g_c(t)$ and A is true in **M** at (w,i); it is false at (w,i) if either i ≠ the x relative to $g_c(t)$ or A is false at (w,i); and otherwise it is undefined.

(33a) ON d (A) is true in **M** at (w,i) if i is a subinterval of d and A is true in **M** at (w,i); it is false at (w,i) if either i is not a subinterval of d or A is false at (w,i); and otherwise it is undefined.

(33b) ON x_t (A) is true in **M** at (w,i) if i is a subinterval of the x relative to $g_c(t)$ and A is true in **M** at (w,i); it is false at (w,i) if either i is not a subinterval of the x relative to $g_c(t)$ or A is false at (w,i); and otherwise it is undefined.

(34a) BEFORE d (A) is true in **M** at (w,i) if i is earlier than d and A is true in **M** at (w,i); it is false at (w,i) if either i is not earlier than d or A is false at (w,i); and otherwise it is undefined.

(34b) BEFORE x_t (A) is true in **M** at (w,i) if i is earlier than the x relative to $g_c(t)$ and A is true in **M** at (w,i); it is false at (w,i) if either i is not earlier than the x relative to $g_c(t)$ or A is false at (w,i); and otherwise it is undefined.

Examples of these are the following:

(35) ON tomorrow$_t$ (A) is true in a model **M** at (w,i) if i is a subinterval of the day after the day of $g_c(t)$ and A is true in **M** at (w,i); it is false at (w,i) if i is not a subinterval of the day after $g_c(t)$ or A is false at (w,i); and otherwise it is undefined.

(36) ON today$_t$ (A) is true in a model **M** at (w,i) if i is a subinterval of the day of $g_c(t)$ and A is true in **M** at (w,i); it is false at (w,i) if i is not a subinterval of the day of $g_c(t)$ or A is false at (w,i); and otherwise it is undefined.

(37) AT now$_t$ (A) is true in a model **M** at (w,i) if $i = g_c(t)$ and A is true in **M** at (w,i); it is false at (w,i) if $i \neq g_c(t)$ or A is false at (w,i); and otherwise it is undefined.

It was stated above that t is the right parameter for almost all temporal indexicals: the only exception might be *then*. It might be argued that the choice of deictic referent is unconstrained by speech time; however, it might be that there is one constraint on the referent of *then* and that is that it *cannot* be $g_c(t)$. If this were so, then even *then* would be properly represented with the parameter t attached to it. Having established the correct parametric representation for unbound indexicals, and thereby fixed upon the proper distinction between dates and indexicals, we can proceed to represent unbound indexicals in a wide variety of contexts.

3.5 Two Unbound Indexicals

In this section, two examples will be dealt with. First, it will be demonstrated that the representation chosen not only captures the right truth conditions for utterances involving indexicals, but also blocks semantically utterances which would involve a mismatch of tense and indexical. Secondly, a rather different apparent case of indexical-tense mismatch will be treated.

3.5.1 A Simple Example

A particular advantage of introducing parameters into the representation of indexicals can be discovered in the elegant exclusion of anomalous sentences. (38) is semantically well-formed, but (20) is not.

(38) John ate his breakfast today

(20) ?John ate his breakfast tomorrow

Let (39) represent (38):

(39) $PAST_{(v,t)}$ [ON $today_t$ (John eat his breakfast)]

(39) is true in model **M** at (w,i) if w = $g_c(v)$ and i = $g_c(t)$ and there is a j earlier than i such that (40) is true at (w,j).

(40) ON $today_t$ (John eat his breakfast)

(40) is true at (w,j) if j is a subinterval of the day of $g_c(t)$ and (23) is true at (w,j).

(23) John eat his breakfast

(23) is true at (w,j) if John eats his breakfast at that time.

In this case, all is well; the past tense can match up with an interval before the utterance, but on the same day. However, the tense and indexical are incompatible when the interval specified by the tense cannot include the interval specified by the indexical; in such cases, a mismatch occurs. That this is so counts in favour of the chosen representation, because it means that the representation of an utterance of a sentence such as (20) is semantically ill-formed. Let (41) represent (20):

(41) $PAST_{(v,t)}$ [ON $tomorrow_t$ (John eat his breakfast)]

(41) is true in model **M** at (w,i) if w = $g_c(v)$ and i = $g_c(t)$ and there is a j earlier than i such that (42) is true at (w,j).

(42) ON $tomorrow_t$ (John eat his breakfast)

(42) is true at (w,j) if j is a subinterval of the day after the day of $g_c(t)$ and (23) is true at (w,j).

(23) John eat his breakfast

Again, (23) is true at (w,j) if John eats his breakfast at that time.

Clearly, (20) must be semantically ill-formed, since the conditions that must be placed on j cannot be met. On the one hand, i = $g_c(t)$, and j is earlier than i. On the other, j is a subinterval of the day *after* the day of $g_c(t)$, so that j must be later than i. j cannot be both before and after i, and so (20) is incoherent. It was observed in section 3.2 that examples such as (20) can only be blocked by Richards by using world knowledge. The parametric representation of indexicals, by contrast, blocks the examples automatically. Furthermore, the blocking, here described in terms of semantic ill-formedness, or incoherence, is given an explicit characterisation in terms of unsatisfiability in Chapter 3.

3.5.2 The Present Future

If we now have an adequate representation for unbound indexicals, then there is a problem associated with the representation of the sentence (43):

(43) Tom finishes his PhD next year

The sentence cannot be represented with a simple present tense operator, since this clashes with the obvious parametric representation of the indexical expression *next-year*, given in (44).

(44) ON next-year$_t$ (A) is true in model **M** at (w,i) if i is a subinterval of the year after the year of $g_c(t)$; it is false at (w,i) if i is not a subinterval of the year after the year of $g_c(t)$; and otherwise it is undefined.

On the other hand, to represent (43) with a future tense operator not only does violence to the syntactic present tense, but also conflates its representation with that of the distinct sentence (45):

(45) Tom will finish his PhD next year

Given the need to capture (43), we have a problem; one way of solving that problem is suggested below. The commitment the solution brings with it is that, while they are represented differently, (43) and (45) are rendered truth-conditionally equivalent. It is still possible to argue that while (45) is a straightforward claim about an event that occurs later than the utterance, (43) is a more subtle assertion about a plan for the later time that is actually held now. (45), but perhaps not (43), would be falsified if no PhD were produced in the year after putative utterance. We suggest below that IQ can go a little way towards capturing this point.

So, one solution to the problem is to represent the main tense of the sentence as present, but to introduce an additional future tense within the representation. Naturally, to ensure syntactic well-formedness, it is necessary to deparametrize the inner tense. Thus, it is suggested that (46) portrays the form of (43).

(46) PRES$_{(v,t)}$ [Gv't'FUT$_{(v',t')}$ [ON next-year$_t$ (Tom finish his PhD)]]

(46) is true in model **M** at (w,i) if w = $g_c(v)$ and i = $g_c(t)$ and (47) is true at (w,i).

(47) FUT$_{(w*,i*)}$ [ON next-year$_t$ (Tom finish his PhD)]

(47) is true at (w,i) if w = $g_c(w^*)$ and i = $g_c(i^*)$ and there is a j later than i such that (48) is true at (w,j).

(48) ON next-year$_t$ (Tom finish his PhD)

(48) is true at (w,j) if j is a subinterval of the year after $g_c(t)$ and (49) is true at (w,j).

(49) Tom finish his PhD

With (46) as the representation for (43), the indexical correctly locates the PhD completion within an interval later than the time of utterance, while at the same time maintaining the main tense of the sentence as present. That there should be a future tense lurking within the representation of (43) is perhaps a little surprising, but evidence from indirect speech reports indicates that this is indeed the case. Suppose that Ewan uttered the sentence (43) in 1985. Late in 1986, Mary can report Ewan's utterance by uttering the sentence (50). She cannot report the original utterance by using the sentence (51), for that would not report what Ewan said.

(50) Ewan said that Tom would finish his PhD this year

(51) Ewan said that Tom finished his PhD this year

To report indirectly an utterance of a sentence such as (43), it is necessary to use a construction which will involve a future tense operator in its representation. The intricacies of indirect speech reports will examined at greater length in section 4; suffice it for the moment that our intuitive understanding of such reports tends to support the representation adopted here for sentences such as (43).

There is one remaining problem concerning the relation between (46) and the simple future sentence (45). If the representation is of a true utterance of (43), is (45) true as well? The answer is not clear. However, even if the present future sentence did imply the simple future sentence, it would be possible to mount a defence of the representation by arguing that utterances of present future sentences are assertions about currently obtaining dispositions which happen to concern the future, whereas utterances of simple future sentences are assertions about properties of objects that need not obtain at the present time at all, dispositional or no.[2]

This is certainly the case at the representational level. The main tense of a simple future sentence is $\text{FUT}_{(v,t)}$. We can interpret such an operator in the following way: 'The present time is such that there is a later time at which the following value-free proposition evaluates to true'. By contrast, the main tense of a present future sentence is $\text{PRES}_{(v,t)}$. That operator would be interpreted in this way: 'The present time is such that the following value-free proposition evaluates to true here'. The value-free proposition which then follows the tense operator is a bare proposition in the case of the simple future, and a proposition involving tense information in the case of the present future. So, the different types of sentence involve asserting that different (but related) propositions evaluate to true at different intervals. The truth-value of a given present future utterance may be the same as its simple future analogue, but we will reach that truth-value by a rather different route.

The distinction between simple future and present future is akin to the distinction between de re and de dicto in at least one important respect.[3] In the de dicto reading of an alethic modality, we allow the modal operator to scope over an entire proposition; in the de re case, we pull some of the elements out of the proposition, and give them maximal scope. In the present future, we allow a tense operator to scope over a complex value-free proposition; in the simple future, the tense information in that complex value-free proposition is abstracted, and given maximal scope. What makes a de re and a de dicto reading true may be the same, but it makes truth in different ways. As we have just seen, this is also the case with our diverse futures. The issue of the

2 This is roughly what Dowty (1979: 157) proposes, following Ellen Prince.

3 I am indebted to David McCarty for this observation. In a rather different framework, Tichy (1980: 363) also trades on a temporal de re/de dicto distinction.

relationship between the present future utterance and its simple future analogue may be murky, then, but it is no murkier than the relationship between de re and de dicto. A logic for the language of IQ may settle the question. In the meantime, we shall adhere to the representation of present futures adopted in this section, for two main reasons. First, it is structurally adequate. Secondly, it is compatible with the treatment of indirect speech reports adopted in section 4.1.

And it is to indirect speech reports containing both tenses and indexicals that we now turn, as we attempt to characterise a particular case of a bound indexical.

§4 Bound Indexicals in IQ

This section deals with the incorporation of bound indexicals into the IQ framework elaborated above. The previous section dealt with the issue of the representation of indexical expressions in general, and unbound occurrences of indexicals in particular. Certain decisions were taken then concerning the nature of the representation which can only be vindicated now, by considering those bound indexicals which were introduced in section 2.2. An examination of the rôle of propositions in indirect speech reports is now required, in order to represent the bound indexical in (11). This discussion is orthogonal to Richards' treatment of subordinate tenses in Chapter 4, and is included partly to illustrate that more than one way of representing indirect speech reports is possible in IQ.

4.1 The Representation of Indirect Speech Reports

There seem to be some problems lurking in the propositional undergrowth. One of these becomes apparent when an attempt is made to supply the truth conditions for an indirect speech report such as (52):

(52) Sagan said that he needed a telescope

In Chapter 1, Richards discusses a similar example at some length, in order to explicate the equation of the value-free proposition with what is actually said. However, he never supplies truth conditions for the utterance, and it is this that we shall now attempt to do. Presupposing no particular analysis of the occurrence of the pronoun *he* in (52), we may take the representation of (52) to be (53), and then work out the conditions in the obvious way.

(53) $PAST_{(v,t)}$ [Sagan say that [Gv't'$PAST_{(v',t')}$ (he need a telescope)]]

(53) is true in model **M** at (w,i) if $w = g_c(v)$ and $i = g_c(t)$ and there is a j earlier than i such that (54) is true at (w,j).

(54) Sagan say that [Gv't'$PAST_{(v',t')}$ (he need a telescope)]

When is (54) true at (w,j)? Presumably, it is true at that interval if Sagan stands in the relation of saying to the proposition whose name is given by (55).

(55) that [Gv't'$PAST_{(v',t')}$ (he need a telescope)]

Richards' view of propositions would dictate that (55) is the name of what was said at the interval. In other words, it is the name of the content of Sagan's utterance. More obviously, (54) is true at (w,j) if what Sagan said at (w,j) was the proposition represented by (56)

(56) Gv't'$PAST_{(v',t')}$ (he need a telescope)

As far as the truth of (52) goes, this is all that matters. But if we want to find out whether what Sagan said was true or false, it is necessary to unpack the truth conditions for (56). Since truth is relativised to a model, world and interval, of course, the interval at which (56) is to be evaluated must be determined. The obvious choice is j. (56) is true at (w,j) if (57) is true at (w,j).

(57) $PAST_{(w*,j*)}$ (he need a telescope)

(57) is true at (w,j) if w = $g_c(w*)$ and j = $g_c(j*)$ and there is a k earlier than j such that (58) is true at (w,k).

(58) he need a telescope

So what Sagan said is true if he needed a telescope at an earlier time than his utterance. Sagan would have said (59). Suppose, on the other hand, he had said (60).

(59) I needed a telescope

(60) I need a telescope

If he had said (60), and (52) is used to report that distinct utterance, then (52) would have to be assigned the different representation (61).

(61) $PAST_{(v,t)}$ [Sagan say that [Gv't'$PRES_{(v',t')}$ (he need a telescope)]]

And the proposition which Sagan expressed would be that in (62).

(62) Gv't'$PRES_{(v',t')}$ (he need a telescope)

What he said was true at (w,j) if (63) was true at (w,j).

(63) $PRES_{(w*,j*)}$ (he need a telescope)

(63) is true at (w,j) if w = $g_c(w^*)$ and j = $g_c(j^*)$ and (58) is true at (w,j). So what Sagan said was true if he needed a telescope at the same time as he spoke, which is just as would be expected. However, the fact that instances of (52), with its embedded past tense, should be taken to be an adequate report of either (59) or (60) means that (52) is ambiguous, in the sense that it can be assigned the two truth-conditionally distinct representations (53) and (61). And if (52), with that embedded past tense, reports (60), then there may be a problem over the representation of (64).

(64) Sagan said that he needs a telescope

(64) cannot be represented by (61) if the truth conditions of what he said are those which have been suggested. After all, what Sagan said could be true at the time he spoke if he needed a telescope at that time, without any suggestion that it must still be the case at the time (64) is uttered. There are essentially three responses that can be made to this position.

First, it is possible to reject the claim that (61) fails to represent (64), and maintain that what has gone wrong can be traced to the attempt to give the truth conditions for what was said in terms of the time of the embedded speech. If the proposition is taken to be evaluated relative to the speech time of the *whole* utterance, then the truth conditions fall out correctly. However, if this is the case, then problems arise if (52) is a report of an utterance of (60), and (60) is taken to be represented by (61).

(52) Sagan said that he needed a telescope

(60) I need a telescope

(61) $PAST_{(v,t)}$ [Sagan say that [Gv't'$PRES_{(v',t')}$ (he need a telescope)]]

(62) Gv't'$PRES_{(v',t')}$ (he need a telescope)

(52) would be true if what Sagan said was the proposition represented by (62). What he said would be taken to be true if it were true at the time of the utterance of (52), rather than at the time of Sagan's utterance of (60). This

cannot be right, not least since it would imply that (52) and (64) are truth-conditionally equivalent. In response, an adherent of this position could hold that the difference between (52) and (64) lies not in their structure, but in the interval relative to which Sagan's proposition should be considered. For (52), the proposition should be evaluated relative to (w,j). For (64), it should be considered relative to (w,i). The problem with this response is that there is no indication as to when (w,i) should be used instead of (w,j). The most obvious strategy to follow would be to use (w,j) at all times, except when the tense of the subordinate clause is present, in which case it is necessary to switch to (w,i). But this policy fails with sentences such as (65), when the *tomorrow* is seen as making more precise the time of speech, rather than the time of need.

(65) Billy will say that he needs the football tomorrow

Final discussion of the correct representation of this example, in which the indexical falls outside the scope of *says* will be deferred until the rôle of indexicals *inside* subordinate clauses has been illustrated.

Secondly, it would still be possible to maintain that (61) correctly represents (64), while claiming that (64) would only be true if j and i were sufficiently close together. Since there is nothing in the structure or the truth clauses to ensure this, such a claim represents an attempt to relegate the problem to pragmatics. Even if this second response did not suffer from the same problems as the first with respect to (65), it is not one that lies comfortably with the general approach of this chapter and the next, which is to leave as little as possible to pragmatics.

Thirdly, it might be agreed that (64) is not properly represented by (61). Such a response would only be acceptable in tandem with an adequate alternative representation for (64). This last response is the avenue which we shall follow, for three reasons. First, the treatment of (64) will offer a solution which may be generalised to deal with other constructions. Secondly, the actual representation given for (64) will dictate the interval at which the value-free proposition is to be evaluated. Lastly, the solution will not run into any trouble over (65).

The first step towards deriving an adequate representation for (64) is to note the existence of other pairs of examples which have certain features in common with the pair (52) and (64).

(52) Sagan said that he needed a telescope

(64) Sagan said that he needs a telescope

(66) Martin said that Marc would visit Glasgow tomorrow

(67) Martin said that Marc will visit Glasgow tomorrow

The embedded tense of *need* seems as though it ought to be present in (64) *and* in the second reading of (52). Similarly, both (66) and (67) seem to require an embedded future tense in their representations. But if they share a representation, then there is again no immediate explanation for the difference in the English speech reports. The difference may be described in the following way: in the first member of each pair, the embedded tense seems as though it ought to be considered relative to the embedded speech time. In the second member of each pair, the embedded tense ought to be considered with respect to the embedding speech time, just like normal, unembedded tenses. To put the point a little more vividly, the former tenses are dead, as far as the reporter of the utterance is concerned; the latter tenses are, by contrast, very much alive. When a tense is dead, it bears no essential relation to speech time; when it is alive, the relation lives on, even in embedded contexts. So in both (64) and (67), the utterer of the indirect speech report is placing herself (not just the reported speaker) in some temporal relation to the individuals and relations mentioned in the report.

What, then, is the life support mechanism that keeps a tense alive, even after it has been embedded? The tense cannot still be fully parametric, since this is forbidden at both the linguistic and propositional level. An embedded tense cannot be fully parametric because tense iteration is explicitly ruled out of the language of IQ. This in turn corresponds to the fact that a parametric tense turns a value-free proposition into a value-specific proposition; and the latter should not occur as part of an indirect speech report, since it is merely a (temporally relativised) truth-value.

A parametric representation cannot be used to provide life support for the tense. However, there is a possibility which is both syntactically and semantically admissable. With the resources of IQ, we may create tenses that are, so to speak, semi-parametric. In all the structures so far proposed, indirect speech reports have contained tenses that have both their parameters bound out by the G-operator. This is not the only possible state of affairs. If the world parameter is bound out by G, and the temporal parameter left free, we obtain a structure that is syntactically well-formed, in that *that* applies to a sentence of IQ that is by definition context-free; furthermore, the structure is also semantically well-formed, since the proposition corresponding to what was said is still value-free, on the definition given by Richards. It will be temporally specific, to be sure, but the discussion in Oberlander (1987: 109–23) argues that it is not a value-specific proposition. Therefore, we can now frame a proposal which will deal with pairs of sentences such as (52) and (64) or (66) and (67). Dead tenses should be represented in the logical form with fully deparametrized tense operators. Live tenses should be represented with semi-parametric tense operators. The former category includes the English past tense, where the original utterance being reported contained a present tense; and also the English future-oriented construction *would*. The latter category includes cases of the English present tense occurring within indirect speech reports, and cases of *will* occurring in those contexts.

To see that this proposal represents the correct solution to the problem presented by pairs such as (52) and (64), consider the representations assigned to these sentences by the proposal:

(61) $PAST_{(v,t)}$ [Sagan say that [Gv't'$PRES_{(v',t')}$ (he need a telescope)]]

(68) $PAST_{(v,t)}$ [Sagan say that [Gv'$PRES_{(v',t)}$ (he need a telescope)]]

The only difference between the representation of the second reading of (52) and the new representation (68) for (64) is that in (68), only one of the parameters on the embedded tense is bound out by G. So we have provided a new representation of (64) to replace (61), but it is different in only a small respect. To see what a difference that difference makes, let's examine what is reported to have been said in each case. According to (61), what was said is the value-free proposition in (62); according to (68) (which represents a distinct utterance), what was said is the value-free proposition in (69).

(62) $Gv't'PRES_{(v',t')}$ (he need a telescope)

(69) $Gv'PRES_{(v',t)}$ (he need a telescope)

The two value-free propositions are true under different circumstances: the truth of (62) can be considered at any world-interval pair; (69) is temporally specific, and can be true at many world indices, but only one temporal index. To see that this is so, consider whether (69) is true at the speech time of (64), and at the time of Sagan's speech reported by (64). Let's look at the latter of these first. What would have to be the case for (69) to be true at Sagan's speech time (w,j)? (69) is true at (w,j) if (70) is true at (w,j).

(70) $PRES_{(w^*,t)}$ (he need a telescope)

(70) is true at (w,j) if $w = g_c(w^*)$, and $j = g_c(t)$. Now, the utterance of the sentence (64) was true if $i = g_c(t)$, and by the definition of the past tense operator, j is earlier than i. Thus, trying to make (69) true at (w,j) generates inconsistent truth-conditions. So, (69) cannot be made true at (w,j), the index at which Sagan himself spoke. However, it is simple to show that (69) *can* be made true at (w,i), the time of the reporter's speech. In fact, this is the only temporal index at which the value-free proposition evaluates to true. It should now be obvious why embedding speech time is sometimes the place to find out whether what was said is true. When a tense is live, there is only one temporal index at which what was said is true: embedding speech time. In the

normal case, when the tense is dead, what was said is less specific, and it makes sense to find out whether it was true at the time of the reported speech. So, with the representation for (64) proposed here, we do have an procedure for determining where to find out whether what was said is true. If the tense operator is rendered as deparametrized, then we consider what was said at (w,j); if the tense operator is semi-parametric, we can only consider what was said at (w,i).

This solution to the problem of the present tense in (64) generalises to the apparently standard future tense in (67). The future tense operator in the representation of (66) will be deparametrized; the operator in the representation of (67) will be semi-parametric:

(71) $PAST_{(v,t)}$ [Martin say that [Gv't'$FUT_{(v',t')}$ [ON $tomorrow_t$ (Marc visit Glasgow)]]]

(72) $PAST_{(v,t)}$ [Martin say that [Gv'$FUT_{(v',t)}$ [ON $tomorrow_t$ (Marc visit Glasgow)]]]

The presence of the indexical *tomorrow* in the value-free proposition contained in both representations does not disrupt the smooth analysis; again, a semi-parametric tense operator forces us to look at the truth value of what was said at the time of the utterance of the indirect speech report.

The introduction of semi-parametric tenses is, of course, quite compatible with the existence of examples such as (65).

(65) Billy will say that he needs the football tomorrow

In these cases, the embedded present tense is dead, not alive. So what is reported to have been said is to be evaluated at the time of Billy's speech, not at the time of the utterance of (65). We shall return to this example below. To summarise, it has been shown that we can deal with the embedded present tense of (64) by using a strategy which dictates in a systematic manner the interval at which what is said is to be evaluated; thus, we have here a semantic explanation for the sequence of tense phenomena examined by, for instance, Costa (1972). Furthermore, we have seen that the strategy generalises to cover other cases of embedded but living tenses; and happily, it can be demonstrated that sentences such as (65), which contains a dead present tense, can be represented in the obvious way.

We have assumed that when a tense is dead, the only interval relevant to determining the truth value of what was said is the embedded speech time. To show that this is so, it is necessary to consider indirect speech reports which contain indexical expressions. In so doing, we shall attempt to prove two points in turn. First, that contrary to one interpretation of Richards' assertion in section 6 of Chapter 1, temporal adverbs can be embedded within indirect speech in such a way as to determine the time relative to which the value-free proposition is to be considered. Secondly, it will be shown that the temporal indexicals which determine the correct interval in these cases force the use of the embedded speech time at the expense of the embedding speech time.

(73) Someone will say that Bush was a great President

(74) Bush was a great President

(75) Someone will say on 17th May 2000 that Bush was a great President

(76) Someone will say that Bush was a great President on 17th May 2000

In considering sentences (73)–(76), Richards could be seen as claiming that the temporal adverb in (76) cannot be thought of as modifying the contained occurrence of (74) so that it is to be considered relative to 17th May 2000. That is, (76) cannot be read as meaning that someone will assert (at some time after 2000) that Bush was a great President on the 17th of May, even if that date turns out to be Bush's moment of resolution and glory. So, on this analysis, (76) can only be read as (75).

By considering indirect speech reports which contain occurrences of temporal indexicals, however, it can be shown that such a contention must be false.

(77) Terry said that he would need a terminal tomorrow

Clearly, the *tomorrow* in (77) cannot be thought of as making the time of reported speech more precise, which is the function Richards assigns to the temporal adverb in (75). Rather, it modifies the value-free proposition to be considered, which is to be thought of as what Terry said. If (78) and (79) are rival representations of (77), it can easily be shown that while (78) is semantically coherent, (79) is not.

(78) $PAST_{(v,t)}$ [Terry say that [Gv't'$FUT_{(v',t')}$ [ON $tomorrow_t$ (he need a terminal)]]]

(79) $PAST_{(v,t)}$ [ON $tomorrow_t$ [Terry say that [Gv't'$FUT_{(v',t')}$ (he need a terminal)]]]

It should be noted, of course, that temporal indexicals can also be used to locate the interval of reported speech, as in (80).

(80) Terry said yesterday that he would need a terminal tomorrow

An example such as (81) may therefore be ambiguous, and could be represented either as in (82) or (83).

(81) Keith said that he would visit Cambridge yesterday

(82) $PAST_{(v,t)}$ [Keith say that [Gv't'$FUT_{(v',t')}$ [ON $yesterday_t$ (he visit Cambridge)]]]

(83) $PAST_{(v,t)}$ [ON $yesterday_t$ [Keith say that [Gv't'$FUT_{(v',t')}$ (he visit Cambridge)]]]

Thus, it has been shown that temporal adverbs can occur within the scope of the *says* relation. It is still necessary to prove that the interval at which what Keith said should be evaluated is the interval of embedded speech, and not the speech time for an utterance of (81). This can be done by unpacking the truth conditions for (82); this will also demonstrate that embedded indexicals are indeed semantically coherent. (82) is true in model **M** at (w,i) if w = $g_c(v)$ and i = $g_c(t)$ and there is a j earlier than i such that (84) is true at (w,j).

(84) Keith say that [Gv't'FUT$_{(v',t')}$ [ON yesterday$_t$ (he visit Cambridge)]]

(84) is true at (w,j) if Keith stands in the relation of saying to the value-free proposition named in (85).

(85) that [Gv't'FUT$_{(v',t')}$ [ON yesterday$_t$ (he visit Cambridge)]]

What Keith said at (w,j) was the value-free proposition represented by (86).

(86) Gv't'FUT$_{(v',t')}$ [ON yesterday$_t$ (he visit Cambridge)]

(82) is true at (w,i) if what Keith said at (w,j) was (86). It is now possible to show that the embedded indexical uniquely fixes j as the interval for determining the truth value of what Keith said. Suppose that the interval is (w,i). Then (86) is true at (w,i) if (87) is true at (w,i).

(87) FUT$_{(w^*,i^*)}$ [ON yesterday$_t$ (he visit Cambridge)]

(87) is true at (w,i) if w = $g_c(w^*)$ and i = $g_c(t)$ and there is a k later than i such that (88) is true at (w,k).

(88) ON yesterday$_t$ (he visit Cambridge)

(88) is true at (w,k) if k is a subinterval of the day before the day of $g_c(t)$. But this cannot be so, since it has already been stated that k is later than i, which is the value of $g_c(t)$. Thus, what Keith said is semantically incoherent, if its truth is to be determined relative to (w,i). On the other hand, if (86) is evaluated relative to (w,j), then the conditions are more favourable: (86) is true at (w,j) if (89) is true at (w,j).

(89) FUT$_{(w^*,j^*)}$ [ON yesterday$_t$ (he visit Cambridge)]

(89) is true at (w,j) if w = g_c(w*) and j = g_c(j*) and there is an l later than j such that (88) is true at (w,l). (88) is true at (w,l) if l is a subinterval of the day before the day of g_c(t), and (90) is true at (w,l).

(90) he visit Cambridge

So, if the value-free proposition which represents what Keith said is evaluated relative to (w,j), the conditions which result are those which accord with intuition. What Keith said is true if he spoke before the occasion of his visit to Cambridge, and that visit took place the day before the utterance of (81) which reports his utterance.

Thus it can be seen that the occurrence of temporal indexicals within indirect speech reports counts in favour of using (w,j) in examples as diverse as (52) and (80). What is more, the occurrence of indexicals *outside* the scope of the *says* relation counts against the use of embedding speech time as the interval for evaluation of the temporally neutral value-free proposition expressed. One reading of examples such as (65) sees the indexical *tomorrow* as locating the interval of the reported utterance. (91) is a representation of this reading.[4]

(65) Billy will say that he needs the football tomorrow

(91) $FUT_{(v,t)}$ [ON $tomorrow_t$ [Billy say that [Gv't'$PRES_{(v',t')}$ (he need the football)]]]

(91) is true in model **M** at (w,i) if w = g_c(v) and i = g_c(t) and there is a j later than i such that (92) is true at at (w,j).

(92) ON $tomorrow_t$ [Billy say that [Gv't'$PRES_{(v',t')}$ (he need the football)]]

4 Note that the present tense in this example cannot be live, and so should not be represented with a semi-parametric PRES. Such a representation would denote a distinct, temporally specific value-free proposition. Indeed, (97) could be used to report someone's expressing that proposition.

(92) is true at (w,j) if j is a subinterval of the day after the day of $g_c(t)$ and (93) is true at (w,j).

(93) Billy say that [Gv't'PRES$_{(v',t')}$ (he need the football)]

(93) is true at (w,j) if what Billy says at (w,j) is the value-free proposition represented in (94).

(94) Gv't'PRES$_{(v',t')}$ (he need the football)

If we want to find out whether what Billy says at (w,j) is true, we must evaluate the value-free proposition. It is simple to show that the interval at which (94) should be evaluated is not the embedding speech time (w,i). If it were, then (94) would be true at (w,i) if (95) is true at (w,i).

(95) PRES$_{(w*,i*)}$ (he need the football)

(95) is true at (w,i) if w = $g_c(w^*)$ and i = $g_c(i^*)$ and (96) is true at (w,i).

(96) he need the football

Clearly, if what is said is evaluated relative to (w,i), it is only true if Billy needed a football at embedding speech time (w,i), and this is certainly not the intuitive sense of (65). If this were indeed the situation, it would be appropriate to predict Billy's utterance by uttering an instance of (97).

(97) Billy will say that he needed the football, tomorrow.

It can also be shown that with (91) as a structure for (65), if what is said is evaluated relative to (w,j), the predicted time of speech, the truth-conditions coincide with intuition. (94) would be true at (w,j) if (95) were true at (w,j), which would be the case if w = $g_c(w^*)$ and j = $g_c(j^*)$ and if (96) were true at (w,j). This is the correct way to consider whether what Billy will say would be true.

And if this is so, the first approach to sentences such as (64) has been falsified, for it predicted that an embedded present tense would force a switch to the embedding speech time. On the other hand, the embedded present tense in (65) is quite consistent with the approach which we have adopted: the tense is dead, and so the value-free proposition can happily be evaluated at any interval; it so happens, of course, that the interval of interest is the time of embedded speech. From the treatments above of the examples (81) and (64), it can be concluded that (w,i) is only used as the interval for evaluation of the value-free proposition reported when the proposition itself forces it. This occurs when the value-free proposition is so specific as to evaluate to true only at (w,i). Such a proposition is denoted by a sentence of IQ which contains a semi-parametric tense, and this in turn represents a sentence of English which harbours a live tense.

So, a truth-conditionally respectable account of indirect speech reports has now been derived. It can accommodate unbound indexicals, both inside and outside the reported speech, and it can account for anomalous sentences such as (64). The structure proposed for (64) generalises to a variety of other cases, and yet remains quite compatible with the existence of examples such as (65). The account of indirect speech reports will generalise to provide a treatment of tense and indexicals in other propositional attitude reports; what is more, it will allow us to represent the cases of *bound* indexicals such as (11).

(11) Max always said that he would be rich tomorrow

4.2 A Bound Indexical

The previous section furnished us with a clear picture of the rôle of unbound indexicals in indirect speech reports. It is now possible to deal with those cases of bound indexicals which occur in indirect speech reports, which were first noted in section 2.2.

(11) Max always said that he would be rich tomorrow

There are, it seems, two possible readings of (11). The first takes an utterance of (11) on the 18th of August 1985 to be an assertion that throughout some interval of the past, Max claimed every so often that he would be rich on the 19th of August 1985. The second reading of an utterance of (11) has no such intimate relation to the 19th of August. Rather, it is taken to say that throughout some interval of the past, Max claimed every so often that he would be rich on the day after each of those claims. The first reading takes *tomorrow* to act normally, as a parameter. The second takes *tomorrow* to act non-parametrically, and it counts as a paradigm case of what we have termed a bound indexical. Corresponding to each of these readings, we have the representations in (98) and (99) respectively.

(98) $PAST_{(v,t)}$ [$ALWAYS_r$ [Max say that [Gv't'$FUT_{(v',t')}$ [ON $tomorrow_t$ (he be rich)]]]]

(99) $PAST_{(v,t)}$ [$ALWAYS_r$ [Max say that [Gv't'$FUT_{(v',t')}$ [ON $tomorrow_{t'}$ (he be rich)]]]]

It can be seen that (98) and (99) differ in only one detail: in (98), *tomorrow* is rendered as a parameter, while in (99), that parameter is bound by the G-operator; it is no longer a parameteric referring expression, but is now part of a quantifier expression. To demonstrate the difference, it is only necessary to unpack the truth-conditions for (98), and then (99). (98) is true in model **M** at (w,i) if $w = g_c(v)$ and $i = g_c(t)$ and there is a j earlier than i such that (100) is true at (w,j).

(100) $ALWAYS_r$ [Max say that [Gv't'$FUT_{(v',t')}$ [ON $tomorrow_t$ (he be rich)]]]

(100) is true at (w,j) if $j = g_c(r)$ and there exists a partition P of $g_c(r)$ such that for all $p \in P$, (101) is true at (w,p).

(101) Max say that [Gv't'$FUT_{(v',t')}$ [ON $tomorrow_t$ (he be rich)]]

(101) is true at (w,p) if Max stood in the *says* relation at (w,p) to the value-free proposition named in (102).

(102) that [Gv't'FUT$_{(v',t')}$ [ON tomorrow$_t$ (he be rich)]]

As far as the truth of this reading of (11) goes, this is all that matters. But is what Max said at (w,p) true? Given the view of indirect speech reports derived in the previous section, we need to evaluate the proposition in (103) at (w,p) in order to determine whether what Max said is true.

(103) Gv't'FUT$_{(v',t')}$ [ON tomorrow$_t$ (he be rich)]

(103) is true at (w,p) if (104) is true at (w,p).

(104) FUT$_{(w*,p*)}$ [ON tomorrow$_t$ (he be rich)]

(104) is true at (w,p) if w = g_c(w*) and p = g_c(p*) and there is a q later than p such that (105) is true at (w,q).

(105) ON tomorrow$_t$ (he be rich)

(105) is true at (w,q) if q is a subinterval of the day after the day of g_c(t) and (106) is true at (w,q).

(106) he be rich

Things are very nearly, but not quite the same for the second reading of (11). (99) is true in model **M** at (w,i) if w = g_c(v) and i = g_c(t) and there is a j earlier than i such that (107) is true at (w,j).

(107) ALWAYS$_r$ [Max say that [Gv't'FUT$_{(v',t')}$ [ON tomorrow$_{t'}$ (he be rich)]]]

(107) is true at (w,j) if j = g_c(r) and there exists a partition P of g_c(r) such that for all p $\in$ P, (108) is true at (w,p).

(108) Max say that [Gv't'FUT$_{(v',t')}$ [ON tomorrow$_{t'}$ (he be rich)]]

(108) is true at (w,p) if Max stood in the *says* relation at (w,p) to the value-free proposition named in (109).

(109) that [Gv't'FUT$_{(v',t')}$ [ON tomorrow$_{t'}$ (he be rich)]]

Again, as far as the truth of this reading of (11) goes, this is all that matters. What Max said is true if (110) is true at (w,p).

(110) Gv't'FUT$_{(v',t')}$ [ON tomorrow$_{t'}$ (he be rich)]

(110) is true at (w,p) if (111) is true at (w,p).

(111) FUT$_{(w^*,p^*)}$ [ON tomorrow$_{p^*}$ (he be rich)]

(111) is true at (w,p) if $w = g_c(w^*)$ and $p = g_c(p^*)$ and there is a q later than p such that (112) is true at (w,q).

(112) ON tomorrow$_{p^*}$ (he be rich)

(112) is true at (w,q) if q is a subinterval of the day after the day of $g_c(p^*)$ and (106) is true at (w,q). The difference between (98) and (99) comes down to this: what Max is portrayed as saying in (98) is true if he is rich on the day after utterance of (11); what he is portrayed as saying in (99) is true if, for each of *his* utterances, he is rich on the day following that utterance. (113) represents a paraphrase of this reading of (11).

(113) Max always said that he would be rich the day after his speaking

We are now in a position to cash the full value of the representation of indexicals adopted in section 3. The parametric t represents a position into which the G-operator may substitute the name of an interval of time; with it, IQ can represent bound indexicals. In essence, a G'd t' replacing a t for a sentence like (11) represents the fact that in such cases the indexical derives its value from the speech time of the embedded utterance, instead of the speech time of the embedding utterance. In this case, the parametric nature of *tomorrow* is frustrated by its being embedded as part of someone else's utterances.

Conclusion

In section 4 we showed that unbound indexicals within indirect speech reports can be perspicuously represented in IQ, and we then demonstrated that a bound indexical in a quantified indirect speech report can also be represented. This has allowed us to see that IQ, suitably altered in the ways indicated in section 3, is a framework which allows us to treat two types of natural language indexical behaviour. IQ can capture unbound indexicals and single-sentence bound indexicals. The obvious next step is to apply the new mechanisms developed in Chapter 5 to deal with multisentence bound indexicals. It should be clear, however, that Kamp and Rohrer's 1983 claim, which might have been true then, has now been overtaken by IQ.

3

Two Theories of Indexicals

JON OBERLANDER

Introduction

In the last chapter, we discussed a possible way of representing temporal indexical expressions. It was demonstrated there that IQ could successfully represent both bound and unbound indexicals. The task here is slightly more formal. We can say that the system we have developed embodies a particular theory of indexical function, and the object of this chapter is to compare a language reflecting that theory with another language reflecting a more orthodox theory. To acheive this object, we shall be specifying a syntax and semantics for a fragment of the IQ system we have already discussed. This will allow us to compare IQ with David Kaplan's Logic of Demonstratives, LD (Kaplan (1977; 1979)), a classic formal treatment of demonstratives and indexicals. In particular, taking the two languages to exemplify two distinct theories of indexicals, we can uncover a vital aspect of IQ's propositions, whereby they can be forced to be true at unique indices; this property, as we shall see, is not shared by the classical theory. It is a property which brings our theory of indexicality closer to the indexicality of natural language; and lets IQ, unlike LD, give a semantic explanation of the oddness of a sentence like:

The Prime Minister will leave Britain yesterday

In this chapter we therefore explore the differences between IQ and LD which arise from a property which only the former possesses. We do not investigate here those other differences that arise from properties which only the latter possesses. In a sense, this chapter presents only half the story; nevertheless this part of the story seems to be an interesting one.

For the purposes of comparison, we won't be discussing full versions of either IQ or LD themselves; instead, we will compare and contrast variants on the systems, which we will call IQ* and LD*, respectively.

§1 Overview of the Differences between LD* and IQ*

Before presenting the formal systems, it's useful to establish the major points of difference and similarity between them. In this section, therefore, we'll consider briefly the syntax and semantics of the systems, and stake out a general view of the comparative approaches to tenses and indexicals.

1.1 Semantics

The first major point to note is that, in what follows, we are taking the two systems to share the same models. Both systems require metalinguistic reference to not only the index of utterance, but also the index of evaluation. As a result, an element of the model is taken to be a pair, composed of a context-index and a circumstance-index. Since LD* is a temporal fragment of Kaplan's LD, all the apparatus which he had to include in order to deal with locational and personal indexicals has been jettisoned. Amongst other things, this means that contexts can be rendered as world-time pairs rather than as *n*-tuples, since these are the only aspects of context which are relevant to the operators of the LD* object-language. On this basis, both LD* and IQ* are being viewed as varieties of double-indexing systems, following Kamp (1971). This doesn't mean that context is conflated with circumstance, since they are represented as distinguished pairs, but it does mean that they are both pairs of worlds and times.

A second point is that IQ* uses integers for times, in order to facilitate the comparison with LD*. This means that questions cannot be raised concerning the homogeneity of temporal intervals, or the effects of temporal quantifiers over intervals. Given the indexical operators in each of the object-languages, we may wish to think of the integral times as complete 'days'. At the same time, we move back from partial functions to total functions.

These moves considerably simplify the task of comparing the representational power of the systems; we need only consider the syntactic translation functions from LD* to IQ* and back again, since the semantic transformation is the identity function, either way.

Having said this, it should be noted that the systems differ slightly in what they take to parameters. Following on from Chapter 1, we assume that in IQ* there is a contextual function which takes parameters (elements of the object-language) to values. Here, the function g_c is a two-place function on contexts and a restricted set of linguistic expressions, returning elements of the model. By contrast, in LD*, there will be two contextual functions, both taking contexts to elements of the model. It is these functions that Kaplan calls 'parameters'. In fact, each function will be a one-place function on contexts, returning, in the first case, worlds, and in the second case, times. It should be clear that the IQ* function's extra place (for the linguistic parameters) allows a simpler expression of Kaplan's 'parameters'; in addition, of course g_c allows for the distinction between parametric and non-parametric occurrences of the same expression.

Significantly, the parametric nature of the indexicals and tenses of IQ* ensures that a tensed wff of IQ* will be true, relative to a context, at only one context-circumstance pair. In LD*, however, it will tend to be the case that tensed wffs are true, relative to a context, at many context-circumstance pairs.

This difference leads to major divergence in the satisfiability conditions of wffs in the two systems; it is central to the new approach to indexicality embodied by IQ* and IQ in general. Put in terms we introduce in §5.2, our language takes tenses and indexicals to be *eternity-disturbing*, in sharp contrast to the *eternity-preserving* operators in LD*. The divergence can only be resolved by adding new expressions to the object-language of LD*. These new expressions involve singular reference to times and worlds, and are required in order to simulate the parametric nature of tense and indexicals in IQ*.

We shall urge that a theory which takes tenses and indexicals to be eternity-disturbing comes rather closer to the facts of natural language tense than a theory which does not.

1.2 Syntax: Tense and Indexicals

Turning to syntax, the most important difference concerns the treatment of tense and indexicals. In IQ*, but not LD*, tenses are rendered as indexical expressions; the presence of parameters within their form guarantees their indexicality. The effects of this difference can be seen in the way that LD* allows the truth of a tensed wff to depend on the truth of the untensed wff relative to a time which need have no connexion to context at all; IQ*, by contrast, requires more from this time, namely, that it be related in a relevant way to the time of the context.

§2 Formulation of LD*

The following section outlines a version of David Kaplan's Logic of Demonstratives which can be directly compared with the formulation of IQ given in the next section. Let's call this version of LD 'LD*'. LD* contains four tense operators, including a *day before* and a *day after* operator; and it has four indexical operators, including an *actually* operator.

2.1 Syntax

PRIMITIVE SYMBOLS FOR PREDICATE LOGIC

0 Punctuation),(

1 Infinite set of variables V

2 Infinite, possibly empty, set of n-place predicates, for all natural numbers n.

3 Infinite, possibly empty, set of n-place functors, for all natural numbers n.

4 Sentential connectives: $\wedge, \vee, \neg, \rightarrow, \leftrightarrow$

5 Quantifiers: $\forall, \exists$

6 A definite description operator: *the*

7 Identity: =

PRIMITIVE SYMBOLS FOR TENSE LOGIC

8 Tense Operators: P, F, K, L
(Respectively: past, future, day before, day after[1])

PRIMITIVE SYMBOLS FOR LOGIC OF DEMONSTRATIVES

9 1-Place Sentential Operators: A, N, Y, T

NON-KAPLANIAN PRIMITIVE SYMBOLS FOR LD*/IQ* EQUIVALENCE

10 An infinite set of temporal constants: V_T

11 An infinite set of world constants: V_V

1 Notice that K and L are classed as tense operators, rather than demonstratives. As we shall see in the semantics, this is because they work off the circumstance index, rather than the context index.

WELL-FORMED EXPRESSIONS OF LD*

We will take $\neg$, $\wedge$ and $\exists$ as primitives and take the other logical constants to be definable as usual. We let 'nk' abbreviate 'non-Kaplanian'.

1 1.1 If $\alpha \in V$, then α is an individual term.

1.2 Let $U = V_V \cup C_T$; if $\alpha \in U$ then α is an nk term.

2 If R is an n-place predicate, and $\alpha_1,\ldots, \alpha_n$ are individual terms, then $R\alpha_1\ldots\alpha_n$ is a wff.

3 If S is an n-place functor, and $\alpha_1,\ldots, \alpha_n$ are individual terms, then $S\alpha_1\ldots\alpha_n$ is a term.

4 If φ, ψ are wffs, then $\varphi \wedge \psi$ and $\neg\varphi$ are wffs.

5 If φ is a wff, and $\alpha \in V$, then $\exists\alpha\varphi$ is a wff.

6 If φ is a wff, then if $\alpha \in V$, then *the* α φ is a term.

7 If $\alpha, \beta \in V \cup U$, then $\alpha = \beta$ is a wff.

8 If φ is a wff, then $P\varphi$, $F\varphi$, $K\varphi$, $L\varphi$ are wffs.

9 If φ is a wff, then $A\varphi$, $N\varphi$, $Y\varphi$, $T\varphi$ are wffs.

MODELS FOR LD*

An LD*-model **M** is a tuple $\langle C, W, I, D, J\rangle$ such that:

1 C is a non-empty subset of $W \times I$, the set of permissable contexts.

2 If $\langle w,i\rangle \in C$, then w and i are the world and time of the context; where there is no danger of confusion, we shall abbreviate $\langle w,i\rangle$ by c.

3 W is a nonempty set of world states.

4 I is the set of integers (the set of times).

5 D is a nonempty set of individuals.

6 J is a function that assigns to each predicate and functor an appropriate intension as follows:

6.1 If R is an n-place predicate, J_R is a function such that for each $w' \in W$ and $i' \in I$, $J_R(w'i') \subseteq D^n$.

6.2 If S is an n-place functor, J_S is a function such that for each $w' \in W$ and $i' \in I$, $J_S(w'i') \in (D \cup \{\dagger\})^{D^n}$.[2]

2.2 Truth

TRUTH AND DENOTATION IN A CONTEXT

We write: $[\![\varphi]\!]^{<c,c'>,f,\mathbf{M}} = T$

for: φ when taken in context c (i.e. $<w,i>$) (under assignment f and structure **M**) is true with respect to the circumstance c' (the world-time pair $<w', i'>$). Only when the indices are not of this form will we draw attention to the full form (e.g. $<w',i'-1>$).

In the style of Kaplan, this could also be written: $\models^{\mathbf{M}}_{<c,c'>f} \varphi$.

In general, we write: $[\![\alpha]\!]^{<c,c'>,f,\mathbf{M}}$

for: the denotation of α in context c (under f and **M**), with respect to circumstance c'.

Let: $\mathbf{M} = <C, W, I, D, J>$

We say that f is an assignment with respect to **M** iff $f \in D^V$

Futhermore, f^{α}_{x} is the assignment which is exactly equal to f except possibly for its value at x. More formally, $f^{\alpha}_{x} = (f \sim \{<\alpha,f(\alpha)>\}) \cup \{<\alpha,x>\}$.

NB: There will be a pair of 'parameters' Wp, Tp which constitute functions from contexts to elements of W and I respectively. Reference to these 'parameters' is suppressed in what follows, but their effects can be traced in the truth conditions of those operators which are indexical in nature.

---

2 Following Scott and Kaplan, the symbol † represents an alien entity, not in the domain D.

2.3 Semantics for LD*

In what follows, the following are fixed: c (i.e.<w,i>) $\in$ C, f is an assignment, w, w' $\in$ W and i, i' $\in$ I. c' (i.e. <w',i'>) $\in$ W $\times$ I. Notice that clause 1 covers only individual terms; the additional nk-terms are covered by clauses 10 to 13, echoing the divisions in the syntax of §2.1 above. In every clause but 7, 10 and 11, a term α will be taken to be an individual term.

1 If $\alpha \in$ V, then $\llbracket \alpha \rrbracket^{<c,c'>f} = f(\alpha)$

2 $\llbracket R\alpha_1,\ldots,\alpha_n \rrbracket^{<c,c'>f} = T$

iff

$<\llbracket \alpha_1 \rrbracket^{<c,c'>f} \ldots \llbracket \alpha_n \rrbracket^{<c,c'>f}> \in J_R(w'i')$.

3 $\llbracket S\alpha_1\ldots\alpha_n \rrbracket^{<c,c'>f} = J_S(w'i')\ (<\llbracket \alpha_1 \rrbracket^{<c,c'>f} \ldots \llbracket \alpha_n \rrbracket^{<c,c'>f}>)$,

if none of $\llbracket \alpha_m \rrbracket^{<c,c'>} = \dagger$, and $\dagger$ otherwise.

4 4.1 $\llbracket \varphi \wedge \psi \rrbracket^{<c,c'>f} = T$ iff $\llbracket \varphi \rrbracket^{<c,c'>} = T$ and $\llbracket \psi \rrbracket^{<c,c'>} = T$.

4.2 $\llbracket \neg\varphi \rrbracket^{<c,c'>f} = T$ iff it's not the case that $\llbracket \varphi \rrbracket^{<c,c'>f}$.

5. If $\alpha \in$ V, then $\llbracket \exists\alpha\varphi \rrbracket = T$

iff

for some x $\in$ D, $\llbracket \varphi \rrbracket^{<c,c'>f^{\alpha}_{x}} = T$.

6 If $\alpha \in$ V, then $\llbracket \textit{the}\ \alpha\ \varphi \rrbracket^{<c,c'>}$ = the unique x $\in$ D

such that

$\llbracket \varphi \rrbracket^{<c,c'>f^{\alpha}_{x}} = T$, if there is one, and $\dagger$ otherwise.

7 If $\alpha \in (V \cup U)$, then $\llbracket \alpha = \beta \rrbracket^{<c,c'>} = T$ iff $\llbracket \alpha \rrbracket^{<c,c'>} = \llbracket \beta \rrbracket^{<c,c'>}$.

For the remaining clauses, we give the context-circumstance indices in full.

8 8.1 $\llbracket P\varphi \rrbracket^{<<w,i>,<w',i'>>} = T$

iff

$\exists i'' < i'$ such that $\llbracket \varphi \rrbracket^{<<w,i>,<w',i''>>} = T$.

8.2 $\llbracket F\varphi \rrbracket^{<<w,i>,<w',i'>>} = T$

iff

$\exists i'' > i'$ such that $[\![\varphi]\!]^{<<w,i>,<w',i''>>} = T$.

8.3 $[\![K\varphi]\!]^{<<w,i>,<w',i'>>} = T$ iff $[\![\varphi]\!]^{<<w,i>,<w',i'-1>>} = T$.

8.4 $[\![L\varphi]\!]^{<<w,i>,<w',i'>>} = T$ iff $[\![\varphi]\!]^{<<w,i>,<w',i'+1>>} = T$.

9 9.1 $[\![A\varphi]\!]^{<<w,i>,<w',i'>>} = T$ iff $[\![\varphi]\!]^{<<w,i>,<w,i'>>} = T$.

9.2 $[\![N\varphi]\!]^{<<w,i>,<w',i'>>} = T$ iff $[\![\varphi]\!]^{<<w,i>,<w',i>>} = T$.

9.3 $[\![Y\varphi]\!]^{<<w,i>,<w',i'>>} = T$ iff $[\![\varphi]\!]^{<<w,i>,<w',i-1>>} = T$.

9.4 $[\![T\varphi]\!]^{<<w,i>,<w',i'>>} = T$ iff $[\![\varphi]\!]^{<<w,i>,<w',i+1>>} = T$.

10 10.1 There is a distinguished constant $t_s \in C_T$, such that $[\![t_s]\!]^{<<w,i>,<w',i'>>} = i$

10.2 For all other $t_e \in C_T$, $[\![t_e]\!]^{<<w,i>,<w',i'>>} = i'$

11 11.1 There is a distinguished constant $v_s \in C_V$, such that $[\![v_s]\!]^{<<w,i>,<w',i'>>} = w$

11.2 For all other $v_e \in C_V$, $[\![v_e]\!]^{<<w,i>,<w',i'>>} = w'$

2.4 Remarks

LD* is, essentially, a faithful temporal fragment of Kaplan's LD. Interestingly enough, the new world and temporal terms t_s and v_s have treatments very much like *I* and *Here* in Kaplan's original LD: they're constants whose interpretation depends on the context of speech. The other new 'non-Kaplanian' terms (nk-terms) are rather different: their interpretation depends not on the context of speech, but on the circumstance of evaluation; in a manner of speaking, t_e plays definite description to t_s's rigid designator. The new symbols are introduced in order to allow equivalence between LD* and IQ*. Without them, as we shall see in §5, LD* cannot represent the distinctions representable in IQ*. Notice also the subtle but critical difference between, for instance, $K\varphi$ and $Y\varphi$. The former is true at a circumstance index if φ is true at another circumstance index related directly to that of $K\varphi$; the latter is true at a circumstance index if φ is true at another circumstance index related, not to $Y\varphi$'s circumstance index, but to its *context* index.

§3 Formulation of IQ*

The following section outlines a version of IQ designed to be directly compared with the formulation of LD. Let's call this version of IQ 'IQ*'. IQ* has three tense operators, three indexical operators, and *actually* and *now* operators whose truth-conditions are the same as those of Kaplan's operators.

3.1 Syntax

PRIMITIVE SYMBOLS FOR PREDICATE LOGIC

These are exactly as for LD*

PRIMITIVE SYMBOLS FOR INDEXICAL/TENSE LOGIC

8 1-Place Tense Operators: $PRES_{(v,t)}$, $PAST_{(v,t)}$, $FUT_{(v,t)}$

9 1-Place Indexical Operators: N_t, Y_t, T_t

10 Deparametrizing Operator: G

11 Infinite sets of temporal variables: V_T, and constants C_T

Let $Term_T = (V_T \cup C_T)$

12 Infinite sets of world variables: V_V, and constants C_V

Let $Term_V = (V_V \cup C_V)$

ADDITIONAL PRIMITIVE SYMBOLS FOR IQ*/LD* EQUIVALENCE

13 1-Place Intensional Operators: A, N

WELL-FORMED EXPRESSIONS OF IQ*

1 If $\alpha \in$ V, then α is a term

Clauses 2 to 7 are as for LD*. However, note that only members of V are terms; so whereas LD* allows identities involving what we called nk-terms, IQ* has none.

8 If φ is a wff, $v \in Term_V$, $t \in Term_T$, and $B \in \{PRES, PAST, FUT\}$, then $B_{(v,t)}\varphi$ is a wff.

9 If φ is a wff and $t \in Term_T$, then $N_t\varphi$, $Y_t\varphi$, $T_t\varphi$ are wffs.

10 If φ is a wff, $v' \in V_V$, and $t' \in V_T$, then $Gv'\varphi$ and $Gt'\varphi$ are wffs.

11 If φ is a wff, then $A\varphi$ and $N\varphi$ are wffs.

MODELS FOR IQ*

An IQ* model is exactly the same as an LD* model.

3.2 Truth

TRUTH AND DENOTATION IN A CONTEXT

The remarks in §2.2 apply as before. In addition,
we write: φ_s^{u*} for: the result of substituting u* for every instance of s in φ. We let u* be a name for u, where $u^* \in Term_V \cup Term_T$.
We write: $Gv't'\varphi$ for: $Gv'Gt'\varphi$

DEFINITION: g_c is an assignment of values to contextual parameters, with respect to the model **M** and the context <w,i> (rendered as subscripted c), iff g_c is a 2-place function, from contexts c and expressions n, to elements of the model, such that:

$g_c(n) =$

- w, if $n = v$
- i, if $n = t$
- u, if $n = u^*$

• †, otherwise

3.3 Semantics for IQ*

Let $<w,i> \in C$, f be an assignment, g_c be a contextual function assigning values to parameters, w, w' ∈ W and i, i' ∈ I. Note that the c in g_c stands for the context <w,i>. Now, clauses 1 to 7 are exactly as in LD*; the differences in the systems only emerge in their treatments of tense and indexicality. In what follows, recall that $g_c(v) = w$ and $g_c(t) = i$, always, and that $.g_c(u^*) = u$.

8 8.1 $[\![PRES_{(v,t)}\varphi]\!]^{<<w,i>,<w',i'>>f,gc} = T$

iff

$g_c(v) = w'$, $g_c(t) = i'$ and $[\![\varphi]\!]^{<<w,i>,<w',i'>>f,gc} = T$.

8.2 $[\![PAST_{(v,t)}\varphi]\!]^{<<w,i>,<w',i'>>f,gc} = T$

iff

$g_c(v) = w'$, $g_c(t) = i'$ and $\exists i'' < i'$

such that

$[\![\varphi]\!]^{<<w,i>,<w',i''>>f,gc} = T$.

8.3 $[\![FUT_{(v,t)}\varphi]\!]^{<<w,i>,<w',i'>>f,gc} = T$

iff

$g_c(v) = w'$, $g_c(t) = i'$ and $\exists i'' > i'$

such that

$[\![\varphi]\!]^{<<w,i>,<w',i''>>f,gc} = T$.

9 9.1 $[\![N_t\varphi]\!]^{<<w,i>,<w',i'>>f,gc} = T$

iff

$g_c(t) = i'$ and $[\![\varphi]\!]^{<<w,i>,<w',i'>>f,gc} = T$.

9.2 $[\![Y_t\varphi]\!]^{<w,i>,<w',i'>f,gc} = T$

iff

$g_c(t) = i'+1$ and $[\![\varphi]\!]^{<<w,i>,<w',i'>>f,gc} = T$.

9.3 $[\![T_t\varphi]\!]^{<<w,i>,<w',i'>>f,gc} = T$

iff

$g_c(t) = i'-1$ and $[\![\varphi]\!]^{<<w,i>,<w',i'>>f,g_c} = T$.

10 10.1 $[\![Gv'\varphi]\!]^{<<w,i>,<w',i'>>f,g_c} = T$

iff

$[\![\varphi^{w'*}_{v'}]\!]^{<<w,i>,<w',i'>>f,g_c} = T$.

10.2 $[\![Gt'\varphi]\!]^{<<w,i>,<w',i'>>f,g_c} = T$

iff

$[\![\varphi^{i'*}_{t'}]\!]^{<<w,i>,<w',i'>>f,g_c} = T$.

11 11.1 $[\![A\varphi]\!]^{<<w,i>,<w',i'>>f,g_c} = T$

iff

$[\![\varphi]\!]^{<<w,i>,<w,i'>>f,g_c} = T$.

11.1 $[\![N\varphi]\!]^{<<w,i>,<w',i'>>f,g_c} = T$

iff

$[\![\varphi]\!]^{<<w,i>,<w',i>>f,g_c} = T$.

3.4 Remarks

We should note here the crucial 'diagonalising' aspect of the semantic clauses for tenses. By forcing the values returned by g_c from the context index to equal elements of the circumstance index, we ensure that a tensed wff can be true only at context-circumstance pairs where the context and the circumstance are the same. Thus, in a cartesian space where the co-ordinates are context-circumstance pairs, tensed wffs are true, if at all, only on the diagonal. This feature of IQ tense is not shared by LD tense.

It is also interesting to note that condition 8 in the well-formedness clauses in §3.1 departs from Chapters 1 and 2, and says that whatever the form of φ, $B_{(v,t)}\varphi$ is well-formed. This means that for $B_1, B_2 \in$ {PRES, PAST, FUT}, a wff ψ of the form $B_{1(v,t)}B_{2(v,t)}\varphi$ is well-formed. This doesn't in fact constitute a radical departure from the version of IQ presented earlier, for where $B_1 \neq$ PRES, ψ is unsatisfiable (cf. §4.2). Nevertheless, IQ* is not faithful to the context-sensitive/context-free distinction.

A final point is that the operators A and N introduced as additional primitive symbols for IQ*/LD* equivalence, and given their semantics in clause 11 above, are identical to Kaplan's operators. They are treated separately from IQ*'s indexical operators because they don't have the same type of semantic effect: since they are not parametric, they do not place conditions on the circumstance indices in the way that IQ*'s indexicals do. They are both Kaplan indexicals; but that does not make them proper IQ* indexicals. We examine in more detail the difference between the semantics of indexicals in the two systems in §6 below. Here, the two significant facts are first, the operator in IQ* does *not* have the effects of the evil 'actual$_V$' indexical discussed in Oberlander (1987: 118–23). It isn't really on a par with IQ*'s indexicals; but it does make the translation into IQ* truth-condition preserving. Secondly, the operator N is carried over from Kaplan's system because it possesses a characteristic not possessed by IQ* indexicals. On the one hand, this means that the full IQ* actually has something that IQ itself hasn't; on the other, we don't really pursue this side of the story in this chapter. We concentrate only on those features of IQ* which are difficult to capture in LD*; suffice it that adding something like N to IQ* is necessary to make the translation truth-condition preserving.

§4 Properties of the Systems

In comparing the expressive power of two systems, we want to find out whether it's possible to define the functions σ (sigma) and τ (tau). σ provides a syntactic translation of expressions of one language into expressions of the other, preserving satisfaction; τ provides a semantic transformation of a model for one language into a model for the other.

(1) $\mathbf{M}$ $\qquad\qquad$ $\tau(\mathbf{M})$

(2) $[\![\varphi]\!]^{\mathbf{M}} = \text{True}$ iff $[\![\sigma(\varphi)]\!]^{\tau(\mathbf{M})} = \text{True}$

Now, in designing the models for LD* and IQ*, a conscious decision was taken to ensure that LD*-contexts were identical to IQ*-contexts. As a result, τ can be taken to be the identity function. With regard to the syntax, it's clear that the presence of parameters in the object-language operators of IQ* requires σ to do rather more work than τ. In §4.1, we shall exhibit a translation theorem which would guide the satisfaction-preserving syntactic translation from LD* into IQ*; in the subsequent sections, we'll look at the way IQ* represents Kaplan's definitions for validity and necessary truth. Looking slightly further ahead, §5 will examine reasons for thinking that while IQ* can translate LD*, the converse is not true. §6 will then propose the extensions to LD* that are required to enable it to translate expressions of IQ*.

4.1 Translation Theorem

Above we observed that we must investigate the syntactic translation in some detail. It is proposed that any translation scheme from LD* into IQ* should respect the following theorem. For all LD* formulae φ:

$$[\![\varphi]\!]^{<<w,i>,<w',i'>>} = T \text{ iff } [\![(\sigma(\varphi))]\!]^{<<w,i>,<w',i'>>} = T$$

A wff of LD*, which may be true at more than one context-circumstance pair, must be translated by a wff of IQ* which can also be true at more than pair. Thus, a deparametrized wff is appropriate. In general, if the formula φ is tensed (i.e. of the form $P\psi$ or $F\psi$), the IQ* translation will contain a deparametrized tense as the initial operator.[3] The translation σ from LD* to IQ* does at least contain the following:

(3) $\quad P \quad \Rightarrow \quad Gv't'PAST_{(v',t')}$

3 Cf. for instance the IQ* translation of the LD* representation of the example in §5.1 below.

$$F \Rightarrow Gv't'FUT_{(v',t')}$$
$$\varphi \Rightarrow \sigma(\varphi)$$

We'll see in more detail in §7 the full scheme for translation. We do not prove there that the translation functions comply with the theorem. But a proof would be relatively simple, proceeding by induction on the complexity of formulae. For the moment it should suffice to note that we are effectively in the position to carry out a top-down translation from LD* to IQ*. For instance, omitting subscripts for brevity,

(4) $P\varphi \wedge F\psi \quad \Rightarrow \quad GPAST\varphi \wedge GFUT\psi$

4.2 Validity and Satisfiability

An LD* formula φ is valid iff $\forall wi\ [\![\varphi]\!]^{<<w,i>,<w,i>>} = T$
iff
$\forall wi\ [\![\sigma(\varphi)]\!]^{<<w,i>,<w,i>>} = T$

Validity in LD* is just as Kaplan defined it. By equivalence of truth-conditions, an untensed IQ* expression will be true at the index <<w,i>,<w,i>> just in case its tensed analogue is true at that index. That is:

$[\![Gv't'PRES_{(v',t')}\ (\sigma(\varphi))]\!]^{<<w,i>,<w,i>>} = T$
if
$[\![PRES_{(v,t)}\ (\sigma(\varphi))]\!]^{<<w,i>,<w,i>>} = T$

The question of validity may be said to arise when we want to know, for some sentence, whether it will always be true whenever it is uttered. This last equivalence shows why, when posed in IQ*, the question of validity seems to arise for *tensed* sentences of the theory.

An LD* formula φ is satisfiable iff $\exists wi\ [\![\varphi]\!]^{<<w,i>,<w,i>>} = \text{True}$
iff

$\exists wi\ [\![\sigma(\varphi)]\!]^{<<w,i>,<w,i>>} = \text{True}$

This result is straightforward: a wff is satisfiable iff there is at least one context at which it evaluates to true. This result will be of use in §5.

4.3 Necessity

An LD* formula φ is necessary iff $\forall wiw'i'\ [\![\varphi]\!]^{<<w,i>,<w',i'>>} = \text{True}$
iff
$\forall wiw'i'\ [\![\sigma(\varphi)]\!]^{<<w,i>,<w',i'>>} = \text{True}$

Kaplan distinguished a formula's validity (truth in every possible context of utterance) from its necessity (truth in every circumstance for every context). This was an essential part of his program devoted to showing that there are truths which are valid, but not necessary. His examples of such formulae included *I am here now* and *I exist*. Thomason (1974: 65–8) and Montague (1968: §3) also discuss the desirability of representing the special status of such truths. What Kaplan calls 'validity', they call 'pragmatic validity'; and what Kaplan calls 'necessity', they call 'semantic validity'. Their usage is closer to general custom, since Kaplan's 'necessity' is very similar to what is generally called 'validity', tout court. We could follow them, and perhaps coin the terms *P-valid* and *S-valid* (and *P-satisfiable* and *S-satisfiable*). However, a good deal of our discussion will be about what we would then have to call P-satisfiability. On grounds of mere economy, we therefore follow Kaplan in talking of validity, satisfiability and necessity.

Having removed personal and locational indexicals from the object-language to derive LD*, we cannot prove the particular results about *I am here now* and *I exist*. However, for some formula φ of LD*, it can be shown that (5) is valid, but not necessary.

(5) $\neg(N\varphi \leftrightarrow K\varphi)$

The proof is simple: (5) is valid iff, for all contexts, it's not the case that the truth value of Nφ is the same as that of Kφ. That is, (5) is valid iff for all contexts, Nφ and Kφ differ in truth value. For this to be the case, all that is required is that φ be picked so that its truth value alternate from day to day. But with the same φ, (5) is necessarily true iff, for all contexts and circumstances, Nφ and Kφ differ in truth value. Suppose φ is true at some context-circumstance pair. Then Nφ will be true for all context-circumstance pairs sharing the same context. Take the context-circumstance pair at which the circumstance's time index is the day after the context's time index. Kφ will be true at this pair also. Thus Nφ and Kφ will share a truth value at some context-circumstance pair. Thus (5) is not necessarily true. (In the terms suggested above, it is P-valid, but not S-valid).

So we can see that LD* can contain formulae which are not necessary truths. And by the equivalence given at the beginning of this section, IQ* can capture them also. The IQ* representation of LD* necessity differs in an interesting respect from the IQ* representation of LD* validity. While in the latter case, we could show that validity effectively arose only for tensed sentences of IQ*, this is not so for necessity. And this is an intuitively appealing result: for Kaplan, the issue of necessity arises when we ask whether, for the content (proposition) expressed by a wff in a context, that content is true in all circumstances. In IQ*, then, this result is captured by the fact that the wffs of the theory which might be necessarily true are *detensed* wffs.

§5 How Not to Kaplan an IQ

In §4, we showed how to represent various formal properties of the system based on Kaplan's LD within the system based on IQ. In this section, however, we shall consider an example which indicates that the resources of LD* are not sufficiently powerful to represent all the formal properties of

IQ*. Thus while we can, to a certain extent, IQ a Kaplan, we cannot Kaplan an IQ. In what follows, we are considering LD* without the terms included in §2.1 under the heading 'Non-Kaplanian Primitive Symbols for LD*/IQ* Equivalence', and thus without the semantic clauses supplied for those expressions. If we were being more precise, we might refer to this fragment of LD* as LD^-; but in general, there should be no risk of confusion in calling it LD*. The additional symbols are in fact the *solution* to the problem outlined in this section. They will be introduced in §6.

5.1 A Counterexample

Consider the English sentence (6).

(6) It will rain yesterday

In §3.5.1 of Chapter 2, it was observed that IQ gives sentences such as (6) representations whose truth conditions cannot be met, since they involve a mismatch between the intervals specified by the tense and the indexical. On these grounds, such sentences were deemed to be semantically incoherent. Using only the resources of IQ*, we are now in a position to be rather more precise about this notion of incoherence: (6) is anomalous because it is unsatisfiable in IQ*. And it is here that a significant difference between IQ* and LD* emerges: LD* leaves (6) satisfiable. In the face of this fact, and the fact that neither theory renders the content of (6) necessarily false, serious problems seem to arise for LD*.

Let us take (6) both ways: first we shall represent it in LD*, and translate it into IQ*; then we shall represent it in IQ* directly, and translate it into LD*. The LD* representation of (6) will be (7). By the translation theorem, and the translation of Y given in §7.1, (7)'s IQ* translation is (8).

(7) FY (It rain)

(8) $Gv't'FUT_{(v',t')}$ [N $[Gv''t''PAST_{(v'',t'')}Y_{t''}$ (It rain)]]

Is (7) satisfiable, and if so, is its translation satisfiable? To see whether this is so, consider the definition of satisfiability given in §4.2. A wff will be satisfiable iff there exists a context <w,i> such that the wff is true there. Now, this means that, if we can show that (7) can be true with respect to some index <<w,i>,<w,i>>, (7) is satisfiable. What would have to be the case for this to be so? By the definitions in §2.3, (7) is true at <<w,i>,<w,i>> iff there is some i' > i such that (9) is true at <<w,i>,<w,i'>>.

(9) Y (It rain)

(9) is true at <<w,i>,<w,i'>> iff (10) is true at <<w,i>,<w,i–1>>.

(10) It rain

So, if it rained the day before the context of utterance of (6), LD* could make its representation (7) true; hence the formula (7) is satisfiable.

Now, is (7)'s IQ* translation (8) satisfiable? It will be, so long as there is some context <w,i> such that (8) is true at <<w,i>,<w,i>>. By the definitions in §3.3, (8) will be true there iff w = w, i = i and there is some i' > i such that (11) is true at <<w,i>,<w,i'>>.

(11) N [Gv''t''$\mathrm{PAST}_{(v'',t'')}\mathrm{Y}_{t''}$ (It rain)]

By the definition of N, (11) is true at <<w,i>,<w,i'>> iff the formula within N's scope is true at <<w,i>,<w,i>>. By applying the definition of G, that formula is (12):

(12) $\mathrm{PAST}_{(w^*,i^*)}\mathrm{Y}_{i^*}$ (It rain)

(12) is true at <<w,i>,<w,i>> iff w = w, i = i and there is some i'' < i such that (13) is true at <<w,i>,<w,i''>>.

(13) Y_{i*} (It rain)

This will be the case if iff i" = i–1 and 'It rains' is true at <<w,i>,<w,i">>. Now, since there is no relationship specified between i' (the index 'supplied' by the tense) and i" (the index 'supplied' by the indexical), there is no reason why i" cannot be earlier than i'. Thus the IQ* translation of the LD* representation of (6) is also satisfiable.

The situation is completely different if we give (6) its IQ* representation *directly*. Let this representation be (8').

(8') $FUT_{(v,t)}$ [Y_t (It rain)]

Is *this* formula satisfiable in IQ*, and if it is, is its LD* translation satisfiable in LD*? This time, let us answer the first question before attempting the second. (8') will be satisfiable if there is a context <w,i> for which it is true. By definitions, (8') is true at <<w,i>,<w,i>> iff $g_c(t)$ = i = i, $g_c(v)$ = w = w and there is some i' > i such that (14) is true at <<w,i>,<w,i'>>.

(14) Y_t (It rain)

(14) will be true at <<w,i>,<w,i'>> iff i' = i–1 and (10) is true at <<w,i>,<w,i'>>.

(10) It rain

This time, the conditions cannot be met. For i' > i, yet i' = i–1, so i' < i. (8') cannot be made true for any <w,i>. So the IQ* representation of (6) is *not* satisfiable.

The question now re-presents itself: is the LD* translation of (8') satisfiable? This question can only be answered if we know what the LD* translation of (8') is, and armed with a good translation, it might prove possible to give an LD* expression which is also unsatisfiable, while explaining why the asymmetry should have arisen.

An obvious explanation for the anomaly lies in the parametric nature of IQ* tense. (8') contains parametric tense; (8) did not. So it is natural to argue that it is on these grounds that (8') is unsatisfiable, and infer from this that all that LD* needs to capture this property is some apparatus to simulate full parametric tense. Once this position has been reached, it only remains to choose the appropriate combination of operators to stand in for parametric tense. One possibility might be to prefix any LD* wff φ with A and N to form ANφ; this would certainly ensure that, rather than considering the truth of a formula relative to an arbitrary context-circumstance pair, we must look at its truth relative to the particular context-circumstance pair where the circumstance *is* the context. But above, we started off with just that index, and it did us no good in LD*.

The operator Y can always afford to 'throw away' whatever index has been handed to it by the truth-conditions: Kaplan's style of indexicals always take wide scope, whereas IQ-style indexicals are rather different. In LD*, therefore, no relationship is required between the index at which (10) is true and the index supplied by the tense operator F. A and N are not enough. Indeed, as we shall see in the next section, no combination of the operators LD* has at its disposal is sufficient to capture the unsatisfiability of the IQ* formula.

Before proceding to this general proof, it is worth noting in passing that the unsatisfiability problem is not a trivial one. For although (8') is not satisfiable in IQ*, (8) is not necessarily false; in the case of (8), the tenses are not parametric, and thus the LD*/IQ* asymmetry disappears. This fact suggests that IQ* should manage to explain a fact about English for which LD* is lost for words. Consider (15a) and (15b).

(15) (a) ?Sam said that it will rain yesterday

(b) Sam said that it would rain yesterday

Although we do not enter into the intricacies of embedded reports here, it should be clear that, since LD* doesn't rule out (6), it won't rule out (15a).

IQ* should rule it out alright, because it rules out (6). On the other hand, neither LD* nor IQ* should rule out (15b); LD* certainly won't, and the fact that (8) is not necessarily false in IQ* suggests that (15) could be true there too.

5.2 Proof of Untranslatability

The intuition that A and N might simulate a tense has a certain appeal to it. The difference between IQ* and LD* is that tensed formulae of IQ* considered relative to a context will take only one context-circumstance pair to true, whereas a tensed formula of LD* will take many to true. The same difference holds for indexicals: in IQ*, a formula of the form $Y_t\varphi$ will go to true at an index only if the time of the circumstance is the day before the time of the context, and φ is true at the time of the circumstance; by contrast, in LD*, a formula of the form $Y\varphi$ will go to true at *any* index whatsoever, so long as φ is true at the possibly distinct index at which the time of the circumstance is the day before the time of the context.

While IQ* can make its formulae evaluate to true, relative to a context, at only one circumstance, LD* seems unable to prevent its formulae evaluating to true, relative to a context, at many indices. We shall now prove that, with only its current temporal operators, LD* cannot define a tense of IQ*.

With regard to semantic definability, there are two varieties that are of interest: general and structure-relative. We shall pursue only the former. A notion O (such as a modal or tense operator) is *generally definable* in terms of the notions $O_1,\ldots,O_n$ (a list which does not contain O) just in case there is a formula $\varphi[O_1,\ldots,O_n]$ involving only $O_1,\ldots,O_n$ such that

$$\models \varphi[O_1,\ldots,O_n] \leftrightarrow \psi[O]$$

'$\models$' means 'is valid', as before. So, in our case, $\text{PRES}_{(v,t)}\varphi$ will be generally definable in terms of some LD*-operators $O_1,\ldots,O_n$ just in case there is an LD* wff $\psi[O_1,\ldots,O_n]$ such that

$$\psi[O_1,\ldots,O_n] \leftrightarrow \text{PRES}_{(v,t)}\varphi$$

is true in every structure. We can say, then, that if $\text{PRES}_{(v,t)}\varphi$ is generally definable in LD*, then we can understand $\text{PRES}_{(v,t)}\varphi$ wholly on the basis of LD*-operators without making any presuppositions concerning the atomic wffs. To put it another way, if $\text{PRES}_{(v,t)}\varphi$ (which is, after all, a wff of IQ*, not LD*, as it stands) were to be added to LD*, then two possibilities are opened up. Either it adds expressive power to LD*, or it is redundant. It is redundant iff it can be generally defined as above.

Now, it is easy to show that if we pick some tautology T, $\text{PRES}_{(v,t)}\text{T}$ is not generally definable in LD*. Thus, to add it to LD* would be to add expressive power; LD* and IQ* are not, as it stands, intertranslatable. In what follows, we shall ignore world indices, for the sake of clarity and brevity; we can think of the model structures as simply $I \times I$; the model will be an assignment from pairs of indices to truth values. This means, of course, that we do not deal with the LD* operator A, since it is cashed in terms of worlds; but what applies to LD*'s N with respect to temporal indices applies to A with respect to world indices.

DEFINITION: A wff φ denotes an *eternal* proposition
iff
$\forall i$, (if $\exists i'$ such that $[\![\varphi]\!]^{<i,i'>} = T$, then $\forall j$, $[\![\varphi]\!]^{<i,j>} = T$).

It can be proved from this that, if φ denotes an eternal proposition and $[\![\varphi]\!]^{<i,i'>} = F$, then $\forall j$, $[\![\varphi]\!]^{<i,j>} = F$. Suppose the conclusion does not follow. Then $\exists j$ such that $[\![\varphi]\!]^{<i,j>} = T$; and since φ denotes an eternal proposition, it follows from the fact that $[\![\varphi]\!]^{<i,j>} = T$ that $\forall j'$, $[\![\varphi]\!]^{<i,j'>} = T$.

But this contradicts the premise $[\![\varphi]\!]^{<i,i'>} = F$, since there must be at least one index at which φ is false. □

CONVENTION: With the interpretation function J, we can write $[\![\varphi]\!]^J$, or just φ^J for the proposition assigned to the wff φ.

LEMMA: Let $\psi[\varphi_1,\ldots,\varphi_n]$ be a LD* wff ψ containing atomic wffs φ_1 to φ_n, and let J assign eternal propositions to each of $\varphi_1,\ldots,\varphi_n$. Then $[\![\psi]\!]^J$ is eternal.

Once we have proved this lemma, we will have shown that if LD*'s atomic wffs denote eternal propositions only, then its complex wffs also denote eternal propositions only.

PROOF: By cases, with respect to the wff φ and the operators $\wedge$, $\neg$, N, Y, T, K, L, F and P (A is not required). There are five types of case; we will show it for one example in each type.

CASE 1: Atomic wffs
The atomic wffs have the property of eternity by assumption.

CASE 2: $\wedge$, $\neg$
Assume: $[\![\varphi]\!]^J$ and $[\![\psi]\!]^J$ are eternal. Now we prove: so are $[\![\varphi \wedge \psi]\!]^J$ and $[\![\neg\varphi]\!]^J$.
The result for $\neg$ follows from the remarks about eternal falsehood above.
Let's show that it holds for $\wedge$;
Let $[\![\varphi \wedge \psi]\!]^{J<i,i'>} = T$. Then $[\![\varphi]\!]^{J<i,i'>} = T$ and $[\![\psi]\!]^{J<i,i'>} = T$
By assumption, φ^J and ψ^J are eternal.
So $\forall j$, $[\![\varphi]\!]^{J<i,j>} = T = [\![\psi]\!]^{J<i,j>}$
Hence $\forall j$, $[\![\varphi \wedge \psi]\!]^{J<i,j>} = T$
So $[\![\varphi \wedge \psi]\!]^J$ is eternal.

CASE 3: N, Y, T

Assume: $\llbracket\varphi\rrbracket^J$ is eternal. Now we prove: so are $\llbracket N\varphi\rrbracket^J$, $\llbracket Y\varphi\rrbracket^J$ and $\llbracket T\varphi\rrbracket^J$.
Let's show it for Y;
Let $\llbracket Y\varphi\rrbracket^{J\langle i,i'\rangle} = T$. Then by definition of Y, $\llbracket\varphi\rrbracket^{J\langle i,i-1\rangle} = T$
Hence $\forall j$, $\llbracket Y\varphi\rrbracket^{J\langle i,j\rangle} = T$
So $\llbracket Y\varphi\rrbracket^J$ is eternal.

CASE 4: K, L
Assume: $\llbracket\varphi\rrbracket^J$ is eternal. Now we prove: so are $\llbracket K\varphi\rrbracket^J$ and $\llbracket L\varphi\rrbracket^J$.
Let's show it for K; the proof is like that for Y, except we deal with i' instead of i. Let $\llbracket K\varphi\rrbracket^{J\langle i,i'\rangle} = T$. Then by definition of K, $\llbracket\varphi\rrbracket^{J\langle i,i'-1\rangle} = T$
By assumption, φ^J is eternal and time is infinite in both directions.[4]
Hence $\forall j$, $\llbracket\varphi\rrbracket^{J\langle i,j-1\rangle} = T$
It follows that $\forall j$, $\llbracket K\varphi\rrbracket^{J\langle i,j\rangle} = T$
So $\llbracket K\varphi\rrbracket^J$ is eternal.

CASE 5: F, P
Assume: $\llbracket\varphi\rrbracket^J$ is eternal. Prove: so are $\llbracket P\varphi\rrbracket^J$ and $\llbracket F\varphi\rrbracket^J$.
Let's show it for F;
Let $\llbracket F\varphi\rrbracket^{J\langle i,i'\rangle} = T$. Then by definition of F, $\exists j > i'$ such that $\llbracket\varphi\rrbracket^{J\langle i,j\rangle} = T$
By assumption, φ^J is eternal and time is infinite.
So $\forall k$ $\llbracket\varphi\rrbracket^{J\langle i,k\rangle} = T$
And $\forall k$, $\exists k' > k$ such that $\llbracket\varphi\rrbracket^{J\langle i,k'\rangle} = T$
Thus $\forall k$, $\llbracket F\varphi\rrbracket^{J\langle i,k\rangle} = T$
Hence $\llbracket F\varphi\rrbracket^J$ is eternal. □

Taking together cases 1 to 5, the lemma is proved. We have shown that if a wff φ is interpreted so that it is true everywhere, then a wff of the form Operator-φ will be true everywhere also. *Mutatis mutandis* for falsehood.

---

4 Time simply has an integer structure in the models for LD* and IQ* given in sections 2 and 3 above; it could have a more complex structure if necessary; but if it is simple and finite in extent, we could define IQ* operators by a process of enumerating the indices at which the IQ* metalanguage equations hold. So, we might say that IQ* + finite time = LD*.

Now it's easy to show that there are IQ* operators which do not conform to this pattern. This means that they cannot be generally defined in LD*, and that IQ* is therefore more expressive than LD*.

THEOREM: Where T is a tautology such as $(\varphi \vee \neg\varphi)$, PRES_tT is not generally definable in LD*.

PROOF: Assume PRES_tT is definable. Then there is an LD* wff ψ such that
$\models \psi \leftrightarrow \text{PRES}_t\text{T}$
Take a model **M** in which all atomic wffs θ are eternal. From the lemma, it follows that all wffs of any form are eternal. So, in particular, $[\![\psi]\!]^J$ is eternal. However, $[\![\text{PRES}_t\text{T}]\!]^J = \{\langle i,i\rangle : i \in I\}$ is clearly *not* eternal. We know that for $\models \psi \leftrightarrow \text{PRES}_t\text{T}$ to be true, the left hand side and right hand side must give the same proposition in all models. But, as is shown, this fails for **M**. The assumption of definability leads to contradiction. □

So, from the lemma and the theorem, we can see that $\text{PRES}_{(v,t)}\varphi$ is not generally definable in LD*; to add it to LD* would be to increase LD*'s expressive power. The reason for this lies in the basic difference between LD* and IQ* which can be expressed in terms of the eternity property. In a model (for both LD* and IQ*) which happened to make each atomic wff true at all indices (or false at all indices), the operators of LD* would make *all* complex wffs true at all indices (or false at all indices) as well. By contrast, the operators of IQ* would *not* preserve the eternity property in this way. So, in the general case, we shall say that LD* logical operators are *eternity-preserving*, and IQ* tense and indexical operators are *eternity-disturbing*.

We may therefore say that, if an atomic wff taken relative to a context evaluates to true at every (or no) circumstance-index, the following result holds. Taking LD* without the added 'Non-Kaplanian Primitive Symbols', the complex sentences of LD* formed will also be able to evaluate to true at every (or no) index. So LD* simply doesn't have the ability to restrict the truth of sentences taken in contexts to one index only.[5] This is a direct reflection of the fact that Kaplan's tense and indexical operators do not place restrictions on the intervals at which wffs evaluate to true; and it is because of this that formulae remain P-satisfiable which IQ* would deem P-unsatisfiable on grounds of indexical/tense mismatch.

Indeed, the indexical operators of LD* are not just eternity-preserving; they are eternity creating, in the following sense. If the atomic wffs upon which they operate go to true at at least one context-circumstance pair, the indexical wffs will go to true for that context at *all* circumstance indices. Showing that $\text{PRES}_{(v,t)}$ is not generally definable within the unaugmented LD* of this section has demonstrated that LD* doesn't have tenses or indexicals which will limit the truth of wffs to single indices. As things stand, this property leads to the difference in expressive power evinced by the conflicting satisfiability conditions examined in §5.1; the two systems are not currently mutually translatable, in the sense that there is no satisfaction-preserving translation in both directions. In the next section, we introduce the new primitive symbols which allow LD* the luxury of single-index truths. With these in hand, it seems as though it might after all be possible to represent an IQ-like system in Kaplan's system.

§6 How To Do It

In the previous section, we showed that unless something is added to it, the object-language of LD* would be unable to represent the property of parametric IQ* wffs which allows them to evaluate to true at one context-circumstance index only. In this section, we shall first indicate how the restrictions work in IQ*, then introduce into LD* the additional, non-

5 If an LD* atomic formula were false at just one index, then its negation would be true at just one index. But this kind of 'single index truth' is accidental compared to the systematic single index truth forced by IQ*'s eternity-disturbing operators.

Kaplanian primitive symbols which can replicate these restrictions, and finally apply them to the sentence *It will rain yesterday*.

The way tenses and indexicals work in IQ* is by placing restrictions on the intervals at which a formula may evaluate to true; this often involves equational conditions on the temporal (and, in the case of tenses, world) indices at which the formula is being evaluated. To see what this means, and to compare it with what LD* does with indexicals, take the semantic clauses each system gives for *yesterday* :

(16) $[\![Y_t\varphi]\!]^{<<w,i>,<w',i'>>f,g_c} = T$

iff

$g_c(t) = i'+1$ and $[\![\varphi]\!]^{<<w,i>,<w',i'>>f,g_c} = T$

(17) $[\![Y\varphi]\!]^{<<w,i>,<w',i'>>} = T$

iff

$[\![\varphi]\!]^{<<w,i>,<w',i-1>>} = T.$

In IQ*, $g_c(t)$ will return i; so the restriction stated is that $i = i'+1$; meanwhile the contained formula φ must be true at i'—the same index at which $Y_t\varphi$ had to be true. In LD*, on the other hand, φ has to be true at $i-1$; but there is no demand that Yφ be true at that index, nor that $i-1 = i'$ (ie that $i = i'+1$). So, as we saw in §5.2, Yφ can be true-in-LD* at many indices; $Y_t\varphi$ can be true-in-IQ* at an index only if the time of the circumstance *equals* the day before the time of the context.[6] To reiterate: what's missing from LD* is an object-language expression which can invoke these metalanguage equations, in the way the parametric expressions of IQ* do.[7] And the 'Non-Kaplanian Primitive Symbols' included in the formulation of LD* in §2 in fact fill this restrictive role. Recall that these symbols are:

---

6 In IQ proper, of course, 'yesterday' is defined in terms of subintervals rather than equations. But the point stands: a restriction is placed on the existing interval of evaluation; we don't evaluate relative to a brand-new interval.

7 The operators A and N, borrowed from LD* by IQ*, are not parametric, and thus do not resemble true indexicals in this way. Like the Kaplan operators in general, they don't invoke metalanguage equations.

10 An infinite set of temporal constants: V_T

11 An infinite set of world constants: V_V

The constants are rather like the *I* and *Here* which Kaplan included in the original formulation of LD. t_s and v_s have semantic clauses which allow them to pick out the time and world of the context of speech; t_e and v_e, however, have semantic clauses which allow them to pick out the times and worlds of the circumstances relative to which they are evaluated. This last feature is rather subtle: different occurrences of t_e within the same wff may sometimes be evaluated with respect to different circumstances of evaluation, if, for instance, one of them falls within the scope of an operator that switches the circumstance. A correct treatment of this in the translation from IQ* into LD* requires distinct constants to be syntactically distinguished; we return to the import of this after the translation has been given.

With the additional devices, it is quite simple to express, in the LD* object-language, equations which will have the same effects in the metalanguage as the parametric expressions of IQ*.

(18) $[\![t_s = t_e]\!]^{<<w,i>,<w',i'>>}$

(19) $[\![v_s = v_e]\!]^{<<w,i>,<w',i'>>}$

(18) will be true iff i = i'; (19) will be true iff w = w'. If the parametric tenses of IQ* are to be simulated, then the ordinary Priorian tenses of LD* need to be accompanied by occurrences of both (18) and (19). If a parametric indexical is to be simulated, then a suitably embedded occurrence of (18) must be used.

The use of these expressions can be made much clearer by example; and the obvious case to treat is (6), whose IQ* representation is (8'):

(6) It will rain yesterday

(8') $FUT_{(v,t)}$ $[Y_t$ (It rain)]

§7 gives a translation function from IQ* into LD*; for the moment it will suffice to recognise the following (assume that φ is atomic):

(20) $FUT_{(v,t)}\varphi \Rightarrow (t_S = t_e) \wedge (v_S = v_e) \wedge F\varphi$

$Y_t\varphi \Rightarrow L[(t_S = t_e) \wedge K\varphi]$

Notice that the L (day after) and K (day before) operators ‘cancel’, so that in the translation of $Y_t\varphi$, φ is to be considered relative to the same index as $Y_t\varphi$ would have been, while speech time and circumstance time are equated at the day after that index (that is: today!). Now, (8') will be translated as (21):

(21) $(t_S = t_e) \wedge (v_S = v_e) \wedge FL[(t_S = t_e) \wedge K\varphi]$

This formula is unsatisfiable in LD*. For, relative to an index <<w,i>,<w,i>>, it will be true only if i = i, w = w, and there is some i' > i such that i = i'+1, and φ is true at i'+1. But i is then both earlier and later than i'. Inconsistency results: the LD* translation of the IQ* wff preserves unsatisfiability.

So, one coherent way for LD* to portray the previously elusive properties of IQ* formulae is by adding these new primitive symbols to the LD* object-language. The extension might be thought non-conservative, since wffs which were previously satisfiable are no longer satisfiable; but of course, the old wffs are still satisfiable; we have merely added new wffs which aren't satisfiable (and of course, new wffs which are satisfiable too). In the next section, we give the full translation functions from LD* into IQ*, and back again.

§7 The Translation Functions

Both σ_1 and σ_2 are top-down translation functions.

LD* OPERATORS

A = actually	N = now
P = past	F = future
K = day before	L = day after
Y = yesterday	T = tomorrow

NEW LD* TERMS

t_s = speech time	t_e = evaluation time
v_s = speech world	v_e = evaluation world

7.1 σ_1: from LD* into IQ*

Where α is an LD* individual term and φ is any LD* wff,

$\alpha \Rightarrow \alpha$

the $\alpha\ \varphi \Rightarrow$ *the* $(\sigma_1(\alpha)(\sigma_1(\varphi)))$

Where φ is an atomic LD* wff,

$\varphi \Rightarrow \varphi$

Where φ and ψ are any LD* wffs,

$\varphi \wedge \psi \Rightarrow \sigma_1(\varphi) \wedge \sigma_1(\psi)$

$\neg\varphi \Rightarrow \neg(\sigma_1(\varphi))$

$\exists\alpha\varphi \Rightarrow \exists\alpha(\sigma_1(\varphi))$

Other cases:

$P\varphi \Rightarrow Gv't'PAST_{(v',t')}(\sigma_1(\varphi))$

$F\varphi \Rightarrow Gv't'FUT_{(v',t')}(\sigma_1(\varphi))$

$K\varphi \Rightarrow Gv't'PAST_{(v',t')}[Y_{t'}(\sigma_1(\varphi))]$

$L\varphi \Rightarrow Gv't'FUT_{(v',t')}[T_{t'}(\sigma_1(\varphi))]$

$A\varphi \Rightarrow A(\sigma_1(\varphi))$

$N\varphi \Rightarrow N(\sigma_1(\varphi))$

$Y\varphi \quad \Rightarrow \quad N(Gv't'PAST_{(v',t')}[Y_{t'}(\sigma_1(\varphi))])$

$T\varphi \quad \Rightarrow \quad N(Gv't'FUT_{(v',t')}[T_{t'}(\sigma_1(\varphi))])$

Let $\Gamma = (t_s = t_e)$ and $\Delta = (v_s = v_e)$; then

$\Gamma \quad \Rightarrow \quad Gv'PRES_{(v',t)}(\alpha = \alpha)$

$\Delta \quad \Rightarrow \quad Gt'PRES_{(v,t')}(\alpha = \alpha)$

7.2 σ_2: from IQ* into LD*

Where α is an IQ* term and φ is any IQ* wff,

$\alpha \quad \Rightarrow \quad \alpha$

$\mathit{the}\ \alpha\ \varphi \quad \Rightarrow \quad \mathit{the}\ (\sigma_2(\alpha)(\sigma_2(\varphi)))$

Where φ is an atomic IQ* wff,

$\varphi \quad \Rightarrow \quad \varphi$

Where φ and ψ are any IQ* wffs,

$\varphi \wedge \psi \quad \Rightarrow \quad \sigma_2(\varphi) \wedge \sigma_2(\psi)$

$\neg\varphi \quad \Rightarrow \quad \neg(\sigma_2(\varphi))$

$\exists\alpha\varphi \quad \Rightarrow \quad \exists\alpha(\sigma_2(\varphi))$

Other cases, where $v' \in Term_V$ and $t' \in Term_T$:

$PRES_{(v',t')}\varphi \quad \Rightarrow \quad (\sigma_2(t') = t_e) \wedge (\sigma_2(v') = v_e) \wedge \sigma_2(\varphi)$

$PAST_{(v',t')}\varphi \quad \Rightarrow \quad (\sigma_2(t') = t_e) \wedge (\sigma_2(v') = v_e) \wedge P(\sigma_2(\varphi))$

$FUT_{(v',t')}\varphi \quad \Rightarrow \quad (\sigma_2(t') = t_e) \wedge (\sigma_2(v') = v_e) \wedge F(\sigma_2(\varphi))$

$N_{t'}\varphi \quad \Rightarrow \quad (\sigma_2(t') = t_e) \wedge \sigma_2(\varphi)$

$Y_{t'}\varphi \quad \Rightarrow \quad L[(\sigma_2(t') = t_e) \wedge K(\sigma_2(\varphi))]$

$T_{t'}\varphi \quad \Rightarrow \quad K[(\sigma_2(t') = t_e) \wedge L(\sigma_2(\varphi))]$

$Gv'\varphi \quad \Rightarrow \quad \sigma_2(\varphi^{w'*}_{v'})$[8]

$Gt'\varphi \quad \Rightarrow \quad \sigma_2(\varphi^{i'*}_{t'})$

---

8 Where w'* doesn't already occur within φ. *Mutatis mutandis* for i'* in the next clause.

$A\varphi$	$\Rightarrow$	$A(\sigma_2(\varphi))$
$N\varphi$	$\Rightarrow$	$N(\sigma_2(\varphi))$

Where v' = v and/or t' = t:

t'	$\Rightarrow$	t_s
v'	$\Rightarrow$	v_s

Otherwise, (where v' = w'* and/or t' = i'*) the function is identity:

i'*	$\Rightarrow$	i'*
w'*	$\Rightarrow$	w'*

7.3 Remarks

There are three points to note: first, σ_1 is the function from LD* into IQ* which was less precisely referred to as σ in sections 4 and 5.

Secondly, the translation from IQ* into LD* depends crucially on the fact that the translation is itself relativised to extra-linguistic context. This is clear where G is concerned: in order to get it over to LD*, we must substitute constants for the variables within subformulae; and these constants are the names of the indices with respect to which the formula is to be evaluated (the indices themselves are, of course, the same in each language). This point is rather interesting, because it means that we may need to use several such constants within the same formula, each generated from a different index of evaluation, and each equated with another constant whose interpretation is a possibly distinct evaluation index.

The third point is rather significant: the translations for Kaplan's indexicals require the use of Kaplan's N in IQ*. This reflects the fact that the full IQ could not fully represent LD* (although we do not prove this here), since N is added to IQ* for precisely this reason. All the other translations will work, but it seems that without it, IQ* actually couldn't quite capture the particular features of Kaplan-style indexicals. It seems that Kaplan's indexicals, while they lack the strong property of disturbing eternity, do have some 'descoping' feature that cannot be captured by a judicious combination of parameters and G-operators. That difference is a matter for further investigation; basically, it involves the fact that LD*'s N forces the formula within its scope to be evaluated with repect to an index which is speech time; IQ*'s N_t, by contrast, while placing a restriction on the index of evaluation, still lets the formula within *its* scope evaluate with respect to the same index as before. The IQ* *now* disturbs eternity, but it can never 'throw away' an index the way LD* operators do.

We hope eventually to present a system which combines both kinds of indexical in a more systematic manner than IQ*. Chapter 9 represents a move in that direction, but for the moment it suffices to note once again the central point of this chapter: whatever else Kaplan's view of indexicality entails, it makes tenses and indexicals eternity-preserving; and whatever else the IQ* view of indexicality entails, it makes tenses and indexicals eternity-disturbing.

Given these observations, we can say that since σ_1 and σ_2 are translations functions which deliver truth-conditional equivalents in the two systems, it should be possible to translate from LD* to IQ* and back again (or vice versa). In so doing, we would see what effect the 'second language' had upon the wffs of the first system; we could derive for LD*, for instance, the IQ*-normal form of wffs. Thus it looks as though we can Kaplan an IQ after all, and IQ it back. But there are some further issues which we may help us contrast the systems. It is to these issues that we now turn.

§8 Outstanding Issues

We have demonstrated that, with an extension to a simple fragment of Kaplan's LD, we can generate a formal system LD* with which it is possible to compare the formal system IQ* based on the system IQ discussed at length elsewhere. Amongst other things, we have seen that notions of validity and necessary truth can be carried over from LD* into IQ*, and that certain subtle properties of IQ* tense and indexicals can apparently be simulated by introducing indexical equations into the object-language of LD*. However, there are a number of outstanding problems which seem to prevent the claim that LD* and IQ* are 'notational variants' from going through. The first relates to the representation of scope relations in LD*; the second relates to the issue of temporal quantification and the question of bound indexicals.

8.1 Scope in LD*

A point in favour of IQ* is that it allows us to carefully model the relationships between tenses and indexicals in such a way as to be able to say *which* tense an indexical (or its non-indexical equivalent) is related to; and which tenses are related to which other ones. It is of course the use of G which allows this flexibility; and the possibilities offered by this approach to temporal scope relations should be manifest from the other chapters in this part of the book which deal with scope in subordinate clauses. Now, in comparing LD* with IQ*, we have gone some way towards reproducing these relationships within LD*. But it may well be that LD*'s indexicals, even if they do not correspond to IQ*'s, can do things with scope that IQ* cannot. Whether or not this is so, we will argue below that at least some of the scope relations LD* contains do not correspond to any natural language readings; a possible explanation of this fact will be canvassed. In considering this explanation, we will consider the wisdom of correlating the tense operators of LD* with the tenses of natural language.

Consider the following two wffs of LD* and the English sentence (32):

(30) PY (Fiona eat breakfast)

(31) YP (Fiona eat breakfast)

(32) Fiona ate breakfast yesterday

Intuitively, both these formulae represent (32). But if we assume the temporal structure for LD* given in §2.1 and paraphrase (30) and (31) as Kaplan advises us, we must read them respectively as 'It was the case that yesterday it was the case that Fiona ate breakfast' and 'Yesterday it was the case that it was the case that Fiona ate breakfast'. On the one hand, the latter reading makes it clear that (31) is no representation for (32), for it says that at some time *before* yesterday, Fiona ate breakfast. And this certainly doesn't catch the meaning of (32). On the other hand, if we strictly interpret LD* in terms of its rational temporal structure, the reading we gave of (30) also leads us astray, for the indexicals in Kaplan's system basically *ignore* any preceding temporal operators (this is one way of expressing the spurious satisfiability of example (6) in §5.1).

There are at least two explanations we can give for these impressions. First, we might argue that (30) and (31) are not the representations LD* would assign to the English sentence (32). We have jumped to this representational conclusion, perhaps encouraged by the representation Dowty (1979: 323–25) considers (and ultimately rejects) for such sentences within a Montague framework. The correct representation might rather be (33):

(33) Y (Fiona eat breakfast)

This is read as 'Yesterday it was the case that Fiona ate breakfast'. Now such an argument suggests that LD* and IQ* are actually giving the semantics for very different operators: IQ* may indeed give a successful semantics for English tenses and indexicals, but LD* just isn't doing the same thing. LD* is actually giving the semantics for *It was the case that* and *Yesterday it was the case that*. Thus, what differences remain between IQ* and LD* could be explained by analogy to the difference between the enterprise of giving a semantics for quantified modal logic, and the enterprise of providing a semantic representation for the English words *possibly* and *necessarily*.

Secondly, a stronger version of such an explanation can be derived from the following position: not only are (30) and (31) not the representations LD* would assign to (32), but the fact of the matter is that LD* would not assign representations to (32) at all. That is not the function of LD*. LD* is a model of a fragment of English, but there is no promise that we should be able to translate from natural language into the formal language. Perhaps such a move might be encouraged by the Montague style of natural language semantics; but LD was not designed as a representational intermediate like IL, and LD* has inherited its parent's functions and added no new ones to its repertoire. LD* tells us how *It was the case that* interacts with *Yesterday it was the case that*, and that is the end of the matter.

There is at least one further reason why we might wish to drive a wedge between the tense operators of LD*, and natural language tense. Consider a free hydrogen atom, which floats in empty space far, far away from any galaxy. Call the hydrogen atom 'Harry'. It is matter of chance that Harry never combines with another atom to form a molecule; however, this means that (34) is a sentence which would, in LD*, denote a proposition of the type we called eternal:

(34) Harry is free.

(35) Harry was free.

Now, in natural language, if a speaker uses a past tense, as in (35), there is a very strong suggestion that, for one reason or another, the speaker is not committed to the truth of (34) at any time other than those times which fall *before* the time of speech. That is to say, the speaker is committing herself to the truth of the proposition denoted by (34) at only a *subset* of the set of temporal indices. If this intuitive view of tense is correct, natural language tense is an eternity-disturbing device. In LD*, however, the tense operators (and the indexical operators) are eternity-preserving. Since the proposition denoted in LD* by (34) is eternal (true at all temporal indices), so too is the proposition denoted by any sentence formed from it by an LD* operator. Thus, LD* would say that what is said in an utterance of (35) is, by chance, an eternally true proposition. And this conflicts with our intuitions about natural language discourse.

There is of course a solution to this, even within LD*, and that involves the introduction of the new primitive symbols of §6, which simulate the eternity-disturbing character of the parametric expressions of IQ*. Doubtless, the wisdom of taking Harry's uncombined state to underwrite non-eternal contents for tensed English sentences may be questioned. But given that we are right to use parameters to semantically block our old example (6),

(6) It will rain yesterday

it should be clear from the argument above *on their own*, the Priorian tense operators and Kaplanian indexical operators cannot correspond very closely to natural language tenses and indexicals.

If the position suggested under the second option were to be adopted, then perhaps its adherents could consistently maintain their isolation from natural language semantics, together with an unaugmented version of LD*. Or they could even adopt LD* as presented here, but still stick to discussing the semantics of the artificial logical operators such as *It was the case that.* But it would certainly remain true that the tense operators of LD* would not directly reflect the tenses which occur in natural language, and which are represented in IQ*. On this basis, those whose interests do lie in the provision of semantics for natural languages could at the very least study IQ* as well as LD*, not because of internal deficiencies in the latter, but because IQ* possesses a view of tense and indexicals which captures something interesting about natural language which LD* doesn't. This need not preclude the possibility that LD* contains something IQ* doesn't; but whatever that is, it doesn't upset the truth about eternity.

8.2 Temporal Quantification and Bound Indexicals

We adverted to the temporal structure of LD* (and also, implicitly, of IQ*) above, in discussing scope relations. That structure currently uses integers to stand for elements of the set I, intuitively interpreted as moments of time. Now, the full IQ system, of which IQ* is but a fragment, gained a certain appeal from its treatment of temporal quantification in English. The quantifiers, in keeping with the interval basis of IQ, were defined in terms of (deictically picked out) intervals of quantification. Indeed, the use of relations defined over intervals is vital to their utility. At the same time, the temporal quantifiers can stand in scope relationships too, as they may be bound by the operator G.

The point is that neither IQ*, nor LD*, has intervals at its root, and to add suitably restricted temporal quantifiers to either system would be a major task. However, since this has not been attempted, it is perhaps worth noting how LD* would have to represent the bound indexicals of Chapter 2. We have mentioned the non-parametric analogues of *yesterday* and *tomorrow* in IQ*, and they form part of the IQ* translations of K and L from LD*. These non-parametric expressions are, of course, the expressions which IQ would use to represent bound indexicals. In IQ, they could occur in their classic contexts of temporal quantification, but in IQ* they have merely appeared as the representations of non-indexical constructions of English (or LD*).

What could LD* do about these expressions? The answer, of course, is that they would probably have to be treated in terms of K and L, and so any connexion between bound indexicals and unbound indexicals would effectively be lost in an extended object-language for LD*. Kaplan himself states that the resemblance between Y and K (G, in his presentation) is merely superficial (Kaplan (1977: 84)); thus, we would be forced to conclude that the resemblance between unbound indexicals and bound indexicals is also merely superficial. Perhaps this would correctly reflect the fact that Kaplan never considered them as falling into the domain of his semantics for indexicals.

But it would mean missing a generalisation that really should be explained by any theory of indexicals.

Conclusions

The purpose of this chapter has not been to demonstrate the superiority of one indexical system over another, but to compare and contrast their distinctive features. From what has been said, three main points can be drawn. First, if we treat both systems as double-indexing, we can see that IQ* is adequate to represent much, but perhaps not all, of what LD* can represent. Of course, IQ* makes an unusual double-indexing system, since the second index can be viewed as being wholly dependent on the first.

Secondly, it seems that LD* might not be as appropriate a tool as IQ* for modelling tense and indexicality in English; on this point, superiority might conceivably be claimed for IQ*, but cf. the discussion in §8.1. And equally, we added a Kaplanian indexical to IQ* to fix the translation functions; this indicates that LD* contains a descoping operator which is missing from IQ*. So LD* might be a more appropriate tool for modelling phenomena *other* than indexicals.

Lastly, the significance of the eternity result is that it allows us to see the deep-seated difference between LD* and IQ* which also, by implication, divides the full systems LD and IQ from one another, and hence the classical view of indexical function from our own. To be sure, both IQ* and LD* are *possible* representations for English. But IQ* represents the pragmatic unsatisfiability of anomalous sentences, which LD* cannot, without extra primitive symbols. So while IQ* and the full LD* are indeed intertranslatable, the result reflects back onto the original IQ and LD, and the theories of indexicality they exemplify. For this reason alone, IQ and LD just can't be intertranslatable; and the differing semantics they give their indexicals is the major cause of this.

In LD, the truth of an indexical formula φ with respect to a context-circumstance pair <<w,i>,<w',i'>> does not require any relation to hold between the context index <w,i> and the circumstance index <w',i'>. In IQ, by contrast, the truth of an indexical formula with respect to a context-circumstance pair <<w,i>,<w',i'>> requires some relation between the time index of the contextual pair <w,i> and the time index of the circumstantial pair <w',i'>. This then means that IQ's indexicals (and tenses) can disturb eternity, while LD's cannot. It is from this difference in the theoretical approach to indexicality that the other differences arise, and we have seen that LD* can contain new 'non-Kaplanian' terms which will invoke the appropriate relations.

4

Subordinate Tenses

BARRY RICHARDS

Introduction

Subordinate clauses provide one of the more testing environments for a theory of tense. The principal cases are of two types, relative clauses and oblique contexts, and the basic issue is how tenses in subordinate positions are related semantically to those in main clauses. We propose to explore this matter with a view to characterizing the phenomena within the temporal theory IQ, which was first developed in Richards (1986).[1]

To illustrate what is at issue, consider these two sentences.

(1) Every student who would pass on Friday failed on Monday.

(2) Every student who will pass on Friday failed on Monday.

The meaning of (2) seems clear enough. A teacher might use (2) on Wednesday to make a prediction about what is going to happen on Friday's test: every student who will pass Friday's test failed Monday's test. The meaning of (1) is a little more subtle. The intended reading emerges in the following parenthetical context.

---

1 Reprinted in revised form as Chapter 1.

(1') Unbeknownst to Max, every student who would pass on Friday failed on Monday.

Here *would* is naturally interpreted relative to the past tense of *failed*.[2] That is, (1') can be used on some past Wednesday to report this state of affairs: unbeknownst to Max, every student who would pass Friday's test was one who failed Monday's test. Note, in contrast, that *will* in (2) must be interpreted relative to the time of speech (the present time).

Our task is to see how the difference between (1) and (2) can be rendered in IQ and whether the result is in any way illuminating. Among the underlying issues is whether there exists a syntactic explanation for the semantic difference between (1) and (2). Are there distinct syntactic analyses which give rise to their respective interpretations? It would seem reasonable to expect some structural difference, otherwise it would be unclear how the sentences come to have the particular meanings they have. But what sort of structure might that be, surely not phrase structure? Contrast (1) with this sentence.

(3) Every student who failed on Monday would pass on Friday.

If uttered on some past Wednesday, (3) could be used to report this situation: any student who failed the test on Monday was one would pass Friday's test. Although the meanings of (3) and (1) are plainly different, the relation between *would* and *failed* is the same in both sentences; that is, the future form *would* is interpreted relative to the past tense of *failed*. How is this to be explained?

The problem is complicated by the relation between the tenses and the common noun *student*. Note that (1) can be understood as an assertion about either past students or present students. That is, it can be read, on the one hand, as a claim about students at some past time, viz. that everyone who was

---

2 It should be mentioned that occurrences of *would* can sometimes be interpreted relative to past tenses in other sentences. We shall consider one or two examples below.

a student at that time and who would pass on Friday failed on Monday. It can also be read as a statement about students at the present time, viz. that everyone who is now a student and who would pass on Friday failed on Monday. There is a similar distinction in (2): it can be understood as an assertion about present students or about students at some future time. Is this difference to be explained as a 'byproduct' of the relation between the tenses and their place in the syntactic analyses of (1) and (2)? Or is there some other explanation? The problem here is just one aspect of a more general one: how is the syntactic status of tenses to be related to their semantic import?

Oblique contexts complicate matters even further. Note that the tenses in the following two sentences appear to be connected in a way analogous to the tenses of (1) and (2).

(4) Max said that every student would pass.

(5) Max said that every student will pass.

In (4) *would* must be interpreted relative to the past tense of *said*, while *will* in (5) is to be interpreted with respect to speech time. But here the syntactic status of the subordinate clauses is not the same as that of the clauses in (1) and (2). The clauses in (4) and (5) occupy nominal positions, while those in (1) and (2) do not. This would suggest that the scope relations between the tenses in (4) and (5) cannot be represented in the same way as they can in (1) and (2). But then how is the apparent similarity between (4) and (5), on the one hand, and (1) and (2), on the other, to be explained? Perhaps they are not as similar as they appear?

One of the revealing aspects of oblique contexts is the way tenses interact with indexicals, as in this sentence.

(6) Adam will say that someone ate an apple now.

Why is it that the sentence,

(7) Someone ate an apple now.

is anomalous when it stands as a main clause but not when it occurs in (6)? Note that in both cases the indexical *now* is to be interpreted as referring to the time of speech. This suggests that the status of the past tense must be different in the two kinds of occurrence. Intuitively, the past tense in (6) is not to be understood relative to speech time but to the future tense *will* of the main verb. It is interesting to observe that the same does not hold with respect to the relative clause in this anomalous sentence.

(8) Someone who ate an apple now will regret it.

The past tense in the subordinate clause *who ate an apple now* must be interpreted relative to speech time, which conflicts with the interpretation of the indexical *now*. In effect, the past tense in (8) is not related to the future tense of the main clause in the the same way that the past tense in (6) How is this to be accounted for?

Our primary objective is to explore these and other puzzles with a view to testing two hypotheses.

(I) Tenses which occur in relative clauses of subject noun-phrases are not semantically subordinate to other tenses.[3]

(II) Tenses which occur in oblique contexts are always semantically subordinate to the tense of the main verb.

From the perspective of formal semantics the first hypothesis implies that tenses in subject relative clauses should not be represented as falling within the scope of other tenses.[4] In contrast, the tenses in oblique contexts should always be so represented. Below we shall indicate how the distinction can be

3 We take (1)–(3) to be paradigm instances of such relative clauses. Although the concept of subject position may be difficult to define precisely, the intuitive idea is sufficient for our immediate purposes. It should be noted, however, that passives may give rise to problematic cases.

4 Tenses which occur in relative clauses of object noun-phrases behave rather differently. They can be read as having either wide or narrow scope relative to the tenses in the main clause and hence, the sentences concerned are genuinely ambiguous.

captured within IQ, and argue that the approach reflects an important semantic generalization.

Since the discussion will turn on certain syntactic considerations, it will be helpful to fix the issues within a particular syntactic theory. We shall opt for Montague's PTQ as formulated in Dowty et al. (1981). There are at least two reasons for doing so. First, Montague translates tenses as sentential operators and this coincides with their treatment in IQ. Although the semantic analysis of tenses in IQ differs from that in Montague's system IL, their common status as operators is significant. Second, Montague assumes that the scope of tenses is determined by syntactic structure, and his approach helps to reveal the basic problems. One interesting feature is the special rôle of the rule of quantifier-phrase insertion, i.e. rule S14.[5] This rule (or something like it) seems to be indispensable for any theory which treats tense in terms of scope. For those who believe that tenses are rightly seen as operators, the rule S14 (or some equivalent) is more than a convenience. From a syntactic perspective, however, S14 may seem less than satisfactory since it is know to ‘overgenerate’. The tension here between syntactic and semantic considerations may lead to a disappointing conclusion, viz. that a rule-to-rule fit between syntax and semantics may be impossible to achieve.

§1 Relative Clauses in Subject Position

Let us begin by considering sentence (2). To capture the correct interpretation of this sentence it is necessary to appeal both to the tense rule S17 and the quantifier rule S14.[6]

(2) Every student who will pass on Friday failed on Monday.

---

5 See Dowty et al. (1981:204)
6 For S17 see Dowty et al. (1981:244)

Neither tense in (2) should be represented as falling within the scope of the other. Both *will pass* and *failed* are to interpreted relative to the time of speech and hence, the tenses are effectively independent of each other. There is only one way to reflect this situation in PTQ and that is by the analysis given in Figure 1. The expedient of rendering *who* as *such that he* is of no immediate relevance.

To translate this analysis into IQ we follow a simple procedure. First, we translate (9) into Montague's system IL and 'boil' the result down to its simplest form; that is, we transform it into a formula belonging to the modal fragment of IL with standard conventions. We then replace all occurrences of IL-tenses with their counterparts from IQ, making the index-parameters of the IQ-tenses the same. In the case of (9) there is no need for further adjustments, although in other cases there will be. We shall indicate what these are at the appropriate time.

To appreciate the import of (9) with respect to the tenses, it may be helpful to trace its translation into IL through the relevant applications of lambda conversion. Since we are only interested in the tenses, it is convenient to adopt a version of IL in which certain English constructions have the status of abbreviations. These will be obvious and hence need no special comment. We shall use R and Q for property expressions, ∃ and ∀ for the existential and universal quantifiers, and P and F for the past and future tense operators.[7] Recall that the translation of the quantifier *every* is as follows.

(10) $\lambda R \lambda Q \forall x[R\{x\} \rightarrow Q\{x\}]$

This is applied to the translation of *student such that he will pass on Friday*

(11) $\lambda x[\text{student}(x) \wedge F[x \text{ pass on Friday}]]$

to yield the translation of *every student such that he will pass on Friday.*

7 Other deviations should be self-explanatory.

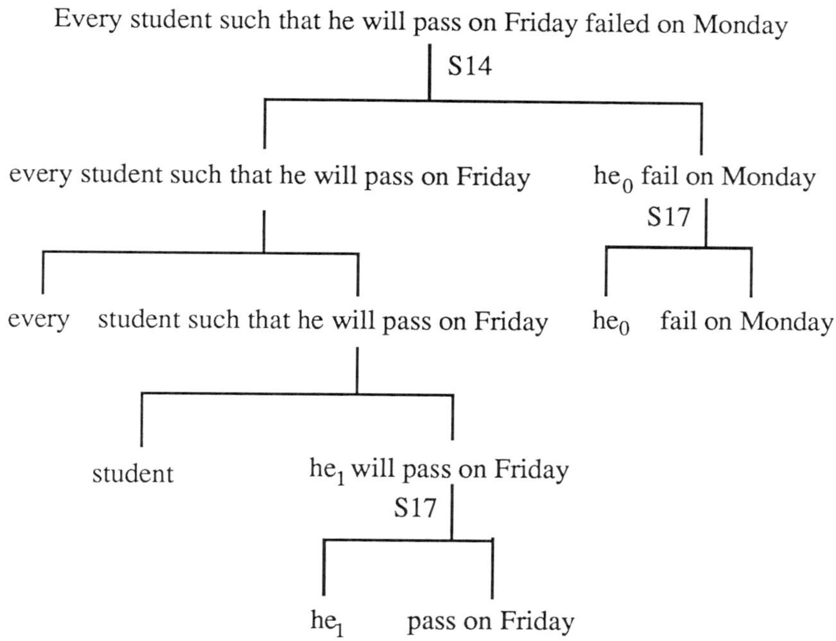

Figure 1

(12) $\lambda R\lambda Q\forall x[R\{x\} \rightarrow Q\{x\}](^\wedge\lambda x[\text{student}(x) \wedge F[x \text{ pass on Friday}]])$

By lambda conversion, together with other conventions, (12) 'boils down' to the following.

(13) $\lambda Q\forall x[[\text{student}(x) \wedge F[x \text{ pass on Friday}]] \rightarrow Q\{x\}]$

This is then applied to the translation of *he_0 italic failed on Monday*,

(14) $P[x \text{ fail on Monday}]$

to yield the full translation of (2).

(15) $\lambda Q\forall x[[\text{student}(x) \wedge F[x \text{ pass on Friday}]] \rightarrow Q\{x\}](^\wedge\lambda xP[x \text{ fail on Monday}])$

By lambda conversion (15) reduces to the desired formula.

(16) $\forall x[[student(x)\ F[x\ pass\ on\ Friday]] \rightarrow P[x\ fail\ on\ Monday]]$

The point to be noted here is that the tense operators are independent of each other, neither falling within the scope of the other.

By replacing the tense operators in (16) with their counterparts in IQ under the restriction of parameter agreement, we reach the translation of (2) in IQ.

(17) $\forall x[[student(x) \wedge FUT_{(v,t)}[x\ pass\ on\ Friday]] \rightarrow PAST_{(v,t)}[x\ fail\ on\ Monday]]$

Since all the occurrences of v and t pick up the same values at the time of speech, the two tense operators function relative to the same index. But what about the status of the subformula *student(x)* which is outside the scope of both tenses? Given the form of the truth definition in IQ, in particular the treatment of v and t, this subformula is effectively rendered as 'present tensed'. This implies that (17) is an assertion about those individuals who are students at the present time. Whether this coincides with the intuitive reading of (2) is a matter we shall discuss below.

Let us now consider sentence (1) where the future *would* is understood relative to the past *failed.*

(1) Every student who would pass on Friday failed on Monday.

There may be reason to think that *would* is perhaps some past form of *will*, but it would be wrong to conclude that there are two independent past tenses in (1), one in the main verb and the other in the subordinate verb. The envisaged reading dictates that *would* be interpreted as a subordinate tense. Although the grammar of PTQ is not defined for such occurrences of *would*, the semantics of IL is. Bearing this in mind, one might propose extending the grammar to allow for the analysis of (1) as given in Figure 2.

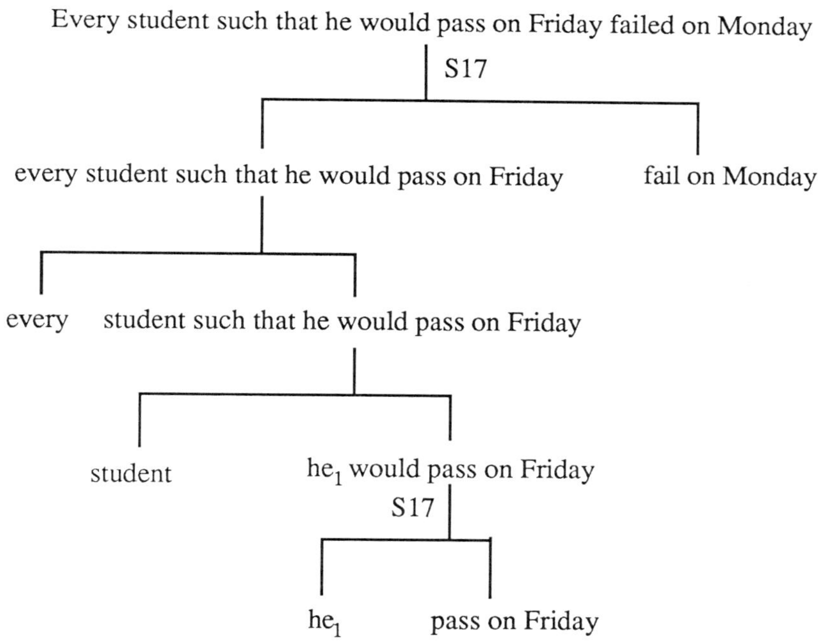

Figure 2

The introduction of *would* rather than *will* in the initial application of 'S17' anticipates that the future will eventually fall within the scope of the past tense. This is realized right at the top of the tree when *every student such that he would pass on Friday* is combined with *fail on Monday*. As indicated, the rule employed is S17.

Let us assume that the translation of *every student such that he would pass on Friday* is the same as the similar quantifier phrase in (9), where *will* occurs in place of *would*.

(19) $\lambda Q \forall x[[\text{student}(x) \wedge F[x \text{ pass on Friday}]] \rightarrow Q\{x\}]$

By the translation rule T17 the meaning of (1) would be given by this formula.

(20) $P[\lambda Q \forall x[[\text{student}(x) \wedge F[x \text{ pass on Friday}]] \rightarrow Q\{x\}](\hat{}\text{fail on Monday})]$

Reducing (20) by lambda conversion, we can see that it is arguably the desired translation of (1).

(21) $P[\forall x[[student(x) \wedge F[x \text{ pass on Friday}]] \rightarrow x \text{ fail on Monday}]]$

Here the future tense operator falls within the scope of the past tense operator and hence must be interpreted relative to it. This is just what intuition requires.

To transform (21) into IQ, however, we cannot simply replace the tense operators with their IQ counterparts. It will be remembered that the system, as presented in Chapter 1, does not allow tense operators to occur within the scope of other tense operators unless their indices are 'bound'. The restriction, formulated in terms of context-free formulas, says that tense operators can only apply to formulas that are context free. The original definition, given in (27) of Chapter 1, will be slightly amended for reasons that will emerge below. We first define the concept of a subformula of IQ. Let A, B and C be any formulas.

(22) (i) If A is the result of applying a *unary* logical operator to B (e.g. *Not*, G, and the universal and existential operators), then B is a subformula of A;

(ii) If A is the result of applying a *binary* logical operator to B and C (e.g. *and* and *or*), then B and C are subformulas of A;

(iii) Nothing else is a subformula of A.

Let $Q_{(c,t')}$ be any tense operator where t' is an interval *variable* and c any kind of world expression (variable, name or parameter). Q takes as its substitution instances PRES, PAST and FUT. A context-free formula is then defined is this way.[8] (27) A is context free if each occurrence of a tense operator in a subformula is of the form $Q_{(v',t')}$ where v' and t' are variables.[9]

(23) A is a context-free formula if each occurrence of a tense operator in a subformula is of the form $Q_{(c,t')}$.[10]

With (23) in hand, we can now specify the full procedure for translating the IL formula (21) into IQ.

The first step is as before: replace the tense operators of IL by their counterparts in IQ. The second step is to check for subformulas of the form $Q_{(c,t)}B$ which fall within the scope of a tense operator, and replace each one with a formula of the form $Gt'[Q_{(v,t')}B]$. Note that t' is an interval variable bound by the operator G. In the case of (21) this two-step process yields first the ill-formed formula

(24) $PAST_{(v,t)}[\forall x[[student(x) \wedge FUT_{(v,t)}[x \text{ pass on Friday}]] \rightarrow x \text{ fail on Monday}]]$

and then the following well-formed translation.

(25) $PAST_{(v,t)}[\forall x[[student(x) \wedge Gt'FUT_{(v,t')}[x \text{ pass on Friday}]] \rightarrow x \text{ fail on Monday}]]$

To see whether (25) is intuitively correct, i.e. as far as the tenses are concerned, let us partially 'unpack' its import. By the definition of the past tense (25) will be true in a model **M** at an index (w,i) only if there is an interval $j < i$ such that

---

8 The definition in Chapter 1 is slightly, though significantly, different.

9 The revised definition is intended to reflect the view that the only genuine contextual coordinate is speech time. Since a world parameter can only take the actual world as its value, it can hardly be regarded as contextually determined. It does, nevertheless, play an important role, which we shall consider below.

10 It should be noted that truth is defined only for formulas where all the variables are bound.

(26) $\forall x[[\text{student}(x) \wedge Gt'FUT_{(v,t')}[x \text{ pass on Friday}]] \rightarrow x \text{ fail on Monday}]$

is true at (w,j) in **M**. This obtains if

(27) $[\text{student}(b) \wedge Gt'FUT_{(v,t')}[b \text{ pass on Friday}]] \rightarrow b \text{ fail on Monday}$

is true at (w,j) for every model $\mathbf{M}^b$.[11] Here we must define implication, which is not defined in Chapter 1. To coincide with the numbering of the truth definition there, the clause is numbered (vii).

(vii) $(A \rightarrow B)$ is true in **M** at (w,i) if B is true at (w,i) or A is false at (w,i); it is false at (w,i) if A is true at (w,i) and B is false at (w,i); and otherwise it is undefined.

According to (vii), (27) is true at (w,j) in $\mathbf{M}^b$ if

(28) b fail on Monday

is true at (w,j) given that

(29) $\text{student}(b) \wedge Gt'FUT_{(v,t')}[b \text{ pass on Friday}]$

is true at (w,j). And by the definition of conjunction, (29) is true at (w,j) only if the second conjunct is, i.e. only if

(30) $Gt'FUT_{(v,t')}[b \text{ pass on Friday}]$

is true at (w,j), which holds only if there is $k > j$ such that

(31) $FUT_{(v,k^*)}[b \text{ pass on Friday}]$

is true at (w,k). Here we see that the future tense is evaluated, as required, relative to the past tense, i.e. relative to the past interval j.

---

11 For the definition of the universal quantifier see (16v) of Chpater 1.

But all may not be as required. Since the past-tense operator in (25) has widest scope, embracing both the universal quantifier and the predicate *student*, (25) is tantamount to the following assertion: at some past time all those individuals who at that time *were* students and *would* pass on Friday failed on Monday. Thus (25) characterizes its analysandum,

(1) Every student who would pass on Friday failed on Monday

as a statement about certain past students. There is a question, however, whether this is the only admissible interpretation. Although (1) might have a 'past tense' feel about it, there seems to be no intuitive impediment to interpreting it as referring to current students. One might assert (1) with the intention of remarking on the past performance of one's current students, perhaps for the purpose of contrasting it with their present performance. Suppose that a teacher has the practice of testing his class every Monday and Friday. He might make the following report.

(32) Last term every student who would pass on Friday failed on Monday. This term they always pass.

There is a formula of IQ which may seem to capture the intended reading of (1).

(33) $\forall x[\text{student}(x) \rightarrow [\text{PAST}_{(v,t)}[\text{Gt}'\text{FUT}_{(v,t')}[x \text{ pass on Friday}] \rightarrow x \text{ fail on Monday}]]]$

But there is no PTQ analysis of (1) which yields (33) as its translation. Indeed, given the way relative clauses are formed in PTQ, viz. by the rule S3, it is not easy to see how the grammar could be adjusted to yield (33) without changing it in some radical way.

Note that (33) differs from (25) in more than its interpretation of the common noun *student*. Since the universal quantifier has widest scope in (33), there is no requirement that every student have failed on the same past

Monday, as there is in (25). For (33) to be true it is enough that for each current student there is some past Monday on which he failed, i.e. one which is followed by a Friday on which he passed. To be sure, (33) is compatible with that Monday being the same for all the students; it is just not necessarily so, as it is in (25). This may suggest that (33) is not an admissible alternative translation to (25); at least, it is perhaps not the desired one. It is significant that PTQ also does not admit an analysis of (1) which leads to a translation which is like (25) except that the universal quantifier has widest scope.

(34) $\forall x[PAST_{(v,t)}[[student(x) \wedge Gt'FUT_{(v,t')}[x \text{ pass on Friday}]] \rightarrow x \text{ fail on Monday}]]$

If this represents an admissible reading of (1), one is bound to ask whether there can be an underlying syntactic explanation.

As one might expect, the quantifier *every* leads to similar ambiguities in (2), whose 'preferred' analysis is (17).

(17) $\forall x[[student(x) \wedge FUT_{(v,t)}[x \text{ pass on Friday}]] \rightarrow PAST_{(v,t)}[x \text{ fail on Monday}]]$

According to (17), the sentence,

(2) Every student who will pass on Friday failed on Monday.

is an assertion about current students: each current student who will past on Friday is one who failed on Monday. But this is not the only interpretation of (2); it can also be read as an assertion about future students, i.e. as reflected in this formula.

(35) $\forall x[FUT_{(v,t)}[student(x) \wedge x \text{ pass on Friday}] \rightarrow PAST_{(v,t)}[x \text{ fail on Monday}]]$

According to (35), (2) asserts of any individual who will be a student and pass on Friday is someone who failed on Monday. This allows that the individuals may not have been students on Monday. Perhaps they had not yet matriculated. Those who will have matriculated by Friday and pass on that day were ones who failed on Monday.

It should be observed that there is no interpretation of (2) in which the universal quantifier occurs inside the scope the future-tense operator. The only way to realize a well-formed formula with this permutation is to give the future-tense operator scope over the past-tense operator.

(36) $FUT_{(v,t)}[\forall x[[student(x) \wedge x \text{ pass on Friday}] \rightarrow Gt'PAST_{(v,t')}[x \text{ fail on Monday}]]]$

Plainly (36) cannot distinguish an admissible reading of (2), because the tenses in (2) must be interpreted as independent of each other.

The point of this 'digression' is twofold. The first is to indicate how tenses in certain kinds of sentences interact semantically with quantifiers and common nouns. And the second is to show how this interaction relates to the strategies in PTQ for capturing the relative scope of tenses. There is a tendency to feel that there must be a syntactic explanation for the scope relations between the tenses (although perhaps not for their scope relations with quantifiers and common nouns). But is the relative scope of tenses always syntactically tractable? Consider sentence (3) again.

(3) Every student who failed on Monday would pass on Friday.

Lest (3) be thought unusual, we note two contexts in which it occurs felicitously.

(37) Max stopped giving tests on Monday because every student who failed on Monday would pass on Friday.

(38) Last term Max noticed a curious pattern: every student who failed on Monday would pass on Friday.

In both cases the future form *would* is naturally interpreted relative to the past tense of *failed*. In the circumstance, the tenses in (3) are related exactly as they are in (1), notwithstanding the 'switch' in syntactic position. This suggests that the scope of tenses may not be purely a matter of grammatical structure, at least not of the sort characterized in PTQ.

There are only two basic ways to analyze a sentence like (3) in PTQ. The first is by the rule S14, where the quantifier phrase *every student who failed on Monday* is inserted into a structure of this form.

(39) he_0 would pass on Friday.

Here the two tenses are represented as independent.[12] The second is by the tense rule S17, where *every student who failed on Monday* is combined with the verb phrase *pass on Friday*. In this case the future is represented as having scope over the past, rather than the other way round as required.[13] Neither strategy yields an analysis which gives a plausible interpretation (3). Arguably there are three possible readings, which can be represented in IQ as follows.

(40) $PAST_{(v,t)}\forall x[[student(x) \wedge x$ fail on Monday$] \rightarrow Gt'FUT_{(v,t')}[x$ pass on Friday$]]$

(41) $\forall x PAST_{(v,t)}[[student(x) \wedge x$ fail on Monday$] \rightarrow Gt'FUT_{(v,t')}[x$ pass on Friday$]]$

(42) $\forall x[student(x) \rightarrow PAST_{(v,t)}[x$ fail on Monday $\rightarrow Gt'FUT_{(v,t')}[x$ pass on Friday$]]]$

Observe that in all three the future tense falls within the scope of the past tense and hence, the G operator must be invoked to render the 'future' subformula context free. The future tense is thereby 'bound' to the past tense in just the way required. This implies that the past tense is the principle tense operator, a

12 The construction is illustrated in (9).
13 The construction is illustrated in (18).

status reflected in its indexical parameters which pick up their values from the context of utterance. This suggests that the main verb of (3) is actually *failed* and not *would pass*, at least from a semantic point of view. Though syntactically subordinate, the past tense here is semantically superordinate. This 'mismatch' between syntax and semantics may lead one to wonder whether there can be a rule-to-rule relation between syntax and semantics which covers both (1) and (3).

It may be ventured that the problem lies not with the idiosyncrasies of syntax but with the strategy of treating tenses as having scope. In IQ the requisite translations of (1) and (3) must represent the past tense as having scope over the future tense. But this may not be the only way of characterizing their relationship. It might be captured by invoking a more complex array of temporal reference. Suppose that tenses introduce two references to time, one to speech time and the other to 'reference time'.[14] In the case of the past tense, for example in the sentence,

(43) Max failed on Monday.

an utterance may be seen to engender distinct references to speech time and 'reference time', which in (43) are related as follows: (43) will be true for the time of speech if the 'reference time' is a Monday earlier than the time of speech at which the present-tense sentence,

(44) Max fails on Monday

is true. Let us suppose that the analyses of (43) and (44) contain explicit explicit referring expressions which designate speech time and 'reference time'. In the circumstance, it is is not hard to see how the relation between the tenses in

14 See Reichenbach (1947) for an account of the distinction. A more recent account can be found in Steedman (1982).

(3) Every student who failed on Monday would pass on Friday.

may be specified. One can simply make the term referring to the speech time of *would pass* anaphoric for the term referring to the 'reference time' of *failed*. This can be achieved in two ways. If the terms are distinct, one could make them co-referential; alternatively one could change one of the terms, identifying it with the other.

Either way the tenses are given the right relationship. But there is a problem with this strategy, which is not unlike the one confronted by IQ. Recall that IQ can offer a plausible translation of (3) but it remains to be seen how this translation can be syntactically motivated. What syntactic analysis of (3) would give *failed* scope over *would pass*? A similar question arises for the anaphoric proposal. What principle of syntax would restrict the range of possible anaphoric relations to the uniquely admissible one? Note that (3) is unambiguous as to the relation between the tenses and hence the range of possible anaphoric connections must be uniquely restricted. This also holds for

(1) Every student who would pass on Friday failed on Monday.

where the relation is exactly the same. What procedure of 'co-referencing' would yield both results uniquely?

From a syntactic viewpoint co-referencing seems as much of a mystery as the phenomenon of scope. As a result, there is no advantage to be gained at this point by forsaking the semantic strategy of IQ for an anaphoric approach of the sort outlined. Indeed, we suggest in Chapter 5 that IQ may actually be able to treat certain types of anaphoric connection that currently lie beyond the reach of referential theories. Be that as it may, it remains to be seen whether IQ offers any special insight into the cases at hand.

So far we have considered just one type of tense subordination involving subject relative clauses, viz. the subordination of the future tense to the past tense. It is natural to ask whether there are any other types, for example, whether the past tense can be subordinated to the future tense. Can the past be interpreted relative to the future in this sentence?

(45) Every student who failed on Monday will pass on Friday.

Obviously not. Both tenses must be read as fixed to the time of speech and as such, they are semantically independent of each other. From the perspective of PTQ this requires that S14 be invoked at the final step of the syntactic analysis of (45), i.e. as exemplified in (9). If the tense rule S17 were used instead, it would result in the future tense having scope over the past tense.

But what is it about the tenses here which 'forces' them to be read as independent? If they are understood in terms of the double-reference structure envisaged above, i.e. in terms of speech time and 'reference time', the question is one of reference, why can there be no anaphoric connection between them? Singular terms can always enter into co-referential relations with each other, although sometimes not without a certain awkwardness. But (45) can never be so construed, and thus the above referential theory of tense seems unable to offer an explanation. Significantly, IQ requires all embedded tenses to be 'bound' by occurrences of G. Using S17 instead of S14 in the final step of the analysis of (45) would portray the past tense as embedded; it would thus give rise to an ill-formed translation in IQ unless there were an appropriate application of G. But invoking G would only yield a translation which (45) does not have. In contrast, by using of S14 in the final step, one achieves an intuitive well-formed translation, one in which the tenses are independent and uniformly related to speech time. IQ may thus be seen to distinguish S14 as the uniquely appropriate rule in the analysis of (45).

Although (45) cannot be interpreted as an instance of tense subordination, perhaps this sentence can.

(46) Every student who will fail on Monday will pass on Friday.

It is not unnatural to read the two future tenses as successive, i.e. to interpret *will pass* as future to *will fail*. This could be captured in IQ by treating the latter as having scope over the former. On the referential approach it would be rendered by taking the speech time of the former to be identical with the 'reference time' of the latter. While both are technically possible, neither seems necessary since the tenses are arguably independent of each other, notwithstanding the possibility of a 'sequential' reading. Note that the two occurrences of the future tense in (46) can be regarded as having a common relation to speech time; in fact, there seems no choice in the matter since both Monday and Friday must be understood as future relative to the time of speech. The question is whether the intended Friday must be read after the envisaged Monday. If it must, the two occurrences of the future are arguably successive. But if that Friday can also be read as before the Monday, it is natural to regard the tenses as independent and attribute successiveness to the particular interpretations of *Monday* and *Friday*.

It does not seem difficult to imagine a situation where Monday follows Friday. Suppose that every student who is good at history is poor at physics, and suppose that the history exam is on Friday, followed by the physics exam on Monday. Then one might assert (46), believing that only history students will fail the physics exam. Of course the situation could be different. It might be that all good physics students are poor at history, and the history exam is on Monday, followed on Friday by the physics exam. One might then assert (46), believing that only physics students will fail the history exam. The difference between the two readings of (46) can be attributed to the different interpretations of *Monday* and *Friday*. There is no need to invoke any special relation between the tenses other than that they are both linked to the same speech time. The relevant futures are picked out by the referents of *Monday* and *Friday*. In the circumstance, the syntactic analysis of (46) in PTQ must be through the rule S14.

The same applies to this sentence whose content is rather similar to (46).

(47) Every student who fails on Monday will pass on Friday.

The present tense in the relative clause is here a futurate and is to be read as independent of the future in the main clause. Moreover, it can be understood either as preceding or succeeding the main future tense.[15] In this respect the tenses in (47) are related exactly like those in (46), which is not to say of course that (46) and (47) mean the same thing. The reason for considering (47), however, is not merely to compare it with (46); it is rather to identify an example where the present tense might be mistaken as subordinate to the future. Plainly, the present tense does not have a subordinate status in (47).

At this point it seems reasonable to conjecture that tenses in subject relative clauses are generally independent of main-clause tenses, except perhaps for the future *would*.[16] When *would* occurs in a subject relative clause, we have seen that it can be read as subordinate to a past tense in the main clause. But we have seen that this does not change when the positions are reversed, i.e. when *would* appears in the main clause and the past tense in the subordinate clause. This would suggest that the nature of the subordination here, i.e. its semantic character, may not be a matter of syntactic structure. It should be noted that the envisaged subordination may hold even when the tenses are both in main clauses.

(48) Only one student failed on Monday and he would pass on Friday.

And it continues to hold when the clauses stand as distinct sentences.

(49) Only one student failed on Monday. Fortunately, he would pass on Friday.

---

15 For those who doubt that both are possible, consider these two sentences.

(i) Every student who graduates on Monday will pay his fees on Friday.

(ii) Every student who graduates on Monday will get a job on Friday.

In the case of (i) the paying of fees is naturally understood to be before the graduating. But in (ii) the order of events is intuitively read the other way round.

16 Compare hypothesis I in the introduction.

The status of *would* as a subordinate future seems to have nothing to do with sentential position. As a result, one might justifiably strengthen the above conjecture about subject relative clauses: tenses in such clauses are never subordinate in respect of their position alone.

From the point of view of PTQ this would suggest that sentences like (1), (2) and (3) should all be analyzed in a uniform way, i.e. by a uniform application of the rule S14. The basic semantic independence of the tenses emerges from S14 since it represents neither tense as falling within the scope of the other. This is significant from the perspective of IQ, which contains no devices for removing one tense from the scope of another, i.e. no device like Kamp's 'now' operator.[17] Such a device could, in fact, only be regarded as an ad hoc accretion to IQ.

Of course it remains to be seen how to characterize *would*. From an intuitive viewpoint two things seem evident. First, *would* always seems semantically subordinate to a past tense, one that may occur either in the same sentence or in a sentence of previous discourse. In effect, *would* does not itself introduce a past tense. Second, although the G operator of IQ captures the subordinate relation between the tenses in such sentences as,

(1) Every student who would pass on Friday failed on Monday.

(3) Every student who failed on Monday would pass on Friday.

it does not explain why subordination is always to the past tense, nor how this can transcend sentential boundaries. While a referential approach to the analysis of tense may offer a way round the latter problem, it appears ill-suited to deal with the former. As we mentioned above, it admits ambiguities that do not exist.

Before speculating further about the formal characterization of *would*, we should look first at the status of tenses in oblique contexts, such as in

---

17 See Kamp (1971).

(6) Adam will say that someone ate an apple now.

Note that the oblique clause contains a past tense together with the indexical *now*, which may refer to the time of speech. While this combination is not generally acceptable, it is so in (6), and this plainly has something to do with the future tense in the main clause. Here the past tense can be read as semantically subordinate to the future tense, even though the interpretation of *now* remains fixed to the time of speech. It is interesting that no similar possibility holds for the following sentence.

(8) Someone who ate an apple now will regret it.

There is no construal of this sentence which allows the past tense to be interpreted relative to the future tense. We shall explore the import of this below with a view to characterizing oblique tenses in general and the semantics of *would* in particular.

§2 Oblique Contexts

The hypothesis we shall explore is that tenses in oblique contexts are uniformly subordinate to main-clause tenses.[18] Take the following example.

(50) Max will say that he likes physics.

This sentence might be used as a prediction about what Max will say next year regarding his view of physics at that time. In the event, the present tense in the oblique clause,

(51) he likes physics

---

18 Compare hypothesis II in the introduction.

is not to be understood relative to the time of speech but rather with respect to the saying event in the future. To capture this reading in IQ, (51) must be made context free; that is, the interval parameter of the present-tense operator must give way to a variable bound by the G operator. But this is not sufficient: when formulas occur in intensional contexts, it is also necessary to bind into the position held by the world parameter. The effect of such double binding will be said to render a formula both context free and intension free.

An intension-free formula is defined as follows. Let $Q_{(v',c)}$ be any temporal operator with v' a world *variable* and c any interval expression, i.e. any such variable, name or parameter.

(52) A is an intension-free formula if each occurrence of a tense operator in a subformula is of the form $Q_{(v',c)}$.

Given (52), we introduce a new syntactic restriction into IQ, i.e. new with respect to the formulation in Chapter 1. Where M is any non-temporal modal operator in IQ, e.g. the operators of necessity and possibility,

(53) M(A) is a well-formed formula of IQ only if A is intension free.

When characterizing the logical form of sentences of propositional attitude, we shall treat the complementizer *that* as a unary modal operator and hence allow it to apply only to intension-free formulas. Where A is any such formula, the expression 'that A' is a term which refers to the proposition expressed by A.

With these refinements in hand, we propose the following as the logical form of (50).

(54) $FUT_{(v,t)}$[Max say that Gv't'$PRES_{(v',t')}$[he like physics]]

Here *say* is to be read as a two-place relation between Max and the proposition expressed by (55), which represents the logical form of the occurrence of (51) in (50).

(55) $Gv't'PRES_{(v',t')}$[he like physics]

Note that (55) is not only intension free but also context free. In this connection it should be emphasized, perhaps contrary to expectation, that the tense operators in (54) are not strictly iterated, even though $PRES_{(v',t')}$ might be regarding as falling within the scope of $FUT_{(v,t)}$. That is, the truth value of (54) at an index does not depend upon the truth value of (55) at any index. What (54) requires is that Max (at some future interval in the actual world) have the saying relation to the proposition expressed by (55), not that (55) be true at any particular index.

But what kind of a proposition does (55) express? It is sometimes said that tensed propositions are those that can change their truth value from time to time. This holds in the case of (55). Where w* is some fixed world, it is possible for (55) to be true at (w^*,i_1) and false at (w^*,i_2), for distinct intervals i_1 and i_2. What marks (55) as expressing a present-tense proposition is the fact that it is true at an index (w,i) just in case the subformula,

(56) he like physics

is true at that very same index. The 'presentness' of (55) is captured in the requirement that (55) and (56) are always evaluated at the same interval. This becomes clearer when we substitute the past tense for the present tense in (55).

(57) $Gv't'PAST_{(v',t')}$[he like physics]

This formula is true at an index (w,i) if and only if there is some earlier interval j such that

(56) he like physics

is true at (w,j). The 'pastness' of (57) is reflected in the fact that (56) is to be evaluated at an interval earlier than (57).

One may of course agree with all of this and yet still wonder if (54) captures the intended reading of,

(50) Max will say that he likes physics.

The question is not whether the intension-free formula (55) expresses a present-tense proposition, but whether it expresses such a proposition with respect to the future. We claim that this is resolved by the future tense of the main clause, i.e. as represented in (54). Recall that (54) is true at an index (w,i) only there is some future interval j such that

(58) Max say that Gv't'$PRES_{(v',t')}$[he like physics]

is true at (w,j). The requisite saying relation is thus located in the future, where the relata are Max and the present-tense proposition expressed by (55).

To get a clear view of what is going on here, it is useful to consider the 'past-tense' version of (50), i.e.

(59) Max will say that he liked physics.

This assertion is true at an index (w,i) only if Max has a saying relation to the past-tense proposition expressed by

(57) Gv't'$PAST_{(v',t')}$[he like physics]

at some future index (w,j). Thus Max is represented as saying something about the past relative to the future. Note that the past might just be the present. That is, one might utter (59) with the intention of making a claim about what Max will say about his present view of physics. In the event, (59) would be tantamount to asserting,

(60) Max will say that he liked physics now.

Here *now* is to be read as referring to the time of speech. The logical form of (60) is analyzed in this way.

(61) $FUT_{(v,t)}$[Max say that Gv't'$PAST_{(v',t')}$[AT now [he like physics]]]

The formal treatment of the operator 'AT now' follows the pattern of 'AT then' as it is defined in Chapter 1.[19] Hence, there is no need for any special comment on the definition. Let A be any context-free formula.[20]

(62) AT now (A) is true in a model **M** at (w,i) if i = now and A is true at (w,i); it is false at (w,i) if i ≠ now or A is false at (w,i); and otherwise it is undefined.

It can be readily seen that the formula,

(63) Gv't'$PAST_{(v',t')}$[AT now [he like physics]]

may be true for suitable choices of i, i.e. those choices where i is later than now. Observe that (63) is true for an index (w,i) if there is an interval j earlier than i such that j is now and

(56) he like physics

is true at (w,j). Since i is not fixed relative to speech time, there is no necessary clash between the past tense in (63) and the interpretation of *now* as referring to speech time. Thus, (63) can express a proposition to which Max can have a future saying relation, i.e. as asserted in (60).

The oblique clauses of (50), (59) and (60) must, it seems, be translated by formulas that are both intension free and context free.[21] But this may not be the case for all oblique clauses. Consider this example.

---

19 See (97) in Chapter 1. For a more subtle analysis see Oberlander (1987).

20 Note that any formula which is intension free is also context free.

21 Not everyone may agree with our readings of (50) and (59). In the case of

(50) Max will say that he likes physics.

some may feel that *likes* can be interpreted relative to speech time, i.e. as involving a 'real' present tense. A similar thing might be said of the past tense *liked* in,

(68) Max said that he likes physics.

Suppose that Max uttered the sentence,

(69) I like physics.

with the intention of asserting at the time of speech that he likes physics; and suppose, furthermore, that one believes he would utter the same sentence now and at every intervening time, i.e. between now and then. To indicate this situation one could appropriately assert (68). In the event, the present tense in the oblique clause has a double rôle. It determines the proposition to which Max is said to have a past saying relation; and it indicates that this relation is somehow presently relevant. The question is whether both aspects should be reflected at the level of logical form.

If we follow the pattern of the two earlier examples, viz. (50) and (60), the logical form of (68) would be characterized as follows.

---

(59) Max will say that he liked physics.

It may be read relative to speech time and hence be a 'real' past tense. Although intuition is always slippery, the case in regard to (59) seems rather weak. The subordinate reading is clear and indisputable, particularly with the addition of *now*.

(60) Max will say that he liked physics now.

Plainly *liked* in (60) cannot be a 'real' past tense. Note that (59) can also be modified by *last year* which locates the event in the more distant past.

(64) Max will say that he liked physics last year.

It seems evident that the burden of location is carried by the adverb, not by the tense. As for (50), the subordinate reading is equally clear and indisputable. But the situation in regard to adverbial modification is more difficult to decipher. Consider the use of *tomorrow*.

(65) ? Max will say that he likes physics tomorrow.

This makes perfectly good sense in IQ but not everyone will find it an acceptable sentence. IQ treats *tomorrow* as an indexical and hence as referring to the tomorrow of current speech time, i.e. of the speech time of (65). The effect is that (65) locates the present-tense proposition somewhere in the interval of tomorrow. Some English speakers find (65) an odd way of saying this. It would seem better to use the following sentence.

(66) Tomorrow Max will say that he likes physics.

The same applies with respect to the other future indexicals like *next year*.

(67) Next year Max will say that he likes physics.

In both cases *likes* must be read as subordinate to the future *will* in the main clause. There is obviously much more that needs to be considered here, e.g. past indexicals like *yesterday*, but we shall leave such matters to another time.

(70) $PAST_{(v,t)}$[Max say that Gv't'$PRES_{(v',t')}$[he like physics]]

Here Max is represented as having a past saying relation to the present-tense proposition expressed by (55).

(55) Gv't'$PRES_{(v',t')}$[he like physics]

But there is nothing which identifies this proposition as purportedly holding at the speech time of the main sentence, i.e. of (68). Does this mean that (70) is not a fully adequate characterization of (68)? Not necessarily. The aspect of present relevance is not obviously a matter of semantics. Arguably it is a pragmatic factor and hence should not be rendered as part of logical form. There is, however, a way of realizing current perspective as a semantic factor, viz. by uttering (71) instead of (68).

(71) Max said that he now likes physics.

Max is here asserted to have a past saying relation to the present-tense proposition expressed by (72).

(72) Gv't'$PRES_{(v',t')}$[AT now [he like physics]]

As it is used in (71), *now* seems more of an 'extended now' than a 'punctual now': it is understood to encompass a period of time around the time of speech. This reading requires no adjustment in the definition of the indexical operator 'AT now', since it is catered for by the structure of IQ.[22] Given that *now* is interpreted as the 'extended now', (72) expresses a proposition which may be a suitable relatum of the saying relation attributed to Max.[23] While this proposal may seem broadly acceptable, it allows (68) to be interpreted in two

---

22 The property of homogeneity requires that a formula of the form 'AT now (A)' will be true at an interval i only if A is true throughout i, in effect throughout now.

23 There are several issues that remain to be clarified. One is the relation between Max's utterance of (69) and the proposition expressed by (72). Could Max have meant to express this proposition by uttering (69)? This is a question not only about IQ but about the nature of indirect discourse. We shall not pursue the matter here.

possible ways. One interpretation, rendered as (70), imputes no present relevance to the proposition expressed in the oblique clause: there may be an 'implicature' of present relevance but that is purely a pragmatic factor. It is a moot point whether (70) is really a genuine reading of (68). The more natural interpretation, paraphrased as (71), gives semantic status to the 'implicature' of present relevance. Indeed, it seems that it must be semantic in character since (68) appears never to be interpreted without it. Does this mean then that (68) is really 'elliptical' for (71)?

It seems to be, although there is a possible alternative. One might try to represent the logical form of (68) so as to reflect the special status of speech time. Consider the following formula in which the complementizer *that* applies to a subformula that is intension free but not context free.

(73) $PAST_{(v,t)}$[Max say that Gv'$PRES_{(v',t)}$[he like physics]]

In (73) Max is portrayed as having a past saying relation to a proposition related to the current time of speech, i.e to the speech time of (73). This holds because the occurrence of the parameter t in the subformula,

(74) Gv'$PRES_{(v',t)}$[he like physics]

receives the same value as the occurrence in the past-tense operator. But note that, as a consequence, (74) does not express a proposition which relates to Max's speech time. That is, it does not say anything about his taste for physics at that time, only at the speech time of (68). This seems curious, if not anomalous: it implies that (68) attributes to Max an assertion about his tastes now but not at the time he spoke. Surely this is strange reading, perhaps even an impossible one.

Let us suppose now that Max uttered the sentence,

(69) I like physics.

intending only to make an assertion about his taste for physics at that time. One would not report his assertion by means of the sentence,

(68) Max said that he likes physics.

but rather with the sentence,

(75) Max said that he liked physics.

where the tense in the oblique clause agrees with the tense of the main clause, i.e. where they are both past tenses. There is a sense, however, in which the past tense in the oblique clause masks its semantic rôle. Consider this translation of (75).

(76) $PAST_{(v,t)}$[Max say that Gv't'$PAST_{(v',t')}$[he like physics]]

Here Max is given to have a past saying relation to a past-tense proposition. But this is not what was intended in the report. To reflect its content Max must be portrayed as having a past saying relation to a *present-tense* proposition. In effect, the desired analysis is actually (70).

(70) $PAST_{(v,t)}$[Max say that Gv't'$PRES_{(v',t')}$[he like physics]]

But how can this be justified syntactically?

There is an explanation to hand, although to be sure a rather slippery one. It has been suggested that the present tense (of English) in oblique contexts may be subject to a sequence-of-tense rule. When the main verb is in the past tense, the present tense in oblique position may be governed by a principle of agreement; that is, it may be transformed morphologically to the past although remaining semantically the present. Thus (75) may be seen to be a 'derivative' of (68). This is not to say that (68) and (75) mean the same thing. While the two are closely related, they differ in a subtle though significant respect: (68) is an assertion relating to the 'extended now', as in the paraphrase (71), while (75) is an assertion relating to past speech time, viz. that of the utterance reported. We conjecture, in effect, that (68) is really 'elliptical' for (71) and that (75) has a reading with a 'suppressed' present tense.

Of course (75) need not always be interpreted in this way. One might utter (75) intending to use the past tense essentially, that is, to assert Max to have a past saying relation to a *past-tense* proposition. In the event, the correct translation of (75) would be (76). It is interesting to note that only by using a temporal adverb can one disambiguate whether the past tense occurs essentially.

With a view to considering two problematic cases, we should note the following example which conforms to the general pattern of subordination.

(77) Max will say that he will like physics.

There is only one admissible interpretation of (77), viz. that which asserts Max to have a future saying relation to a future-tense proposition. Its unique translation into IQ is given by this formula.

(78) $FUT_{(v,t)}$[Max say that Gv't'$FUT_{(v',t')}$[he like physics]]

According to (78), the future in the oblique context of (77) is semantically subordinate to the future in its main clause. This, we venture, is characteristic of their relationship in a syntactic configuration like (77).

But the same does not necessarily hold when there is a past tense in the main clause, as in the following sentence.[24]

(79) Max said that he will like physics.

Here the future can only be interpreted relative to speech time. One who utters (79) asserts Max to have a past saying relation to a future-tense proposition, where the future is interpreted as after current speech time. This future is the 'real' one, not the 'relative' one. The two tenses in (79) are thus independent

[24] Not everyone may find this sentence acceptable, but some do and that is enough to take it seriously.

of each other in that they have the same relation to speech time. But they are not completely independent since the future is essential to the proposition to which Max is purported to be related. While the latter aspect is reflected in (80), the former is not.

(80) $\text{PAST}_{(v,t)}$[Max say that Gv't'$\text{FUT}_{(v',t')}$[he like physics]]

Note that (78) does not mark the proposition expressed by,

(81) Gv't'$\text{FUT}_{(v',t')}$[he like physics]

as future relative to the time of speech. The future is represented as subordinate to the past in just the way that it is represented as subordinate to the future in (78).

The question then is how the future aspect of (79) is to be captured. It must be said that some would doubt whether this feature ought to be captured at all. There are those who would not accept (79) as well-formed, even though it may be semantically coherent. They would suggest that the following is a more appropriate sentence, if not uniquely preferable.

(82) Max said that he would like physics.

For this sentence (80) is the correct translation: it captures the fact that the future in (82) is relativized to the past. As such, it need not be the 'real' future, although of course it may be. That is, (82) could be used with the intention of attributing to Max a saying relation to a future-tense proposition which may be located either in the past or in the future. To indicate that it is in the future, one can invoke an appropriate temporal adverb, e.g. *tomorrow*.

(83) Max said that tomorrow he would like physics.

That *tomorrow* is interpreted relative to speech time is reflected in the translation of (83).[25]

(84) $PAST_{(v,t)}$[Max say that Gv't'$FUT_{(v',t')}$[ON tomorrow [he like physics]]]

Since the operator 'ON tomorrow' is always interpreted relative speech time, the required interpretation is captured.

In contrast to (82), there is no need in (79) to add any future reference to fix its perspective as relative to the 'real' future. The oblique clause can only be read in this way. Of course, it may still be informative to add such a reference; the sentence,

(85) Max said that he will like physics tomorrow.

is a more precise assertion than (79). This does not of course obviate the need to characterize (79), given that it is taken to be well-formed. As we illustrated in the case of (68), IQ may be adjusted to represent the required connection between current speech time and the subordinate future tense.

(86) $PAST_{(v,t)}$[Max say that Gv'$FUT_{(v',t)}$[he like physics]]

Since the interval parameter t in the formula,

(87) Gv'$FUT_{(v',t)}$[he like physics]

receives speech time as its value, (86) attributes to Max a past saying relation to future-tense proposition fixed to the current time of speech. This may seem to be just what is needed, but there is still a residual curiousity about (86). It represents Max as actually saying something about now (the present time of

---

25 The definition of the operator 'ON tomorrow' is as follows, with A understood as a context-free sentence.

> ON tomorrow (A) is true in a model M at (w,i) if i is a subinterval of tomorrow and A is true in M at (w,i); it is false at (w,i) if i is not a subinterval of tomorrow or A is false at (w,i); and otherwise it is undefined.

Note that this conforms to the pattern of definition (98) in Chapter 1.

speech) while it is highly unlikely that he had any such intention. Normally he would only have intended to say something about the future, viz. the future relative to his speech time. He could hardly have had intentions with respect to the speech times of those who would report him. In this respect (86) would typically misrepresent Max's intentions. Note that the same cannot be said of (80), where current speech time is irrelevant to the embedded formula. Perhaps (80) is, after all, the correct translation both of

(82) Max said that he would like physics.

and of

(79) Max said that he will like physics.

Perhaps the status of *will* in (79) is just a pragmatic curiosity. We are inclined to think so.

As yet, we have failed to identify any clear evidence that oblique clauses should be represented as anything other than context free. We stipulated from the beginning that all such clauses must be characterized as intension free but left it open whether they should also be represented as context free. At this point it seems reasonable to conjecture that the semantics of oblique clauses warrant both restrictions. Here we might perceive an important semantic generalization.

§3 Some Residual Problems

Let us try to summarize the current situation in regard to tenses in subordinate positions. Tenses in subject relative clauses are generally independent of the tenses in superordinate clauses. The only exception is the future *would*, but the nature of the dependence suggests that it has nothing particular to do with relative clauses. In fact, it seems to be a special relation which *would* has only with the past tense. Significantly, *would* can have this dependence relation to a past tense that occurs anywhere in the sentence, or even in a previous discourse.

The status of tenses in oblique contexts is just the opposite of their status in subject relative clauses. They are not generally independent but semantically subordinate to tenses in superordinate position. The only possible exceptions are the present tense and future *will* when the main verb is in the past tense. However, these have been seen not to be clear counterexamples. Indeed, they seem more appropriately treated as genuine subordinate tenses. The future form *would* is again subordinate, and always to a past tense. There is, nevertheless, a difference: in oblique contexts *would* must always be read as subordinate to the past tense of the main verb; semantic subordination cannot transcend sentence boundaries.

This has to be qualified slightly to cover multiple occurrences of *would*, as in this sentence.

(88) Max said that he would say that he would like physics.

Here the only admissible reading is the one which interprets the second *would* as semantically subordinate to the first and this one as subordinate to the main past tense. The required translation is represented by this formula.

(89) $PAST_{(v,t)}$[Max say that Gv't'$FUT_{(v',t')}$[he say that Gv't'$FUT_{(v',t')}$[he like physics]]]

Observe that (89) portrays Max as having a past saying relation to a future-tense proposition, viz. the one expressed by this formula.

(90) Gv't'$FUT_{(v',t')}$[he say that Gv't'$FUT_{(v',t')}$[he like physics]]

In turn (90) attributes to Max a future saying relation to a future-tense proposition, viz. the one expressed by the following formula.

(91) $Gv't'FUT_{(v',t')}$[he like physics]

IQ seems to give a fair characterization of the meaning of (88), where the first occurrence of *would* is subordinate to the past tense and the second occurrence subordinate to the first.

It should be emphasized that (88) is unambiguous in this respect: there is only one admissible sequence of subordination. This underlines our conjecture that the occurrences of *would* in oblique contexts have a somewhat different status than the occurrences in relative clauses. While the latter can be interpreted as subordinate to a past tense in a variety of syntactic positions, the former can only be read as subordinate to the tense of the superordinate verb. In all cases, *would* must be 'anchored' to some past tense, although its relation to this tense is not uniform. When *would* occurs in a relative clause, the relation is one of tense iteration, but when it occurs in an oblique context, this is not the case.

To say the least, this is a puzzling collection of facts. But significantly, they do not challenge the general hypotheses we set out to explore. As we conjectured, tenses in subject relative clauses are uniformly independent of other tenses regardless of where they occur, with the exception of *would*. In this case subordination does not arise as a feature of relative clauses but from the curious nature of *would*. Its subordinate status in relative clauses is a fact about *would*, not about syntactic structure. Tenses in oblique clauses, on the other hand, are in general semantically subordinate. Although two cases may be seen to fall into a somewhat 'grey' area, these are arguably not counterexamples.

As a last observation on this matter, it is interesting to consider the following sentence which is similar in structure to (88).

(92) Max will say that Sam will say that he likes physics.

Here the present tense in the most deeply embedded oblique clause is to be read as subordinate to the immediately superordinate *will* which in turn must be interpreted relative to the *will* of the main verb. This sequence is just like that of (88), which lends support to our hypothesis that all oblique clauses should be translated into IQ by formulas that are both intension free and context free.

By way of conclusion we turn finally to a problem arising from relative clauses in object position. Consider this sentence.

(93) Jocelyn will pass every student who passed physics.

There are two interpretations of the past tense in the relative clause, one where it is semantically subordinate to the future of the main clause and one where it stands as an independent tense. The latter leads to a reading of (93) which may be paraphrased in this way: every student who at some earlier time passed physics is such that at some future time Jocelyn will pass him. The former gives rise to a different reading which is conveyed by the following paraphrase: at some future time every student who at an earlier time had passed physics is one whom Jocelyn will pass. Both are intuitive readings of (93) and both can be given appropriate analyses in PTQ.

Where the tenses are understood as independent, S14 plays an essential rôle. The analysis is as in Figure 3, with *such that* replacing *who*.

By the translation rules of PTQ, (94) leads to a formula in Montague's system IL which reduces to the following, with j understood as referring to Jocelyn.

(95) $\forall x[[\text{student}(x) \wedge P[x \text{ pass physics}]] \rightarrow F[\text{pass}(j, {}^\wedge\lambda R[R\{x\}])]]$

Since *pass* is an extensional verb, the meaning postulate MP1 can be invoked to simplify (95) further.[26] The simplification proceeds in two stages. By MP1 the subformula

26 See Dowty et al. (1981:226).

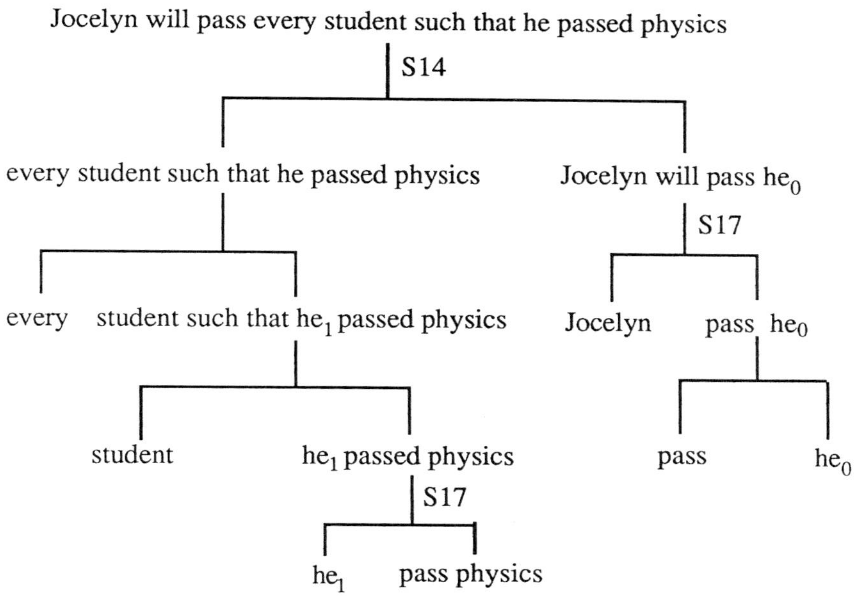

Figure 3

(96) $F[\text{pass}(j, {}^\wedge\lambda R[R\{x\}])]$

is replaced by the formula,

(97) ${}^\wedge\lambda R[R\{x\}]\{{}^\wedge\lambda x F[\text{pass}*(j,x)]\}$

which by lambda conversion and the brace convention reduces to this.

(98) $F[\text{pass}*(j,x)]$

Since PTQ treats all transitive verbs as intensional, MP1 introduces a new verb to capture the extensional sense of *pass*, viz. *pass*∗. The fully reduced translation is then as follows.

(99) $\forall x[[\text{student}(x) \wedge P[x \text{ pass physics}]] \rightarrow F[\text{pass}*(j,x)]]$

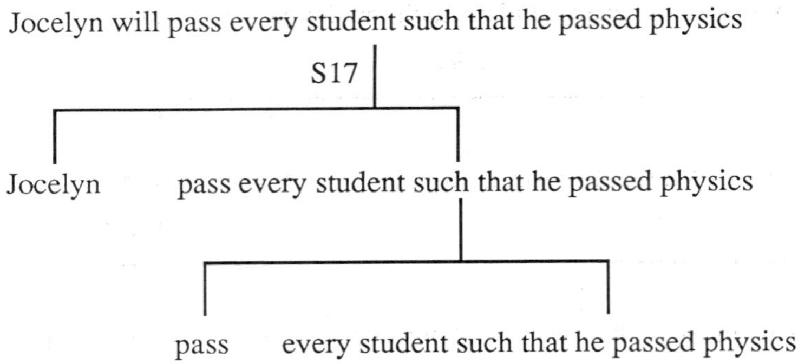

Figure 4

Clearly (99) reflects the intended relation between the tenses since neither falls within the scope of the other. Moreover, it gives an admissible reading of the relation between the past tense and the universal quantifier, and also the relation that between the past tense and the predicate *student*. We shall leave the other possibilities to one side.

Since it is obvious how to translate (99) into IQ, we shall not bother to do so here. Now what about the other reading of (93)? There is only one syntactic analysis that might be appropriate and it is given by the tree in Figure 4. Since the analysis of the quantifier phrase *every student who passed physics* is the same as in (94), we abbreviate it accordingly.
By the translation rules (100) yields the IL formula,

(101) $F[\text{pass}(j,{}^\wedge\lambda Q\forall x[[\text{student}(x) \wedge P[x \text{ pass physics}]] \rightarrow Q\{x\}])]$

which by MP1 reduces to this formula.

(102) $F[\forall x[[\text{student}(x) \wedge P[x \text{ pass physics}]] \rightarrow \text{pass}{*}(j,x)]]$

Though (102) reflects the desired reading, it is arguably not the only alternative to (99), i.e. as a reading of (93). What about this one?

(103) $\forall x[\text{student}(x) \rightarrow F[P[x \text{ pass physics}] \rightarrow \text{pass}{*}(j,x)]]$

Here the past tense is embedded under the future tense, but the universal quantifier and the predicate *student*, are outside the scope of both tenses. This seems to capture an intuitive reading of (93), although one that is difficult to paraphrase without reference to (103) itself. The problem is finding an analysis of (93) which yields (103). At this point none is in hand, nor even envisaged.

5

Temporal Connection

BARRY RICHARDS

Introduction

One way to analyze the semantic structure of a sentence is to characterize its logical form. This at least is the assumption underlying the application of formal semantics to natural language. As commonly stated, the basic aim is to show how the meaning of a sentence arises compositionally from the meanings of its parts, and in so doing reveal what logically implies what. It is presumed that the meanings of the parts of a sentence can be independently specified, although to be sure not without reference to the context of use. It is recognized that context will sometimes be relevant to determining the particular content of an expression.

What has not been generally recognized is that the relation to context may in some cases be a matter of logical form. Kaplan was one of the first to appreciate that this holds for indexical expressions, in particular for temporal expressions like *yesterday* and *two hours ago*.[1] It also holds, we would suggest, for temporal quantifiers and indeed for temporal expressions generally. This emerges clearly in the context of discourse where the nature of temporal connection leads directly to questions of logical form. We shall

1 See Kaplan (1977).

consider some selected examples below with a view to exploring an alternative to Kaplan's account of temporal indexicality.

In Richards (1986) we adumbrated a framework, now known as IQ, in which we attempted to regiment and characterize a wide variety of temporal phenomena, including tenses, quantifiers, connectives and time adverbs. Here we shall extend that framework to comprehend certain typical instances of temporal connection.[2] The exercise will be twofold in nature. The first objective is to gain some insight into the logical form of the devices of temporal connection. Here we would hope to indicate their relation to each other and their common connection with indexical reference. The second objective is more theoretical in character: it is to explore the resources of the framework IQ in connection with features of discourse. Some would argue that such features can only be handled within formal approaches rather antithetical to Montague-type semantics, for example, Kamp's discourse representation theory. While admitting that there may be reasons for abandoning the Montague approach, we would conjecture that the phenomenon of temporal connection is not one of them. Indeed, we shall suggest that one of the 'descendants' of this approach, viz., the framework IQ, may yield insights that are difficult to replicate in other paradigms.

IQ is an interval-based semantics 'shaped' in the style of Montague, where propositions are functions from indices into truth values. In IQ the indices are world-interval pairs and the theory is constructed so as to exploit the special features of intervals. It must be stressed, however, that IQ is only superficially similar to other interval-based accounts, e.g. Cresswell (1977) and Dowty (1979). Intervals are treated differently in these theories and hence, it is difficult to make a straightforward comparison with IQ. There is, nevertheless, a broad common purpose, viz. to give a comprehensive formalization of temporal phenomena. In the particular case of IQ the aim is to provide an integrated characterization of tenses and temporal expressions such

---

2 IQ might be read as abbreviating several things, of which the most immediately relevant is indexical quantification.

as quantifiers, connectives and indexicals. To this end, reference to intervals plays a special rôle, one that seems to allow most intra-sentential phenomena to be comprehended. But when the aim is broadened to inter-sentential phenomena, the same does not appear to hold. Here it seems necessary to introduce reference to propositions. It is this extension, and its motivation, that we shall discuss below.

§1 Some Problems

Let us consider a simple example of temporal connection, viz. one arising from the temporal adverb *later*.

(1) (a) Yesterday Max went home early.
(b) Later he went back to the office.

The content of this discourse is intuitively clear, indeed so clear as to render any paraphrase otiose. Nevertheless, there is a question as to how these two sentences are connectioned, i.e., as to how *later* functions. It is natural to suppose that it functions with respect to some time reference in the first sentence, say to the time yesterday at which Max purportedly went home early. In the circumstance the second sentence is understood to assert that Max went back to the office sometime after that time.[3] Another equally natural hypothesis is that *later* works with respect to a reference to an event-type, here that of Max's going home early yesterday.[4] In this case the second sentence is understood to assert that Max went back to the office later than this event type occurred.

[3] It should be mentioned that the time reference here need not necessarily be regarded as definite. On Kamp's theory it would be possible to accommodate indefinite reference, such as would arise from the quantifier *sometime*. Whether this is intuitively sustainable is not a matter we need comment on.

[4] The concept of an event-type is perhaps somewhat elusive but the basic idea is clear enough: it invokes kinds of events as opposed to particular instances of them.

Prima facie both proposals seem to be intuitive and viable. The first treats *later* as a relation between times and hence is committed to finding analyses of (1a) and (1b) which reveal the appropriate relata. The second regards *later* as some kind of relation between event types and thus is bound to seek alternative analyses of (1a) and (1b). Each proposal is interesting and faces a non-trivial challenge. For reasons associated with IQ we shall opt for the second proposal and as a result take up only the second challenge. Tempting though it may be to regard *later* as a relation between times, it is not clear how this idea can be realized in IQ without assuming definite reference to past time in (1a), i.e. to the time at which Max went home. We are not at all convinced that there is any such reference and thus by 'default' we are bound to look to the alternative view. The task then is to show how this can be captured within IQ. Although IQ does not explicitly contain an ontology of event types, it does contain something similar, viz. 'tenseless' propositions. It is not unreasonable to suppose that each event type can be distinguished by a 'tenseless' proposition. Given this assumption, we shall seek to discover how the intended sense of *later* can be characterized within IQ.

To this end it is useful to consider another example of temporal connection, one involving *three hours before*.

(2) (a) Sam bought some traveler's cheques yesterday.
(b) Three hours before he booked a flight to Boston.

On the relevant interpretation of (2b) there seems to be an 'anaphoric' reference back to something in (2a). This comes to the surface in the following paraphrase of (2b)

(2) (c) Three hours before *that* he booked a flight to Boston.

Here the pronoun *that* is understood to refer not to an interval of time but to the proposition expressed by sentence (2a).[5] In effect (2c) is equivalent to (2d)

(2) (d) Three hours before Sam bought some traveler's cheques yesterday he booked a flight to Boston.

This raises two questions. What is the relation between the occurrence of *three hours before* in (2d) and the one in (2c)? And what is the connection between these occurrences and the one in (b)?

Let us take the first question first. On the assumption that the pronoun *that* in (2c) refers to the proposition expressed by the sentence,

(2) (a) Sam bought some traveler's cheques yesterday.

it is difficult to distinguish (2c) from (2d) on semantic grounds. Nevertheless, there is an obvious difference: in (2c) the sentence (2a) has no syntactic status while in (2d) it does. If syntax is a clue to logical form, then (2c) and (2d) have different logical forms and hence, *three hours before* does not have a univocal semantic rôle. In (2d) it functions as a sentential connective while in (2c) it has a rather different status. Within the framework of IQ the phrase *three hours before that* can be treated as a complex sentential operator, with *that* taken as a referring expression. We shall indicate the details below, at which time the relation between the two forms will become clear.

Having distinguished two possibly different senses of *three hours before*, we must now consider the occurrence in (2b). Although it is syntactically unlike those in (2c) and (2d), there is a certain semantic connection. As we noted above, the occurrence of *three hours before* seems in (2b) to involve a certain anaphoric element, one which functions to invoke the sentence,

---

5 Actually this is not quite as we shall characterize it below, but for the moment it will do.

(2) (a) Sam bought some traveler's cheques yesterday.

The question is what kind of element this might be. Is it a form of pronoun anaphora, like that found in *three hours before that* or is it more a version of ellipsis, similar to the occurrence in (2d)?

(2) (d) Three hours before Sam bought some traveler's cheques yesterday, he booked a flight to Boston.

Intuitively both alternatives seem plausible and hence, if we are to make a non-arbitrary choice, we shall have to look to other considerations.

Fortunately this is not something we need settle here. As will subsequently emerge, both choices can be made to fit into IQ and thus we are free to chose whichever seems the more convenient. In the present context we shall opt for the 'pronominal' solution. Thus the occurrence of *three hours before* in (2b) will be analyzed as equivalent in status to *three hours before that* in (2c).

It is interesting to note that temporal quantifiers also seem to have a certain anaphoric use. Consider the following discourse.

(3) (a) Harry had a headache five times last week.
(b) Twice he took some aspirin.

On the intended reading *twice* is to be understood relative to the occasions on which Harry had a headache last week. The anaphora, if that is what it is, comes to the surface in this paraphrase of (3b).

(3) (c) On two of those occasions he took some aspirin.

Roughly speaking, the phrase *those occasions* refers to the cases over which *two* quantifies. But how does it identify those cases? Surely not by just referring to intervals, but rather by invoking the nature of the cases at issue, viz, those on which Harry had a headache last week. It distinguishes the range of quantification by relativizing it to those intervals during which the proposition expressed by *Harry had a headache last week* is true. In this respect *those occasions* may be seen to have a rôle not unlike that of *that* in (2c): both invoke a proposition, the latter by referring to it and the former in some other way. The difference from the point of logical form may be seen to be irrelevant. This at least is what we shall suggest when we come to formalize these ideas below. For the moment it is enough to point to the analogy between *on two of those occasions* and *three hours before that*. They seem to function in much the same way.

Before we turn to more technical matters, it is worth noting the discourse which results from (3) by adding this sentence.

(3) (d) Each time he felt better afterwards.

Plainly the temporal quantifier *each time* is to be understood as 'quantifying' over just those occasions last week on which Harry had a headache and took some aspirin. For each of these he is said to have felt better afterwards. But how are we to understand *afterwards*? After what did Harry feel better? Surely after he took some aspirin. To explain how this connection arises, we might paraphrase *afterwards* as *after that*, with the pronoun *that* taken to refer to the relevant proposition. But what proposition is that? Is it the one expressed by the sentence *Harry took some aspirin* or is it the more complex one expressed by the sentence *Last week Harry had a headache and took some aspirin*? We shall claim that it is actually the latter, although immediately the former may seem the more natural. This subtlety aside, however, the envisaged structure of (3d) is clear enough; it is that given by this paraphrase.

(3) (e) On each of those occasions he felt better after that.

Although (3e) may not be a particularly elegant paraphrase, it does indicate how (3d) fits into the discourse (3). The expression *those occasions* invokes the complex proposition expressed by the sentence *Last week Harry had a headache and took some aspirin*, thereby restricting the range of the quantifier *each* to the relevant intervals. And the occurrence of *that* refers to the same proposition, thereby indicating after what Harry felt better. The question is how all this arises from the logical form of the constituents of the discourse.

§2 Some Solutions

To implement the suggestions adumbrated in the previous section we shall have to extend the account of IQ given in Chapter 1. As it stands, IQ does not allow reference to propositions in the way envisaged in temporal connection. However, it is a straightforward matter to incorporate this facility into the theory. Note that IQ has three distinct kinds of variables, each ranging over different domains: there are individual variables, world variables and interval variables. Let us now add a fourth type, viz. propositional variables, and a corresponding set of deictic parameters. Following the conventions of IQ, we take p' to be any propositional variable and p any such parameter. Since it is important to distinguish nominal positions from sentential positions, we restrict the legitimate occurrences of p and p' to nominal positions only.

To identify the propositions over which they range we must extend the definition of a model for IQ. In addition to the nonempty sets D (objects), W (worlds) and I (intervals), a model will also contain the set P of all propositions definable on W × I (the cartesian product of worlds and intervals). Since propositions are characterized as functions from world-interval pairs into truth values, P will contain all the total functions from W × I into the set of truth values {true, false, undefined}. A model will therefore be a septuple (D, W, I, P, <, g_c, f), where the content of P depends upon the choice of W and I. For any deictic parameter p, its value relative to a context will be some element g_c(p) belonging to P.[6]

[6] The definition of a model here deviates in other aspects from the definition in Chapter 1. For example, 'undefined' is now explicitly treated as a truth value, rather than as a truth value gap. In addition, contexts constitute part of a model in the form of g_c. Validity is

With these adjustments we can now indicate the logical form of *later*. We assume that its underlying semantic structure is revealed in the paraphrase *later than that*, where the pronoun *that* is understood to refer to some proposition. It is in virtue of such reference that connection with previous discourse is realized. To reflect this in the analysis of *later* we represent it by a complex propositional operator LATER$_{(p)}$, with p read as a deictic propositional parameter. Since p occurs in a nominal position, the operator LATER$_{(p)}$ is not unlike the representations of other time adverbials, e.g. BEFORE 1492 and AT 9.0. While *1492* and *9.0* refer to times, (p) refers to a proposition. Nevertheless, all three operators are similar in being defined as operators over propositions.

The content of LATER$_{(p)}$ is defined as follows, with A taken as any context-free sentence.

(5) LATER$_{(p)}$ A is true in a model **M** at (w,i) if there is a unique subinterval j of i such that g_c(p) is true at (w,j) and another subinterval k of i such that j < k and A is true at (w,k); it is false at (w,i) is there is no unique subinterval j of i for which g_c(p) is true at (w,j) or another subinterval k of i for which j < k and A is true at (w,k); (and otherwise it is undefined).[7]

Note that the value of p relative to a context, i.e. g_c(p), is some proposition from P and that this proposition is picked out deictically. How this reference is achieved is not a matter we shall speculate about here. It is enough to

---

then defined as follows: a formula is valid just in case it is never false in a model. A more rigorous account of the logic of IQ is given Chapter 6.

7 The definition of a context-free sentence is given in (27) in Chapter 1.
What it is for a proposition to be true at a unique interval is given in definition (127) of Chapter 1. The motivation is traced to the complexities introduced by such temporal quantifiers as *twice* and temporal connectives like *when*. These are discussed in detail in the section 'Temporal quantifiers and connectives' of Chapter 1.
The reason for including the phrase *and otherwise it is undefined* in parentheses is to conform to the style of the original paper. For some propositional operators the definitions yield only partial functions, and for others they yield total functions. Where the functions are total, we put redundant qualification in parentheses.

understand that deixis is seen as the means by which *later* achieves temporal connection.

Let us now return to discourse (1), whose constituent sentences are analyzed in this way.[8]

(6) (a) $PAST_{(v,t)}$[ON yesterday (Max go home early)]

(b) $PAST_{(v,t)}$[$LATER_{(p)}$(he go back to the office)

The question is what the value of p should be in order to capture the intended reading of the discourse. Plainly it cannot be the proposition expressed by (6a), as we intimated above. For particular values of v and t (6a) will express a value specific proposition, that is, a proposition which will evaluate to true at most at one index, viz. at (g_c(v), g_c(t)). Such a proposition is obviously not a suitable relatum of comparison since it is not sufficiently discriminating. At the index (g_c(v), g_c(t)) all true indicative sentences will express one proposition and all false ones another.[9] There is, however, an appropriate value for p, viz. the proposition expressed by this subformula of (6a).

(7) ON yesterday (Max go home early)

On this assignment (6b) will 'unpack' as follows. Relative to g_c(v) and g_c(t) (6b) will be true at an index (w, i) if w = g_c(v) and i = g_c(t) and there is an interval $j < i$ such that

(8) $LATER_{(p)}$(he go back to the office)

---

8 The logical form of *yesterday* is represented as ON yesterday, whose definition is given in (98) in Chapter 1.

(i) ON yesterday A is true in a model **M** at (w,i) if i is a subinterval of yesterday and A is true in M at (w,i); it is false at (w,i) if i is not a subinterval of yesterday or A is false at (w,i); and otherwise it is undefined.

For a more subtle account of *yesterday*, see Chapter 2.

9 For a detailed discussion of the concept of a value specific proposition see Chapter 1.

is true at (w,j). This holds just in case there is a unique subinterval k of i such that $g_c(p)$, viz. the proposition expressed by (7), is true at (w,k) and another subinterval l of i such that that k < l and

(9) he go back to the office

is true at (w,l). What this implies, relative to the time of speech, is that Max went back to the office at some time in the past and that that time was after the time of his going home early yesterday. Note that Max's returning to the office is not necessarily portrayed as having occurred yesterday; it might have happened in the early hours of this morning. Of course it could have happened yesterday and this is allowed for in the definitions. What is not significant is any occurrence of Max's going back to the office which happened before yesterday. All this seems to conform to natural intuitions about discourse (1).

The temporal adverb *three hours before* will be treated exactly like *later*. Its structure, as mentioned above, is assumed to be given by the paraphrase *three hours before that*. Thus we represent it by the complex propositional operator THREE-HOURS-BEFORE$_{(p)}$, with p understood as a propositional parameter, and define it as follows, where A is any context-free sentence.

(10) THREE-HOURS-BEFORE$_{(p)}$ A is true in a model **M** at an index (w,i) if there is a unique subinterval j of i such $g_c(p)$ is true at (w,j) and another subinterval l of i such that l is three hours before k and A is true in M at (w,l); it is false at (w,i) if there is no unique subinterval j of i such $g_c(p)$ is true at (w,j) or another subinterval l of i such l is three hours before k and A is true at (w,l); (and otherwise it is undefined).

It should perhaps be noted that we could have analyzed THREE-HOURS-BEFORE$_{(p)}$ into the components THREE-HOURS and BEFORE$_{(p)}$, and defined these separately. But this would involve an unnecessary distraction from our immediate objectives.

With (10) in hand let us consider discourse (2) whose component sentences are characterized as one would expect.

(11) (a) $PAST_{(v,t)}$[ON yesterday (Sam buy some traveler's cheques)]

(b) $PAST_{(v,t)}$[THREE-HOURS-BEFORE$_{(p)}$ (he book a flight to Boston)]

As before, the content of the discourse turns on the value of p. The natural reading of the discourse emerges by taking $g_c(p)$ to be the proposition expressed by this formula.

(12) ON yesterday (Sam buy some traveler's cheques)

On this assumption (11b) will be true at (w,i), relative to $g_c(v)$ and $g_c(t)$, if $w = g_c(v)$ and $t = g_c(t)$ and and there is a $j < i$ such that

(13) THREE-HOURS-BEFORE$_{(p)}$(he book a flight to Boston)

is true at (w,j) where $g_c(p)$ is the proposition expressed by (12). This obtains if there is a unique subinterval k of j such that the proposition expressed by (12) is true at (w,k) and another subinterval l of j which is three hours before k and

(14) he book a flight to Boston

is true at (w,l). Note that it is possible for l to be a subinterval of yesterday (provided that k is sometime after 3 a.m. yesterday) but that this is not necessary for the truth of (11b). This would seem to be in conformity with the intuitive reading of (2b), whose logical analysis (11b) is.

Finally we come to discourse (3) and here the situation becomes a little more complex. In Chapter 1 we analyzed *twice* as a temporal quantifier ranging over an indexically determined interval. Its structure was represented as $TWICE_r$, where r was interpreted as a deictic parameter taking intervals as values. But this characterization is not sufficient to capture the content of the occurrence of *twice* in the second sentence of discourse (3), i.e. on its intended interpretation.

(3) (a) Harry had a headache five times last week.

(b) Twice he took some aspirin.

As we mentioned above, *twice* here is not just quantifying over last week; it is rather quantifying over those occasions last week on which Harry had a headache. There is a sort of 'double anaphora' which invokes both the interval last week and the event of Harry's having a headache. To reflect this at the level of logical form we shall adjust the original approach and analyze *twice* as $\text{TWICE}_{(p,r)}$, where r remains an interval parameter and p is a propositional parameter. Its definition is as follows, with A taken as any context-free sentence.

(15) $\text{TWICE}_{(p,r)}$A is true in a model **M** at (w,i) if $i = g_c(r)$ and there is a cover Q of $g_c(r)$ such that for two elements q_1 and q_2 in Q $g_c(p)$ and A are both true at (w,q_1) and (w,q_2); it is false in M at (w,i) if $i \neq g_c(r)$ or there is no cover Q of $g_c(r)$ such that for two elements q_1 and q_2 in Q $g_c(p)$ and A are both true at (w, q_1) and (w, q_2); (and otherwise it is undefined).[10]

The quantifier *five times* will be treated in a similar way; it will be represented as $\text{FIVE-TIMES}_{(p,r)}$, and its definition will follow the same pattern as (15) mutatis mutandis.[11] We can now indicate the logical forms of (3a) and (3b).

(16) (a) $\text{PAST}_{(v,t)}[\text{FIVE-TIMES}_{(p,r)}$[ON last-week (Harry have a headache)]]

(b) $\text{PAST}_{(v,t)}[\text{TWICE}_{(p,r)}$(he take some aspirin)]

---

10 The concept of a cover is specified in definition (120) in chapter 1.

11 Note that we have really defined the temporal quantifiers *at least twice* and *at least five times*. Other definitions could be introduced to define *exactly twice* and *exactly five times*. Since these are not immediately relevant, we shall not specify them here.

In (16b) there is no question about what the value of p must be to reflect the desired interpretation: it must be the proposition expressed by the formula

(17) ON last-week (Harry have a headache).[12]

But what about the value of p in (16a)? On the assumption that there is no previous discourse there are apparently no candidate propositions to refer to. Here one might entertain two possibilities. First one might suppose that the temporal quantifier *five times* actually has two related but different senses, one where there is 'double anaphora' and one where there is not. The first would be represented as $\text{FIVE-TIMES}_{(p,r)}$ and the second as FIVE-TIMES_r. This is certainly a viable alternative, although perhaps a bit clumsy. The second alternative is to suppose that there is just one sense of *five times*, viz. the one represented as in (16a), and seek for an appropriate referent for p. Since p plainly has a vacuous semantic rôle in (16a), the task is to find a suitably vacuous referent. What better candidate than (17) itself? It can be readily determined that the resulting truth conditions will be as required: (16a) will be true relative to (w,i) only if $g_c(r)$ is some past interval for which there is a cover Q containing at least five intervals q such that (17) is true at (w,q). Treating p in this way obviates the need to multiply senses and yet yields two significantly different uses, one where the referent of p is semantically redundant and one where this is not the case. Here there seems to be economy with insight and hence, this is the strategy we shall adopt.

Finally let us consider the third sentence of the discourse consisting of (3a), (3b) and (3d).

(3) (d) Each time he felt better afterwards.

On the reading of (3) considered above, the interpretations of *each time* and *afterwards* are both conditioned by previous discourse. What (3) means, in effect, is that each time last week that Harry had a headache and took some

---

12 ON last-week is defined similar to ON yesterday, whose definition is given above.

aspirin he felt better after that. Following the pattern of analysis for *later*, we shall represent the adverbial *afterwards* as $\text{AFTER}_{(p)}$; moreover, we shall define it exactly as we defined $\text{LATER}_{(p)}$.[13] Intuitively there would seem to be no semantic distinction between *later* and *afterwards*, although there may be some stylistic differences.

The semantic rôle of *each time* is similar to that of *twice* and hence is represented similarly, i.e. as $\text{EACH-TIME}_{(p,r)}$. Its definition is as follows, with A being any context-free sentence.

(18) $\text{EACH-TIME}_{(p,r)}$A is true in a model **M** at (w,i) if $i = g_c(r)$ and there is a cover Q of $g_c(r)$ such that for each element q of Q if there is a unique subinterval m of q where $g_c(p)$ is true then there is a subinterval n of q where A is true; it is false $i \neq g_c(r)$ or if there is no such cover Q; (and otherwise it is undefined).[14]

Before we attempt to illustrate this definition, let us first consider the logical form of (3d). The fundamental question is how to treat the occurrences of the propositional parameters in the operators $\text{EACH-TIME}_{(p,r)}$ and $\text{AFTER}_{(p)}$: are they to be distinguished or identified? To guarantee that the right interpretation emerges we shall opt to identify them, although it would be possible to distinguish the parameters and achieve the same result. But this alternative would admit some rather bizarre readings and for that reason is perhaps less preferable. What these are need not concern us just now since we only wish to adumbrate the 'shape' of the proposal, not argue matters of fine detail. The logical form of (3d) is thus rendered in this way.

(19) $\text{PAST}_{(v,t)}[\text{EACH-TIME}_{(p,r)}[\text{AFTER}_{(p)}$(he feel better)]]

Now (19) will be true at an index (w,i) only if there is an interval $j < i$ such that,

---

13 See the definition given in (5).

14 Note that n, m and q need not be distinct intervals.

(20) $\text{EACH-TIME}_{(p,r)}[\text{AFTER}_{(p)}(\text{he feel better})]$

is true at (w,j). This holds if there is a cover Q of $g_c(r)$ such that for each element q in Q if there is a unique subinterval m of q where $g_c(p)$ is true then there is a subinterval n of q (not necessarily distinct from m) where

(21) $\text{AFTER}_{(p)}(\text{he feel better})$

is true. And (21) is true at (w,n) just in case there is a unique subinterval k of n such that $g_c(p)$ is true at (w,k) and another subinterval l of n such that $k < l$ and

(22) He feel better

is true at (w,l). What all this amounts to can be summarized is this way: each instance of Harry's having a headache last week and taking some aspirin was an instance of his feeling better after doing so, that is, after taking some aspirin on those occasions when he had a headache last week. Though a bit clumsy in paraphrase, this seems a fair rendering of the truth conditions of (3d) as it occurs in the extended discourse.

§3 Some Residual Matters

Having reconceived the logical form of *twice*, we must envisage similar adjustments in the case of the other temporal quantifiers, e.g. for *always*. To capture its interaction with discourse we must, as before, introduce a deictic propositional parameter into its analysis. Following the pattern illustrated in the analysis of *twice*, we shall represent *always* as $\text{ALWAYS}_{(p,r)}$ and define it in this way, with A being any context-free sentence.[15]

---

15 The original definition is given in (121) in Chapter 1.

(23) $ALWAYS_{(p,r)}A$ is true in a model M at (w,i) if $i = g_c(r)$ and there is a cover Q of $g_c(r)$ such that for each element q in Q if there is a unique subinterval m of q where $g_c(p)$ is true then there is a subinterval m of q where A is true; it is false at (w,i) if $i \neq g_c(r)$ or there is not such cover Q of $g_c(r)$; (and otherwise it is undefined).

It will be noted that that the definitions of $ALWAYS_{(p,r)}$ and $EACH\text{-}TIME_{(p,r)}$ are exactly the same. This reflects our view that that *always* and *each time* are semantically identical in content, although differing perhaps in other respects. It remains to be seen, however, whether (23) actually coincides with the intuitive meaning of *always*.

Let us consider the simple assertion

(24) Max always went home early.

Suppose that (24) is intended as an assertion about the period when Max worked in the Treasury. This would be the interval assigned to r in the logical analysis of (24) which is as follows.

(25) $PAST_{(v,t)}[ALWAYS_{(p,r)}(\text{Max go home early})]$

The question is what the appropriate assignment to p is. On the assumption that there is no previous discourse there is no obvious contextual candidate. Certainly (24) can be understood without reference to earlier discourse; that is, it can be intended as an 'isolated' simple assertion. In the event the value of p must be essentially redundant; it can play no significant rôle in determining the truth conditions of (22). Given the definition of $ALWAYS_{(p,r)}$, the obvious candidate for this rôle is the logically true proposition, i.e. the proposition which is true at every index.[16] To see that the result is as it should be, let $g_c(p)$ be this proposition. Then (25) will be true at an index (w,i), modulo the assignments to v and t, if there is an interval $j < i$ such that

16 In IQ there is of course just one such proposition.

(26) $ALWAYS_{(p,r)}$(Max go home early)

is true at (w,j). This is the case if there is a cover Q of $g_c(r)$ such that for each element q of Q if there is a unique subinterval m of q where $g_c(p)$ is true then there is a subinterval n of q where

(27) Max go home early

is true.[17] Note that $g_c(p)$, as a logically true proposition, will be true throughout $g_c(r)$ and hence throughout each element of Q. As a result, (25) can be true only if (27) is also true throughout each element of Q and thus throughout $g_c(r)$. But this is just what is required to capture the intended meaning of (24).

It might be thought that there are perhaps two meanings for the temporal quantifier *always*, one where it is related to previous discourse and one where it is not. We would suggest, however, that the distinction is not really one of meaning. What may seem to be a difference of senses is simply a difference of reference. Where previous discourse is relevant the value of p will be significant to the truth conditions of the sentence; this we saw in the case of (3d) whose logical form was analyzed as (17). Where previous discourse is irrelevant, on the other hand, the value of p will be effectively redundant; this is reflected in the choice of the logically true proposition as the value of p. This should not be seen as merely a technical ploy since it coincides so plainly with the intuitive meaning of *always*. The logically true proposition is always true, no matter what the interval. What is interesting for a particular chosen interval is what else, besides the logically true proposition, is always true throughout it. This concern is reflected in the definition of $ALWAYS_{(p,r)}$.

As a last example, we shall consider a case involving the temporal connective *before*.

---

17 Here (27) must be read dispositionally; that is, it must be understood as attributing to Max the property of having the disposition to go home early. This he might have at all times throughout $g_c(r)$, even though he is not at that time actually going home early.

(28) When Max ate a pizza, he always got a headache later.

On current reckoning the logical form of (28) should be rendered in this way.

(29) $\text{PAST}_{(v,t)}[\text{ALWAYS}_{(p_1,r)}[[\text{LATER}_{(p_2)}$(he get a headache) *when* (Max eat a pizza)]]]

There are two things to be noted here. First, the deictic propositional parameters are distinguished, reflecting the fact that their values are to be thought of distinctly. Second, *when* has the status of a sentential connective. For convenience we reproduce the definition as given in Chapter 1. As usual, A and B are any context-free sentences.

(126) (A *when* B) is true in a model **M** at (w,i) if there is a unique subinterval j of i such that B is true at (w,j) and at least one subinterval k of i such that A is true at (w,k); it is false at (w,i) if there are no j and k of i which satisfy the indicated conditions; (and otherwise it is undefined).

Before we 'unravel' (29), we must fix the values of p_1 and p_2. On the assumption that there is no relevant previous discourse, we let $g_c(p_1)$ be the logically true proposition. But what about $g_c(p_2)$? In the circumstance there is a uniquely suitable candidate, viz. the proposition expressed by the sentence,

(30) Max eat a pizza.

Given these assumptions, (29) will true at an index (w,i), modulo $g_c(v)$ and $g_c(t)$, if there is a $j < i$ such that

(31) $\text{ALWAYS}_{(p_1,r)}[[\text{LATER}_{(p_2)}$(he get a headache) *when* (Max eat a pizza)]]

is true at (w,j). This obtains if there is a cover Q of $g_c(r)$ such that for each element q of Q if there is a unique subinterval m of q where $g_c(p_1)$ is true then there is a subinterval n of q where

(32) $\text{LATER}_{(p_2)}$(he get a headache) *when* (Max eat a pizza)

is true. Here it is plain that n, m and q must be identical. Now (32) will be true at (w,q) if there is a unique subinterval k of q such that

(28) Max eat a pizza

is true at (w,k) and a subinterval l of q such that

(33) $\text{LATER}_{(p_2)}$(he get a headache)

is true at (w,l). Here k must be subinterval of l. On this assumption (33) is true at (w,l) if there is a unique subinterval y of l, viz. k, such that $g_c(p_2)$ is true at (w,y) and another subinterval z of l such that y < z and

(34) He get a headache

is true at (w,z). This somewhat elaborate formulation is tantamount to the following 'reduction': for the period $g_c(r)$, which is earlier than the time of speech $g_c(t)$, each instance of Max's eating a pizza was following by an instance of his having a headache. Surely this is just what the assumed reading of (28) amounts to.

By way of a final comment we would venture to claim that temporal connection is typically achieved by propositional reference. While reference to time may be an essential ingredient, it is not always a sufficient one. This holds, for example, in the case of all temporal quantifiers, such as *twice* and *always*, and for some uses of temporal adverbials, such as those indicated for *later* and *before*. These are not of course the only uses of these adverbs but they are nevertheless genuine and common. Any adequate account of temporal connection seems bound to invoke propositional reference in some form. This extended version of IQ is one way to achieve this, although perhaps not the only way.

Part Two

Formal Aspects

6

The Temporal Logic IQ

BARRY RICHARDS & INGE BETHKE

Introduction

Natural language has motivated the development of a wide variety of 'modal' logics, and the temporal system IQ is one such logic. IQ is designed to provide an intuitive and comprehensive account of the semantics of temporal expressions, including not only tenses but temporal adverbs, connectives and quantifiers. The system was first adumbrated in Richards (1986) where the envisaged applications were used to introduce and justify the basic strategy.[1] Although the fundamental concepts were outlined and partly formalized, revealing the general 'shape' of the theory, certain essential details were left vague or unspecified. With a view to identifying the logic of IQ we now propose to fill in some of the gaps and provide a more precise technical characterization.

Before we present the system, it might be helpful to survey some of the fundamental ideas. The hypothesis underlying IQ is that intervals are essential to an adequate theory of temporal expressions. While some temporal expressions may be analyzed solely in terms of points, this is not generally the case. One need think only of such adverbs as *on Monday* and *last week,*

1 Reprinted in revised form as Chapter 1.

each of which invokes an interval of time. The semantics of these expressions involves more than just reference to intervals; it also involves quantification over them. Consider the sentence *Max arrived on Monday*. An assertion of this sentence will be true on an occasion of utterance only if Max arrived sometime during the intended Monday. Here there is explicit reference to that interval and implicit quantification over it. A similar situation holds for *Max arrived last week*, where an utterance will be true only if Max arrived sometime during the previous week. Again there is both reference to and quantification over the intended interval.

Which interval this is of course depends upon the occasion of utterance. The semantic import of *last week* can only be understood relative to the time of utterance. How utterance time comes to play this semantic rôle is a matter of some debate. Some argue that utterance time is only of pragmatic significance and hence does not itself have any semantic status. We venture, on the contrary, that it is in fact a semantic notion since it is invoked by reference at the time of speech, viz. by indexical reference. The interval associated with *last week* is defined in terms of the time of utterance, which is identified indexically at the time of utterance.

A similar relation holds in the case of tenses. To understand what is asserted in uttering the sentence *Max arrived on Monday* one must understand when it is uttered. The past tense can be interpreted only with reference to the time of utterance. Such reference is seen to be an 'indexical' feature of tense, which ought to be reflected at the level of logical form. In Chapter 1 we make a somewhat bold proposal. We suggest that tenses involve indexical reference not only to the interval of utterance but also to the actual world. The intuitive idea is that assertions (in contrast to other kinds of utterances) are always statements about the actual world, even the modal ones. Assertions make reference to the actual world. Of course tenses also appear in sentences which cannot be asserted, for example, in subordinate constructions like *Sam said that Max arrived on Monday*. One who asserts this sentence does not assert that Max arrived on Monday. The difference is seen to be partly a matter of reference: there is no indexical reference to the actual world in the subordinate verb *arrived*, although there is in the main verb *said*. For a detailed discussion see Chapter 4.

Indexical reference is one of the basic semantic features of natural language, and IQ is tailored to yield analyses of the various kinds of indexical expressions. There are two different sorts of referring expressions in IQ, viz. constants and parameters, and they are treated in slightly different ways. Intuitively, constants are like proper names and parameters are like simple indexicals. While proper names and simple indexicals both refer, they do so in different ways, the former in terms of their meaning and the latter in virtue of context. This is reflected in the semantics of IQ, where constants are assigned intensions but parameters are not. As for complex indexical expressions, like the tenses of natural language, their analyses in IQ involve parameters essentially and their meanings are defined accordingly. In the subsequent version of IQ we attempt only to lay the foundations for a comprehensive treatment of complex indexicals. We consider just tenses, but these are felt to be typical of all complex indexicals.

In Part I we explored the semantics of tenses with respect to both worlds and intervals. As far as the tenses of natural language are concerned, possible worlds (or something analogous to them) were taken to form an essential component in their analysis. The need for worlds was seen to be independent of their rôle in formalizing the alethic modalities (necessity and possibility). In effect, worlds were understood to have a fundamental status with respect to the semantics of natural language. Having said that, we shall ignore possible worlds in the subsequent formalization of IQ. In Part II we propose to concentrate on the temporal structure of IQ and hence shall 'slim' the language accordingly. By capturing the temporal complexity of IQ, we may 'unmask' its special properties and richness. Since worlds introduce no new structural considerations, we shall continue to refer to the 'slim' language, and its logic, as IQ. This is to emphasize that IQ in Part II is intended to formalize the temporal structural of IQ in Part I.[2]

Although IQ is an interval-based system, it should be stressed that temporal points play an important rôle. The semantics of IQ is defined in terms of a point structure, where the points can be regarded as the limiting case of intervals. This is not to suggest, however, that intervals can be reduced to the status of derived entities. They are as essential to IQ as the points which constitute them. This is reflected in the fact that there is temporal reference only to intervals.

§1 Basic Syntax of IQ

The language of IQ is based on a two-sorted first-order language. Two separate domains are involved, viz. individuals (D) and intervals (I), and for each sort there are three different kinds of basic terms: variables, constants and parameters. Variables and constants are understood in the usual way, while parameters are treated as a kind of hybrid. As we mentioned above, parameters are like simple indexicals, whose special character emerges only at the semantic level. From a syntactic point of view, parameters are just like variables and constants; they can occur wherever variables and constants can.

Let us now define the language of IQ, henceforward referred to as L_{iq}, more precisely. The basic expressions of L_{iq} are as follows.

2 There is another reason for not bringing worlds into the current analysis. Since the modalities of necessity and possibility will not be considered, worlds would seem to be an unnecessary technical accretion. While certain applications of IQ to natural language may require worlds, the logic of the envisaged fragment of IQ can be specified without them. When the fragment is extended to the alethic modalities, worlds will then become logically significant. At that time we shall have to consider the relationship between these modalities and the temporal ones. We have intimated elsewhere, e.g. in Chapters 1 and 4, that the connection will be seen to be 'mediated' through reference to worlds. How this is realized in detail is a matter we shall not examine here. Let it be enough to emphasize that reference to worlds is an essential feature of the IQ strategy.

(i) Two countably infinite sets of variables: V_D and V_I.
For $k \geq 0$ x_k is a variable in V_D, and t_k a variable in V_I.
We let x and t range arbitrarily over these sets.

(ii) Two (possibly empty) sets of name constants: C_D and C_I.
For $k \geq 0$ d^*_k is a constant from C_D, and i^*_k a constant from C_I.
We let d^* and i^* range arbitrarily over these sets.

(iii) Two (possibly empty) sets of parameters: P_D and P_I.
For $k \geq 0$ $d^\dagger_k$ is a parameter from P_D, and $i^\dagger_k$ a parameter from P_I.
We let $d^\dagger$ and $i^\dagger$ range arbitrarily over these sets.

(iv) For $n \geq 0$ a countably infinite set P^n of n-place predicate constants. We let p^n be an arbitrary member of P^n.

(v) Sentential connectives: $\wedge, \vee, \neg, \rightarrow, \leftrightarrow$

(vi) Quantifiers: $\exists, \forall$, G

We read $\exists$ and $\forall$ as 'some' and 'all' respectively. G has no natural reading; its status is somewhat analogous to the lambda operator. It is convenient to distinguish the terms of L_{iq} according to their type.

(vii) The set of D-terms is $V_D \cup C_D \cup P_D$, and the set of I-terms $V_I \cup C_I \cup P_I$.

The tenses in L_{iq} take the standard form of sentential operators, but they have a more complex syntax. Where i is any I-term,

(viii) The tense operators are: $PRES_{(i)}$, $PAST_{(i)}$, $FUT_{(i)}$.

We let Π range over these tense operators. The well-formed formulas (wffs) of L_{iq} can now be defined inductively in the familiar way.

(i) Where p^n is an n-place predicate constant and $d_1,\ldots,d_n$ are D-terms, $p^n(d_1,\ldots, d_n)$ is an atomic wff.

(ii) Where A and B are wffs, so are $(A \wedge B)$, $(A \vee B)$, $\neg A$, $(A \rightarrow B)$, and $(A \leftrightarrow B)$.

(iii) Where A is a wff and x belongs to V_D, $\exists x\, A$ and $\forall x\, A$ are wffs.

(iv) Where A is a wff and t belongs to V_I, $Gt\, A$ is a wff.

(v) If A is a wff and Π a tense operator, ΠA is a wff.

§2 Semantics of IQ

To define the semantics of L_{iq} we first introduce the concept of an IQ-structure. Although IQ is an interval-based system, points play an essential rôle: intervals are seen to be 'built' out of points and are taken to be ordered in terms of the order of the points. In effect the semantics of IQ assumes the notion of a point-structure.

(i) A point-structure **T** is a pair $\langle T, <\rangle$ consisting of a nonempty set T which is strictly ordered by <.

Relative to **T**, an IQ-structure **M** is defined as follows.

(ii) **M** is a quintuple $\langle D, I_T, «, ç, f\rangle$ such that

 (a) D and I_T are disjoint nonempty sets (intuitively the sets of individuals and intervals);

 (b) I_T is a subset of $\boldsymbol{P}_T$, the power set of T, such that
 • all singletons in $\boldsymbol{P}_T$ belong to I_T,
 • i is in I_T only if for all t' and t'' belonging to i and all t such that

$t' \leq t \leq t''$, then t is in i,

- Ø (the empty set) does not belong to I_T;

(c) « is the partial ordering of I_T induced by **T**, i.e.

- for all i and j belonging to I_T i « j if and only if for all t in i and t' in j $t < t'$;

(d) ç is a function (the 'indexical' function) from the parameters of L_{iq} such that

- ç($d^\dagger$) is in D, where $d^\dagger$ in P_D,
- ç($i^\dagger$) is in I_T, where $i^\dagger$ in P_I;

(e) ***f*** is a function which assigns to the constants of L_{iq} (possibly partial) intensions from I_T such that for j in I_T where the intension is defined,

- ***f***(d*)(j) belongs to D, for d* in C_D,
- ***f***(i*)(j) belongs to I_T, for i* in C_I,
- ***f***(p^n)(j) is a subset of D^n, for an n-place predicate p^n;

f is subject to the following *homogeneity* restrictions:

- for every name constant b* and predicate constant p^n, ***f***(b*)(j) and ***f***(p^n)(j) are defined for all (j) in I_T where j is a singleton;
- for all name constants b*, if ***f***(b*)(j) = b, then ***f***(b*)(k) = b for all k included in j (all subintervals of j);
- for any predicate constant p^n, if ***f***(p^n)(j) = S, then for all k included in j (all subintervals of j) ***f***(p^n)(k) includes S.

Where the homogeneity conditions are not satisfied, the intensions will be undefined and thus partial, thereby engendering truth value 'gaps' with respect to formulas. There may be a temptation to think of these 'gaps' as arising from a lack of information and thus as something that can be filled in by making ***f*** more complete. This, however, is not the case. Failure to satisfy the homogeneity conditions is not due to ***f***'s being incomplete but to its being unsuitably specified. That is, the 'gaps' cannot be filled by extending f but only by altering the existing assignments. This suggests that the appropriate valuation space for an IQ-stucture is one with three truth-values: true **t**, false **f** and undefined **u**. A formula will have the value **u** whenever any of its non-logical constants are undefined. It is important to stress that **u** is not a truth value gap but a third truth value.[3]

The truth definition for IQ is based on Kleene's strong three-valued logic and proceeds in terms of the notion of an IQ-interpretation.

(iii) An IQ-interpretation is a pair $\langle \mathbf{M},\mathbf{g} \rangle$ such that
  (a) **M** is an IQ-structure,
  (b) **g** is a function which assigns values to the variables of L_{iq} with
    • $\mathbf{g}(x)$ belongs to D, for x in V_D,
    • $\mathbf{g}(t)$ belongs to I_T, for t in V_I.

We shall write $\mathbf{g}(\delta,e)$ for the assignment which is just like **g** except that it assigns the value e to the variable δ. Given an IQ-interpretation, the denotation of a well-formed expression β is defined recursively in the following way. We let $[\![\beta]\!]^{\mathbf{M},\mathbf{g}}(j)$ be the denotion of β in the IQ-interpretation $\langle \mathbf{M},\mathbf{g} \rangle$ with respect to the interval j of I_T.

(iv) (a) Where β is a variable, $[\![\beta]\!]^{\mathbf{M},\mathbf{g}}(j) = \mathbf{g}(\beta)$.

(b) Where β is either a name constant or a predicate constant, $[\![\beta]\!]^{\mathbf{M},\mathbf{g}}(j) = f(\beta)(j)$.

(c) Where β is a parameter, $[\![\beta]\!]^{\mathbf{M},\mathbf{g}}(j) = \varsigma(\beta)$.

(d) Where β is an atomic wff $p^n(d_1,\ldots,d_n)$, $[\![\beta]\!]^{\mathbf{M},\mathbf{g}}(j) =$

---

3 The homogeneity condition on predicates might be strengthened in two different ways. The first would be to regard it as a condition on admissible models. Any model in which f does not satisfy homogeneity is not an admissible model. The second would take the value of $f(p^n)(j)$ to be the empty set if homogeneity cannot be satisfied otherwise. For a detailed discussion see Chapter 8.

• **t**, if $\langle [\![d_1]\!]^{\mathbf{M},g}(j),\ldots,[\![d_n]\!]^{\mathbf{M},g}(j)\rangle$ belongs to $[\![p^n]\!]^{\mathbf{M},g}(j)$,
• **f**, if $\langle [\![d_1]\!]^{\mathbf{M},g}(j),\ldots,[\![d_n]\!]^{\mathbf{M},g}(j)\rangle$ does not belong to $[\![p^n]\!]^{\mathbf{M},g}(j)$,
• **u**, if $[\![d_i]\!]^{\mathbf{M},g}(j)$ is undefined for any i where $1 \leq i \leq n$ or $[\![p^n]\!]^{\mathbf{M},g}(j)$ is undefined.

(e) Where β is a wff $\neg A$, $[\![\beta]\!]^{\mathbf{M},g}(j) =$
• **t**, if $[\![A]\!]^{\mathbf{M},g}(j) = \mathbf{f}$,
• **f**, if $[\![A]\!]^{\mathbf{M},g}(j) = \mathbf{t}$,
• **u**, otherwise.

(f) Where β is a wff $(A \wedge B)$, $[\![\beta]\!]^{\mathbf{M},g}(j) =$
• **t**, if $[\![A]\!]^{\mathbf{M},g}(j) = \mathbf{t}$ and $[\![B]\!]^{\mathbf{M},g}(j) = \mathbf{t}$,
• **f**, if $[\![A]\!]^{\mathbf{M},g}(j) = \mathbf{f}$ or $[\![B]\!]^{\mathbf{M},g}(j) = \mathbf{f}$,
• **u**, otherwise.

(g) Where β is a wff $(A \vee B)$, $[\![\beta]\!]^{\mathbf{M},g}(j) =$
• **t**, if $[\![A]\!]^{\mathbf{M},g}(j) = \mathbf{t}$ or $[\![B]\!]^{\mathbf{M},g}(j) = \mathbf{t}$,
• **f**, if $[\![A]\!]^{\mathbf{M},g}(j) = \mathbf{f}$ and $[\![B]\!]^{\mathbf{M},g}(j) = \mathbf{f}$,
• **u**, otherwise.

(h) Where β is a wff $(A \rightarrow B)$, $[\![\beta]\!]^{\mathbf{M},g}(j) =$
• **t**, if $[\![A]\!]^{\mathbf{M},g}(j) = \mathbf{f}$ or $[\![B]\!]^{\mathbf{M},g}(j) = \mathbf{t}$,
• **f**, if $[\![A]\!]^{\mathbf{M},g}(j) = \mathbf{t}$ and $[\![B]\!]^{\mathbf{M},g}(j) = \mathbf{f}$,
• **u**, otherwise.

(i) Where β is a wff $(A \leftrightarrow B)$, $[\![\beta]\!]^{\mathbf{M},g}(j) =$
• **t**, if $[\![A]\!]^{\mathbf{M},g}(j) = [\![B]\!]^{\mathbf{M},g}(j) = \mathbf{t}$ or $[\![A]\!]^{\mathbf{M},g}(j) = [\![B]\!]^{\mathbf{M},g}(j) = \mathbf{f}$,
• **f**, if $[\![A]\!]^{\mathbf{M},g}(j) = \mathbf{t}$ and $[\![B]\!]^{\mathbf{M},g}(j) = \mathbf{f}$ or $[\![A]\!]^{\mathbf{M},g}(j) = \mathbf{f}$ and $[\![B]\!]^{\mathbf{M},g}(j) = \mathbf{t}$,
• **u**, otherwise.

The quantifiers ∃ and ∀ are understood in terms of possibly infinite disjunctions and conjunctions. Given the definitions of ∧, ∨ and ¬, they are inter-definable (with negation) when assigned the following 'strong' senses.

(iv) (j) Where β is a wff $\exists x\, A$ with individual variable x,
$[\![\beta]\!]^{\mathbf{M},\mathbf{g}}(\mathrm{j}) =$
• **t**, if $[\![A]\!]^{\mathbf{M},\mathbf{g}(x,\mathrm{e})}(\mathrm{j}) = \mathbf{t}$ for some e belonging to D,
• **f**, if $[\![A]\!]^{\mathbf{M},\mathbf{g}(x,\mathrm{e})}(\mathrm{j}) = \mathbf{f}$ for all e belonging to D,
• **u**, otherwise.

(k) Where β is a wff $\forall x A$ with individual variable x,
$[\![\beta]\!]^{\mathbf{M},\mathbf{g}}(\mathrm{j}) =$
• **t**, if $[\![A]\!]^{\mathbf{M},\mathbf{g}(x,\mathrm{e})}(\mathrm{j}) = \mathbf{t}$ for all e belonging to D,
• **f**, if $[\![A]\!]^{\mathbf{M},\mathbf{g}(x,\mathrm{e})}(\mathrm{j}) = \mathbf{f}$ for some e belonging to D,
• **u**, otherwise.

The G quantifier may appear to be somewhat curious. On the one hand, it seems similar to the standard quantifiers in that it forms formulas from formulas by binding occurrences of the relevant variables. On the other hand, it seems to function more like lambda abstraction, except there is neither type changing nor function application. Despite this syntactic singularity, G is semantically defined to 'simulate' the effect of function application; here there is a certain essential interaction between the object language and the metalanguage. As we shall see, G is used to remove or 'abstract' a formula away from certain indexical factors, viz. those arising from indexical reference to intervals. By replacing all the occurrences of interval parameters with variables and then binding them with G, one renders the indexical coordinate **ç** of an IQ-structure redundant. Here one may see a certain analogy between the semantic status of parameters and free variables. As free variables are interpreted by the assignment function **g,** so parameters receive their content from the indexical function **ç**. We shall explore the expressive power of G below by showing how it can be 'Skolemized' away.

(iv) (l) Where β is a wff $Gt\,A$ with t an interval variable, $[\![\beta]\!]^{\mathbf{M},g}(j) =$
- **t**, if $[\![A]\!]^{\mathbf{M},g(t,j)}(j) = \mathbf{t}$,
- **f**, if $[\![A]\!]^{\mathbf{M},g(t,j)}(j) = \mathbf{f}$,
- **u**, otherwise.

Finally we come to the tense operators. These are defined roughly as one would expect, although certain modifications are necessary to preserve the standard properties of interdefinability. In the case of IQ these properties are not just desirable but fundamental to the subsequent definition of validity.

(iv) (m) Where β is the wff $PRES_{(i)}\,A$ with I-term i, $[\![\beta]\!]^{\mathbf{M},g}(j) =$
- **t**, if $[\![i]\!]^{\mathbf{M},g}(j) = j$ and $[\![A]\!]^{\mathbf{M},g}(j) = \mathbf{t}$,
- **f**, if $[\![i]\!]^{\mathbf{M},g}(j)$ is defined but either $[\![i]\!]^{\mathbf{M},g}(j) \neq j$ or $[\![A]\!]^{\mathbf{M},g}(j) = \mathbf{f}$,
- **u**, otherwise.

(n) Where β is a wff $PAST_{(i)}\,A$ with I-term i, $[\![\beta]\!]^{\mathbf{M},g}(j) =$
- **t**, if $[\![i]\!]^{\mathbf{M},g}(j) = j$ and there is a k with $k \ll j$ and $[\![A]\!]^{\mathbf{M},g}(k) = \mathbf{t}$,
- **f**, if $[\![i]\!]^{\mathbf{M},g}(j)$ is defined but either $[\![i]\!]^{\mathbf{M},g}(j) \neq j$, or there is at least one k such that $k \ll j$ and $[\![A]\!]^{\mathbf{M},g}(k) = \mathbf{f}$ and for no l where $l \ll j$ does $[\![A]\!]^{\mathbf{M},g}(l) = \mathbf{t}$,
- **u**, otherwise.

(o) Where β is a wff $FUT_{(i)}\,A$ with I-term i, $[\![\beta]\!]^{\mathbf{M},g}(j) =$
- **t**, if $[\![i]\!]^{\mathbf{M},g}(j) = j$ and there is a k with $j \ll k$ and $[\![A]\!]^{\mathbf{M},g}(k) = \mathbf{t}$,
- **f**, if $[\![i]\!]^{\mathbf{M},g}(j)$ is defined but either $[\![i]\!]^{\mathbf{M},g}(j) \neq j$, or there is at least one k such that $j \ll k$ and $[\![A]\!]^{\mathbf{M},g}(k) = \mathbf{f}$ and for no l where $j \ll l$ does $[\![A]\!]^{\mathbf{M},g}(l) = \mathbf{t}$,
- **u**, otherwise.

To define validity in IQ we identify a subset of the set of truth values as the designated values; these might be seen as the 'truth-like' values. In the case of IQ the designated values are **t** and **u**. When a formula has the truth value **u**, it is taken to be more 'truth-like' than 'false-like'. The definition of validity now proceeds in two stages.

(v) (a) A wff β has a *designated value* in an IQ-structure **M** iff for every IQ-interpretation ⟨**M**,**g**⟩ and every index (j) $[\![\beta]\!]^{\mathbf{M},\mathbf{g}}(j)$ = **t** or **u**.

(b) A wff β is *IQ-valid* iff for every IQ-structure **M** β has a designated value in **M**.

This completes the semantics of IQ. Below we explore some of the implications of the theory and as a first step, introduce into IQ the equivalents of the tense operators 'it will always be the case' and 'it has always been the case'. In the language L_{iq} these are represented respectively as $FUT\text{-}ALWAYS_{(i)}$ and $PAST\text{-}ALWAYS_{(i)}$. Although they may be somewhat clumsy to write, they are easy to remember and not frequently used in the applications of IQ. Their immediate significance lies in the perspective they offer on the logic of IQ. The definitions of the standard tenses allow these additional tense operators to be introduced by definition.

(vi) Where A is a wff,

(a) $FUT\text{-}ALWAYS_{(i)}A =_{df} \neg FUT_{(i)}\neg A$

(b) $PAST\text{-}ALWAYS_{(i)}A =_{df} \neg PAST_{(i)}\neg A$.

To appreciate the import of (v) let us consider an IQ-structure where I_T is finite, and take a j for which there is no k such that j « k. From a 'classical' point of view, i.e. a bivalent one, the interpretation of $FUT\text{-}ALWAYS_{(i)}A$ would be true at the index j, but in an IQ-interpretation this will not be the case. By (a), $FUT\text{-}ALWAYS_{(i)}A$ will be undefined at j: $FUT_{(i)}\neg A$ is undefined at j, because there is no k 'later than' j at which $\neg A$ is false, and thus $\neg FUT_{(i)}\neg A$ is also undefined. As a result, $FUT\text{-}ALWAYS_{(i)}A$ should not be read as 'it will always be the case that *A* is true' but rather as 'it will never be the case that *A* is false'. The same holds mutatis mutandis for the formula $PAST\text{-}ALWAYS_{(i)}A$. These interpretations coincide with the definition of validity which says that *A* is valid just in case it is never false.

§3 Some Consequences

Although we do not propose to elaborate a proof theory for IQ, it may be helpful to take the first steps in that direction, if only to illustrate the rôle of the quantifier G. We shall consider just the propositional fragment of IQ, i.e. those formulas of L_{iq} which are built up from atomic formulas containing only individual constants (no variables or parameters). Such formulas may, however, contain I-terms. One of the more distinctive aspects of IQ concerns the iteration of tenses. Since tenses are indexed, iteration requires special attention, especially in connection with the temporal axioms. To see what is involved, take the formula,

(1) $PAST_{(i^{\dagger})}PAST_{(i^{\dagger})}A$.

It can be readily shown that (1) is *unsatisfiable*. Note that (1) will be true in an IQ-interpretation $\langle \mathbf{M},\mathbf{g}\rangle$ at an index (j) only if $[\![i^{\dagger}]\!]^{\mathbf{M},g}(j) = j$ and there is a k such that k « j and $[\![PAST_{(i^{\dagger})}A]\!]^{\mathbf{M},g}(k)$ is true; and this will hold only if $[\![i^{\dagger}]\!]^{\mathbf{M},g}(k) = k$. But clearly these conditions are incompatible since $i^{\dagger}$ is required to have two different assignments in the same interpretation. To avoid such a 'clash' of assignments it is sufficient to invoke the quantifier G and alter (1) to the following.

(2) $PAST_{(i^{\dagger})}\ \mathrm{G}t\ PAST_{(t)}A$

Since *t* is bound by G in the embedded formula, no 'clash' can arise with respect to the assignment to $i^{\dagger}$. As we shall see below, G will be used not only to formulate the temporal axioms containing iterated tenses but also to characterize the rule of 'necessitation'.

Let us assume that the only I-terms in A and B, if any, are variables which are bound by occurrences of G. On this assumption the following are representative axiom schemas of the system IQ^m which correspond to the axioms of minimal temporal logic. If i is a variable, we take it to be distinct from all the I-variables in A and B; note that where this does not obtain, it can always be made so.

(3) $FUT\text{-}ALWAYS_{(i)}(A \rightarrow B) \leftrightarrow (FUT\text{-}ALWAYS_{(i)}A \rightarrow FUT\text{-}ALWAYS_{(i)}B)$

(4) $PAST\text{-}ALWAYS_{(i)}(A \rightarrow B) \leftrightarrow (PAST\text{-}ALWAYS_{(i)}A \rightarrow PAST\text{-}ALWAYS_{(i)}B)$

(5) $PRES_{(i)}A \leftrightarrow FUT\text{-}ALWAYS_{(i)}\ \mathrm{G}t\ PAST_{(t)}A$

(6) $PRES_{(i)}A \rightarrow PAST\text{-}ALWAYS_{(i)}\ \mathrm{G}t\ FUT_{(t)}A$

(7) $FUT_{(i)}\ \mathrm{G}t\ FUT_{(t)}A \rightarrow FUT_{(i)}A$ (axiom of transitivity)

The corresponding axioms in more familiar environments are sometimes represented as follows, where C and D are any formulas.

(3') $G(C \rightarrow D) \rightarrow (GC \rightarrow GD)$

(4') $H(C \rightarrow D) \rightarrow (HC \rightarrow HD)$

(5') $C \rightarrow GPC$

(6') $C \rightarrow HFC$

(7') $FFC \rightarrow FC$

Here 'G' is read as 'it will always be the case', 'H' as 'it has always been the case', 'F' as 'it will be the case' and 'P' as 'it was the case'. Since there is no tense iteration in the distribution axioms (3') and (4'), there is no need to invoke the quantifier G in their IQ correlates (3) and (4). But in schemas (5)-(7), where there is iteration, G plays an essential rôle, as we have indicated.

The same holds for the rule of 'necessitation', which for convenience we formulate relative to the above axiom schemas. We assume that IQ^m contains, in addition to the schemas (3)-(7), all truth-functional tautologies plus the rule of modus ponens.

(8) If A is derivable from the schemas (3)-(7), then so are $FUT\text{-}ALWAYS_{(i)}$ Gt A and $PAST\text{-}ALWAYS_{(i)}$ Gt A , where all the occurrences of i in A are replaced by a variable t not already occurring in A

These occurrences of t become bound by Gt. The need for G is again to avoid possible 'clashes' of assignments to i. In some cases of course G will occur vacuously, viz. when A contains no ocurrences of i, but this is harmless, although perhaps clumsy.

We shall leave it to another occasion to verify that all the instances of the schemas (3)-(7) and the 'necessitation' rule (8) are IQ-valid. By imposing a certain restriction on the range of IQ-structures, we can also validate the schema corresponding to density.

(9) $FUT_{(i)}A \rightarrow FUT_{(i)}\, \mathrm{G}t\, FUT_{(t)}A$ (axiom of density)

The standard corresponding schema is the following.

(9') $FC \rightarrow FFC$

To validate (9') it is necessary to restrict temporal quantification to dense sets. In the case of the IQ schema (9), the range of I_T must be restricted to dense sets which respect the relation «. The proof that this is sufficient is again left to another time. It is interesting to note that the schema which may seem to require an infinite future is not quite what it appears to be.

(10) $FUT\text{-}ALWAYS_{(i)}A \rightarrow FUT_{(i)}A$

It is easy to see that (10) may hold in IQ-interpretations where I_T is finite. Let j be an element of I_T such that for no k is j « k. Then

(11) $[\![FUT_{(i)}A]\!]^{\mathbf{M},\mathbf{g}}$

is undefined at j and thus so too is

(12) $[\![FUT\text{-}ALWAYS_{(i)}A]\!]^{\mathbf{M},\mathbf{g}}$

In the circumstance (10) is itself undefined and hence has a designated value. The validity of (10) does not therefore guarantee that the future is unlimited. This is in direct contrast to the status of the schema which corresponds to (10) in bivalent systems.

(13) $GC \rightarrow FC$

In bivalent logics (13) is valid only if there are no future maximals. Here we see one of the significant consequences of introducing a third truth value into IQ.

§4 Eliminating G

We suggested earlier that G might be eliminated from IQ by invoking a form of Skolemization. We shall now prove a Skolem result which holds for a restricted subclass of IQ formulas, which we call *admissible formulas*. Before defining this subclass, we note that IQ, like classical predicate logic, is complete with respect to ¬, ∧, and ∃ and hence, it is convenient to take these as primitive. The other logical symbols, viz. ∨, →, ↔ and ∀, are introduced in the standard way. The class Adm(L_{iq}) of admissible formulas is then defined as follows.

(i) Adm(L_{iq}) is the smallest set of formulas of L_{iq} containing the atomic formulas and closed under these formation rules:

- If A and B belong to Adm(L_{iq}) then so do $\neg A$, $(A \wedge B)$, $\exists x\, A$ and $\prod A$;
- If A belongs to Adm(L_{iq}) and t does not occur free in A, then $\mathrm{G}t\, PRES_{(t)}A$, $\mathrm{G}t\, PAST_{(t)}A$ and $\mathrm{G}t\, FUT_{(t)}A$ belong to Adm(L_{iq}).

Let $A\ (c/v)$ be the formula obtained from A by replacing all free occurrences of the variable v in A by the constant c. Consider now this schema for G-introduction.

(ii) G-introduction: $A\ (i^*/t) \leftrightarrow \mathrm{G}t\, A$

It can be shown that (ii) is not IQ-valid for all substitution instances, in particular, for the following case.

($\mathrm{ii_a}$) $PAST_{(i^*)}FUT_{(i^*)}B \rightarrow \mathrm{G}t\, PAST_{(t)}FUT_{(t)}B$

Let $\langle \mathbf{M},\mathbf{g}\rangle$ be an IQ-interpretation in which $[\![i^*]\!]^{\mathbf{M},\mathbf{g}}(\mathrm{j}) = \mathrm{j}$ and for some k « j $[\![i^*]\!]^{\mathbf{M},\mathbf{g}}(\mathrm{k}) = \mathrm{k}$. Assume, furthermore, that $[\![B]\!]^{\mathbf{M},\mathbf{g}}(\mathrm{l}) = \mathbf{t}$ for some l such that k « l. Then the antecedent of ($\mathrm{ii_a}$) is true and its consequent is false, i.e.

- $[\![PAST_{(i^*)}FUT_{(i^*)}B]\!]^{\mathbf{M},\mathbf{g}}(\mathrm{j}) = \mathbf{t}$
- $[\![\mathrm{G}t\, PAST_{(t)}FUT_{(t)}B]\!]^{\mathbf{M},\mathbf{g}}(\mathrm{j}) = \mathbf{f}$.

Such counterexamples do not arise if we restrict (ii) to substitution instances where the constituent formulas belong to Adm(L_{iq}). The restriction can be stated as follows, where c is an interval constant and t is an interval variable.

(iii) THEOREM. (Restricted G-introduction) Let $A\ (c/t)$ and $\mathrm{G}tA$ be members of Adm(L_{iq}).

(a) If $[\![A\ (c/t)]\!]^{\mathbf{M},\mathbf{g}}(\mathrm{j}) = \mathbf{t}$, then $[\![\mathrm{G}t\, A]\!]^{\mathbf{M},\mathbf{g}}(\mathrm{j}) = \mathbf{t}$, for every IQ-interpretation $\langle \mathbf{M},\mathbf{g}\rangle$ and every index (j);

(b) $(A\ (c/\mathrm{t}) \rightarrow \mathrm{G}t\, A)$ is IQ-valid.

PROOF. (b) clearly follows from (a). To prove (a) let us assume that $\mathrm{G}t\, A \approx \mathrm{G}t\, FUT_{(t)}\, B$, where B does not contain t free ('≈' means syntactic identity). Suppose that $[\![FUT_{(c)}\, B]\!]^{\mathbf{M},g}(\mathrm{j}) = \mathbf{t}$, i.e. $[\![c]\!]^{\mathbf{M},g}(\mathrm{j}) = \mathrm{j}$ and there is a k such that j « k and $[\![B]\!]^{\mathbf{M},g}(\mathrm{k}) = \mathbf{t}$. Then $[\![t]\!]^{\mathbf{M},g(t,\mathrm{j})}(\mathrm{k}) = \mathrm{j}$ and $[\![B]\!]^{\mathbf{M},g(t,\mathrm{j})}(\mathrm{k}) = \mathbf{t}$, since t does not occur free in B. Hence, $[\![FUT_{(t)}\, B]\!]^{\mathbf{M},g(t,\mathrm{j})}(\mathrm{j}) = \mathbf{t}$ and so $[\![\mathrm{G}t\, FUT_{(t)}\, B]\!]^{\mathbf{M},g}(\mathrm{j}) = \mathbf{t}$. The remaining cases are proved similarly. □

We now expand the language $\mathrm{L_{iq}}$ to a new language $\mathrm{L^*_{iq}}$ by adding new interval constants. Let c^i be a mapping from the set of admissible formulas of the form $\mathrm{G}t\, A$ to a list of new interval-constants. We assume that c^i is one-to-one and call the expansion $\mathrm{L^*_{iq}} = \mathrm{L_{iq}} \cup \{c^i(A) \mid A \approx \mathrm{G}t\, B\}$ in $\mathrm{Adm(L_{iq})}$ a Skolem expansion of $\mathrm{L_{iq}}$.

The set $\mathrm{Adm(L^*_{iq})}$ of admissible formulas of $\mathrm{L^*_{iq}}$ is determined by definition (i) with the appropriate amendments. Since these are straightforward, we need not reproduce the definition. Note that Restricted G-introduction holds as well for $\mathrm{Adm(L^*_{iq})}$.

The Skolem theory $\Sigma(\mathrm{L_{iq}})$ of the language $\mathrm{L_{iq}}$ in the language $\mathrm{L^*_{iq}}$ has the following formulas of $\mathrm{L^*_{iq}}$ as axioms.

(iv) Let $A \approx \mathrm{G}t\, B$ be an admissible formula of $\mathrm{L_{iq}}$: $A \rightarrow B\, (c^i(A)/t)$

We shall say that a formula is G-free if G does not occur anywhere in the formula. The definition proceeds by induction.

(v) Where A is any formula of $\mathrm{L_{iq}}$, the G-free formula μ_A of $\mathrm{L^*_{iq}}$ =
- A, if A is atomic,
- $\neg\mu_B$, if $A \approx \neg B$,
- $(\mu_B \wedge \mu_C)$, if $A \approx (B \wedge C)$,
- $\exists x\, \mu_B$, if $A \approx \exists x\, B$,
- $\mu_B(c^i(A)/t)$, if $A \approx \mathrm{G}t\, B$,
- $\prod\mu_B$, if $A \approx \prod B$.

Clearly μ_A is G -free. Moreover, where t is an interval variable,

(vi) If $\mathrm{G}t\, A$ belongs to Adm(L_{iq}), then $\mathrm{G}t\, \mu_A$ belongs to Adm(L^*_{iq}).

We prove now that G can be Skolemized away in admissible formulas of L_{iq}. To this end we define the concept of a *witness model.*

(vii) (a) Let **M** be an IQ-structure and Ω a set of formulas of L^*_{iq}. Then **M** is a model for Ω iff every A in Ω has a designated value in **M**.

(b) Let **M** be a model for $\Sigma(L_{iq})$. **M** is called a *witness model* provided that $[\![c^i\,(\mathrm{G}tA\,)]\!]^{\mathbf{M},\mathbf{g}}(\mathrm{j})$ is defined, if $[\![\mathrm{G}tA]\!]^{\mathbf{M},\mathbf{g}}(\mathrm{j}) = \mathbf{t}$, for every $\mathrm{G}t\, A$ belonging to Adm(L_{iq}), every IQ-interpretation $\langle\mathbf{M},\mathbf{g}\rangle$ and every index (j).

The Skolem Theorem is then as follows.

(viii) THEOREM. Let **M** be a witness model for $\Sigma(L_{iq})$ and assume Ω to be the set $\{A \leftrightarrow \mu_A \mid A$ belongs to Adm(L_{iq})$\}$. **M** is then a model for Ω.

PROOF. We have to prove that $[\![A \leftrightarrow \mu_A]\!]^{\mathbf{M},\mathbf{g}}(\mathrm{j}) = \mathbf{t} \mid \mathbf{u}$ for every IQ-interpretation $\langle\mathbf{M},\mathbf{g}\rangle$ and every index (j). In view of the truth definition it would suffice to prove that if $[\![A]\!]^{\mathbf{M},\mathbf{g}}(\mathrm{j}) = \mathbf{t}$ then $[\![\mu_A]\!]^{\mathbf{M},\mathbf{g}}(\mathrm{j}) = \mathbf{t} \mid \mathbf{u}$ and if $[\![A]\!]^{\mathbf{M},\mathbf{g}}(\mathrm{j}) = \mathbf{f}$ then $[\![\mu_A]\!]^{\mathbf{M},\mathbf{g}}(\mathrm{j}) = \mathbf{f} \mid \mathbf{u}$. For technical reasons we shall prove a slightly stronger result: $[\![A]\!]^{\mathbf{M},\mathbf{g}}(\mathrm{j}) = \mathbf{t}$ iff $[\![\mu_A]\!]^{\mathbf{M},\mathbf{g}}(\mathrm{j}) = \mathbf{t}$. The proof is by induction on A .

(a) A is atomic: Then $A \approx \mu_A$ and hence $[\![A]\!]^{\mathbf{M},\mathbf{g}} = [\![\mu_A]\!]^{\mathbf{M},\mathbf{g}}$.

(b) A is $\neg B$, $(B \wedge C)$, $\exists x\, B$, $\prod B$: The property can be shown to hold in these cases by straightforward applications of the induction hypothesis.

(c) A is $\mathrm{G}t\, B$. First we prove the result 'right to left'. Suppose that $[\![\mu_B\, (c^i(A)/\mathrm{t})]\!]^{\mathbf{M},\mathbf{g}}(\mathrm{j}) = \mathbf{t}$. Then $[\![\mathrm{G}t\, \mu_B]\!]^{\mathbf{M},\mathbf{g}}(\mathrm{j}) = \mathbf{t}$ since $\mathrm{G}t\, \mu_B$ belongs to Adm(L^*_{iq}). Thus $[\![\mu_B]\!]^{\mathbf{M},\mathbf{g}(t,\mathrm{j})}(\mathrm{j}) = \mathbf{t}$ and hence, by the induction hypothesis $[\![B]\!]^{\mathbf{M},\mathbf{g}(t,\mathrm{j})}(\mathrm{j}) = \mathbf{t}$. So $[\![\mathrm{G}t\, B]\!]^{\mathbf{M},\mathbf{g}}(\mathrm{j}) = \mathbf{t}$.

To simplify the proof 'left to right', let us assume that $\mathrm{G}t\, B \approx \mathrm{G}t\, FUT_{(t)}\, C$. The other cases are again similar. Suppose $[\![\mathrm{G}t\, FUT_{(t)}\, C]\!]^{\mathbf{M},\mathbf{g}}(\mathrm{j}) = \mathbf{t}$. Then $[\![FUT_{(c^i(A))}C]\!]^{\mathbf{M},\mathbf{g}}(\mathrm{j}) = \mathbf{t} \mid \mathbf{u}$ since **M** is a model for

$\mathrm{G}t\, FUT_{(t)}C \rightarrow FUT_{(c^i(A))}\, C$. Observe that $[\![FUT_{(c^i(A))}C]\!]^{\mathbf{M},g}(\mathrm{j}) = \mathbf{u}$ only if $[\![c^i(A)]\!]^{\mathbf{M},g}(\mathrm{j})$ is undefined. Hence $[\![FUT_{(c^i(A))}\, C]\!]^{\mathbf{M},g}(\mathrm{j}) = \mathbf{t}$ since **M** is a witness model for $\Sigma(\mathrm{L_{iq}})$. Thus $[\![c^i(A)]\!]^{\mathbf{M},g}(\mathrm{j}) = \mathrm{j}$ and $[\![C]\!]^{\mathbf{M},g}(\mathrm{k}) = \mathbf{t}$ for some k such that j « k. It follows by the induction hypothesis that $[\![\mu_C]\!]^{\mathbf{M},g}(\mathrm{k}) = \mathbf{t}$. So $[\![FUT_{(c^i(A))}\mu_C]\!]^{\mathbf{M},g}(\mathrm{j}) = \mathbf{t}$, i.e.$[\![\mu_A]\!]^{\mathbf{M},g}(\mathrm{j}) = \mathbf{t}$. □

Lest it be thought that Theorem (viii) is too restricted, it should be noted that there are lots of witness models for $\Sigma(\mathrm{L_{iq}})$. In fact every IQ-interpretation ⟨**M**,**g**⟩ can be trivially made into a witness model for $\Sigma(\mathrm{L_{iq}})$ by the following stipulation.

(ix) For Gt A belonging to $\mathrm{Adm}(\mathrm{L_{iq}})$, $f(c^i(\mathrm{G}t\,A))(\mathrm{j}) = \mathrm{j}$.

That is, $f(c^i(\mathrm{G}t\,A))$ is the projection of every index. This of course does not affect the interpretation of any formula of $\mathrm{L_{iq}}$ simply because Skolem constants do not occur in them. To prove that **M** is a model for $\Sigma(\mathrm{L_{iq}})$ let us again look at an admissible formula A of the form $\mathrm{G}t\, FUT_{(t)}B$. Suppose $[\![\mathrm{G}t\, FUT_{(t)}B]\!]^{\mathbf{M},g}(\mathrm{j}) = \mathbf{t}$. Then $[\![B]\!]^{\mathbf{M},g}(\mathrm{k}) = \mathbf{t}$ for some k such that j « k. But $[\![c^i(A)]\!]^{\mathbf{M},g}(\mathrm{j}) = f(c^i(A))(\mathrm{j}) = \mathrm{j}$. From this it therefore follows that $[\![FUT_{(c^i(A))}B]\!]^{\mathbf{M},g}(\mathrm{j}) = \mathbf{t}$. Since interpretations of Skolem constants are everywhere defined, **M** is clearly a witness model for $\Sigma(\mathrm{L_{iq}})$.

This completes the basic formalization of IQ. In the next chapter we shall explore its significance for temporal databases.

7

Temporal Databases: An IQ Approach

BARRY RICHARDS & INGE BETHKE

Introduction

Natural language has given rise to a wide range of logics which attempt to formalize intuitive patterns of reasoning. Some systems are based on detailed syntactic analyses, such as one finds in the tradition of Montague grammar. Others are less well-rooted in grammar but are nevertheless linguistically motivated; the aim is still to characterize the logical structure of linguistic data. The system IQ is of the latter sort, and the constructions concerned are temporal expressions. These come in various forms, e.g. tenses, adverbs, quantifiers and connectives, and the task is to show how IQ can provide an adequate treatment of all their instances. Recent work within the IQ framework would suggest that there may be special insights to be gained from an integrated theory. Some of these are theoretical in nature and hence are reflected in the structure of IQ itself. Others arise as a result of attempting to relate the analysis of one type of expression to that of another. For details see Chapters 1-5. Since IQ has been shown to be technically well-founded and linguistically rich, we propose to use the strategy to develop what may be a new approach to temporal databases.

To locate the venture within a familiar context we shall formulate our proposals with respect to a standard version of PROLOG, viz. that in Clocksin and Mellish (1981). It will subsequently become evident that there is a special syntactic connection between PROLOG and IQ, one which is mediated by the 'metatheoretic' resources of PROLOG. For this reason our theory might be called IQ-Prolog, although it should not in any sense be taken as a version of PROLOG. In the first part of the paper we shall introduce IQ-Prolog in an informal way, mainly by example, and relate it to another PROLOG-based approach, viz. the Event Calculus of Kowalski and Sergot (1985). The two approaches converge on the belief that intervals play an essential rôle in the representation of temporal information. They also agree that 'instantaneous' events mark the boundaries of intervals, although not necessarily in quite the same way. Where the theories appear to diverge is on the concept of an interval. Kowalski and Sergot regard intervals as primitive, while we treat them with respect to a point structure. It is sometimes argued that our approach involves a degree of specificity not usually found in temporal representation. Points commit one to locating events precisely in time, but one is not always, or even typically, able to do this. One may know that one event occurred before another and yet have no precise idea of when either happened. Kowalski and Sergot feel that the Event Calculus is better suited to represent this state of affairs than a point-based system. We shall endeavor to show that the envisaged difference in respect of IQ-Prolog is illusory. In fact, we shall suggest that there may not be much in the debate over whether intervals are more 'naturally' treated as primitive or as sets of points. There is, however, a real question about which is the richer theory, the Event Calculus or IQ-Prolog. This is a matter we shall explore in some detail.

In the second part of the paper we shall relate IQ-Prolog to the version of IQ formulated in Chapter 6; this offers a precise characterization of the logic adumbrated in Chapter 1. Although it is not the only possible formulation, nor the one necessarily to be preferred, it is ideal for our purposes, both formal and informal.[1] To reveal the nature of the connection between IQ and IQ-Prolog we shall develop a system IQ^E which has a modal semantics similar to IQ. We shall then show how IQ can be translated into IQ^E. Among the significant aspects of IQ^E is the capacity to define the tense operators of IQ; they are strictly redundant in IQ^E. Not all the tenses of IQ^E, however, are redundant; IQ^E is essentially a modal system and in this respect is like IQ. The tenses in IQ-Prolog will be interpreted in a similar (though not identical) way to the tenses in IQ, but the formulation will be given in IQ^E. From the perspective of IQ^E we can provide a precise characterization of IQ-Prolog. We can identify its basic well-formed formulas and interpret their relation to the procedures which involve the tenses and other temporal expressions. We can also give a formal interpretation of IQ-Prolog which is compatible with the intuitive semantics of PROLOG.

How the formal semantics of PROLOG relates to the semantics of IQ-Prolog is a question we shall address at a later stage. Although the semantics of PROLOG must embrace the semantics of IQ-Prolog, the significance of this may not be entirely obvious. As we shall see below, IQ^E attributes a non-classical, modal semantics to IQ-Prolog; one may wonder what this implies about the semantics of PROLOG. We hope to clarify the issue as we explore IQ-Prolog.

Part I

§1 IQ-Prolog

Let us begin by illustrating how temporal information can be represented in IQ-Prolog. As we mentioned above, we use the syntax of Clocksin and

---

1 For another formulation see Chapter 8.

Mellish (1981) since it is both standard and perspicuous. Consider the following example.

(1) Sally was promoted on 1st October 1987

Here the temporal information concerning the event of Sally's being promoted is twofold, first that it occurred on 1st October 1987 and second that it was in the past (relative to the present). To represent this situation we need a way of picking out the event qualified, and what better way than by this formula.

(2) promote(sally).

Events, like other entities, can only be picked out by the properties that differentiate them, and (2) would seem to invoke the essential ones. Although (2) is not a referring phrase, it distinguishes the envisaged event by predicating the relevant property of the subject of the event, i.e. by expressing a proposition.[2] It is this proposition which is then qualified by the phrase 'on 1st October 1987'. We might think of 'on' as indicating a relation which holds between the 1st of October 1987 and the proposition expressed by (2), viz. that the proposition held on this day. There is a certain metatheoretical 'flavour' about this analysis which may be seen to be reflected in its PROLOG formulation.

(3) on(1st _october_1987, promote(sally)).

There is a question about the status of the expression 'promote(sally)', viz. whether it has the same status in (3) as it does in (2). Plainly they are intended to invoke the same proposition, but do they do so in the same way? This is a

---

2 The implication of this strategy is that events are not given an independent semantic status; that is, they emerge in the form of propositions, not as objects of reference. This should not be taken to reflect a metaphysical worry about the nature of such objects, i.e. whether they are legitimate candidates for reference. Certainly they are, and subsequently we may have occasion to treat them so. But with respect to the analysis of sentence (1) we prefer to resort to propositions, to be sure, propositions which depict events.

deep issue which, having noted, we shall set aside for the moment. Let it be enough to say that it is not unnatural to want to think of 'promote(sally)' as ocurring unambiguously. Under these circumstances, it seems that the context 'on(1st_october_1987, __)' is more of a sentential operator than a predicate. But more about this later.

As for the past tense, this can be understood as a property of the complex proposition expressed by (3). The past tense places this proposition at some time earlier than now. As such, it may be analyzed as having a structure not unlike that of 'on 1st october 1987'; that is, it may be seen to be composed of a relation, say 'past' and an expression referring to time, in this case 'now'. Accordingly, (1) has the following PROLOG formulation.

(4) past(now, on(1st_october_1987, promote(sally))).

Again there is a question about the status of the contained occurrence of (3), an issue which is made more complex by the fact that (3) contains an occurrence of (2). Nevertheless, the intuitive interpretation of (4) seems clear enough and so let us press on.

Since (3) can be entered directly as an assertion, it allows for useful queries, for example, these.

(5) ? on(1st_october_1987, X).

(6) ? on(X, promote(sally)).

The first asks what happened on the 1st of October 1987, and the second when Sally was promoted. Significantly, (5) and (6) contain no representation of tense, even though they are intuitively read in terms of the past tense. This is due to the fact that we know that 1987 is in the past; but strictly speaking, the queries are with respect to the date only, independent of whether it is past or future. What about this query then?

(7) ? past(now, on(1st_october_1987,X)).

It may be more appropriate to read (7) as a query about the past, but this assumes that 1st October 1987 is actually in the past relative to now. What guarantees this to be so? Clearly the situation is fixed by the content of (4). One who asserts (4) reflects a belief that 1st October 1987 is before now. He may, nevertheless, have got it wrong, in which case his assertion would be false and the corresponding query incoherent.

This points up a weakness in using tenses and dates together to enter information into a database. There may arise a conflict, albeit a rather unlikely one. This would suggest that there must be a certain redundancy here. For example, if one has dates to hand, does one also need tenses? Is it not enough, say, to assert (3) alone? Since it locates the event of Sally's being promoted at a precise time, locating it also in the past, viz. by asserting (4), may seem to be unnecessary. It is important to appreciate, nevertheless, that the past tense does add new information; it locates the date, and thus the event, relative to the time of assertion, i.e. relative to now. This may be crucial in some contexts, in particular, in legal testimony. For such cases one may have to resort to formulas like (4) and thus run the risk of conflict. Still for most cases it may be good practice to use either dates or tenses, but not both, to record temporal information.

The special usefulness of tenses becomes apparent when dates are not available. Consider this case.

(8) Sally was promoted.

One who asserts (8) may not know exactly when Sally was promoted, except that it was sometime in the past. This of course is just what (8) says, that the event of Sally's being promoted occurred sometime in the past. Since the past is always understood relative to the time of speech, i.e. now, the content of (8) is perspicuously represented in this way.

(9) past(now, promote(sally)).

To define the predicate 'past' in IQ-Prolog we invoke a primitive relation 'at' which, like 'past', holds between intervals and propositions: 'at(Y,A)' may be read as 'A holds at Y'.[3] We also need the relation 'is strictly earlier than', abbreviated '«', which holds between intervals. Intuitively we say that Y « X if all the moments in Y are earlier than all the moments in X. It will be possible to make this more precise below.

(10*)[4] past(X,A) :- at(Y,A), Y « X.

What (10*) identifies, in effect, are the conditions sufficient for the truth of a formula of the form 'past(X,A)' where X is an interval and A a formula. Such a formula is true if A holds at the interval Y and Y is strictly earlier than X.[5] Using this definition, we can translate (9) into two assertions which reflect its intended interpretation.

(11) at(u, promote(sally)).
u « now.

Here 'u' is to be read as a Skolem constant which replaces the existentially quantified variable 'Y', and its admissible interpretations are determined relative to now, which represents the time of speech.

At this point we can ask an interesting question: should we allow (8) to be represented in two ways, that is, in terms of either (9) or (11)? This question has two aspects, one which concerns the entry of temporal information into a database and the other which involves its retrieval. In regard to the former it

---

3 It is perhaps tempting to think of 'at' as the present tense, but that is not quite how we shall use it.

4 We shall adopt the convention of marking procedures with an asterisk.

5 It is worth noting that (10*) may also be interpreted as a 'translation' of the basic temporal axiom $A \rightarrow GP(A)$, where 'G' is read as 'it will always be the case that' and 'P' as 'it was the case that'. What (10*) asserts is given by the following formula, which is just what the axiom means.

$$\forall x\, (\exists y\, (y \ll x \wedge at(y,A)) \rightarrow past(x,A))$$

would seem that (9) suffers a certain limitation. Consider this two-sentence discourse.

(12) Sally was promoted.

(13) She became a professor.

The intended interpretation here is that she became a professor at the time she was promoted. Note that this cannot be captured if we represent (13) on the pattern of (9).

(14) past(now, become_professor(sally)).

Even though 'now' is interpreted as referring to the same interval in both (9) and (14), the relation of the two events remains unspecified, except that they both occurred in the past. Nothing is said about their being simultaneous. This can be remedied if we translate (14) into the following formulas.

(15) at(u, become_professor(sally)).
u « now.

Given that (9) is translated as (11), the Skolem constant 'u' places the two events at the same time in the past. This suggests that translation provides a richer and more practical approach to representing temporal information.

In the case of queries, however, the past tense may play a useful rôle. Suppose one wanted to find out whether Sally had been promoted. If the information were stored as (11) and there were no procedure such as (10), it would be necessary to pose two queries, the first one being,

(16) ? at(X, promote(sally)).

Given that some 'v' is assigned to 'X', one would then have to ask,

(17) ? v « now.

Depending on the state of the database, one may be required to undertake a tedious search before finding an appropriate occasion of Sally's being promoted. By invoking procedure (10*), however, one can reduce the effort. In response to the query,

(18) ? past(now, promote(sally)).

(10*) functions to find the appropriate instances. Indeed, it serves to retrieve the desired information in a perspicuous and efficient manner.[6]

Let us turn now to another issue. Imagine that Sally's promotion was from reader to professor. How is one to represent the relation between the earlier state and the later one? And how is one to relate both of these to the event of her being promoted? To appreciate the problem we must first define what an interval is. From the point of view IQ-Prolog intervals will be discriminated with respect to a linearly ordered point structure. This may be the set of integers, rationals or reals. It may also be the set of calendar days, hours or minutes. Which set is the more suitable will depend on the application. We let (P,<) be any point structure, where P is a nonempty set and < a linear ordering on P. Intervals are distinguished by pairs of points and come in four varieties: closed, open, open only on the left, and open only on the right. These are represented respectively as follows on the assumption that i and j are elements of P and i < j: [i,j], (i,j), (i,j] and [i,j). We also admit [i,i] as a minimal interval, viz. the interval which embraces only the point i. It is now possible to specify the interval relation '«' precisely by reference to the kinds of intervals involved and the pairs of points which identify them. Since the definition is obvious, we need not indicate all the details here. Let it be enough to say that [i,j] « [k,l] if j < k, and [i,j) « [k,l] if j ≤ k.

---

6 In view of this (10*) may also be used to provide appropriate database representations for past-tensed formulas.

Using this structure, one might consider depicting the adjacent states surrounding Sally's promotion in terms of two open intervals which share a common boundary.

(19) at((i,j), reader(sally)).
at((j,k), professor(sally)).

Within IQ-Prolog it is assumed that if a formula holds with respect to an interval, it holds with respect to all of its subintervals including the minimal ones.[7] Since j belongs to neither (i,j) nor (j,k), (19) is not contradictory, but it does give rise to a puzzling situation. There is an interval between (i,j) and (j,k) at which Sally was neither a reader nor a professor, viz. the interval [j,j]. Surely this seems counterintuitive. Some would argue that it warrants excluding [j,j] as a legitimate interval; it should only be taken as having the abstract status of a 'limit' between adjacent states.[8] But its status would seem more than abstract with respect to the event of Sally's being promoted. It is conventional practice to represent this event as occurring at the limit.

(20) at([j,j], promote(sally)).

Sally is thus represented as being neither a reader nor a professor at the time of her promotion. Since her promotion was a real event, there must be a real interval where she had no rank at all.

This anomaly can be naturally remedied by assigning j to the interval of her being a professor, i.e. by letting that interval be [j,k) which is open only on the right. Consider again the proposition,

(1) Sally was promoted on 1st October 1987.

If Sally were not a professor on the 1st of October, she would not receive a professorial salary for the full month, only for thirty days. But as one knows,

---

7 This assumption will be reflected in a procedure which is defined below.
8 See Allen and Hayes (1987).

it is standard practice to regard events of promotion as belonging to the states assumed and hence, to arrange payment accordingly. By convention (1) implies that Sally is a professor on 1st October 1987, and for the whole day.

Some would argue, however, the conventional relation exemplified in (1) does not generalize to other causal situations. Consider this statement.

(21) Jane switched on the light.

Is the event of switching on the light rightly located as belonging to the state of the light's being on? It is common knowledge that the light does not come on at the precise instant the switch is thrown; it takes time for the electricity to flow. Moreover, everyone knows that throwing the switch does not always give rise to the light's coming on; there are unfortunately faulty switches and circuits. The event of throwing the switch must be represented as preceeding the state of the light's being on. But what about the event of switching on the light, as opposed to that of just throwing the switch? It seems a truism to say that if Jane succeeded in switching on the light, then the light went on. If there really were an event of switching it on, and not just an attempt to do so, then the light was on. Would it not be right to say that the event succeeded at the time the light came on? Indeed, if there were a delay, success would not be actual, only possible. Possibility characterizes the event of throwing the switch; it might succeed, but it need not. The event of switching on the light, on the other hand, is different; it actually succeeds, i.e. at the very instant the light came one, and hence is essentially part of the state of the light's being on.

These considerations suggest the following strategy for temporal representation. Some events, like being promoted and switching on the light, are appropriately represented as occurring at minimal closed intervals, i.e. those of the sort [j,j].[9] Such intervals consist of a single 'atomic' point and

---

9 This is not to say that everything which is intuitively an event should be so represented. The appropriate cases are sometimes referred to as accomplishments to differentiate them from other candidates, distinguished as processes or activities. The

thus have no subintervals other than themselves. That events are regarded as 'instantaneous' may seem counterintuitive to those would think of them as taking a certain amount of time, i.e. more than an indivisible instant. Our aim, however, is not to reflect naive metaphysical intuitions; it is rather to capture temporal relations as they are conventionally understood. For this purpose the envisaged events are best characterized as instantaneous.[10] As for states, like being a professor or the light's being on, they are represented by intervals which are closed on the left and open on the right, viz. by intervals of the form [i,j) where i < j. The fact that i belongs to this interval and j does not should not be seen as grounded on any metaphysical intuitions, naive or otherwise, but on the need to capture the temporal relations between states and events (or rather between the sentences which discriminate them). The difficult question is how one distinguishes an 'event' sentence from a 'state' sentence. The temporal system IQ offers one perspective from which to answer this question, although not of course the only one.

To see how the strategy applies let us consider a situation and its successive updates. Suppose we are initially told that Max used to be a lecturer but is one no longer; we are not told when he became a lecturer nor when he ceased to be one. This situation is represented by these assertions, where the interval [n,n] identifies the present moment.

(22) at([i,j), lecturer(max)).
[j,j] « [n,n].

Being a lecturer is plainly a state, not an event; it typically holds over some period of time. Since we do not know how long the period was, we use the Skolem constants i and j to identify that interval. Still we do know that the interval was before now, a fact which is recorded in (22).

---

metaphysics of events is, however, an area fraught with difficulty, and thus it would be foolish to regard these distinctions with any confidence. Nevertheless, it is natural to think of certain things as being true only at points, and these we shall call events.

10 It may also be the metaphysically correct way to characterize them. This is the IQ view which is elaborated in Chapter 1.

Later we are told that Max resigned. It would be natural to assume that it was from the post of lecturer that he resigned, in which case we would insert the following assertion.

(23) at([j,j], resign(max)).

Relative to the assumed point structure, [j,j] is the interval, in effect the point, which limits the state of Max's being a lecturer.[11] But we might wish to be more cautious; Max may have resigned at some other stage in his career. To allow for this we would update with the following assertions.

(24) at([k,k], resign(max)).
[k,k] « [n,n].

Here we indicate that the interval [k,k] need not terminate the state of Max's being a lecturer. He may have resigned from another position held later on; he may also have resigned from a position held earlier.

What if we subsequently learn that the resignation at [k,k] occurred between i and j? What does this entail about Max's status as a lecturer? Before we answer this, recall that we said above that in IQ-Prolog if a state holds for an interval, it is assumed to hold for all its subintervals. To formalize this assumption, known as the homogeneity condition, we invoke the following procedure.

(25*) at_hom(X,A) :- at(Y,A), sub(X,Y).

We read 'sub(X,Y)' as 'X is a subinterval of Y' and interpret the subinterval relation relative to the given point structure, i.e. the one used to specify the intervals X and Y. Let X and Y be intervals open only on the right, represented respectively as [a,b) and [c,d). Then

---

11 There may or may not be a last interval of Max's being a lecturer. If the point structure is dense, there is no such interval; if it is not dense, there is.

(26*) sub([a,b), [c,d)) :- c ≤ a, b ≤ d.[12]

If X and Y are both closed intervals, the conditions in the body remain the same, as they do when Y is closed and X is open only on the right. But where X is closed and Y is open only the right, the second condition must be adjusted.

(27*) sub([a,b], [c,d)) :- c ≤ a, b < d.

We shall not bother to extend the definition to the other cases since they are not immediately relevant.[13] Since it is convenient to formulate temporal queries in terms of tenses, we let the tenses call the procedure (25).

(28*) pres(X,A) :- at_hom(X,A).
(29*) past(X,A) :- at_hom(Y,A), Y « X.

It is easy to see how the future tense would be added.

Let us now consider the IQ-Prolog database consisting of (22) and (24) together with the new information that Max's resignation occurred somewhere between i and j.[14]

```
(30)  at([i,j), lecturer(max)).
      [j,j] « [n,n].
      at([k,k], resign(max)).
      [k,k] « [n,n].
      [i,i] « [k,k].
      [k,k] « [j,j].
```

---

12 Strictly speaking, (26*) is an abbreviation of two clauses since '≤' refers disjunctively to two relations, each of which must be defined separately.

13 These will be found in the full specification of IQ-Prolog, as will the definition of an interval, which has so far been assumed.

14 If we want to allow the event to coincide with [i,i] or [j,j], we would have to define a relation on intervals other than '«' which means 'strictly earlier than'. While this can be easily done, it would distract us from relevant issues.

The first thing to note is that (28) is not an inconsistent database, even though it would verify the following two queries.

(31) ? pres([k,k], lecturer(max)).

(32) ? pres([k,k], resign(max)).

Observe that the Skolem constant j identifies the limit of Max's being a lecturer and that [j,j] « [k,k]. Together these facts imply that the position Max resigned from is not the lecturership he held through the interval [i,j). In effect (30) implies that Max must have held some other position, although we do not as yet know what it was. Suppose we discover that Max actually held another lectureship which he took up at the same time as the other one. Was this the post he resigned from? If we do not know, we would add the following assertion to (30).

(33) at([i,l), lecturer(max))

Since there are no restrictions on l, the post at [i,l) is not identified with the post at [i,j).[15] If we know at the time of update that this other lectureship is the one Max resigned from, we would add (34) instead of (33) to the database.

(34) at([i,k), lecturer(max)).

There is a problem if we first add (33) and then discover that [k,k] was the time at which Max resigned from this lectureship. It would be nice if we could simply add the following fact, with '=' interpreted as semantic identity.

(35) [k,k] = [l,l].

---

15 From a semantic point of view they would turn out to be the same if l and j were assigned the same point. But this cannot be reflected in PROLOG without making a syntactic change, either replacing 'l' by 'j' or vice versa.

Since '=' does not have the desired meaning in PROLOG, another mode of representation must be sought, a quest which we shall postpone for now.

An interesting question emerges if we attempt to update (30) by adding these two assertions.

(36) at([j,j], marry(max)).

(37) at([j,j], promote(max)).

We know that [j,j] is the limit of Max's tenure as a lecturer, i.e. of the period initiated at [i,i]. The question is, which event terminated this state? His marriage or his promotion? Consider the query,

(38) ? at([j,j], A).

Intuitively (38) asks what event (s) occurred at [j,j]. Given that 'marry(max)' is first assigned to A, we could then ask what states this event limits by posing the query,

(39) ? at([I, j), B).

In response, i would be assigned to I and 'lecturer(max)' to B. While this may be taken to suggest that Max's marriage ended his lectureship, the inference does not follow logically from the database. Strictly speaking, the database records only the temporal relations between events and states, not their causal relations. It could be that Max left his lectureship because he was married; the hypothesis may seem more or less probable, depending upon what one knows about Max. But probability notwithstanding, the database has nothing whatever to say on the matter. The same holds for the event of Max's promotion. Although it is very natural to think that this event caused him to cease to be a lecturer, the conclusion is not a valid consequence of the database, compelling though it may be.

This may be seen to be a disadvantage of IQ-Prolog since one may want to extract causal information from a temporal database. It would of course be possible to introduce such information, but it may actually be better to leave it unspecified. One may not know what the cause of a particular state is, even though one may know the events which limit it. Indeed, temporal databases might be used as a way of building up a comprehensive 'picture' of temporal relations with a view to seeking the probable causal relations. IQ-Prolog allows this to be done without preempting the conclusion. Moreover, it frees the user from the need to specify information that may be irrelevant. He may only care about temporal information, in which case he can leave causal matters aside.

For sizable databases IQ-Prolog typically gives rise to an 'avalanche' of Skolem constants, and as we have seen, it may be important to differentiate them when updating. When integrating a new piece of information into a database, one may have to relate the new information to a piece of existing information. This is achieved by first finding the existing information in the database and then using the relevant Skolem constants in some appropriate way. The process of searching the database is straightforward in IQ-Prolog since the Skolem constants are always associated with particular states or events, identified by such clauses as 'lecturer(max)' or 'marry(max)'. This may not remove all complications but it does at least make the search perspicuous.

To highlight some of the characteristics of IQ-Prolog let us reconsider the database consisting of (30), (36) and (37), but supplemented by one additional fact, viz. (40).

(30) at([i,j), lecturer(max)).
[j,j] « [n,n].
at([k,k], resign(max)).
[k,k] « [n,n].
[i,i] « [k,k].
[k,k] « [j,j].

(36) at([j,j], marry(max)).

(37) at([j,j], promote(max)).

(40) at([j,m), reader(max)).

If one wanted to know about Max's career, it would be natural to ask what positions he held. This could be done through the query '? at([I,J), X(max))' or through this present-tensed alternative.

(41) ? pres([I,J), X(max)).

Generally, querying through the present tense yields more information than the corresponding queries with 'at', although in this case there is no difference.[16] Note that '[I,J)' distinguishes both queries as being about states, not events.[17] The first state found would be that of Max's being a lecturer for the period [i,j). One might then want to know what happened at [j,j].

(42) ? pres([j,j], X(max));

Because of the structure of the database the initial reply would be that Max got married. This may not seem to provide an explanation of why he ceased to be lecturer; perhaps there was another reason. So one prompts (42) to look further. One then discovers that Max was also promoted at [j,j], which is a more plausible explanation of the situation. One can find out what state resulted from his promotion by this query.

(43) ? pres([j,L), X(max)).

One is told that for the period [j,m) Max was a reader. But is he still a reader?

---

[16] Where the difference emerges is in ground queries. Since 'pres' calls other procedures, e.g. 'at_hom', while 'at' does not, certain ground queries with 'pres' will succeed but their corresponding queries with 'at' will not.

[17] Note that the same cannot be said of queries using 'past'. In the query '? past([I,J), X(max))' the interval expression '[I,J)' has a different status than it does in (41). Here the query is not about what states hold in [I,J) but rather about what properties hold of Max at some earlier interval. In contrast, (41) is about the states which hold of Max in [I,J).

(44) ? pres([n,n], reader(max)).

Here the answer is no. This arises from the fact that in the database the relation between the points m and n is unspecified, i.e. whether m is earlier than or later than n.[18] Whenever a database does not contain enough information to answer a query positively, it answers negatively. This would seem to be unfortuate since it obscures the distinction between knowing a proposition to be false and not knowing something to be true. As a consequence, the only stable information one can extract from a database is positive information.

The question is whether one wants to be confined to stable information. Kowalski and Sergot suggest that it may be useful to admit unstable information by means of procedures which invoke 'negation as failure'. In certain contexts one may want to allow the response to (44), with respect to the given database, to be yes. Sometimes plans are best formulated on the hypothesis that states hold unless they are explicitly shown not to hold. Of course, in other contexts a more cautious approach might be called for. We propose to take a cautious view of temporal information in IQ-Prolog; in effect, we shall not assume that 'real' temporal information comes only in the positive variety. For applications where this proves to be inconvenient, we can always augment IQ-Prolog by introducing procedures with 'negation as failure'. But for the moment it may be instructive to remain conservative.

Before turning to the Event Calculus, we should perhaps indicate one of the advantages of having intervals explicitly represented. Consider the following assertion.

(45) Max was married in 1985.

Let us assume that we are working with respect to a point structure consisting of days. What (45) says, intuitively, is that there was some day in 1985 on

---

18 Identity is precluded here since 'm' and 'n' are distinct Skolem constants.

which Max was married. How can we represent this in IQ-Prolog? Since we do not know the day of Max's marriage, we must introduce a Skolem constant and qualify it appropriately. What we have to capture is that his marriage occurred sometime before now and during 1985. This can be achieved by the following assertions.

```
(46)    at([q,q], marry(max)).
        [q,q] « [n,n].
        [31_dec_1984, 31_dec_1984] « [q,q].
        [q,q] « [1_jan_1986, 1_jan_1986].
```

It may be noted that we have actually made no essential use of intervals; (45) might just as well have been represented in terms of points alone.

But suppose we want to query the database to find out whether Max got married in 1985. Here we can employ intervals to define a procedure which makes this a simple matter.

```
(47*)   in(X,A) :- at_hom(Y,A), sub(Y,X).
```

The clauses in the body of (47*) were specified above. We must also define an appropriate clause for the past tense.

```
(48*)   past(X,in(Y,A)) :- in(Y,A), Y « X.
```

The requisite query is then the following.

```
(49)    ? past([n,n], in([1_jan_1985,31_dec_1985], marry(max))).
```

We can also ask in which year Max got married.

```
(50)    ? past([n,n], in([X,Y), marry(max))).
```

If we are not interested in whether the event occurred in the past, we could use the present tense to effect the query.

(51) ? pres([Z,Z], in([X,Y), marry(max))).

To all these queries the responses are as we would expect them to be. In IQ-Prolog tenses and intervals work together to make database query clear and uncomplicated. This suggests that perhaps intervals and tenses share an interesting property: while they may not be essential for temporal representation, they are effective, if not indispensable, devices for database query.

§2 The Event Calculus

On the face of it, the Event Calculus looks very different from IQ-Prolog. It invokes a primitive ontology of events and admits intervals only as derived entities. It does not use tenses at all, either for representation or for query. This in fact is a matter of policy since tenses are seen to belong to non-classical logic and the Event Calculus is a first-order theory. Kowalski and Sergot claim that first-order theories have greater expressive power than their non-classical 'competitors' and hence, they see no need to employ tense logics in the service of temporal databases. Moreover, such logics have yet to be rendered computationally useful in the way that first-order logic has. While there are efficient theorem provers for the Horn clause fragment of first-order logic, nothing similar has been shown to hold for any tense logic.

Since IQ-Prolog contains tenses, it might be thought to be among those non-classical systems dismissed by Kowalski and Sergot. Such is not the case, however. IQ-Prolog is not a temporal logic and hence does not treat the tenses as full-fledged logical operators. The tenses are rather like the so-called meta-predicates of the Event Calculus, for example, 'Holds' or 'Initiates': they apply to expressions which may be regarded as well-formed formulas. The semantic status of such predicates may be a matter of some dispute, but it is clear that the systems to which they belong do not typically give them the rôle of logical operators. This is not to imply, however, that there may not be an interesting connection between meta-predicates and logical operators. Indeed, the tenses in IQ-Prolog have a special relation to the temporal operators of tense logic. The nature of this relation will subsequently emerge, and so too will our general view of the connection between non-classical logics and deductive databases.

Having observed that both the Event Calculus and IQ-Prolog employ meta-predicates, we should mention that they also take a similar approach to database updating. Essentially this is an additive process requiring no deletions, a feature which reflects their common status as PROLOG systems. Still there is a difference. The Event Calculus appeals to 'negation as failure' to integrate new information into a database, while IQ-Prolog does not invoke this strategy (at least not yet). What the computational implications may be of this difference is not something we shall consider just now. Let it be enough to say that as far as the frame problem is concerned the difference seems to be negligible. The two systems are identical in the way they circumvent the frame problem, viz. by locally indexing events and states. In IQ-Prolog the local indices are the intervals distinguished by point-names or their Skolem surrogates. In the Event Calculus the indices are Skolem constants which may or may not be associated with temporal points. In both cases the effect is the same.

There is another similarity between the Event Calculus and IQ-Prolog: they both assume a temporal point structure which can be used for locating events. For the Event Calculus this may be the arithmetic of PROLOG, covering the sets of integers, rationals and reals; or it may be the PROLOG calendar, including the sets of minutes, hours, days and years. Whatever the intended set, the natural linear ordering applies, which is fixed in PROLOG. The Event Calculus is, however, unlike IQ-Prolog in that it does not use points to identify intervals. Intervals have no independent status in the system, only in connection with events. While events may be explicitly located with respect to time, intervals are only located implicitly through their relation to events. This leads to a fundamental, though subtle, difference between IQ-Prolog and the Event Calculus.

Let us consider how the following proposition might be represented in the Event Calculus.

(52) Fiona was a lecturer in 1980.

It is natural to assume that there was some event which gave rise to Fiona's being a lecturer, and in the Event Calculus this is explicitly represented by a Skolem constant, say, ‘e’. Being a lecturer is of course not an event; it is rather a state which holds for a period of time initiated by an event. The period initiated by e is referred to as the interval after(e), with e being its left bound.[19] It is assumed that events are ordered by the relation ‘<’, which also orders the days of the year. Given these conventions, one can represent the fact that Fiona was a lecturer by the following assertions, with ‘today’ read in the intended way.

(53) lecturer(fiona, after(e)).
e < today.

But how does one say that the period after(e) overlaps the year 1980? Here it seems one has to explicitly invoke the two bounds of after(e); that is, one has to refer to its start and end points. To this end one may invoke these two clauses.

(54) start(after(e), e).
end(after(e), e').

---

19 In the Event Calculus e is not treated as belonging to the interval ‘after(e)’; in effect, ‘after(e)’ is an interval open on the left. This difference between the Event Calculus and IQ-Prolog is of no immediate significance.

Here e' is the event which bounds after(e) on the right; as in the case of e, e' does not belong to after(e). The full translation of (51) can now be captured by adding these assertions to (53) and (54).[20]

(55) e < 31_dec_1980.
1_jan_1980 < e'.
e' ≤ today.

Although the interval 1980 is not explicitly represented in the translation, its import seems to have been fully reflected in terms of its endpoints, albeit the inclusive ones.

The same is not the case for the interval after(e). Its status is not exhausted by its endpoints alone. In the Event Calculus the clause,

(56) lecturer(fiona, after(e)).

is understood to assert that Fiona was a lecturer throughout the period after(e). To capture this reading Kowalski and Sergot introduce conditions on the predicates ‘start’ and ‘end’.

(57*) start(before(e'), e) :- after(e) = before(e').
end(after(e), e') :- after(e) = before(e').

The expression ‘before(e')’ refers to the open interval bounded on the right by the event e'. The identity of after(e) and before(e') results from this instance of a procedural schema.

(58*) after(e) = before(e') :- lecturer(X, after(e)),
lecturer(X, before(e')),
e < e',
not after(e) << before(e').

20 This is not necessarily the preferred translation, nor perhaps an entirely perspicuous one. It does nevertheless serve our purposes. As the for the relation ‘≤’, we use it as we did in IQ-Prolog, viz. to mean that e' is either earlier than or identical to today.

The relation '<<' says that the two time periods are disjoint, i.e. that the end point of the former is before the start point of the latter. Here we see an essential use of 'negation as failure' in the Event Calculus. Together (57*) and (58*) imply the homogeneity of (56), that is, that it holds throughout the period after(e), which is the same as before(e'). In IQ-Prolog it will be recalled that homogeneity is captured by the following general procedure.

(25*) at_hom(X,A) :- at(Y,A), sub(X,Y).

Since IQ-Prolog has direct access to intervals, there is no need to invoke 'negation as failure'.

At this stage one may begin to wonder whether there is any real difference between the Event Calculus and IQ-Prolog. Both systems use the property of homogeneity, and for the same kind of sentences, viz. those expressing states. Both can represent the content of sentences like (52) which mention intervals explicitly, e.g. by the phrase 'in 1980'. It may be that IQ-Prolog achieves these ends somewhat more concisely than the Event Calculus; on the other hand, it may do so at a computational cost higher than that of the Event Calculus. These are issues that can only be settled by further enquiry. What seems almost immediately evident, however, is that IQ-Prolog offers a more efficient means of database query.

Consider the translation of (52) into IQ-Prolog, where [n,n] is understood as today.

(60) at([i,j), lecturer(fiona)).
[i,j) « [n ,n].
[i,i] « [1_jan_1981, 1_jan_1981].
[1_jan_1980, 1_jan_1980] « [j,j].

If one wanted to ask whether Fiona was a lecturer in 1980, it would not be necessary to initiate four queries. The following would be sufficient.

(61) ? past([n,n], in([1_jan_1980, 31_dec_1980], lecturer(fiona))).

By first calling the procedure,

(48*) past(X,in(Y,A)) :- in(Y,A), Y « X.

next the procedure,

(47*) in(X,A) :- at_hom(Y,A), sub(Y,X).

and finally the procedure,

(25*) at_hom(X,A) :- at(Y,A), sub(X,Y).

(59) would return the answer yes, given an appropriately specified database like (60). It is not clear how the Event Calculus could achieve the same response without initiating multiple queries. In the case of IQ-Prolog the key to efficient and perspicuous query lies in the ability to refer explicitly to intervals, viz. in the form exemplified in (59). Without this capacity there would seem no alternative but to undertake the cumbersome process of formulating and posing several queries.

How might the Event Calculus be adjusted? As it stands, the Event Calculus allows events to be associated directly with points of time, which themselves can be explicitly referrred to. What it does not allow is intervals to be represented explicitly in the point structure. As a result, states cannot be associated directly with intervals of time. Although states are defined with respect to events and events may be assigned time points, there is no way to relate states explicitly to time intervals. If this were changed, the Event Calculus would probably not be very different from IQ-Prolog. To achieve the desired connection between states and intervals there would almost certainly have to be a procedure like (25*). In the circumstance, it would seem redundant to have a procedure like (58) which appears to be necessary only if states are not related explicitly to intervals. In fact, it would appear that 'negation as failure' could be dispensed with altogether, at least with respect to temporal procedures. The only essential uses of 'negation as failure' would seem to arise from the inability to refer to intervals of time. Once this is rectified, there is no reason to think that the metaphysics of the Event Calculus cannot be realized in IQ-Prolog. To be sure, there may have to be some adjustment of detail, for example, in the kinds of intervals associated with states. In IQ-Prolog state intervals are of the form [i,j), while in the Event Calculus they are taken to be completely open. Though we may wish to argue about which is the more suitable interval, [i,j) or (i,j), the dispute would be independent of the resources of IQ-Prolog.

Whether these conjectures can be sustained must remain moot for the time being. Only a more detailed investigation could settle the matter. Nevertheless, there is an issue on which IQ-Prolog and the Event Calculus clearly divide, and that is on the rôle of tenses and temporal intervals. The Event Calculus gives neither any status and as a consequence, can initiate natural queries only in ways that are obscure and inefficient. This is not the case in IQ-Prolog, however, where tenses and temporal intervals are rendered explicitly. It must be emphasized that in regard to representation there is no major difference between IQ-Prolog and the Event Calculus. The representations of the proposition,

(52) Fiona was a lecturer in 1980.

are not significantly distinguished by their complexity. Where the difference emerges is with respect to queries. It is here that one may begin to see the 'figure' of tense logic. The tensed queries in IQ-Prolog have a striking connection with the temporal logic IQ in that the computational procedures of the former reflect some of the essential semantic properties of the latter. The aim in the remainder of this paper is to provide a precise theorectical account of the connection. In the process we hope to reveal how non-classical logics might be used to serve deductive databases.

§3 Some Residual Aspects of IQ-Prolog

Before we address these technical issues, it may be useful to summarize the current status of tenses in IQ-Prolog. Only two tenses have appeared so far, the present and the past. Since the future is treated similarly to the past, mutatis mutandis, it raises no new issues and hence is of no independent theoretical interest. As for the present and past tenses, recall that they have occurred only in the heads of procedures. One may wonder whether this is intended to indicate a restriction on how they may be used. Could tenses be used to make simple assertions, that is, could they occur in unit clauses? The simple answer is obviously no if one wishes to reserve tenses solely for the purpose of query. But perhaps one may wish to be more flexible. After all, natural language contains simple tensed assertions, so it would seem reasonable to admit them into temporal databases. Let us see what this would entail.

If one wanted to represent directly the proposition

(62) Fiona was a lecturer.

one could extend the conventions of IQ-Prolog to admit this clause.

(63) past([n,n], lecturer(fiona)).

To reflect the intuitive status of (63), i.e. as a past-tensed assertion, it would be necessary to add a procedure which would allow queries to succeed at intervals after [n,n]. Where [m,m] is such an interval, one would like the following query to succeed if (63) occurs in the database.

(64) ? past([m,m], lecturer(fiona)).

To insure this outcome one would have to introduce a procedure whose declarative content is equivalent to this conditional.

(65*) past(X,A) :- past(Y,A), Y « X.

Although (65) is not computationally satisfactory, being a left recursive procedure, it serves nevertheless to establish the relevant point. Given the presence of (63) in the database, the query (64) would succeed by calling (65*).[21]

Although (65*) may render (63) an intuitive representation of (62), it remains to be seen whether the strategy usefully extends the resources of IQ-Prolog. Recall that (62) could alternatively be represented by these two assertions.

(67) at([i,j), lecturer(fiona)).
[i,j) « [n,n].

The query (64) would then succeed by calling the already defined procedure,

(29*) past(X,A) :- at_hom(Y,A), Y « X.

So why bother with (63)? There does not seem to be much in the argument that (63) is more a concise representation. Moreover, it seems that any algorithm which would translate (62) into (63) could be easily extended to yield (67). To be sure, there would be more steps but the computational overhead would be almost too small to measure. There are, however, two good reasons for preferring (67) to (63). The first one was illustrated above. Suppose that for the period in which she was a lecturer Fiona was happy. To represent this one need only add the following assertion to (67)

(68) at([i,j), happy(fiona)).

---

21 It is interesting to note that (65*) expresses one of the basic axioms of tense logic, viz. PPA → PA, where 'P' is read as 'it was the case that'. What (65*) asserts is captured by the following formula which reflects the content of the axiom.

$\forall x\ (\exists y\ (y \ll x \wedge past(y,A)) \rightarrow past(x,A))$

Above we indicated that there is a similar relationship between (10*) and the temporal axiom A → GPA .

(10*) past(X,A) :- at(Y,A), Y « X.

It would not be so simple with respect to (63); that is, it would not be enough to add this assertion, even with the procedure (65*).

(69) past([n,n], happy(fiona)).

There is nothing in (63) and (69) which ties the two states to the same period in the past. Moreover, it is not clear how this could be achieved other than by translating them into (67) and (68) respectively.

The other reason for eschewing assertions like (63) is to free oneself from the need to invoke 'awkward' procedures like (65*). To remove its left-recursive character would require restructuring and further complicating the database, thereby obscuring its current conceptual clarity. While this may not be unendurable, it would be an inconvenience with no ostensible benefit. As things stand in IQ-Prolog, temporal facts are represented in a perspicuous manner, and tenses are reserved solely for inference, i.e. queries. Moreover, (63) and (65*) introduce no additional expressive power; indeed, they serve to highlight the extent of the power already available. Surely one can hardly but agree that it is better to confine oneself to these richer resources and avoid (63) and (65*) altogether. While the strategies exemplified by (63) and (65*) may be of some theoretical interest, they are strictly redundant.

Part II

§4 The System IQ^E

To explore the connection between IQ-Prolog and the temporal logic IQ we now define the temporal system IQ^E. As we indicated above, the aim is twofold. First, we show how IQ can be translated into IQ^E.[22] Since IQ^E is itself a tensed system, translation does not imply that all tenses disappear; indeed, IQ^E is essentially tensed, as will subsequently become apparent. Second, we show how IQ^E can be used to regiment and interpret IQ-Prolog. IQ^E is a non-classical system: not only does it contain non-truth-functional operators, it is also non-bivalent. IQ-Prolog can be seen to be just such a system.

The language of IQ^E is essentially the same as the language of IQ with a few deletions and additions.[23] In particular, the following IQ expressions do not belong to IQ^E.

(70) (i) the tense operators $PRES_{(i)}$ $PAST_{(i)}$ $FUT_{(i)}$
(ii) the interval constants C_I
(iii) the quantifier G

Note that although IQ^E does not contain interval and world constants, it does contain variables and parameters of these types. It also has the following expressions which IQ does not.

(71) (i) the tense operators $pres_{(i)}$ $past_{(i)}$ $fut_{(i)}$[24]
(ii) the existential quantifier $\exists^i$ which binds interval variables[25]
(iii) a two-place predicate *earlier* which takes only interval terms as arguments
(iv) a one-place predicate *now* which also takes just interval terms

The atomic well-formed formulas (wffs) of IQ^E are those of IQ plus the new ones arising from the predicates *earlier* and *now*.

---

22 Significantly, all the temporal operators distinguished in Chapter 1 can be defined in IQ^E, although we shall not attempt to prove this here. We do nevertheless consider one such operator below, viz. 'in'.
23 See Chapter 6.
24 These will be treated in a slightly different way than the tenses of IQ.
25 The corresponding universal quantifier can be introduced by definition.

(72) (i) If i and i' are I-terms, *earlier(i, i')* is a wff;

(ii) If i is an I-term, *now(i)* is a wff.

Since the two systems have the same logical connectives and the individual quantifiers $\exists$ and $\forall$, they agree on first-order complexity. Moreover, the clause introducing the tenses of IQ^E reads the same as that in IQ, except that Π ranges over IQ^E tenses. The only new clause in IQ^E is the following one.

(73) If A is a wff and t is an interval variable, then $\exists^i t\, A$ is a wff.

Below we shall see that (73) represents a significant addition.

The semantics of IQ^E is based on IQ-interpretations. Since there are no interval constants in IQ^E, we gain a certain notational simplicity. The I-terms are restricted to variables and parameters and as a result, such terms are always defined and their denotations in any IQ-interpretation $\langle \mathbf{M,g} \rangle$ are the same for all indices. That is, where i is an I-term and $\langle \mathbf{M,g} \rangle$ any IQ-interpretation, the following holds.

(74) (i) $[\![i]\!]^{\mathbf{M,g}}(j)$ is defined for all indices (j);

(ii) $[\![i]\!]^{\mathbf{M,g}}(j) = [\![i]\!]^{\mathbf{M,g}}(j')$ for all indices (j) and (j').

Since the denotation of i is always a constant function, we can reduce the notational clutter by referring to its denotation at an index simply as $[\![i]\!]^{\mathbf{M,g}}$.

The interpretation of present-tensed formulas in IQ^E differs from that in IQ in one crucial respect. In IQ the index of evaluation has a special relation to the index of reference: a present-tensed formula will be true at an index of evaluation only if it is identical with the index of reference. This relation does not hold in IQ^E; if a present-tensed formula is true at the index of reference, it is true at all indices of evaluation.[26] The tenses in IQ^E are defined as follows.

(75) (i) $[\![pres_{(i)} A]\!]^{\mathbf{M,g}}(j) = [\![A]\!]^{\mathbf{M,g}}([\![i]\!]^{\mathbf{M,g}})$;

---

26 In this respect IQ^E is similar to Kaplan's treatment of tenses in 'The Logic of Demonstratives' (1979).

(ii) $[\![past_{(i)}A]\!]^{M,g}(j) =$

- **t**, if there is a k « $[\![i]\!]^{M,g}$ such that $[\![A]\!]^{M,g}(k) = \mathbf{t}$,
- **f**, if there is a k « $[\![i]\!]^{M,g}$ such that $[\![A]\!]^{M,g}(k) = \mathbf{f}$ and for all l « $[\![i]\!]^{M,g}$, $[\![A]\!]^{M,g}(l) = \mathbf{f}$ or **u**,
- **u**, otherwise.

(iii) $[\![fut_{(i)}A]\!]^{M,g}(j) =$

- **t**, if there is k such that $[\![i]\!]^{M,g}$ « k and $[\![A]\!]^{M,g}(k) = \mathbf{t}$,
- **f**, if there is k such that $[\![i]\!]^{M,g}$ « k and $[\![A]\!]^{M,g}(k) = \mathbf{f}$ and for all l such that $[\![i]\!]^{M,g}$ « l, $[\![A]\!]^{M,g}(l) = \mathbf{f}$ or **u**,
- **u**, otherwise.

The new quantifier $\exists^i$ is treated as one might expect, but the predicates *earlier* and *now* have a somewhat special status. They are not assigned a denotation in an IQ-structure and thus are different from the usual predicates. They are defined contextually and in this respect are like the logical constants. As a consequence, every IQ^E-structure is also an IQ-structure, although the converse does not hold since IQ contains interval and world constants which IQ^E does not. Finally recall that $g(\alpha,e)$ is the assignment which is exactly like g except possibly for the assignment of e to the variable α.

(76) (i) $[\![\exists^i t\, A]\!]^{M,g}(j) =$

- **t**, if $[\![A]\!]^{M,g(t,k)}(j) = \mathbf{t}$ for some k belonging to I_T;
- **f**, if $[\![A]\!]^{M,g(t,k)}(j) = \mathbf{f}$ for all k belonging to I_T;
- **u**, otherwise.

(ii) $[\![earlier(i, i')]\!]^{M,g}(j) =$

- **t**, if $[\![i]\!]^{M,g}$ « $[\![i']\!]^{M,g}$;
- **f**, if not $[\![i]\!]^{M,g}$ « $[\![i']\!]^{M,g}$.

(iii) $[\![now(i)]\!]^{M,g}(j) =$

- **t**, if $[\![i]\!]^{M,g} = j$;
- **f**, if $[\![i]\!]^{M,g} \neq j$.

Note that the predicates *earlier* and *now* are never undefined since their arguments are restricted to variables and parameters. Note, moreover, that the interpretation of *earlier(i,i')* is not tied to the index of evaluation; it is a constant function and hence, we can refer to its denotation at an index in the abbreviated way, viz. as $[\![earlier(i, i')]\!]^{\mathbf{M},\mathbf{g}}$.

The result we intend to prove proceeds in terms of the notion of strong IQ-validity which is defined as follows.

(77) DEFINITION. Where A and B are wffs of IQ^E, the wff $A \leftrightarrow B$ is *strong IQ-valid* iff for all indices j and IQ-interpretations $\langle \mathbf{M},\mathbf{g}\rangle$:
$[\![A]\!]^{\mathbf{M},\mathbf{g}}(j) = \mathbf{t}$ iff $[\![B]\!]^{\mathbf{M},\mathbf{g}}(j) = \mathbf{t}$.[27]

The stronger concept of validity is required to preserve transitivity, which is not preserved by the weaker notion of IQ-validity. It can be shown that although $A \leftrightarrow B$ and $B \leftrightarrow C$ are IQ-valid, $A \leftrightarrow C$ may not be.

Within IQ^E the past and future tenses can be seen to be redundant since the following equivalences are strong IQ-valid.

(78) (i) $past_{(i)}A \leftrightarrow \exists^i t\,(earlier(t,i) \wedge pres_{(t)}\,A)$
(ii) $fut_{(i)}A \leftrightarrow \exists^i t\,(earlier(i,t) \wedge pres_{(t)}\,A$

We shall only prove (i), given that (ii) is the mirror case. It is a condition on (i) and (ii) that t not occur in $past_{(i)}A$ and $fut_{(i)}A$, otherwise they may not be strong IQ-valid.[28]

---

27 The definition of IQ-validity can be found in Chapter 6.

28 One may wonder whether the present tense can also be eliminated, i.e. whether the following is strong IQ-valid.

(i) $pres_{(i)}\,A \leftrightarrow (now(i) \wedge A)$

That (i) is not even IQ-valid, much less strongly so, is almost immediately evident. Note that the righthand side of (i) will be true for an index j only if $j = [\![i]\!]^{\mathbf{M},\mathbf{g}}$. Plainly there can be just one such index in any interpretation $\langle \mathbf{M},\mathbf{g}\rangle$. But there is no such constraint on the lefthand side of (i). It will be true for all indices if $[\![A]\!]^{\mathbf{M},\mathbf{g}}$ is true for the index $([\![i]\!]^{\mathbf{M},\mathbf{g}})$.

Although (i) is not IQ-valid, it is interesting to observe that the following identity holds in IQ^E.

$[\![now(i) \wedge pres_{(i)}\,A]\!]^{\mathbf{M},\mathbf{g}}(j) = [\![now(i) \wedge A]\!]^{\mathbf{M},\mathbf{g}}$

This becomes relevant below when we translate the tenses of IQ into IQ^E.

PROOF. (a) Suppose $[\![past_{(i)}A]\!]^{\mathbf{M},g}(j) = \mathbf{t}$. Then $[\![A]\!]^{\mathbf{M},g}(k) = \mathbf{t}$ for some $k \ll [\![i]\!]^{\mathbf{M},g}$. Hence $[\![pres_{(t)}A]\!]^{\mathbf{M},g(t,k)}(j) = \mathbf{t}$ and $[\![earlier(t,i)]\!]^{\mathbf{M},g(t,k)} = \mathbf{t}$. Thus $[\![\exists^i t\ (earlier(t,i) \wedge pres_{(t)}\ A)]\!]^{\mathbf{M},g}(j) = \mathbf{t}$.
(b) For the converse suppose $[\![\exists^i t\ (earlier(t,i) \wedge pres_{(t)}A)]\!]^{\mathbf{M},g}(j) = \mathbf{t}$. Then $[\![earlier(t,i)]\!]^{\mathbf{M},g(t,k)} = \mathbf{t}$ and $[\![pres_{(t)}A]\!]^{\mathbf{M},g(t,k)}(j) = \mathbf{t}$ for some k belonging to I_T. Thus for some k belonging to I_T one has $k \ll [\![i]\!]^{\mathbf{M},g}$ and $[\![A]\!]^{\mathbf{M},g}(k) = \mathbf{t}$. Hence $[\![past_{(i)}A]\!]^{\mathbf{M},g}(t) = \mathbf{t}$. □

We leave it to the reader to verify the need for the requirement that *t* does not occur in $past_{(i)}A$.

§5 Translating IQ into IQ^E

Since IQ^E does not contain interval constants, we shall restrict IQ in a similar way. Let us call this language IQ^S. It should be noted that IQ^S is in this respect more faithful to the system presented in Chapter 1 than the version of IQ under discussion. In that system any expression referring to an interval has the status of a rigid designator. The same holds in IQ^S and IQ^E since all variables and parameters are semantically rigid designators. Whether there is any practical need for non-rigid interval constants is an issue we cannot argue here. The view in Chapter 1 is that they are basically unnecessary, and this is the view we shall adopt here. It is sufficient for our purposes to show how IQ^S can be translated into IQ^E, since it has all the expressive power we require.

Note that the denotation of I-terms in IQ^S is stable in just the way it is in IQ^E; that is, it is fixed by the assignment functions **g** (for variables) and **ç** (for parameters) and hence, it is the same for all indices of evaluation. In effect, (74) holds for IQ^S. Although IQ^E lacks the quantifier G and treats its tenses in a different way than IQ^S, there exists a translation of IQ^S into IQ^E such that the following holds. Where *A* is any wff of IQ^S, ΘA is the translation of A in IQ^E, where $\langle \mathbf{M,g} \rangle$ is any IQ-interpretation $\langle \mathbf{M,g} \rangle$ and j any index

(79) $[\![A]\!]^{\mathbf{M},\mathbf{g}}(j) = [\![\Theta A]\!]^{\mathbf{M},\mathbf{g}}(j)$.

The translation Θ is defined inductively in this way.

(80) If A is a wff of IQ^S, then ΘA is

(i) A, if A is atomic;

(ii) $\neg\Theta B$, if A is $\neg B$;

(iii) $(\Theta B \wedge \Theta C)$, if A is $(B \wedge C)$;

(iv) $\exists x\, \Theta B$, if A is $\exists x B$;

(v) $(now(i) \wedge pres_{(i)}\, \Theta B)$, if A is $PRES_{(i)}B$;

(vi) $(now(i) \wedge past_{(i)}\, \Theta B)$, if A is $PAST_{(i)}B$;

(vii) $(now(i) \wedge fut_{(i)}\, \Theta B)$, if A is $FUT_{(i)}B$;

(viii) $\exists^i t\, (now(t) \wedge \Theta B)$, if A is $\mathrm{G}tB$.[29]

We can now prove (79).

PROOF. The proof proceeds by induction on the complexity of A. The only nontrivial cases are those where A is *I)* ΠB or *II)* $\mathrm{G}tB$.

PROOF OF I). A is ΠB: We shall only consider the case where Π is the past tense; the proof for the future tense proceeds as the mirror of the past tense, while the proof of the present tense is obvious. Let A be the IQ^S wff $PAST_{(i)}B$; then ΘA is the IQ^E wff $(now(i) \wedge past_{(i)}\, \Theta B)$. We prove that for all IQ-interpretations $\langle \mathbf{M,g} \rangle$ and indices j,

* $[\![PAST_{(i)}B]\!]^{\mathbf{M},\mathbf{g}}(j) = [\![(now(i) \wedge past_{(i)}\, \Theta B)]\!]^{\mathbf{M},\mathbf{g}}(j)$.

---

29 In view of the fact that

$[\![now(i) \wedge pres_{(i)}\, A]\!]^{\mathbf{M},\mathbf{g}}(j) = [\![now(i) \wedge A]\!]^{\mathbf{M},\mathbf{g}}$

we could translate $PRES_{(i)}$ in (v) without invoking the present tense $pres_{(i)}$ of IQ^E. But there would be little point is doing so; moreover, it may lead one to believe something false, viz. that $pres_{(i)}$ is redundant in IQ^E.

(a) Suppose $[\![PAST_{(i)}B]\!]^{\mathbf{M},g}(j) = \mathbf{t}$. Then $[\![i]\!]^{\mathbf{M},g} = j$ and $[\![B]\!]^{\mathbf{M},g}(k) = \mathbf{t}$ for some k « j. Hence $[\![now(i)]\!]^{\mathbf{M},g}(j) = \mathbf{t}$. Moreover, for some k « $[\![i]\!]^{\mathbf{M},g}$ it holds that $[\![B]\!]^{\mathbf{M},g}(k) = \mathbf{t}$. By the induction hypothesis, it holds that $[\![\Theta B]\!]^{\mathbf{M},g}(k) = \mathbf{t}$. Thus $[\![past_{(i)}\Theta B]\!]^{\mathbf{M},g}(j) = \mathbf{t}$.
The proof of the converse proceeds by virtually reversing the above.

(b) Suppose $[\![PAST_{(i)}B]\!]^{\mathbf{M},g}(j) = \mathbf{f}$. Then either *(i)* $[\![i]\!]^{\mathbf{M},g} \neq j$ or
(ii) $[\![i]\!]^{\mathbf{M},g} = j$, and $[\![B]\!]^{\mathbf{M},g}(k) = \mathbf{f}$ for some k « t and for all l « j
$[\![B]\!]^{\mathbf{M},g}(l) = \mathbf{f}$ or $\mathbf{u}$.
If (i) holds, then clearly $[\![now(i)]\!]^{\mathbf{M},g}(j) = \mathbf{f}$. Hence
$[\![(now(i) \wedge past_{(i)}\,\Theta B)]\!]^{\mathbf{M},g}(j) = \mathbf{f}$.
If (ii) holds, it follows from the induction hypothesis that $[\![\Theta B]\!]^{\mathbf{M},g}(k) = \mathbf{f}$ for some k « $[\![i]\!]^{\mathbf{M},g}$ and $[\![\Theta B]\!]^{\mathbf{M},g}(l) = \mathbf{f}$ or $\mathbf{u}$ for all l « $[\![i]\!]^{\mathbf{M},g}$. In effect, $[\![past_{(i)}\Theta B]\!]^{\mathbf{M},g}(j) = \mathbf{f}$. As in (a), the proof of the converse proceeds by virtually reversing the above.

(c) Suppose finally that $[\![PAST_{(i)}B]\!]^{\mathbf{M},g}(j) = \mathbf{u}$. This holds if and only if $[\![PAST_{(t)}B]\!]^{\mathbf{M},g}(j) \neq \mathbf{t}$ and $[\![PAST_{(i)}B]\!]^{\mathbf{M},g}(j) \neq \mathbf{f}$. Given (a) and (b), this obtains if and only if $[\![\Theta PAST_{(i)}B]\!]^{\mathbf{M},g}(j) \neq \mathbf{t}$ and $[\![\Theta PAST_{(i)}B]\!]^{\mathbf{M},g}(j) \neq \mathbf{f}$, which holds if and only if $[\![\Theta PAST_{(i)}B]\!]^{\mathbf{M},g}(j) = \mathbf{u}$.

PROOF OF II). Let us now consider the case where A is G$t\,B$. Here we must prove that

$$** \qquad [\![\mathrm{G}t\, B]\!]^{\mathbf{M},g}(j) = [\![\exists^i t\,(now(t) \wedge \Theta B)]\!]^{\mathbf{M},g}(j).$$

(a) Suppose $[\![\mathrm{G}t\, B]\!]^{\mathbf{M},g}(j) = \mathbf{t}$. Then $[\![B]\!]^{\mathbf{M},g(t,j)}(j) = \mathbf{t}$. This means $[\![now(t)]\!]^{\mathbf{M},g(t,j)}(j) = \mathbf{t}$ and by the induction hypothesis $[\![\Theta B]\!]^{\mathbf{M},g}(j) = \mathbf{t}$. Hence $[\![\exists^i t\,(now(t) \wedge \Theta B)]\!]^{\mathbf{M},g}(j) = \mathbf{t}$. The proof of the converse proceeds essentially in reverse.

(b) Suppose $[\![Gt\, B]\!]^{\mathbf{M},g}(j) = \mathbf{f}$. Then $[\![B]\!]^{\mathbf{M},g(t,j)}(j) = \mathbf{f}$, and by the induction hypothesis $[\![\Theta B]\!]^{\mathbf{M},g(t,j)}(j) = \mathbf{f}$.
Let k be any member of I_T. If k = j, then by the induction hypothesis $[\![now(t) \wedge \Theta B]\!]^{\mathbf{M},g(t,k)}(j) = \mathbf{f}$. If k ≠ j, then $[\![now(t)]\!]^{\mathbf{M},g(t,k)}(j) = \mathbf{f}$ and thus $[\![now(t) \wedge \Theta B]\!]^{\mathbf{M},g(t,k)}(j) = \mathbf{f}$. Thus for all k in I_T $[\![now(t) \wedge \Theta B]\!]^{\mathbf{M},g(t,k)}(j) = \mathbf{f}$. That is, $[\![\exists^i t\, (now(t) \wedge \Theta B)]\!]^{\mathbf{M},g}(j) = \mathbf{f}$. The proof of the converse again proceeds essentially in reverse.

(c) Suppose finally that $[\![Gt\, B]\!]^{\mathbf{M},g}(j) = \mathbf{u}$. This holds if and only if $[\![Gt\, B]\!]^{\mathbf{M},g}(j) \neq \mathbf{t}$ and $[\![Gt\, B]\!]^{\mathbf{M},g}(j) \neq \mathbf{f}$.Given (a) and (b), this obtains if and only if $[\![\Theta Gt\, B]\!]^{\mathbf{M},g}(j) \neq \mathbf{t}$ and $[\![\Theta Gt\, B]\!]^{\mathbf{M},g}(j) \neq \mathbf{f}$, which holds if and only if $[\![\Theta Gt\, B]\!]^{\mathbf{M},g}(j) = \mathbf{u}$. □

Anything that can be expressed in IQ^S can thus be expressed by an equivalent wff in IQ^E. This may not come as a great surprise, nor indeed may the next result. In IQ^E no logical connective or quantifier need be represented as falling within the scope of a tense. When a connective or quantifier occurs within the scope of a tense, one can always find another strongly equivalent wff where this does not obtain.

§6 The Scope of Tenses in IQ^E

IQ^E differs from IQ^S in that connectives and quantifiers are not essentially bound within the scope of tense operators. For any IQ^E formula in which a connective or quantifier occurs within the scope of a tense, there is a translation in which the connective or quantifier does not fall within the scope of any tense. Where ⟨**M,g**⟩ is any IQ-interpretation, the denotation of the wff

(81) $Gt\, PAST_{(i)} PRES_{(t)} A$

is always either f or u at an index while the denotation of (82) may be t.

(82) $PAST_{(i)} \mathrm{G}t\, PRES_{(t)} A$

A similar situation holds for $\neg$ which cannot be 'moved outside' the scope of the present tense operator $PRES_{(i)}$ salva veritate. If $[\![i]\!]^{\mathbf{M},g} \neq \mathrm{j}$, the denotation of

(83) $PRES_{(i)} \neg A$

at the index j is f, but the denotation of

(84) $\neg PRES_{(i)} A$

at j is t. We shall now define a *normal form* result for IQ^{E} where tense operators have scope only over atomic wffs.

Where A and B are wffs of IQ^{E}, the following are all strong IQ-valid.

(85) (i) $pres_{(i)} \neg A \leftrightarrow \neg pres_{(i)} A$

(ii) $pres_{(i)} (A \wedge B) \leftrightarrow pres_{(i)} A \wedge pres_{(i)} B$

(iii) $pres_{(i)} \exists x\, A \leftrightarrow \exists x\; pres_{(i)} A$

(iv) $pres_{(i)} \exists^{\mathrm{i}} t\, A \leftrightarrow \exists^{\mathrm{i}} t\; pres_{(i)} A$, provided t is not i

PROOF.

(i) This is almost immediate since $[\![pres_{(i)} \neg A]\!]^{\mathbf{M},g}(\mathrm{j}) = \mathbf{t}$ iff $[\![A]\!]^{\mathbf{M},g}([\![i]\!]^{\mathbf{M},g}) = \mathbf{f}$ iff $[\![\neg pres_{(i)} A\,]\!]^{\mathbf{M},g}(\mathrm{j}) = \mathbf{t}$.

(ii) This can be seen to hold since $[\![pres_{(i)}(A \wedge B)]\!]^{\mathbf{M},g}(\mathrm{j}) = \mathbf{t}$ iff $[\![A]\!]^{\mathbf{M},g}([\![i]\!]^{\mathbf{M},g}) = [\![B]\!]^{\mathbf{M},g}([\![i]\!]^{\mathbf{M},g}) = \mathbf{t}$ iff $[\![pres_{(i)} A \wedge pres_{(i)} B]\!]^{\mathbf{M},g}(\mathrm{j}) = \mathbf{t}$.

(iv) Observe that $[\![pres_{(i)} \exists^{\mathrm{i}} t\, A]\!]^{\mathbf{M},g}(\mathrm{j}) = \mathbf{t}$ iff $[\![A]\!]^{\mathbf{M},g(t,\mathrm{k})}([\![i]\!]^{\mathbf{M},g}) = \mathbf{t}$ for some k in $\mathrm{I_T}$ iff $[\![pres_{(i)} A]\!]^{\mathbf{M},g(t,\mathrm{k})}(\mathrm{j}) = \mathbf{t}$ for some k in $\mathrm{I_T}$ iff $[\![\exists^{\mathrm{i}} t\; pres_{(i)} A]\!]^{\mathbf{M},g}(\mathrm{j}) = \mathbf{t}$.

Note that (iii) is proved in a similar way to (iv); only the domains of quantification are different. □

Given the results in (85) together with the fact that $past_{(i)}$ and $fut_{(i)}$ are definable in terms of *earlier* and $pres_{(i)}$, we obtain the following.

(86) Where A and B are wffs of IQ^E, these are strong IQ-valid.

(i) $past_{(i)}\neg A \leftrightarrow \exists^i t\,(earlier(t,i) \wedge \neg pres_{(t)}A)$,
provided t does not occur in $past_{(i)}\neg A$

(ii) $past_{(i)}(A \wedge B) \leftrightarrow \exists^i t\,(earlier(t,i) \wedge pres_{(t)}A \wedge pres_{(t)}B)$,
provided t does not occur in $past_{(i)}(A \wedge B)$

(iii) $past_{(i)}\exists x\, A \leftrightarrow \exists x\, past_{(i)}A$

(iv) $past_{(i)}\exists^i t\, A \leftrightarrow \exists^i t\, past_{(i)}A$,
provided t is not i

(87) Where A and B are wffs of IQ^E, these are also strong IQ-valid.

(i) $fut_{(i)}\neg A \leftrightarrow \exists^i t\,(earlier(i,t) \wedge \neg pres_{(t)}A)$,
provided t does not occur in $fut_{(i)}\neg A$

(ii) $fut_{(i)}(A \wedge B) \leftrightarrow \exists^i t\,(earlier(i,t) \wedge pres_{(t)}A \wedge pres_{(t)}B)$,
provided t does not occur in $fut_{(i)}(A \wedge B)$

(iii) $fut_{(i)}\exists x\, A \leftrightarrow \exists x\, fut_{(i)}A$

(iv) $fut_{(i)}\exists^i t\, A \leftrightarrow \exists^i t\, fut_{(i)}A$,
provided t is not i

We can now use (86) and (87) to reduce the translations of IQ^S in IQ^E, that is, to reduce the complexity of a formula within the scope of a tense operator. The equivalences below should be read subject to the usual restrictions about renaming variables to avoid unwanted binding.

(88) Where A is a wff of IQ^S, the following translations are strong IQ-valid.

(i) $\Theta(PRES_{(i)}\neg A) \leftrightarrow now(i) \wedge \neg pres_{(i)}\Theta A$

(ii) $\Theta(PAST_{(i)}\neg A) \leftrightarrow now(i) \wedge \exists^i t\,(earlier(t,i) \wedge \neg pres_{(t)}\Theta A)$

(iii) $\Theta(FUT_{(i)}\neg A) \leftrightarrow now(i) \wedge \exists^i t\,(earlier(i,t) \wedge \neg pres_{(t)}\Theta A)$

(89) Where A and B are wffs of IQ^S, the following translations are

strong IQ-valid.

(i) $\Theta(PRES_{(i)}\,(A \wedge B)) \leftrightarrow now(i) \wedge pres_{(i)}\Theta A \wedge pres_{(i)}\Theta B$

(ii) $\Theta(PAST_{(i)}\,(A \wedge B)) \leftrightarrow$

$now(i) \wedge \exists^{i}t\,(earlier(t,i) \wedge pres_{(t)}\,\Theta A \wedge pres_{(t)}\Theta B)$

(iii) $\Theta(FUT_{(i)}\,(\mathrm{A} \wedge B)) \leftrightarrow$

$now(i) \wedge \exists^{i}t\,(earlier(i,t) \wedge pres_{(t)}\,\Theta A \wedge pres_{(t)}\Theta B)$

(90) Where A is a wff of IQ^S, the following are strong IQ-valid.

(i) $\Theta(PRES_{(i)}\mathrm{G}t\,A) \leftrightarrow now(i) \wedge \exists^{i}t\;pres_{(i)}\,(now(t) \wedge \Theta A)$

(ii) $\Theta(PAST_{(i)}\mathrm{G}t\,A) \leftrightarrow now(i) \wedge \exists^{i}t\;past_{(i)}\,(now(t) \wedge \Theta A)$

(iii) $\Theta(FUT_{(i)}\mathrm{G}t\,A) \leftrightarrow now(i) \wedge \exists^{i}t\;fut_{(i)}\,(now(t) \wedge \Theta A)$

The proofs of (88)-(90) will be left to the reader. It will be noted that (88) and (89) conform strictly to the pattern of reduction steps: where the principal tense operator on the lefthand side applies to the wff A, all the occurrences of tenses on the righthand side apply to proper subformulas of A. This is not the case in (90). Here the tenses on the righthand side all have scope over conjunctions which contain a conjunct not appearing on the lefthand side, viz. *now(t)* in (90). However, the wffs on the righthand side can all be further reduced by applying (85), (86) and (87) as appropriate. Though (90) may not strictly reduce the wffs on the lefthand side, it specifies essential steps in their reduction.[30]

In IQ^S one cannot generally shorten arbitrary sequences of tense operators. While the following equivalences hold in IQ^S,

---

30 If we assume that $\mathrm{G}t\,A$ is of the form $\mathrm{G}t\,\Pi B$ and G binds a variable in the tense operator Π, then the tense operators on the righthand side apply to wffs of lower complexity than those on the lefthand side. For example, consider the wff

(a) $PAST_{(i)}\mathrm{G}t\;FUT_{(t)}\,A$

By (90) this can be reduced to the wff,

(b) $now(i) \wedge \exists^{i}t\;past_{(i)}(now(t) \wedge fut_{(t)}\Theta A)$

The conjunction inside the tense operator $past_{(i)}$ happens to be the translation of the wff

(c) $FUT_{(t)}A$

and so the relevant instance of (90) is the following.

(d) $\Theta(PAST_{(i)}\mathrm{G}t\;FUT_{(w,t)}A\,) \leftrightarrow now(i) \wedge \exists^{i}t\;past_{(i)}\,\Theta(FUT_{(t)}A)$

(91) (i) $PRES_{(i)}PRES_{(i)}A \leftrightarrow PRES_{(i)}A$

(ii) $PRES_{(i)}PAST_{(i)}A \leftrightarrow PAST_{(i)}A$

(iii) $PRES_{(i)}FUT_{(i)}A \leftrightarrow FUT_{(i)}A$

there is no way of abbreviating wffs such as $PAST_{(i)}FUT_{(t)}A$. One can, however, reduce the translation of every satisfiable sequence of IQ^S tense operators, i.e. their translations in IQ^E. We state the relevant equivalences in (92)-(94), the first of which relates to the IQ^S sequences indicated in (91).

(92) Where A is a wff of IQ^S, these are strong IQ-valid.

(i) $\Theta(PRES_{(i)}PRES_{(i)}A) \leftrightarrow now(i) \wedge pres_{(i)}\Theta A$

(ii) $\Theta(PRES_{(i)}PAST_{(i)}A) \leftrightarrow now(i) \wedge past_{(i)}\Theta A$

(iii) $\Theta(PRES_{(i)}FUT_{(i)}A) \leftrightarrow now(i) \wedge fut_{(i)}\Theta A$

For sequences of tense operators beginning with $PAST_{(i)}$, we have to invoke the predicate *earlier*.

(93) Where A is an IQ^S wff, these are strong IQ-valid.

(i) $\Theta(PAST_{(i)}PRES_{(t)}A) \leftrightarrow now(i) \wedge earlier(t,i) \wedge pres_{(t)}\Theta A$

(ii) $\Theta(PAST_{(i)}PAST_{(t)}A) \leftrightarrow now(i) \wedge earlier(t,i) \wedge past_{(t)}\Theta A$

(iii) $\Theta(PAST_{(i)}FUT_{(t)}A) \leftrightarrow now(i) \wedge earlier(t,i) \wedge fut_{(t)}\Theta A$

PROOF. We shall only prove (ii) since (i) and (iii) are proved in a similar way.

(a) Suppose $[\![\Theta(PAST_{(i)}PAST_{(t)}A)]\!]^{\mathbf{M},\mathbf{g}}(j) = \mathbf{t}$. Then
$[\![now(i) \wedge past_{(i)}\Theta(PAST_{(t)}A)]\!]^{\mathbf{M},\mathbf{g}}(j) = \mathbf{t}$. Thus
(1) $[\![i]\!]^{\mathbf{M},\mathbf{g}} = j$ and $[\![\Theta(PAST_{(t)}A)]\!]^{\mathbf{M},\mathbf{g}}(k) = \mathbf{t}$ for some k « j. So
$[\![now(t) \wedge past_{(t)}\Theta A]\!]^{\mathbf{M},\mathbf{g}}(k) = \mathbf{t}$; that is, $[\![t]\!]^{\mathbf{M},\mathbf{g}} = k$ and
$[\![past_{(t)}\Theta A]\!]^{\mathbf{M},\mathbf{g}}(k) = \mathbf{t}$. Since $[\![t]\!]^{\mathbf{M},\mathbf{g}} = k$, k « j and $[\![i]\!]^{\mathbf{M},\mathbf{g}} = j$,
(2) $[\![earlier(t,i)]\!]^{\mathbf{M},\mathbf{g}} = \mathbf{t}$. Moreover, since $[\![past_{(t)}\Theta A]\!]^{\mathbf{M},\mathbf{g}}(k) = \mathbf{t}$,
(3) $[\![past_{(t)}\Theta A]\!]^{\mathbf{M},\mathbf{g}}(j) = \mathbf{t}$.
Together (1), (2) and (3) entail
(4) $[\![now(i) \wedge earlier(t,i) \wedge past_{(t)}\Theta A]\!]^{\mathbf{M},\mathbf{g}}(j) = \mathbf{t}$.

(b) Suppose $[\![now(i) \wedge earlier(t,i) \wedge past_{(t)}\Theta A]\!]^{\mathbf{M},g}(j) = \mathbf{t}$.Then $[\![i]\!]^{\mathbf{M},g} = j$, $[\![t]\!]^{\mathbf{M},g} \ll [\![i]\!]^{\mathbf{M},g}$ and $[\![\Theta A]\!]^{\mathbf{M},g}(k) = \mathbf{t}$ for some $k \ll [\![t]\!]^{\mathbf{M},g}$. Then $[\![now(t) \wedge past_{(t)}\Theta A]\!]^{\mathbf{M},g}([\![t]\!]^{\mathbf{M},g}) = \mathbf{t}$; that is, $[\![\Theta(PAST_{(t)}\Theta A]\!]^{\mathbf{M},g}([\![t]\!]^{\mathbf{M},g}) = \mathbf{t}$. Since $[\![t]\!]^{\mathbf{M},g} \ll [\![i]\!]^{\mathbf{M},g}$ and $[\![i]\!]^{\mathbf{M},g} = j$, it follows that $[\![now(i) \wedge past_{(i)}\Theta(PAST_{(t)}A]\!]^{\mathbf{M},g}(j) = \mathbf{t}$; that is, $[\![\Theta(PAST_{(i)}PAST_{(t)}\Theta A)]\!]^{\mathbf{M},g}(j) = \mathbf{t}$. □

For sequences of IQ^S tense operators beginning with $FUT_{(i)}$, the following equivalences hold.

(94) Where A is a wff of IQ^S, these are strong IQ-valid.

- (i) $\Theta(FUT_{(i)}PRES_{(t)}A) \leftrightarrow now(i) \wedge earlier(i,t) \wedge pres_{(t)}\Theta A$
- (ii) $\Theta(FUT_{(i)}PAST_{(t)}A) \leftrightarrow now(i) \wedge earlier(i,t) \wedge past_{(t)}\Theta A$
- (iii) $\Theta(FUT_{(i)}FUT_{(t)}A) \leftrightarrow now(i) \wedge earlier(i,t) \wedge fut_{(t)}\Theta A$.

This completes the formal chararacterization of the translation of IQ^S into IQ^E. We shall now turn our attention to the relation between IQ^E and IQ-Prolog.

§7 IQ^E and IQ-Prolog

We said above that IQ^E can be used to regiment IQ-Prolog. To this end we must extend IQ^E slightly so as to accommodate explicit reference to points. This is a straightforward matter which does not affect any of the technical results established so far. They all carry over to the extended system, which we call IQ^{Et} ('t' for times). Syntactically IQ^{Et} is just like IQ^E with the following additions.

(95) (i) An infinite set of point variables V_T: m and n range arbitrarily over this set.

(ii) An infinite set of point parameters P_T: $m^{\dagger}$ and $n^{\dagger}$ range arbitrarily over this set.

(iii) A two-place predicate *before*.

(iv) A new point quantifier $\exists^t$.

The definition of wff is supplemented by these two clauses.

(96) (i) Where a and b belong to $V_T \cup P_T$, $before(a, b)$ is an atomic wff.

(ii) Where A is a wff, $\exists^t m\, A$ is a wff.[31]

To accommodate these additions semantically we need only adjust the semantics of IQ^E slightly. In the previous chapter we defined an IQ-structure on the basis of an assumed point structure $\langle T, < \rangle$. We now bring this assumption explicitly into the definition of an IQ-structure for IQ^{Et}.

(97) An IQ-structure for IQ^{Et} is a septuple $\langle D, T, I_T, <, \ll, \text{ç}, f\rangle$ which is defined exactly as for IQ^E except for these additions.

(i) T is a nonempty set of elements which is strictly ordered by <;

(ii) $\text{ç}(m^{\dagger})$ is in T, where $m^{\dagger}$ is in P_T.

We also extend the definition of an IQ-interpretation $\langle \mathbf{M,g} \rangle$ such that,

(98) $\mathrm{g}(m)$ is in T, where m is in V_T.

As with all variables and parameters, the denotations of point variables and parameters remain constant across different indices of evaluation.

(99) (i) $[\![m^{\dagger}]\!]^{\mathbf{M,g}}(\mathrm{j}) = \text{ç}(m^{\dagger})$;

(ii) $[\![m]\!]^{\mathbf{M,g}}(\mathrm{j}) = \mathrm{g}(m)$.

For such rigidly denoting expressions we follow the convention above and delete reference to the index of evaluation. The required amendments to the

---

[31] As in the case of the other existential quantifiers, the corresponding universal quantifier can be introduced by the standard definition.

truth definition are as one might expect, except that there is no need to invoke the third truth value **u** since all wffs are either true or false at a point.[32]

(100) (i) $[\![\exists^t m A]\!]^{M,g}(j) =$
- **t**, if $[\![A]\!]^{M,g(m,a)}(j) = t$ for some a in T;
- **f**, if $[\![A]\!]^{M,g(m,a)}(j) = f$ for all a in T.

(ii) $[\![before(a,b)]\!]^{M,g}(j) =$
- **t**, if $[\![a]\!]^{M,g} < [\![b]\!]^{M,g}$;
- **f**, if not $[\![a]\!]^{M,g} < [\![b]\!]^{M,g}$.

We can now proceed to use IQ^{Et} in the service of IQ-Prolog.

The aim is to interpret as much of IQ-Prolog as possible in IQ^{Et}. To begin we must draw a distinction between the *elementary* predicates of IQ-Prolog, those like 'promote' and 'professor', and the so-called *higher-order* predicates, such as 'at' and 'past'. The former are just like the predicate constants of IQ^{Et} and are treated as such, both syntactically and semantically. The latter are rather similar to sentential operators and will be defined accordingly. There are also *reserved* predicates in IQ-Prolog, of which '<' and '«' are two; the first takes point expressions as arguments and the second interval expressions. They are interpreted in IQ^{Et} by relations < and « respectively, i.e. like 'before' and 'earlier'. As for referring expressions, they are all assimilated to parameters in IQ^{Et}: the individual names of IQ-Prolog, e.g. 'sally' and 'max', are assimilated to the individual parameters of IQ^{Et}, while the temporal expressions, those referring to points or intervals, to the corresponding types of IQ^{Et} parameters.[33] Their interpretations are thus uniformly rigid.

The higher-order predicates of IQ-Prolog are defined in a similar way to the tense operators of IQ^S. From a syntactic point of view these predicates when taken together with their first argument may be understood as complex

---

32 See the truth definition for IQ given in Chapter 6.

33 Names are assimilated to parameters because their denotations are required to be rigid. Rigidity does not necessarily hold for individual constants.

sentential operators, and their interpretations will be formulated accordingly. We consider four such operators, viz. 'at' and the three tenses 'pres', 'past' and 'fut'.[34] To define them we invoke the distinction between elementary and higher-order wffs. The *elementary wffs* of IQ-Prolog are the atomic wffs composed of elementary predicates and individual symbols (variables or parameters).[35] The *higher-order wffs* are those of the form *H(i, A)*, where *H* is a higher-order predicate, *i* an interval expression and *A* an elementary wff.

(101) Where i is any interval variable or parameter, and A any elementary wff,

(i) $[\![\mathrm{at}(i, A)]\!]^{\mathbf{M,g}}(\mathrm{j}) = [\![A]\!]^{\mathbf{M,g}}([\![i]\!]^{\mathbf{M,g}})$;

(ii) $[\![\mathrm{pres}(i, A)]\!]^{\mathbf{M,g}}(\mathrm{j}) =$

- **t**, if $[\![i]\!]^{\mathbf{M,g}} = \mathrm{j}$ and $[\![A]\!]^{\mathbf{M,g}}(\mathrm{j}) = \mathbf{t}$;
- **f**, if $[\![i]\!]^{\mathbf{M,g}} \neq \mathrm{j}$ or $[\![A]\!]^{\mathbf{M,g}}(\mathrm{j}) = \mathbf{f}$;
- **u**, otherwise.

(iii) $[\![\mathrm{past}(i, A)]\!]^{\mathbf{M,g}}(\mathrm{j}) =$

- **t**, if $[\![i]\!]^{\mathbf{M,g}} = \mathrm{j}$ and there is a $\mathrm{k} \ll [\![i]\!]^{\mathbf{M,g}}$ such that $[\![A]\!]^{\mathbf{M,g}}(\mathrm{k}) = \mathbf{t}$,
- **f**, if $[\![i]\!]^{\mathbf{M,g}} \neq \mathrm{j}$ or there is a $\mathrm{k} \ll [\![i]\!]^{\mathbf{M,g}}$ such that $[\![A]\!]^{\mathbf{M,g}}(\mathrm{k}) = \mathbf{f}$ and for all other $\mathrm{l} \ll [\![i]\!]^{\mathbf{M,g}}$, $[\![A]\!]^{\mathbf{M,g}}(\mathrm{l}) = \mathbf{f}$ or **u**,
- **u**, otherwise.

(iv) $[\![\mathrm{fut}(i, A)]\!]^{\mathbf{M,g}}(\mathrm{j}) =$

- **t**, if $[\![i]\!]^{\mathbf{M,g}} = \mathrm{j}$ and there is a k such that $[\![i]\!]^{\mathbf{M,g}} \ll \mathrm{k}$ and $[\![A]\!]^{\mathbf{M,g}}(\mathrm{k}) = \mathbf{t}$,
- **f**, if $[\![i]\!]^{\mathbf{M,g}} \neq \mathrm{j}$ or there is a k such that $[\![i]\!]^{\mathbf{M,g}} \ll \mathrm{k}$ and $[\![A]\!]^{\mathbf{M,g}}(\mathrm{k}) = \mathbf{f}$ and for all other l such that $[\![i]\!]^{\mathbf{M,g}} \ll \mathrm{l}$, $[\![A]\!]^{\mathbf{M,g}}(\mathrm{l}) = \mathbf{f}$ or **u**,

---

34 The predicate 'fut' has not been used so far, but we include it for the sake of completeness.

35 Note that '<' and '«' are not elementary predicates but '=' is.

• **u**, otherwise.[36]

It should be noted that the meanings of 'at' and 'pres', although very similar, are different. This is intended to reflect the fact that in IQ-Prolog they are used in slightly different ways. As we illustrated above, 'at' is used to record basic facts in the database, while 'pres' is used only in queries. The difference is of more than procedural significance since tensed queries take a temporal perspective on the database. That is, they are initiated with respect to an interval which is regarded as 'now', the current perspective. This feature is captured in the definitions of the tenses: the requirement that $[\![i]\!]^{\mathbf{M},g}$ be identical to j is tantamount to stipulating that j must be 'now'.[37]

There are two other temporal operators which appear in IQ-Prolog, viz. 'at_hom' and 'in'. The interpretation of 'at_hom' is exactly the same as that of 'at'.

(102) Where *i* is any interval variable or parameter, and *A* any elementary wff, $[\![\text{at}(i, A)]\!]^{\mathbf{M},g}(\text{j}) = [\![\text{at\_hom}(i, A)]\!]^{\mathbf{M},g}(\text{j})$

Unlike 'at', however, 'at_hom' also plays a rôle in an axiom, i.e. a procedure, which expresses an important property of IQ-Prolog. Let us take as given the procedure which specifies the subinterval predicate 'sub' (another *reserved* predicate). Recall that in IQ-Prolog intervals are defined by means of pairs of points, and the subinterval relation is specified by invoking the ordering on those points. Earlier we adumbrated the requisite conditions by means of the following, which are actually abbreviations of several clauses.

(26*) sub([a,b), [c,d)) :- c ≤ a, b ≤ d.

(27*) sub([a,b], [c,d)) :- c ≤ a, b < d.

---

[36] It can be readily verified that these definitions respect the procedures which are associated with the tenses in IQ-Prolog. We shall consider the status of procedures below.

[37] Recall that $[\![now(i)]\!]^{\mathbf{M},g}(\text{j})$ is true if $[\![i]\!]^{\mathbf{M},g} = \text{j}$, and false if $[\![i]\!]^{\mathbf{M},g} \neq \text{j}$.

The following interpretation of 'sub' obviously respects (26*) and (27*). Here it is convenient to identify the reserved wffs of IQ-Prolog since they are involved in the definition. The *reserved wffs* are those of the form *R(i, i')*, where *R* is a reserved predicate, and *i* and *i'* are interval expressions.

(103) Where *i* and *i'* are interval expressions, $[\![\text{sub}(i, i')]\!]^{M,g}(j)$ =
- **t**, if $[\![i]\!]^{M,g}$ is a subinterval of $[\![i']\!]^{M,g}$,
- **f**, if $[\![i]\!]^{M,g}$ is not a subinterval of $[\![i']\!]^{M,g}$.[38]

In contrast to 'sub', there is just one procedural clause for the higher-order predicate 'at_hom'.

(25*) at_hom(X,A) :- at(Y,A), sub(X,Y).[39]

Given that 'at_hom' and 'at' are assigned the same meaning, (25*) can be read as specifying part of the homogeneity condition. That is,

(104) If $[\![\text{at}(i, \text{A})]\!]^{M,g}(j)$ = **t** and $[\![k]\!]^{M,g}$ is a subinterval of $[\![i]\!]^{M,g}$, $[\![\text{at}(k, \text{A})]\!]^{M,g}(j)$ = **t**.[40]

It will be remembered that 'at_hom' occurs in the body in other procedures, e.g. in these two.

(28*) pres(X,A) :- at_hom(X,A).

(29*) past(X,A) :- at_hom(Y,A), Y « X.

[38] Since *i* and *i'* are always defined, so too is the given wff.

[39] Observe that here 'X', 'Y' and 'A' are all variables of the object language; they are not meta-expressions. Because of the status of 'A', the interpretation of (25*) requires special handling.

[40] Note that 'at(*i*,A)' may not always be defined: if the denotation assigned to 'A' is not constant throughout the interval assigned to *i* , then the truth value of 'at(*i*,A)' will be u, viz. undefined.

Plainly, the interpretations of the predicates involved in (25*), (28*) and (29*) respect the intended content of the procedures. The formal status of these procedures will be considered below.

Another example of a higher-order predicate is 'in', which is defined as follows subject to the usual restrictions.

(105) $[\![\text{in}(i, A)]\!]^{M,g}(j) =$

- **t**, if $[\![A]\!]^{M,g}(k) = $ **t** for some k which is a subinterval of $[\![i]\!]^{M,g}$;
- **f**, if $[\![A]\!]^{M,g}(k) = $ **f** for some k which is a subinterval of $[\![i]\!]^{M,g}$ and for all other subintervals l of $[\![i]\!]^{M,g}$, $[\![A]\!]^{M,g}(l) = $ **f** or **u**;
- **u**, otherwise.

There are two procedures in which 'in' occurs; it appears in the head of one and the body of the other.

(47*) in(X,A) :- at_hom(Y,A), sub(Y,X).

(48*) past(X,in(Y,A)) :- in(Y,A), Y « X.

Again it can be immediately seen that the interpretation of 'in' is congruent with the envisaged content of the procedures. In fact, (47*) simply reflects one part of the truth definition.

The two logical connectives in IQ-Prolog are defined by their 'translations' in IQ^{Et}; conjunction and implication have the truth tables for $\wedge$ and $\rightarrow$ respectively.[41] So far we have distinguished the need for three different types of quantifier in IQ-Prolog, and for each type there is an existential and universal quantifer. The individual quantifiers are interpreted by $\exists$ and $\forall$, the interval quantifiers by $\exists^i$ and $\forall^i$, and the point quantifiers by $\exists^t$ and $\forall^t$.[42]

---

[41] Here ':-' is just the arrow read backwards, and conjunction is represented by ','.

[42] Note that the kind of quantifier is determined by the place of the variable in the formula.

Finally, we come to the interpretation of the procedures. Those which do not involve higher-order predicates, e.g. (26*) and (27*), are no problem; their interpretations in IQ^{Et} are fixed by what we have already said. Such is not the case, however, for higher-order procedures such as (29*). How are higher-order variables like 'A' to be interpreted? There are no corresponding variables in IQ^{Et}. It may be tempting to think of them as meta-variables, which take elementary formulas as their values. This approach might work if the range of values could be restricted to ground formulas, i.e. those not containing free variables. Consider the query 'past(i, promote(X))', which would invoke the procedure (29*), assigning 'promote(X)' to 'A'. How is the variable 'X' to be interpreted here? Does it have the status of a genuine free variable, i.e. one available for assignment? Or does it have the status of a quoted expression, which cannot sustain meaningful assignments? We shall not attempt to resolve this issue; instead we adopt an alternative strategy in which occurrences of 'A' are treated as object-language variables ranging over propositions.

To implement this we extend IQ^{Et}, calling the richer system IQ^{Etp} ('p' for propositions). In contrast to previous extensions, IQ^{Etp} is supplemented only with variables of the propositional type; there are no constants or parameters of this type.

(106) Let V_P be an infinite set of propositional variables, with δ ranging arbitrarily over this set.

To bind these variables IQ^{Etp} has the sorted quantifier $\exists^p$ (with $\forall^p$ introduced by definition). The definition of wff includes these two additional clauses.

(107) (i) If Φ^n is an n-place propositional operator and $\delta_1,\ldots,\delta_n$ are propositional variables, then the result of placing the variables in the formula positions, designated as $\Phi^n(\delta_1,\ldots,\delta_n)$, is a wff.[43]

[43] The propositional operators include the logical connnectives and the tense operators, but not the quantifiers.

(ii) Where A is any wff and δ any propositional variable, $\exists^{p}\delta A$.

The definitions of an IQ-structure and IQ-interpretation are amended as one might expect. An IQ-structure for IQ^{Etp} is an octuple $\langle D, T, P, I_T, <, «, ç, \mathbf{f}\rangle$ which is defined exactly as for IQ^{Et} except for this addition.

(108) P is the set of propositions consisting of all functions from I_T to $\{\mathbf{t}, \mathbf{u}, \mathbf{f}\}$.

Since there are no propositional constants or parameters, nothing further is needed. The concept of an IQ-interpretation must, however, be extended to cover assignments to the propositional variables.

(109) $g(\delta)$ is in P, for all δ in V_P.

There are two amendments required to the truth definition, one for the new quantifiers and the other for the propositional operators. In the case of the latter, one general revision is sufficient.

(110) The definitions of the propositional operators are adjusted to allow A to be either a wff or a propositional variable; otherwise they are exactly as before.

In the case of the quantifiers, it is only necessary to give the definition of the existential quantifier since the universal quantifier can be introduced by the usual abbreviation.

(111) $[\![\exists^{p}\delta A]\!]^{M,g}(j) =$

- $\mathbf{t}$, $[\![A]\!]^{M,g(\delta,p)}(j) = \mathbf{t}$ for some p in P;
- $\mathbf{f}$, $[\![A]\!]^{M,g(\delta,p)}(j) = \mathbf{f}$ for all p in P;
- $\mathbf{u}$, otherwise.

Now we are in a position to specify the interpretation of the higher-order procedures of IQ-Prolog. Its higher-order variables, such as 'A', are assimilated to δ and the higher-order quantifiers to $\exists^{p}$ and $\forall^{p}$.

One might wonder whether IQ^{Etp} is potentially inconsistent. The first thing to note is that IQ^{Etp} does not contain the facility for self-reference, at least not as it stands. But even if it did, the system would not thereby become inconsistent, as Kripke (1975) has indicated. IQ^{Etp} is a many-valued system based on Kleene's strong three-valued logic, and Kripke has shown that such a logic can consistently contain its own truth predicate.[44] One might also wonder whether IQ^{Etp} can be translated into a many-sorted first-order system. It is worth emphasizing that whatever form such a translation might take, it would still result in a many-valued system. The homogeneity condition inherited by IQ^{Etp} from IQ requires the third truth value 'undefined'.

To see what we have gained by interpreting IQ-Prolog in IQ^{Etp}, we must now consider the relation of logical consequence. In Chapter 6 we defined the notion of IQ-validity but did not develop its import for consequence. The obvious definition is perhaps the following since it reflects the non-classical character of IQ.

(112) $\Delta \models \varphi$ iff for every IQ-structure **M** whenever all the wffs in Δ have a designated value in **M** so does φ.

Clearly the rule of modus ponens fails in IQ on this definition (as does the deduction theorem). Let Δ consist of the wffs $(A \rightarrow B)$ and A. On the assumption that A has the value u and B the value f, $(A \rightarrow B)$ has the value u, thus giving a counter-example. But the rule of modus ponens holds in PROLOG and hence in IQ-Prolog. This can be accommodated by introducing a stronger notion of logical consequence.

(113) $\Delta \models_S \varphi$ iff for every IQ-structure **M** whenever the value of φ is **f** in **M** there is some wff in Δ which is either **f** or **u** in **M**.[45]

44 As a modal system, IQ^{Etp} is not 'vulnerable' to Montague's result. See Montague (1963).

45 For a detailed study of this definition and its implications, see Chapter 8.

It can be shown that (113) coincides with the classical definition, even though the basic semantics of IQ is many-valued.[46] Significantly, the definition of IQ-validity need not be changed; indeed, some would say that it 'fits' better with (113) than (112).

(114) A wff φ is *IQ-valid* iff in every IQ-structure **M** φ always has a designated value (either **t** or **u**).[47]

By (114) the wff corresponding to the rule of modus ponens is IQ-valid.

(115) $(A \wedge (A \rightarrow B)) \rightarrow B$

In fact, all wffs which are classically valid are IQ-valid. This may suggest that consequence in the system IQ should be defined classically, i.e. as $\models_S$. It is plain, in any event, that $\models_S$ is required for IQ^{Etp} if it is to serve as an interpretation of IQ-Prolog. We therefore let (113) define the notion of consequence in IQ^{Etp}, assuming an appropriately extended concept of an IQ-structure. We also let (114), similarly amended, define the notion of IQ^{Etp}-validity.[48]

At this point the connection between IQ^{Etp} and IQ-Prolog becomes evident: IQ-Prolog is effectively the Horn clause fragment of IQ^{Etp} and as such, is a many-valued, modal system. Among its modal operators are 'at', 'at_hom' and the tenses, which were shown to provide an expressive capability not currently shared by the Event Calculus. IQ-Prolog also contains the resources for introducing an extensive range of new modal operators designed to handle a wide variety of temporal expressions in natural language. In Chapters 1-5 it was shown how various types of temporal expressions in natural language can be analyzed within the IQ framework.

[46] Note that the definitions of the logical constants remain as before, as do the definitions of an IQ-structure and an IQ-interpretation.
[47] The definition of what it is to have a designated value in an IQ-structure is given in Chapter 6.
[48] These definitions of course assume suitable definitions of what it is to be true (have a designated value) in an IQ^{Etp}- structure.

Since these analyses can be formulated within IQ^{Etp}, they are available to enhance IQ-Prolog, subject of course to the Horn clause restriction. Given the relation between IQ-Prolog and IQ^{Etp}, the interface between the temporal fragment of natural language and PROLOG becomes considerably more tractable. The key is the status of the modal operators: their principle rôle (though not necessarily their only rôle) is with respect to database query, not the representation of information. The way this is 'implemented' in IQ-Prolog may serve to indicate how other modalities could be made similarly tractable.

8

On IQ^{int} and Related Systems

JAAP VAN DER DOES

Introduction

The original aim of the system IQ, introduced in Chapter 1 and formally refined in Chapter 6, was to give a satisfactory semantics of both tenses and temporal quantifiers. In Chapter 7 it is shown that this system also provides a promising framework for building temporal databases. The explanation lies in the use of intervals satisfying the 'homogeneity condition', together with a language powerful enough to refer to these intervals. But how do we formalize intervals? Do we take points or intervals as primitives? From a logical point of view, the difference between these approaches must not be exaggerated. When we have intervals, points can be defined and vice versa. As Van Benthem (1983) shows, a liberal stance enables us to enjoy a fruitful interplay between point and periods (i.e. intervals). With a view to applications, however, there may be a significant difference. The choice of which is to be primitive, may not be a matter of taste, but of computational efficiency.

In Chapter 7 the road from IQ to PROLOG, implemented as IQ-Prolog goes via a two sorted partial predicate logic IQ^E. IQ^E allows quantification not only over objects, but also over intervals. The intended semantics of this language coincides by and large with that of IQ. So what about the semantics of IQ-Prolog itself? Does it have an intensional semantics too, or, is the classical (declarative) semantics of PROLOG sufficient? There are reasons to argue for the former, but here we will defend the latter.

As it stands, the semantics of IQ and IQ^E are both based on the notion of an interval, but this notion is not taken to be primitive. Instead, intervals are conceived as the convex sets of a linearly ordered point structure, i.e. they are defined by $[a,b] := \{x \mid a < x < b\}$ and similarly for other sorts of interval. As a result, a full range of intervals is available, among which we have 'point' or singleton intervals. Despite the attractiveness of this approach, in this chapter we adopt a somewhat different stance. Here we take seriously the idea that intervals and not points are basic. The main reason for doing so, besides theoretical interest, is that this move enables us to characterize the interval structure by means of first order axioms, most of which are in the Horn clause fragment.

The precise ramifications of our departure from the original IQ and IQ^E is a subject for further investigation, not to be addressed here. Our immediate aim is to provide precise definitions of the syntax and semantics of the interval-based IQ^{int}, and give an axiom system which is sound and complete with respect to this semantics. These results will be found in Section 2. The completeness proof will make use of a notion of logical consequence which, although defined in regard to a partial environment, equals classical consequence. This consequence relation will be discussed in Section 1. In the last section we provide soundness and completeness results for extensions similar to those of IQ^E defined in Chapter 7, by treating the general case of having denumerable many sorts. Here we extend Smullyan's results that underlie his Unifying Principle and set them in a partial environment. A natural move, since they already had a strong partial flavour.[1]

---

1 See Smullyan (1968: 65), and also van Benthem (1984: 6).

For readers who are acquainted with the completeness proof for classical predicate logic, this chapter can also be viewed as a fairly detailed introduction to the use of downward closed sets (Hintikka sets) in a partial setting.

§1 Partial Predicate Logic

To set the stage, we define the notion of a partial model for a first-order predicate logical language. After discussing the monotonicity of Kleene's strong interpretation with respect to an extension relation between partial models, we highlight an appropriate notion of logical consequence. Next we show that this notion of partial logical consequence coincides with the classical consequence relation. It follows that the partial notion of consequence can be recursively enumerated by means of whatever 'classical' axiom-system one likes to choose.

1.1 Partial Models and Monotonicity

In this section we will limit our attention to first-order predicate languages without function symbols and identity. This enables us to get a clear view of the main features of the semantics. The 'full-blown' case will be treated in Section 3. Now, what is a partial model?

1.1.1 PARTIAL MODELS. A partial model **M** is a tuple $(\mathbf{D},*)$, with **D** a non-empty set and * a partial interpretation function such that:

1. $c^* \in \mathbf{D}$, for all constants c in the domain of *;
2. for all n-place relation symbols R:
   $R^* = \langle R^+, R^- \rangle$ with R^+, R^- disjoint and $R^+, R^- \subseteq \mathbf{D}^n$.

We call R^+ the extension, and R^- the anti-extension of R. The interpretation of an n-place relation symbol is *total*, if $R^- \cup R^+ = \mathbf{D}^n$. **M** is *classical* if all constants are in the domain of * and if all interpretations of relation symbols are total.[2]

As usual, when interpreting a formula in a model, we have to take care of the free variables. To remain in the spirit of this semantics, we use partial instead of total assignments. The value of a term, i.e. variables or individual constants, with respect to a model and an assignment will have the standard definition and notation: $[\![t]\!]^{M,g}$.[3] Given these preliminaries, we can ask ourselves what it means for a sentence to be verified or falsified by a partial model. Kleene's strong interpretation provides an answer.

1.1.2 VERIFICATION AND REFUTATION. Let $\mathbf{M} = (\mathbf{D},*)$ be a partial model and g an assignment for **M**. In regard to g, **M** verifies a formula φ (notation: $\mathbf{M}\models^{+}\varphi$ [g]) or **M** refutes a formula φ (notation: $\mathbf{M}\models^{-}\varphi$ [g]) iff the following holds :

$$\begin{array}{lcl}
\mathbf{M} \models^{+} R(t_1,\ldots,t_n)\ [g] & \Leftrightarrow & \langle [\![t_1]\!],\ldots, [\![t_n]\!]\rangle \in R^{+} \\
\mathbf{M} \models^{-} R(t_1,\ldots,t_n)\ [g] & \Leftrightarrow & \langle [\![t_1]\!],\ldots, [\![t_n]\!]\rangle \in R^{-} \\
\mathbf{M} \not\models^{+} \bot\ [g] & \text{and} & \mathbf{M} \models^{-} \bot\ [g]^{4} \\
\mathbf{M} \models^{+} \psi \rightarrow \chi\ [g] & \Leftrightarrow & \mathbf{M} \models^{-} \psi\ [g] \text{ or } \mathbf{M} \models^{+} \chi\ [g] \\
\mathbf{M} \models^{-} \psi \rightarrow \chi\ [g] & \Leftrightarrow & \mathbf{M} \models^{+} \psi\ [g] \text{ and } \mathbf{M} \models^{-} \chi\ [g] \\
\mathbf{M} \models^{+} \exists x\, \chi\ [g] & \Leftrightarrow & \mathbf{M} \models^{+} \chi\ [g^{x}_{d}] \text{ for a } d \in \mathbf{D} \\
\mathbf{M} \models^{-} \exists x\, \chi\ [g] & \Leftrightarrow & \mathbf{M} \models^{-} \chi\ [g^{x}_{d}] \text{ for all } d \in \mathbf{D}
\end{array}$$

This covers all cases.

The logical constants not mentioned in 1.1.2, are treated as abbreviations in one of the usual ways.[5]

---

2 We can define a meet relation between interpretation functions in a natural way. Thus (**mod**, ⊑), with **mod** the class of partial models, forms a *semi*-lattice. Clearly we do not have a lattice. Union of the (anti-) extensions may cause lack of disjointness.

3 Whenever possible we leave off the superscripts and simply write: $[\![t]\!]$

4 N.B. ⊥ stands for falsum.

5 This holds because *definiendum* and *definiens* are strongly equivalent. That is, they either have the same truth value, or they are both undefined. And, more important, the *definiendum* gets the falsification and verification conditions we want. (See 3.1.9 and 3.2.6)

1.2 Extending Partial Models

When dealing with partial models, it is interesting to think about extension relations between these models. There are several possibilities. For instance, given two partial models **M** = (**D**,*) and **M**' = (**D**',°) one might say that **M**' extends **M** when **D** ⊆ **D**'. It is easily seen that in this case the semantic value of a sentence may change when going from a model to one of its extensions. For existential sentences this is so with respect to refutation, and dually for universal sentences and verification. Thus, the operators T^+(**M**) and T^-(**M**), which assign to each partial model respectively the set of sentences that it verifies and the set of sentences that it refutes, are not monotone with respect to this extension relation. Another possibility, the one we shall pursue here, is captured by the following definition.

1.2.1. EXTENSION RELATION. **M** *extends* **M**', notation **M** ≤ **M**', when **M** and **M**' have the same domain, and the interpretation function ° of **M**' extends the interpretation function * of **M** as follows:

(i) for all c ∈ L: c* is defined ⇒ c* = c°, and

(ii) for all n-place relations R: $R^{*+} \subseteq R^{\circ+}$ and $R^{*-} \subseteq R^{\circ-}$

A straightforward induction on the complexity of formulas shows that the operators T^+(**M**) and T^-(**M**) are monotone with respect to the partial orders ≤ and ⊆. That is, we have the following

1.2.2. MONOTONICITY LEMMA. For all partial models **M** and **M**': **M** ≤ **M**' implies T^+(**M**) ⊆ T^+(**M**') and T^-(**M**) ⊆ T^-(**M**').

PROOF. See 3.2.9. □

For undefined sentences the situation is reversed; **M** ≤ **M**' implies $T^?$(**M**') ⊆ $T^?$(**M**), with $T^?$(**M**) the set of sentences undefined in **M**. As usual, growth of knowledge goes hand in hand with decrease of ignorance.

Although sentences may be undefined, it is not difficult to show that this is not an intrinsic property of any sentence.[6] In Kleene's semantics the logical constants do not introduce truth-value gaps. A model only leaves a sentence undefined if it does not interpret one of the non-logical constants occurring in that sentence. But then we may extend this model so that the sentence obtains a truth-value.

1.2.3. EXTENSION LEMMA. Let $\mathbf{M} = (\mathbf{D},*)$ be a partial model and Γ a set of sentences such that for some $\varphi \in \Gamma$ φ is undefined in $\mathbf{M}$ (notation: $\mathbf{M}?(\varphi)$). An $\mathbf{M}'$ can be found with $\mathbf{M} \leq \mathbf{M}'$ and all $\varphi \in \Gamma$ defined in $\mathbf{M}'$.

PROOF. See 3.2.10. □

1.3 Logical Consequence and Validity

Once we move from total to partial logic, almost all notions familiar from a classical setting have to be rethought. This is especially true for fundamental concepts like that of logical consequence. Since in a partial setting a sentence may be undefined, different notions of logical consequence are available. We are after a notion of consequence which relates the partial semantics of IQ and IQ^E to the semantics of IQ-Prolog. In this respect, most partial consequence relations will not do. A common feature of these relations is that they stay close to Tarski's definition for classical logic. If one reads '**M** verifies' for 'is true in **M**' or Tarski's definition becomes an important definition of entailment in partial logic. Thus '$\Gamma \models \varphi$' might be defined by: for all partial models **M**, if **M** verifies all $\psi \in \Gamma$ then **M** verifies φ. Or dually: for all partial models **M**, if **M** refutes φ then there is a $\psi \in \Gamma$ refuted by **M**. Some authors, for instance Wang, Scott and Blamey, use both definitions to get one 'double-barreled' notion of logical consequence[7]

---

6 For the system $\mathbf{IQ}^{\text{int}}$ the situation is different. See the discussion on strong homogeneity in section 2.2.

7 For Wang and Scott, see Feferman (1984: 263); for Blamey, see Blamey (1985: 58).

Although these consequence relations have several attractive properties, they also have some drawbacks. First of all there is the fact that none of them allow sentence schemas all of whose instances are valid. For all the instances of such a schema would be verified (or refuted) by all models. But due to the existence of the model that leaves all non-logical symbols undefined, no schema can possibly have this property. For example, definition 1.1.2 shows the instance $\bot\vee\neg\bot$ of the schema $\varphi\vee\neg\varphi$ is valid, but the instance $Pc\vee\neg Pc$ is not. The same observation makes plain that the deduction theorem for the arrow as defined in 1.1.2 fails for these consequence relations. Thus these notions of consequence are not classical enough for our purposes. There is, however, a consequence relation with all the classical features we are looking for:

1.3.1 LOGICAL CONSEQUENCE. A sentence φ follows from a set of sentences Γ if and only if for all partial models **M**, if $\mathbf{M} \models^- \varphi$, then there is a $\psi \in \Gamma$ such that $\mathbf{M} \not\models^+ \psi$.[8]

This consequence relation identifies validity with non-refutability, which is very natural when working with Kleene's strong interpretation. The same definition is proposed by Van Benthem (1984: 5) to account for the partial traits of semantic tableaux.

Let us say that φ follows partially from Γ, if φ follows from Γ according to 1.3.1. Even now we are in the position to prove

1.3.2 COINCIDENCE LEMMA. A sentence φ follows partially from a set of sentences Γ precisely when φ follows classically from Γ.

PROOF. From definition 1.1.1 we know that all classical models are special cases of the partial ones. Note that in regard to these models 'non-verifiable' and 'false' are synonyms. Hence, for the partial models that are also classical, the notion of partial logical consequence coincides with the classical

8 For an application of this definition see Chapter 7.

consequence relation. The proof from left to right is therefore obvious. On the other hand, if φ follows classically from Γ, then there cannot be a partial model **M** that refutes φ, while verifying all the sentences in Γ. Since, in view of the monotonicity lemma, the same situation holds in all **M**'s extensions. But it is readily seen that at least one of these extensions is a classical model. So φ must partially follow from Γ. □

Assuming the completeness theorem for classical predicate logic, the Coincidence Lemma shows that the notion of partial logical consequence is complete relative to all deduction systems for this logic.[9] Furthermore, we have as a corollary that partial logical consequence shares all its properties with the classical notion. However, to get a feeling for the type of argument used in this semantics, it is of some interest to prove the most salient features of partial logical consequence directly.

1.3.3 Properties of $\models$

(i) $\models$ is a reflexive and transitive relation

(ii) $\Gamma,\varphi \models \psi \Leftrightarrow \Gamma \models \varphi \rightarrow \psi$

(iii) $\Gamma \models \varphi$ and $\Gamma \subseteq \Delta \Rightarrow \Delta \models \varphi$

(iv) $\Gamma \models \varphi$ and $\Gamma \models \varphi \rightarrow \psi \Rightarrow \Gamma \models \psi$

(v) $\Gamma \models [c/x]\varphi \Rightarrow \Gamma \models \forall x.\varphi$ (c does not occur in Γ or φ)

PROOF. By way of example, we prove (ii)

---

9 Some readers may wonder what the differences are between this approach and the use of supervaluations. As is shown above, the departure of our logic from classical logic is minimal: locally we have a partial interpretation, but at the meta-level the logic is classical. This is the main difference with the supervaluation approach, where local truth and falsity are defined by means of meta-concepts like: all total extensions of a partial valuation. In our logic sentential meta-properties of sentences cannot be determined as regards a partial model. For instance, being a tautology only shows itself on a local level by being non-refutable, i.e. being true or undefined. Of course, relative to partial information some undefined contingent sentence may have the same property. So locally, we cannot distinguish between contingent and necessary non-refutable sentences. But this is mainly due to lack of expressive power of the language used. When we add modal operators implicitly quantifying over the defined extension relation, this deficiency is remedied.

(⇒:) Suppose $\Gamma,\varphi \models \psi$. I.e.:

(*) for all **M**, $\mathbf{M} \models^- \psi \Rightarrow$ there is a $\chi \in \Gamma \cup \{\varphi\}$: $\mathbf{M} \not\models^+ \chi$

Assume $\mathbf{M} \models^- \varphi \rightarrow \psi$. Then $\mathbf{M} \models^+ \varphi$ and $\mathbf{M} \models^- \psi$. Hence via (*): there is a $\chi \in \Gamma\cup\{\varphi\}$: $\mathbf{M} \not\models^+ \chi$. But $\mathbf{M} \models^+ \varphi$, hence such a χ is to be found in Γ. Thus $\Gamma \models \varphi \rightarrow \psi$.

(⇐:) Suppose $\Gamma \models \varphi \rightarrow \psi$. That is:

(*) for all **M**, $\mathbf{M} \models^- \varphi \rightarrow \psi$ there is a $\chi \in \Gamma$: $\mathbf{M} \not\models^+ \chi$.

Assume $\mathbf{M} \models^- \psi$. We have to show that there is $\chi \in \Gamma \cup \{\varphi\}$: $\mathbf{M} \not\models^+ \chi$. There are three possibilities for φ. From $\mathbf{M} \models^- \varphi$ and $\mathbf{M}?\varphi$ the conclusion follows immediately. And in case of $\mathbf{M} \models^+ \varphi$ we have $\mathbf{M} \models^- \varphi \rightarrow \psi$ and by (*) the conclusion follows also. □

The completeness result for partial logical consequence assumed completeness of classical logic. But new light is shed on some known results, when we prove completeness for classical logic via completeness for partial logic. This is done in §3. In the next section we describe how the insights obtained thus far, are related to an interval based variant of IQ^E, viz. IQ^{int}.

§2 IQ^{int}, a Two Sorted Partial Predicate Logic

2.1 The syntax of IQ^{int}

As the title of this section indicates, IQ^{int} is conceived as a two-sorted predicate logic (with a restricted form of identity). So we suppose that there are two infinite sets of variables: the individual and the interval variables, named VAR-O and VAR-I respectively. Variables of the first kind are denoted by an x with or without a subscript. The interval variables are denoted by i, again with or without a subscript. The set of non-logical constants of IQ^{int} consists of possibly empty sets of individual and interval constants, and for each $n \in \omega$ a possibly empty set of n-place relation symbols. It is assumed that the following relation symbols are always available: *now* (one place), *before* (two-place), *sub* (two-place) and E (two-place). *before* and *sub* stand for the well-known relations between intervals. E is a kind of existence predicate, the rôle of which will become clear later on. As usual, the set of individual (interval) terms is the set of individual (interval) constants plus the set of individual (interval) variables. When we talk about variables (terms) simpliciter, we mean individual or interval variables (terms). Next, for each interval term i, at(i) is the so-called *at-operator*. Finally, the logical constants we use are: $\bot$ (falsum), $\rightarrow$ (arrow), $\exists$ (existential quantifier) and = (identity). The definition of (atomic) formula is as expected:

2.1.1 ATOMIC FORMULAS. The set of atomic formulas is the smallest set such that:

(i) $\bot$ (falsum) is an atomic formula;

(ii) if i_1,i_2 are interval terms and x an object term, then $i_1 = i_2$, now(i_1), before(i_1,i_2), sub(i_1,i_2) and E(i_1,x) are atomic formulas;

(iii) if $x_1,\ldots,x_n$ are individual terms, R is an n-place relation symbol and at(i) is a sentence operator, then at(i).R($x_1,\ldots,x_n$) is an atomic formula.

2.1.2 FORMULAS. The set of formulas is the smallest set such that:

(i) all atomic formulas are formulas;

(ii) if φ is a formula not containing *now*, *before*, *sub*, = or E and at(i) is a sentence operator, then at(i).φ is a formula;[10]

(iii) if φ and ψ are formulas, then $(\varphi \rightarrow \psi)$ is a formula;

(iv) if x is an individual or interval variable and φ is a formula, then $\exists x.\varphi$ is a formula.

10 The reason for the condition on φ is that we want to have a clear distinction between the parts of a sentence dealing with the interval structure, and the facts which are related to that structure by means of the sentence operators. Besides that, we do not want to complicate matters by having to treat identity at intervals. [For the general case, see §3].

2.2 The Semantics of IQ^{int}

The semantics defined below, is very much in the spirit of the semantics of IQ as described in chapter 6.

2.2.1 IQ^{int}-MODELS.

An IQ^{int}-model **M** is a sextuple $\langle I, \{O_i\}_{i\in I}, <, \sqsubseteq, n, *\rangle$ such that:

(i) I is a non-empty set (of intervals), and for all $i \in I$ O_i is a non-empty set of objects disjoint from I.

(ii) $\langle I, <\rangle$ is a strict partial order (SPO);

(iii) $\langle I, \sqsubseteq\rangle$ is a partial order (PO);

(iv) $\langle I, <, \sqsubseteq\rangle$ satisfies CONV and MON, i.e.

CONV:

$\forall i_1 i_2 i_3 \in I(i_1 < i_2 < i_3 \rightarrow \forall i_4 \in I(i_1 \sqsubseteq i_4 \wedge i_3 \sqsubseteq i_4 \;.\!\rightarrow\!.\; i_2 \sqsubseteq i_4))$

MON:

left-mon: $\forall i_1 i_2 \in I(i_1 < i_2 \rightarrow \forall i_3 \in I(i_3 \sqsubseteq i_1 \rightarrow i_3 < i_2))$

right-mon: $\forall i_1 i_2 \in I(i_1 < i_2 \rightarrow \forall i_3 \in I(i_3 \sqsubseteq i_2 \rightarrow i_1 < i_3))$

(v) $n = \{i' \in I \mid i' \sqsubseteq i\}$ for a specific $i \in I$; [11]

(vi) $\forall i\, \forall i' \sqsubseteq i$: $O_i = O_{i'}$ [12]

(vii) * is an interpretation function such that:

- now* = n
- before* = <
- sub* = $\sqsubseteq$
- E* = $\{\langle i, d\rangle \mid d \in O_i\}$
- for each interval constant i, $i^* \in I$.
- for each n-place relation sign R, R* is a function from indices to pairs $\langle R^+, R^-\rangle$, notation: $R^*(i) := \langle R_i^+, R_i^-\rangle$, with $R_i^+ \subseteq O_i^n$, R_i^+, R_i^- disjoint and satisfying homogeneity, i.e.: $i' \sqsubseteq i$ only if $R_i^+ \subseteq R_{i'}^+$

11 All the subintervals of the interval now, are now too.

12 All intervals in a $\sqsubseteq$-connected region have the same domain.

- for each object constant o, o* is a partial function with $o^*(i) \in O_i$, also satisfying homogeneity: $o^*(i)$ defined and $i' \sqsubseteq i$ only if $o^*(i) = o^*(i')$

First of all note that we do not require $R_i^- \subseteq O_i^n$. This captures an asymmetry between verification and falsification of an atomic fact at an interval. If an interval verifies the fact that certain objects stand in a particular relation, then the objects must exist at that interval and the relation in question must hold between them. For falsification the situation is different. One reason why objects can fail to stand in a certain relation at an interval is that one of the objects does not exist at that interval. Another possibility is that all objects are present, but they fail to stand in the required relation. If we had stipulated that $R_i^- \subseteq O_i^n$, the former possibility of falsification at an interval would have been excluded.

The constraints on the interval structure, i.e. SPO(<), PO($\sqsubseteq$), CONV and MON, by and large are the minimal conditions on a period structure as defined in Van Benthem (1983). Only his CONJ, stating the existence of a greatest lower bound for two intervals, is missing.

When we compare the above definition with the original definition of an IQ-model, two differences emerge. In contrast to the system in Chapter 6, a domain is associated with each interval. This dissimilarity, however, is a matter of technical expedience only. The use of interval domains together with the use of the E-predicate enables us to give a tractable proof of the homogeneity condition on the interpretations of constants in our completeness proof for IQ^{int}. The difference would be profound, if we were to use the interval domains as domains of quantification. But we shall choose the option of quantifying over the union of the interval domains, which is essentially the same as quantifying over one domain for all intervals, as in IQ.

After this comparison, it is time to go back to the semantics of IQ^{int}.

2.2.2 ASSIGNMENTS. Let **M** be an IQ^{int} model and $O := \bigcup_{i \in I} O_i$. An assignment for **M** is a partial function g: VAR–I $\cup$ VAR-O $\rightarrow I \cup O$, such that $g(i) \in I$ and $g(x) \in O$ for each $i \in$ VAR-I and each $x \in$ VAR-O in the domain of g.

2.2.3 VALUE OF A TERM. Let g be an assignment for an IQ^{int}-model **M** and let $i \in I$. The value of an object term t, denoted by $[\![t]\!]^{M,g}(i)$, is defined to be:

- $[\![x]\!]^{M,g}(i) = g(x)$, if $g(x) \in O_i$ and undefined otherwise for all $x \in$ VAR-O,
- $[\![o]\!]^{M,g}(i) = o^*(i)$, for all object constants o.

The value of an interval term t', denoted by $[\![t']\!]^{M,g}$, is defined to be:

- $[\![v]\!]^{M,g} = g(v)$, for all $v \in$ VAR-I,
- $[\![i]\!]^{M,g} = i^*$, for interval constants i.[13]

From the definitions in (2.2.1) - (2.2.3), it is clear that a formula may lack a truth value at an interval in a model under an assignment. This will be the case if *(a)* it contains an object constant which lacks reference; or *(b)* the interpretation of a relation symbol is undefined for the interpretations of the terms occurring in it; or *(c)* there is an occurrence of a free variable not in the domain of the assignment. (N.B. assignments are partial too!) There are different ways to handle phenomena like this semantically. As in Chapter 6 and the previous section we choose Kleene's strong interpretation. Note, by the way that when we limit ourselves to the interval structure of a model, everything is total.

2.2.4 VERIFICATION AND FALSIFICATION. Let $\mathbf{M} = \langle I, \{O_i\}_{i \in I}, <, \sqsubseteq, n, * \rangle$ be an IQ^{int} model, g an assignment for **M** and $O := \bigcup_{i \in I} O_i$. In regard to g, **M** verifies a formula φ (notation: $\mathbf{M} \models^+ \varphi$ [g]) or **M** refutes a formula φ (notation: $\mathbf{M} \models^- \varphi$ [g]) iff the following holds [14]:

$$\mathbf{M} \models^+ i_1 = i_2\,[g] \quad \Leftrightarrow \quad [\![i_1]\!] = [\![i_2]\!]$$

$$\mathbf{M} \models^+ \mathrm{now}(i)\,[g] \quad \Leftrightarrow \quad [\![i]\!] \in n$$

---

13 Again, when no confusion is possible, we drop the superscripts.

14 When only a verification clause is stated, falsification is equivalent to non-verification. And dually for falsification. For these formulas the interpretation is two valued.

$\mathbf{M} \models^+ \text{before}(i, i')\ [g]$	$\Leftrightarrow$	$[\![i]\!] < [\![i']\!]$
$\mathbf{M} \models^+ \text{sub}(i, i')\ [g]$	$\Leftrightarrow$	$[\![i]\!] \sqsubseteq [\![i']\!]$
$\mathbf{M} \models^+ E(i, t)\ [g]$	$\Leftrightarrow$	$E^*([\![i]\!], [\![t]\!]([\![i]\!]))$ [15]
$\mathbf{M} \models^+ \text{at}(i).R(t_1,\ldots,t_n)\ [g]$	$\Leftrightarrow$	$\langle [\![t_1]\!]([\![i]\!]),\ldots, [\![t_n]\!]([\![i]\!])\rangle \in R_j^+$ [16]
$\mathbf{M} \models^- \text{at}(i).R(t_1,\ldots,t_n)\ [g]$	$\Leftrightarrow$	$\langle [\![t_1]\!]([\![i]\!]),\ldots, [\![t_n]\!]([\![i]\!])\rangle \in R_j^-$
$\mathbf{M} \not\models^+ \text{at}(i).\bot\ [g]$	and	$\mathbf{M} \models^- \text{at}(i).\bot\ [g]$
$\mathbf{M} \models^+ \text{at}(i).\chi\to\zeta\ [g]$	$\Leftrightarrow$	$\mathbf{M} \models^- \text{at}(i).\chi\ [g]$ or $\mathbf{M} \models^+ \text{at}(i).\zeta\ [g]$
$\mathbf{M} \models^- \text{at}(i).\chi\to\zeta\ [g]$	$\Leftrightarrow$	$\mathbf{M} \models^+ \text{at}(i).\chi\ [g]$ and $\mathbf{M} \models^- \text{at}(i).\zeta\ [g]$
$\mathbf{M} \models^+ \text{at}(i).\exists x\chi\ [g]$	$\Leftrightarrow$	$\mathbf{M} \models^+ \text{at}(i).\chi\ [g^x_d]$ for a $d \in O$
$\mathbf{M} \models^- \text{at}(i).\exists x\chi\ [g]$	$\Leftrightarrow$	$\mathbf{M} \models^- \text{at}(i).\chi\ [g^x_d]$ for all $d \in O$ [17]
$\mathbf{M} \models^+ \text{at}(i).\text{at}(i').\chi\ [g]$	$\Leftrightarrow$	$\mathbf{M} \models^+ \text{at}(i').\chi\ [g]$
$\mathbf{M} \models^- \text{at}(i).\text{at}(i').\chi\ [g]$	$\Leftrightarrow$	$\mathbf{M} \models^- \text{at}(i').\chi\ [g]$ [18]

This covers all cases.

The logical constants not mentioned in 2.2.4, are treated as abbreviations (see 3.1.9). Some easy calculations show that within the scope of at(i) the verification and falsification conditions of these abbreviations are as expected. For example, given the definitions $\neg\varphi :=_{\text{def}} \varphi\to\bot$ and $\forall x.\varphi :=_{\text{def}} \neg\exists x.\neg\varphi$ the following are equivalent:

$$\mathbf{M} \models^+ \text{at}(i).\forall x.\varphi\ [g]$$
$$\mathbf{M} \models^+ \text{at}(i).(\exists x.\neg\varphi\to\bot)\ [g]$$
$$\mathbf{M} \models^+ \text{at}(i).(\exists x.\neg\varphi) \to \text{at}(i).\bot\ [g]$$
$$\mathbf{M} \models^- \text{at}(i).(\exists x.\neg\varphi) \text{ or } \mathbf{M} \models^+ \text{at}(i).\bot\ [g]$$
$$\mathbf{M} \models^- \text{at}(i).(\exists x.(\varphi\to\bot))$$

For all $d \in O$: $\mathbf{M} \models^- \text{at}(i).(\varphi\to\bot)\ [g^x_d]$

For all $d \in O$: $\mathbf{M} \models^+ \text{at}(i).\varphi\ [g^x_d]$ and $\mathbf{M} \models^- \text{at}(i).\bot\ [g^x_d]$

For all $d \in O$: $\mathbf{M} \models^+ \text{at}(i).\varphi\ [g^x_d]$

And similarly for the case of falsification.

---

15 For the cases $\bot$, $\chi\to\zeta$ and $\exists x\chi$, see 1.1.2.

16 $j = [\![i]\!]$

17 Analogously for quantification over intervals

18 Iterations of operators 'at(i)' are superfluous, only the innermost operator counts.

Now we are in a position to define an extension relation $\subseteq$ between IQ^{int}-models and prove Monotonicity and Extension Lemmas for these models.

2.2.5 $\subseteq$ FOR IQ^{int}-MODELS. Let $\mathbf{M} = \langle I, \{O_i\}_{i \in I}, <, \sqsubseteq, n, * \rangle$ be an IQ^{int}-model. For each $i \in I$ define $\mathbf{M}^i := \langle O_i, {}^i \rangle$. with ^{i} an interpretation function such that:

$c^i := c^*(i)$ for individual constants c,

$R^i := R^*(i)$ for n-place relation symbols.

Let $\mathbf{M}_1$ and $\mathbf{M}_2$ be IQ^{int}-models that differ only in their interpretation functions. Using definition 1.2.1, we stipulate:

$\mathbf{M}_1 \subseteq \mathbf{M}_2 \Leftrightarrow \forall i \in I$: $\mathbf{M}_1^i \leq \mathbf{M}_2^i$.

Given this ‘intervalwise’ definition of the extension relation, the Monotonicity Lemma generalizes in the following way:

2.2.6 MONOTONICITY LEMMA. For all IQ^{int} models $\mathbf{M}$ and $\mathbf{M}'$:
$\mathbf{M} \subseteq \mathbf{M}' .\Rightarrow. T^+(\mathbf{M}) \subseteq T^+(\mathbf{M}'), T^-(\mathbf{M}) \subseteq T^-(\mathbf{M}')$ and $T^?(\mathbf{M}') \subseteq T^?(\mathbf{M})$

PROOF. On the global level we have the same induction as in the (omitted) proof of 1.2.2. With respect to intervals, we make use of the fact that $\leq$ is defined intervalwise, again giving us an induction as for 1.2.2. □

Due to homogeneity, there is a curious interplay between the extension relation between IQ^{int}-models and the $\sqsubseteq$ relation in those models:

2.2.7 EXTENSION-HOMOGENEITY LEMMA. Let $\mathbf{M} = \langle I, \{O_i\}_{i \in I}, <, \sqsubseteq, n, * \rangle$ be an IQ^{int}-model. For all i, $i' \in I$ such that $i' \sqsubseteq i$ and $\mathbf{M}^{i'} \leq \mathbf{M}^i$ it is the case that:

(i) The same constants are defined at i and i' and in the same way,

(ii) $R_i^+ = R_{i'}^+$

PROOF. Recall that $\mathbf{M}^{i'} \leq \mathbf{M}^i$ means:

- for all individual constants c: if $c^{i'}$ is defined, then $c^{i'} = c^i$
- for all n-place relations: $R_{i'}^+ \subseteq R_i^+$ and $R_{i'}^- \subseteq R_i^-$.

Homogeneity and $i' \sqsubseteq i$ give $R_i{}^+ \subseteq R_{i'}{}^+$ and: for all individual constants c: if c^i is defined, then $c^{i'} = c^i$. From this (i) and (ii) are immediate. □

Homogeneity has as a further consequence that it is impossible to prove general extension lemmas like those in sections 1 and 3. Note that if a constant is undefined at an interval i, it might be that it has different interpretations at different subintervals of i. So, when extending the model, homogeneity forces us to interpret the constant in two different ways. But this is not allowed. Thus we see that in systems satisfying homogeneity terms are often undefined, as is also observed in Chapter 6. There is a way out, however. We could introduce the notion of strong homogeneity for terms.

STRONG HOMOGENEITY An IQ^{int}-model is strongly homogeneous, if it satisfies:
$\forall i{:}\ \forall i' \sqsubseteq i{:}\ \forall i'' \sqsubseteq i{:}\ o^*(i')$ and $o^*(i'')$ are defined only if $o^*(i') = o^*(i'')$.

Intuitively, strong homogeneity captures the idea that, when looking at subintervals, participants with the same name really are the same. Or, to use familiar jargon: names are rigid designators in $\sqsubseteq$-connected regions of intervals. So the interpretation of individual constants in strongly homogeneous models has similarities with both the interpretation of individual constants and the interpretation of parameters in homogeneous models. The former are not rigid at all, while the latter are rigid throughout a model. In comparison the constants in a strongly homogeneous are rigid within $\sqsubseteq$-connected regions of intervals, but they can have different interpretations in different regions.

Strong homogeneity plainly clears the road to an extension lemma.

2.2.8 EXTENSION LEMMA. Let **M** be a strongly homogeneous IQ^{int}-model and Γ a set of sentences such that for some $\varphi \in \Gamma$ φ is undefined in **M**. A strongly homogeneous IQ^{int}-model **M'** can be found with $\mathbf{M} \subseteq \mathbf{M}'$ and all $\varphi \in \Gamma$ defined in **M'**.

PROOF. A simple proof of this lemma would consist of totalizing all the intervals in the model. And it is not difficult to see that this can be done. Here, however, we prefer to introduce interpretations of constants only when we have to.

Recall that $\mathbf{M} \subseteq \mathbf{M}'$ is defined intervalwise. So we have to find an $\mathbf{M}'$ such that for all $i \in I$: $\mathbf{M}^i \leq \mathbf{M}'^i$ and in which all $\varphi \in \Gamma$ are defined. Such an $\mathbf{M}'$ is reached in stages. First fix an enumeration of the sentences undefined in Γ. Due to a normal form result proved in 2.3.3 (viii) below, we may limit our attention to subformulas of sentences in which at-operators only occur in atomic sentences or negations thereof. Hence, let at(i).α be the first such undefined sentence in the first sentence of our enumeration. (The case of negation is similar.) Look at $\mathbf{M}^i$. In $\mathbf{M}^i$ either a constant has no reference, or the interpretations of the terms are neither in the extension nor in the anti-extension of the relation symbol. Due to homogeneity, it is the case that if a constant is undefined at i, it is undefined in all of i's superintervals. So we only have to look at the subintervals of i. At first we try to find a subinterval of i in which the constant is defined. If such a subinterval exists, say it is i', choose the interpretation of the constant at i'. This is allowed, since $O_{i'} = O_i$. If there is no such subinterval, choose an arbitrary interpretation of the constant. We are able to make this choice, since O is non-empty. Due to strong homogeneity, there can not be a 'clash' of this choice with the interpretation of the constant at other places in the model. Furthermore, strong homogeneity is preserved and we can iterate the process, each time using the model that resulted from the previous step until all constants are defined. With respect to relation symbols R, simply set $R^*(i) := \langle R_i{+}, O^n \backslash R_i{+} \rangle$. Then we still have $R_i{+} \subseteq O^n$, and since only anti-extensions are changed, homogeneity remains unaffected.

In the end we have an $\mathbf{M}'$ with $\mathbf{M} \subseteq \mathbf{M}'$. The interpretation of the relation symbols becomes classical, so in the final induction on the complexity of a formula, quantification cannot cause a problem. We can rest assured that the resulting model $\mathbf{M}'$ will do. □

2.3 The Logic IQ^{int}

Now we are going to describe a deduction system, which in the next section we will prove to be sound and complete as regards IQ^{int}-models.

2.3.1 The Deduction System

AXIOMS

Axioms are all the formulas of one of the following forms:

PREDICATE LOGICAL AXIOMS

Any classical system will do. See for instance 3.3.1 (1)-(6) using I and O as sorts.

STRUCTURAL AXIOMS

(7) SPO(before), i.e:

$\forall i.\neg before(i,i)$

$\forall i_1 i_2 i_3\, (before(i_1,i_2) \wedge before(i_2,i_3) .\!\rightarrow\!.\ before(i_1,i_3))$

(8) PO(sub), i.e.:

$\forall i.sub(i,i)$

$\forall i_1 i_2\, (sub(i_1,i_2) \wedge sub(i_2,i_1) .\!\rightarrow\!.\ i_1 = i_2)$

$\forall i_1 i_2 i_3\, (sub(i_1,i_2) \wedge sub(i_2,i_3) .\!\rightarrow\!.\ sub(i_1,i_3))$

(9) CONV:

$\forall i_1 i_2 i_3\, (before(i_1,i_2) \wedge before(i_2,i_3)$

$\rightarrow \forall i_4\, (sub(i_1,i_4) \wedge sub(i_3,i_4) .\!\rightarrow\!.\ sub(i_2,i_4)))$

(10) MON

left-mon: $\forall i_1 i_2\, (before(i_1,i_2) \rightarrow \forall i_3\, (sub(i_3,i_1) \rightarrow before(i_3,i_2)))$

right-mon: $\forall i_1 i_2\, (before(i_1,i_2) \rightarrow \forall i_3\, (sub(i_3,i_2) \rightarrow before(i_1,i_3)))$

(11) HOM(R) with R an n-place relation symbol:

$\forall i_1 i_2\, (sub(i_1,i_2)$

$\rightarrow \forall x_1,\ldots,x_n\, (at(i_2).R(x_1,\ldots,x_n) \rightarrow at(i_1).R(x_1,\ldots,x_n)))$

E-AXIOMS

(12) $\forall i_1 i_2 \forall x\ (sub(i_1,i_2) \rightarrow (E(i_2,x) \leftrightarrow E(i_1,x))$

(13) $\forall i\ \forall x_1,\ldots,x_n\ (at(i).R(x_1,\ldots,x_n)\ .\!\rightarrow\!.\ E(i,x_1) \wedge \ldots \wedge E(i,x_n))$

INTERVAL AXIOMS

(14) $\forall i\ (at(i).\bot \rightarrow \bot)$

(15) $\forall i\ (at(i).(\varphi \rightarrow \psi) \leftrightarrow (at(i).\varphi \rightarrow at(i).\psi))$

(16) $\forall i\ (at(i).\exists x.\varphi \leftrightarrow \exists x.at(i).\varphi)$ for all variables, provided $x \not\equiv i$

(17) $\forall i_1 i_2\ (at(i_1).at(i_2).\varphi \leftrightarrow at(i_2).\varphi)$

(18) $\exists i\ \forall i_1\ (now(i_1) \leftrightarrow sub(i_1,i))$

(19) CONGR(=):

$\forall i\!: i = i$

$\forall i_1 i_2\ (i_1 = i_2 \rightarrow i_2 = i_1)$

$\forall i_1 i_2 i_3\ (i_1 = i_2 \wedge i_2 = i_3\ .\!\rightarrow\!.\ i_1 = i_3)$

$\forall i_1\ i'_1\ i_2\ i'_2\ (i_1 = i_2 \wedge i'_1 = i'_2 \wedge sub(i_1,i'_1)\ .\!\rightarrow\!.\ sub(i_2,i'_2))$

$\forall i_1\ i'_1\ i_2\ i'_2\ (i_1 = i_2 \wedge i'_1 = i'_2 \wedge before(i_1,i'_1)\ .\!\rightarrow\!.\ before(i_2,i'_2))$

RULES OF DERIVATION

The usual two, modus ponens (MP) and universal generalization (UG).

MP: from φ and $\varphi \rightarrow \psi$ infer ψ

UG: from φ infer $\forall x.\varphi$ for both sorts

2.3.2 Some Theorems.

(1) $\forall i\ (at(i).\neg\varphi \leftrightarrow \neg at(i).\varphi)$

(2) $\forall i\ (at(i).(\varphi \wedge \psi) \leftrightarrow (at(i).\varphi \wedge at(i).\psi))$

(3) $\forall i\ (at(i).(\varphi \vee \psi) \leftrightarrow (at(i).\varphi \vee at(i).\psi))$

(4) $\forall i\ (at(i).\forall x.\varphi \leftrightarrow \forall x.at(i).\varphi\ )$ for all variables, provided $x \not\equiv i$

(5) $\forall i_1 i_2\ \forall x\ (i_1 = i_2 \wedge E(i_1,x)\ .\!\rightarrow\!.\ E(i_2,x))$

(6) $\exists! i\ \forall i_1\ (now(i_1) \leftrightarrow sub(i_1,i))$[19]

---

19 As usual '∃!' means: exactly one.

(7) $\forall i_1 i_2 (i_1 = i_2 \wedge now(i_1) .\!\rightarrow\!. now(i_2))$

(8) Call a formula an iq prenex normal form, iq-pnf for short, if it is a disjunctive prenex normal form in which at-operators only occur in atomic formulas. Let φ^{iq} denote an iq-pnf of φ. For each φ there is an φ^{iq} with $\vdash \varphi \leftrightarrow \varphi^{iq}$.

PROOF OF (1) - (4). We only prove (1). (2), (3) and (4) are proved similarly using (1) and axiom (15). The proof of (1) runs:
$at(i).\neg\varphi .\!\leftrightarrow\!. (at(i).\varphi \rightarrow at(i).\bot) .\!\leftrightarrow\!. (at(i).\varphi \rightarrow \bot) .\!\leftrightarrow\!. \neg at(i).\varphi$

PROOF OF (5). Use reflexivity for = and *sub* together with the congruence axiom for *sub* and the first conjunct of the hypothesis to derive $sub(i_1,i_2)$. Now use the second conjunct of the hypothesis and E-axiom (12) to derive theorem $E(i_2,x)$.

PROOF OF (6). Assume there were two. Call them a and b. Thus:
$\forall i_1 (now(i_1) \leftrightarrow sub(i_1,a))$ and $\forall i_1 (now(i_1) \leftrightarrow sub(i_1,b))$. Hence in particular: $now(a) \leftrightarrow sub(a,a)$ and $now(a) \leftrightarrow sub(a,b)$. But *sub* is reflexive, so sub(a,b) follows. Similar reasoning gives sub(b,a), and therefore by antisymmetry a = b as required.

PROOF OF (7). Call the unique interval given by (6) n. Thus (*): $\forall i_1 (now(i_1) \leftrightarrow sub(i_1,n))$. Assume i = i' and now(i). From (*) it follows that sub(i,n). Reflexivity of = and the congruence axiom for *sub* give sub(i',n). Using (*) again we get now(i') and we are done.

PROOF OF (8). Fix a formula φ. Using axioms (14), (15) and (17), show that in φ all occurrences of complex formulas in the scope of an at(i)-operator can be eliminated. If in this process we conjure up an iteration of sentence operators, we remove it by means of axiom (17). Familiar techniques bring the resulting sentence into disjunctive prenex normal form. Clearly we end up with an iq-pnf that is provably equivalent to φ. □

2.4 Correctness and Completeness for IQ^{int}

2.4.1 CORRECTNESS $\Gamma \vdash \varphi \Rightarrow \Gamma \models \varphi$.

PROOF. Here we use induction on the length of derivations. Axioms (1) - (6), the set of axioms CONGR(=) and the derivation rules are classically valid, hence partially valid by the Coincidence Lemma. The other axioms mirror as it were the verification and falsification clauses and the structural constraints.

□

The following completeness result is obtained via a deviation from the common route. Instead of the familiar maximal consistent sets, which induce total models, we shall use a special kind of Hintikka sets that allow the constructed countermodel to be partial.

2.4.2 HINTIKKA SETS. Let L be a language, and I and O interval and object domains. With these domains we associate sets of individual constants $\underline{I} := \{\underline{i} \mid i \in I\}$ and $\underline{O} := \{\underline{d} \mid d \in O\}$ disjoint from L. A *Hintikka set* H of sentences over the language $L \cup \underline{I} \cup \underline{O}$ is a set such that:

(i) $\perp \notin H$ and for no atomic formula α: $\alpha \in H$ and $\neg\alpha \in H$,

(ii) if $\varphi \wedge \psi \in H$ then $\varphi \in H$ and $\psi \in H$,

(iii) if $\varphi \vee \psi \in H$ then $\varphi \in H$ or $\psi \in H$,

(iv) if $\exists x\, \varphi \in H$ then $[\underline{d}/x]\varphi \in H$ for a $d \in O$,

(v) if $\forall x\, \varphi \in H$ then $[\underline{d}/x]\varphi \in H$ for all $d \in O$.

Similarly for interval quantification.

In Section 3 it will be proved that each consistent set of sentences is contained in a Hintikka set; completeness for many sorted logic follows from this. As in a Henkin completeness proof, a model is constructed out of a set of sentences, here a possibly non-maximal Hintikka set. In the proof of the

Consistency Lemma we shall assume these results and concentrate on the special case where we require the constructed model to be an IQ^{int}-model.

2.4.3 CONSISTENCY LEMMA. Every consistent set of sentences has an IQ^{int}-model.[20]

PROOF. Let Γ be a consistent set of sentences, and let $\underline{I}$ and $\underline{O}$ be infinite sets of constants disjoint from each other and from the language used. Without loss of generality we may assume that all the sentences in Γ are in iq-pnf (see 2.3.3.). Using Γ we shall construct a Hintikka set, but such a set need not be deductively closed. We therefore add to Γ the axioms and theorems needed for the model construction beforehand. These added sentences mainly serve two purposes. First they ensure that the resulting model has the structure it ought to have, and second they enable us to properly interpret the non-logical constants within this structure. When reading the list of sentences below, it will be clear which sentence serves which purpose. In this list we sometimes discern between a quantified case and a case for the constants occurring in Γ. We need to do this since in the constructed model the quantifiers range over the sets of new constants or equivalence classes thereof.

Let L_Γ be the set of non-logical constants occurring in a sentence of Γ. Form the union of Γ with iq-pnf variants of the following axioms and theorems:

CONGR(=), $\exists i$: $i = c$ for all interval constants $c \in L_\Gamma$,
SPO(before), PO(sub), CONV, MON, HOM(R) for all $R \in L_\Gamma$,
$\exists! i\ \forall i_1\ (\text{now}(i_1) \leftrightarrow \text{sub}(i_1,i))$,
$\forall i_1 i_2\ \forall x\ (i_1 = i_2 \wedge E(i_1,x) \;.\!\!\rightarrow\!\!.\; E(i_2,x))$,
$\forall i_1 i_2\ (i_1 = i_2 \wedge E(i_1,\underline{d}) \;.\!\!\rightarrow\!\!.\; E(i_2,\underline{d}))$ for all object constants $\underline{d} \in L_\Gamma$,
$\forall i_1 i_2\ \forall x\ (\text{sub}(i_1,i_2) \rightarrow (E(i_2,x) \leftrightarrow E(i_2,x))$,
$\forall i_1 i_2\ (\text{sub}(i_1,i_2) \wedge E(i_2,\underline{d}) \;.\!\!\rightarrow\!\!.\; E(i_1,\underline{d}))$ for all object constants $\underline{d} \in L_\Gamma$,
and finally: $\forall i\ \forall x_1,\ldots,x_n\ [\alpha_i(x_1,\ldots,x_n,c_1,\ldots,c_m)$
$\rightarrow E(i,x_1)\wedge\ldots\wedge E(i,x_n)\wedge E(i,c_1)\wedge\ldots\wedge E(i,c_m)]$

20 N.B. **M** is a model for Γ, if $\mathbf{M} \models^{+} \varphi$ for all $\varphi \in \Gamma$.

with $\alpha_i(x_1,\ldots,x_n,c_1,\ldots,c_m)$ an atomic subformula of a $\varphi \in \Gamma$ which contains the operator at(i) and the constants $c_1,\ldots,c_m$ [not necessarily in that order].

Call the resulting set Γ'. Of course, adding axioms and theorems of IQ^{int} to Γ cannot induce IQ^{int}-inconsistency. Given Γ' together with a two sorted version of the Downward Closure Lemma (3.3.5), we can construct a Hintikka set $\Gamma''\supseteq\Gamma'$. And out of Γ'' we extract an IQ^{int} model by putting $\mathbf{M}: = \langle I,\{O_i\}_{i\in I},<,\sqsubseteq,n,*\rangle$, the precise character of which will be unraveled in the next sequence of definitions.

First we concentrate on the interval structure $\langle I,<,\sqsubseteq,n\rangle$ of **M** and the interpretation of the relevant non-logical constants in this structure. Since we have an identity relation between intervals in our language, we must be sure to get our interval domain right. Due to the relevant axioms in CONGR(=) and downward closedness, $\{i' \mid i' = i \in \Gamma''\}$ is an equivalence class for each $i \in \underline{I}$.[21] Thus for intervals we can set $[i] := \{i' \mid i' = i \in \Gamma''\}$, and define $I = \{[i] \mid i \in \underline{I}\}$. We now interpret the interval constants by $i^* := [i]$. This also gives the desired result for interval constants in L_Γ, since for those we added the axiom $\exists i$: $i = c$. The relations $<$ and $\sqsubseteq$ on I are defined by: $< := \{\langle[i],[i']\rangle \mid \text{before}(i,i') \in \Gamma''\}$ and $\sqsubseteq := \{\langle[i],[i']\rangle \mid \text{sub}(i,i') \in \Gamma''\}$. It is immediate from the relevant axioms in CONGR(=) that these definitions are independent of the representatives of the equivalence classes. That $\langle I, <\rangle$ is a strict partial order, $\langle I, \sqsubseteq\rangle$ a partial order, and that $\langle I, <,\sqsubseteq\rangle$ satisfies CONV and MON is immediate from the fact that SPO(<), PO($\sqsubseteq$), CONV and MON are added to Γ before we downward closed this set. Due to $\exists! i\, \forall i_1\, (\text{now}(i_1)\leftrightarrow\text{sub}(i_1,i))$, there is exactly one interval constant i such that for all interval constants $\underline{i}'$: now($\underline{i}'$) $\in \Gamma''$ iff sub(i',i) $\in \Gamma''$. Thus, using the *sub* axiom in CONGR(=), $n := \{[i'] \mid \text{sub}(i,i') \in \Gamma''\}$ is well-defined and independent of representatives.

Finally we look at the object part of **M** and its interplay with the interval structure defined above. Let O^+ be $\underline{O}$ plus the set of object constants in L_Γ.

---

21 In the sequel, something like 'due to the axioms' will mean: due to the axioms and downward closedness.

For all $i \in \underline{I}$, define $O_i := \{d \in O^+ \mid E(i,d) \in \Gamma''\}$. A consequence of $\forall i_1 i_2 \forall x\ (i_1 = i_2 \wedge E(i_1,x)\ .\!\rightarrow\!.\ E(i_2,x))$ is that intervals which are equal according to Γ in fact have the same object domain. And using $\forall i_1 i_2 \forall x\ (sub(i_1,i_2) \rightarrow (E(i_2,x) \leftrightarrow E(i_1,x)))$ we see that $\forall i \forall i' \sqsubseteq i\ O_i = O_{i'}$. Next we look at the interpretation of the remaining non-logical constants. The interpretation of object constants is easy: for each $c \in O^+$ define $c^*(i){:}c$, if $c \in O_i$, undefined otherwise. We have to prove that c^* satisfies the homogeneity condition. So assume $i' \sqsubseteq i$ and $c^*(i) = c$. Then $c \in O_i = O_{i'}$, since $i' \sqsubseteq i$. Hence $c \in O_{i'}$ and $c^*(i) = c = c^*(i')$. As to the interpretations of n-place relations R, these are defined by: $R^*(i) := \langle R_i^+, R_i^- \rangle$ with

$R_i^+ := \{<d_1,\ldots,d_n> \mid at(i).R(d_1,\ldots,d_n) \in \Gamma''\}$.

$R_i^- := \{<d_1,\ldots,d_n> \mid \neg at(i).R(d_1,\ldots,d_n) \in \Gamma''\}$.

That R_i^+ and R_i^- are disjoint follows from the fact that Γ'' is a Hintikka set. That $R_i^+ \subseteq O_i^n$ is a consequence of the added axioms

$$\forall i\, \forall x_1,\ldots,x_n\, [\alpha_i(x_1,\ldots,x_n,c_1,\ldots,c_m) \rightarrow E(i,x_1) \wedge \ldots \wedge E(i,x_n) \wedge E(i,c_1) \wedge \ldots \wedge E(i,c_m)]$$

And that R^* is also homogeneous, is immediate from the addition of HOM(R). This concludes the model construction.

It remains to be proved that $\varphi \in \Gamma'' \Rightarrow \mathbf{M} \models \varphi$. But this is a routine induction on the complexity of φ. Since $\Gamma \subseteq \Gamma''$, we conclude that $\mathbf{M} \models \Gamma$ and we are done. □

2.4.4 COMPLETENESS $\Gamma \models \varphi \Rightarrow \Gamma \vdash \varphi$.

PROOF. Use 2.4.3 in the familiar way. □

§3 Many Sorted Partial Predicate Logic

In Chapter 7 two extensions of IQ^E are defined, viz. IQ^{Et} and IQ^{Etp}. Both extensions involve introducing new domains and new means in the language of quantifying over these domains. In this section we answer some important logical questions about these systems by treating the more general case where there are denumerably many sorts.

As usual we have two options when it comes to proving things about many sorted logics. Either provide direct proofs, or define an appropriate translation into a first-order logic so that we can use our knowledge about the latter system. Here we treat many sorted logic in its own right and thus prove some of its features in a direct manner. This will also provide some of the results which were assumed in the previous section. In that section it is shown how to arrive at the special kind of structures used in IQ^{int}, so we skip that matter here. Since the main ideas of partial semantics are already introduced, we now change to a 'bare-bones' style of writing, only inserting connecting bits of text when absolutely necessary.

3.1 Syntax

3.1.1 SORTS. S is a denumerable set of sorts. 's' (possibly indexed) is used to refer to sorts, and '**s**' (a bold s) is used to refer to finite sequences of sorts.

3.1.2 LANGUAGE. A *language* is a denumerable set of non logical symbols, with:

(i) for all $s \in S$: C_s a set of individual constants,

(ii) for all $\mathbf{s} = <s_1,\ldots,s_{n+1}>$, $FUN_{\mathbf{s}}$ a set of n-place function symbols,

(iii) for all $\mathbf{s} = <s_1,\ldots,s_n>$, $REL_{\mathbf{s}}$ a set of n-place relation symbols.

Each of the above sets may be empty.

In the sequel, we keep a language L fixed.

3.1.3 VARIABLES. For each $s \in S$, VAR_s is a countable infinite set of (individual) variables. If necessary $x \in VAR_s$ is denoted by x_s or something similar.

3.1.4 LOGICAL ALPHABET. The *logical alphabet* consists of: = (identity), $\perp$ (falsum), $\rightarrow$ (arrow) and $\exists$ (existential quantifier). As *punctuation symbols* we have) (right-hand bracket), , (comma), ((left-hand bracket).

3.1.5 NOTATIONAL DEVICE. To have a concise notation in the following three definitions, we define:

$$Y[X_1,\ldots,X_n] := \{y(x_1,\ldots,x_n) \mid y \in Y \text{ and } x_i \in X_i \ (1 \leq i \leq n)\}$$

3.1.6 TERMS. For each $s \in S$, the set of *terms* of sort s, notation T_s, is the smallest set such that:

(i) $C_s \subseteq T_s$ and $VAR_s \subseteq T_s$,

(ii) $FUN_{\mathbf{s}}[T_{s_1},\ldots,T_{s_n}] \subseteq T_{s_{n+1}}$, with $\mathbf{s} := \langle s_1,\ldots,s_{n+1}\rangle$.

We call a term *closed* if it does not contain variables.

3.1.7 ATOMIC FORMULAS. The set AF of *atomic formulas* is the smallest set such that:

(i) $\perp \in AF$,

(ii) $\{=\}[T_s,T_s] \subseteq AF$, for all $s \in S$.

(iii) $REL_{\mathbf{s}}[T_{s_1},\ldots,T_{s_n}] \subseteq AF$, with $\mathbf{s} := \langle s_1,\ldots,s_n\rangle$.

3.1.8 FORMULAS. The set F of *formulas* is the smallest set such that:

(i) $AF \subseteq F$,

(ii) $\{\rightarrow\}[F,F] \subseteq F$,

(iii) $\{\exists x\}[F] \subseteq F$, for all $s \in S$ and all $x \in VAR_s$.

Sentences are formulas that do not contain free variables.

The above definitions provide prefix notation, but in the sequel we shall use infix notation.

3.1.9 ABBREVIATIONS.

$\neg\varphi :=_{df} \varphi\rightarrow\perp$

$\varphi\wedge\psi :=_{df} \neg(\varphi\rightarrow\neg\psi)$

$\varphi\vee\psi :=_{df} \neg(\neg\varphi\wedge\neg\psi)$

$\forall x_s\varphi :=_{df} \neg\exists x_s\neg\varphi$, for all $s \in S$

3.2 Semantics

3.2.1 MANY SORTED DOMAINS. A *many sorted domain* **D** is a set $\{D_s \mid s \in S\}$ with for each $s \in S$, D_s a non-empty set.

3.2.2 PARTIAL MANY SORTED MODELS. A *partial many sorted model* **M** is a tuple $\langle \mathbf{D}, * \rangle$ with:

(i) **D** a many sorted domain,

(ii) * an interpretation function such that:

- $c^* \in D_s$, for all $c \in C_s$,
- Let $\mathbf{s} := <s_1,\ldots,s_{n+1}>$ and $f \in FUN_\mathbf{s}$: $f^*:D_{s_1}\times\ldots\times D_{s_n}\rightarrow D_{s_{n+1}}$ is a partial function.
- Let $\mathbf{s} := <s_1,\ldots,s_n>$ and $R \in REL_\mathbf{s}$:
  $R^* := \langle R^+, R^- \rangle$ with $R^+, R^- \subseteq D_{s_1}\times\ldots\times D_{s_n}$ and R^+ and R^- disjoint.
  R^* is *total*, if $R^+ \cup R^- = D_{s_1}\times\ldots\times D_{s_n}$.

M is *classical*, if all constants have reference and all functions and relations are total. **M** is *standard*, if all the D_s's are non-empty.

3.2.3 ASSIGNMENTS. Let $\mathbf{M} = \langle \mathbf{D}, * \rangle$ be a many sorted model. An *assignment* for **M** (or for **D**) is a function $g: \bigcup_{s \in S} VAR_s \rightarrow \bigcup_{s \in S} D_s$ such that $g(x_s) \in D_s$.

3.2.4 VALUE OF A TERM. Let $\mathbf{M} = \langle \mathbf{D}, * \rangle$ be a many sorted model and g an assignment for **M**. The *value of a term* t *in* **M** *under g*, notation: $[\![t]\!]^{M,g}$, is defined to be:

$[\![t]\!]^{M,g} = c^*$ if $t \equiv c \in C_s$,

$[\![t]\!]^{M,g} = g(x)$ if $t \equiv x \in VAR_s$,

$[\![t]\!]^{M,g} = f^*([\![t_1]\!],\ldots,[\![t_n]\!])$ if $t \equiv f(t_1,\ldots,t_n)$.[22]

22 We write $[\![t]\!]^{M,g}$ as $[\![t]\!]$, if no confusion can arise.

3.2.5 VERIFICATION AND FALSIFICATION. Let **M** = (**D**,*) be a partial many sorted model and g an assignment for **M**. In regard to g, **M** *verifies* a formula φ (notation: $\mathbf{M} \models^{+} \varphi$ [g]) or **M** *refutes* a formula φ (notation: $\mathbf{M} \models^{-} \varphi$ [g]) iff the following holds :

$\mathbf{M} \models^{+} t_1 = t_2$ [g]	$\Leftrightarrow$	$[\![t_1]\!], [\![t_2]\!] \in \mathbf{D}$ and $[\![t_1]\!] = [\![t_2]\!]$
$\mathbf{M} \models^{-} t_1 = t_2$ [g]	$\Leftrightarrow$	$[\![t_1]\!], [\![t_2]\!] \in \mathbf{D}$ and $[\![t_1]\!] \neq [\![t_2]\!]$
$\mathbf{M} \models^{+} R(t_1,\ldots,t_n)$ [g]	$\Leftrightarrow$	$\langle [\![t_1]\!],\ldots, [\![t_n]\!]\rangle \in R^{+}$
$\mathbf{M} \models^{-} R(t_1,\ldots,t_n)$ [g]	$\Leftrightarrow$	$\langle [\![t_1]\!],\ldots, [\![t_n]\!]\rangle \in R^{-}$
$\mathbf{M} \not\models^{+} \bot$ [g]	and	$\mathbf{M} \models^{-} \bot$ [g]
$\mathbf{M} \models^{+} \psi\to\chi$ [g]	$\Leftrightarrow$	$\mathbf{M} \models^{-} \psi$ [g] or $\mathbf{M} \models^{+} \chi$ [g]
$\mathbf{M} \models^{-} \psi\to\chi$ [g]	$\Leftrightarrow$	$\mathbf{M} \models^{+} \psi$ [g] and $\mathbf{M} \models^{-} \chi$ [g]
$\mathbf{M} \models^{+} \exists x_s\, \psi$ [g]	$\Leftrightarrow$	$\mathbf{M} \models^{+} \psi\ [g^x_d]$ for a $d \in D_s$
$\mathbf{M} \models^{-} \exists x_s\, \psi$ [g]	$\Leftrightarrow$	$\mathbf{M} \models^{-} \psi\ [g^x_d]$ for all $d \in D_s$

This covers all the cases.

3.2.6 ABBREVIATION LEMMA. The verification and falsification conditions of the abbreviations are what we expect them to be:

- $\mathbf{M} \models^{+} \neg\psi$ [g] $\Leftrightarrow$ $\mathbf{M} \models^{-} \psi$ [g]
  $\mathbf{M} \models^{-} \neg\psi$ [g] $\Leftrightarrow$ $\mathbf{M} \models^{+} \psi$ [g]
- $\mathbf{M} \models^{+} \psi\wedge\chi$ [g] $\Leftrightarrow$ $\mathbf{M} \models^{+} \psi$ [g] and $\mathbf{M} \models^{+} \chi$ [g]
  $\mathbf{M} \models^{-} \psi\wedge\chi$ [g] $\Leftrightarrow$ $\mathbf{M} \models^{-} \psi$ [g] or $\mathbf{M} \models^{-} \chi$ [g]
- $\mathbf{M} \models^{+} \psi\vee\chi$ [g] $\Leftrightarrow$ $\mathbf{M} \models^{+} \psi$ [g] or $\mathbf{M} \models^{+} \chi$ [g]
  $\mathbf{M} \models^{-} \psi\vee\chi$ [g] $\Leftrightarrow$ $\mathbf{M} \models^{-} \psi$ [g] and $\mathbf{M} \models^{-} \chi$ [g]
- $\mathbf{M} \models^{+} \forall x\, \chi$ [g] $\Leftrightarrow$ $\mathbf{M} \models^{+} \chi\ [g^x_d]$ for all $d \in D_s$
  $\mathbf{M} \models^{-} \forall x\, \chi$ [g] $\Leftrightarrow$ $\mathbf{M} \models^{-} \chi\ [g^x_d]$ for a $d \in D_s$

PROOF. Straightforward. □

3.2.7 EXTENSION RELATION. Let **D** be a many sorted domain. An *extension relation* $\sqsubseteq$ between interpretation functions into **D** and models on **D**, is defined by:

(i) $* \sqsubseteq \circ$ iff

• for all $c \in L$: c^* is defined $\Rightarrow c^* = c^\circ$,

- for all n-place function symbols $f \in L$: $f^* \subseteq f^\circ$,
- for all n-place relations $R \in L$: $R^{*+} \subseteq R^{\circ+}$ and $R^{*-} \subseteq R^{\circ-}$.

(ii) Let $\mathbf{M}_1 := \langle \mathbf{D}, * \rangle$ and $\mathbf{M}_2 := \langle \mathbf{D}, \circ \rangle$. $\mathbf{M}_1 \sqsubseteq \mathbf{M}_2$ iff $* \sqsubseteq \circ$.

3.2.8 THEORIES OF A MODEL.

$T^+(\mathbf{M}, g) := \{\varphi \mid \mathbf{M} \models^+ \varphi\, [g]\}$

$T^-(\mathbf{M}, g) := \{\varphi \mid \mathbf{M} \models^- \varphi\, [g]\}$

$T^?(\mathbf{M}, g) := \{\varphi \mid \mathbf{M} \not\models^+ \varphi\, [g] \text{ and } \mathbf{M} \not\models^- \varphi\, [g]\}$

3.2.9 MONOTONICITY LEMMA. For all partial models $\mathbf{M}_1$ and $\mathbf{M}_2$: if $\mathbf{M}_1 \sqsubseteq \mathbf{M}_2$ and g is an assignment for $\mathbf{M}_1$ (hence for $\mathbf{M}_2$), then: $T^+(\mathbf{M}_1,g) \subseteq T^+(\mathbf{M}_2,g)$, $T^-(\mathbf{M}_1,g) \subseteq T^-(\mathbf{M}_2,g)$ and $T?(\mathbf{M}_2,g) \subseteq T?(\mathbf{M}_1,g)$

PROOF. First establish, with a term induction that for all $s \in S$ and all $t \in T_s$ that $[\![t]\!]^{\mathbf{M}_1,g}$ is defined only if $[\![t]\!]^{\mathbf{M}_1,g} = [\![t]\!]^{\mathbf{M}_2,g}$. Use this fact to establish the lemma by means of a formula induction. □

3.2.10 EXTENSION LEMMA. Let $\mathbf{M}_1 = (\mathbf{D},*)$ be a many sorted model and Γ a set of sentences such that for some $\varphi \in \Gamma$ φ is undefined in $\mathbf{M}_1$ (notation: $\mathbf{M}?\varphi$). An $\mathbf{M}_2$ can be found with $\mathbf{M}_1 \sqsubseteq \mathbf{M}_2$ and all $\varphi \in \Gamma$ defined in $\mathbf{M}_2$

PROOF. Let L_G be the set of non-logical constants occurring in the sentences of Γ. Choose arbitrary $d \in \mathbf{D}_s$ for the constants in $L_G \cap C_s$ undefined in $\mathbf{M}_1$. Next, look at $f \in FUN_\mathbf{s}$, with $\mathbf{s} = \langle s_1,\ldots,s_{n+1}\rangle$. Choose an arbitrary $d \in D_{s_{n+1}}$. For all $\langle d_1,\ldots,d_n\rangle \in D_{s_1}\times\ldots\times D_{s_n}$ set $f^*(d_1,\ldots,d_n) = d$, if $f^*(d_1,\ldots,d_n)$ is undefined. This will totalize f^*. Finally, make the interpretations of all $R \in L_G \cap REL_\mathbf{s}$ with $\mathbf{s} = \langle s_1,\ldots,s_n\rangle$ total, by setting $R^- = D_{s_1}\times\ldots\times D_{s_n} \setminus R^+$. The model that results is a classical extension of $\mathbf{M}_1$, and hence suffices. □

3.3 Logic

3.3.1 The Deduction System

AXIOMS

(i) $\varphi \to (\psi \to \varphi)$

(ii) $(\varphi \to (\psi \to \chi)) \to ((\varphi \to \psi) \to (\varphi \to \chi))$

(iii) $\bot \to \varphi$

(iv) $((\varphi \to \bot) \to \bot) \to \varphi$

(v) provided t is free for v in φ, for all $t \in T_S$ and $v \in VAR_S$:
$\forall v.\varphi \to [^t/_v]\varphi$,

(vi) provided v does not occur free in φ, for all $v \in VAR_S$:
$\forall v.(\varphi \to \psi) \to (\varphi \to \forall v.\psi)$,

(vii) $EQ_S(=)$, for all $s \in S$:
$\forall x_S\colon x = x$
$\forall x_S y_S\, (x = y \to y = x)$
$\forall x_S y_S z_S\, (x = y \wedge y = z \,.\!\to\!.\, y = x)$

(viii) LL(f) for all $f \in FUN_S$:
$$\forall x_{s_1} y_{s_1},\ldots,x_{s_n} y_{s_n}\, (x_1 = y_1 \wedge \ldots \wedge x_n = y_n \to f(x_1,\ldots,x_n) = f(y_1,\ldots,y_n))$$

(xix) LL(R) for all $R \in REL_S$:
$$\forall x_{s_1} y_{s_1},\ldots,x_{s_n} y_{s_n}\, (x_1{=}y_1 \wedge \ldots \wedge x_n{=}y_n \wedge R(x_1,\ldots,x_n) \to R(y_1,\ldots,y_n))$$

RULES OF DERIVATION

MP: from φ and $\varphi \to \psi$ infer ψ

UG: For all $s \in S$: from φ infer $\forall x_S.\varphi$

The above is essentially a deduction system for classical predicate logic. Hence for each formula φ we can find a formula φ^{pn}, the disjunctive prenex normal form of φ ('dpnf' for short) provable equivalent with φ.

The consequence relation used here is that of 1.3.1. With the help of a many sorted variant of the Coincidence Lemma and the completeness result for classical many sorted predicate logic, we see that the above logic is sound and complete. But, working in a partial environment, it is natural to ask for a non-total partial countermodel in the proof of completeness. In other words, using a Henkin-style argument we do not want to arrive at a *maximal* consistent set, but merely at a suitably rich consistent one. We get such a set by extending the results that underlie Smullyan's Unifying Principle in order to have sorts and identity.

3.3.2 HINTIKKA SETS. Recall that AF is the set of atomic sentences in a language L. Let **D** be a many sorted domain, and for each $s \in S$ let $C_s := \{\underline{d} | d \in D_s\}$ be a set of individual constants disjoint from L. A *Hintikka set* H of sentences over the language $L \cup \bigcup_{s \in S} C_s$ is a set such that:

(i) $\bot \in H$ and for no $\alpha \in$ AF: $\alpha \in H$ and $\neg\alpha \in H$,

(ii) if $\varphi\wedge\psi \in H$ then $\varphi \in H$ and $\psi \in H$,

(iii) if $\varphi\vee\psi \in H$ then $\varphi \in H$ or $\psi \in H$,

(iv) if $\exists x_s\, \varphi \in H$ then $[c/x_s]\varphi \in H$ for a $c \in C_s$,

(v) if $\forall x_s\, \varphi \in H$ then $[c/x_s]\varphi \in H$ for all $c \in C_s$.

Call a formula *basic* if it is an atomic sentence or the negation of an atomic sentence.

3.3.3 EQUALIZED HINTIKKA SETS. Let:

- H be a Hintikka set over a language $L \cup \bigcup_{s \in S} C_s$,
- L_H be the set of non-logical symbols occurring in H, and
- T^s_H be the set of closed terms over L_H of sort s that occur in a basic sentence in H. Call H *equalized* if it satisfies:

(i) For all $t \in T^s_H$ there is a $\underline{d} \in C_s$ with $t = \underline{d} \in H$

(ii) For all $\underline{d} \in C_s$: $\underline{d} = \underline{d} \in H$

(iii) For all $\underline{d}_1, \underline{d}_2 \in C_s$: $\underline{d}_1 = \underline{d}_2 \in H$ only if $\underline{d}_2 = \underline{d}_1 \in H$

(iv) For all $\underline{d}_1,\underline{d}_2,\underline{d}_3 \in C_s$: $\underline{d}_1 = \underline{d}_2 \in H$ and $\underline{d}_2 = \underline{d}_3 \in H$
only if $\underline{d}_1 = \underline{d}_3 \in H$

(v) For all $f \in L_H$: $\underline{d}_1 = \underline{d}'_1 \in H$ and...and $\underline{d}_n = \underline{d}'_n \in H$
only if $f(\underline{d}_1,\ldots,\underline{d}_n) = f(\underline{d}'_1,\ldots,\underline{d}'_n) \in H$[23]

(vi) For all $R \in L_H$:
$\underline{d}_1 = \underline{d}'_1 \in H$ and...and $\underline{d}_n = \underline{d}'_n \in H$ and $R(\underline{d}_1,\ldots,\underline{d}_n) \in H$
only if $R(\underline{d}'_1,\ldots,\underline{d}'_n) \in H$

3.3.4 MODEL LEMMA. Each equalized Hintikka set of dpnf-sentences has a many sorted partial model.

PROOF. Let H be such a set. Having provided the appropriate definition, we can stay close to the procedure in a Henkin-style proof. For all $s \in S$ and all $c \in C_s$ define $[c] := \{c' \in C_s \mid c = c' \in H\}$ Due to 3.3.3 (ii) - (iv), this is an equivalence class. Set $\underline{D}_s := \{[c] \mid c \in C_s\}$ and next $\mathbf{D} := \{\underline{D}_s \mid s \in S\}$. This fixes the domain of the model; now for the interpretation function *. For individual constants c define: $c^* := [c]$ for all $c \in L_H \cup \bigcup_{s \in S}: C_s$. For functions f define: $f^*([t_1],\ldots,[t_n]) = [f(t_1,\ldots,t_n)]$. Given 3.3.3 (i), we can prove that for all $t \in T^s_H$ there is a $[c] \in \underline{D}_s$ with: $[\![t]\!] = [c]$. Also for $f \in FUN_\mathbf{s}$ with $\mathbf{s} = <s_1,\ldots,s_{n+1}>$, $f^* \subseteq \underline{D}_{s_1}\times\ldots\times\underline{D}_{s_n}\times\underline{D}_{s_{n+1}}$. And with the help of 3.3.3 (v) we can show that f* is independent of the representatives of the equivalence classes. * is thus well-defined for all constants and functions. For each n-place relation symbol R define $R^* := \langle R^+, R^- \rangle$ by

$R^+ := \{\langle [t_1],\ldots,[t_n] \rangle \mid R(t_1,\ldots,t_n) \in H\}$ and

$R^- := \{\langle [t_1],\ldots,[t_n] \rangle \mid \neg R(t_1,\ldots,t_n) \in H\}$.

As in the case of functions, it is immediate that $R^+, R^- \subseteq \underline{D}_{s_1}\times\ldots\times\underline{D}_{s_n}$. Using 3.3.2 (i) we see that R^+ and R^- are disjoint. And from 3.3.3 (vi) it follows that R* is independent of the representatives of the equivalence classes. Finally, set $\mathbf{M} := \langle \mathbf{D},* \rangle$. We have defined * in such a way that $[\![t]\!] = [t]$ for all closed terms t. This has as a consequence that for all dpnf-sentences φ:

23 It is understood that these constants are of the proper sort. Idem for (vi)

$\varphi \in H \Rightarrow M \models^{*} \varphi$. For basic sentences, this is true by definition. The other cases are direct consequences of their induction hypotheses. □

The importance of the previous lemma, is mainly due to the Downward Closure Lemma. For the proof of the latter we need some properties of the derivability relation. However, we will not state these properties separately. Instead, we shall use them as we go along and assume that the reader is familiar with their proofs.

3.3.5 DOWNWARD CLOSURE LEMMA. Each consistent set of dpnf sentences is contained in an equalized Hintikka set.

PROOF. First of all we fix the following items:

(i) Γ is a consistent set of dpnf sentences over a countable language L,

(ii) For all $s \in S$, C_s is a countable set of constants c^{s}_{ij} $(i,j \in \omega)$ disjoint from L,[24]

(iii) Γ-FUN_s is the set of $f \in FUN_s$ occurring in Γ,

(iv) Γ-REL_s is the set of $R \in REL_s$ occurring in Γ,

(v) Γ' is the union of Γ with dpnf variants of the following axioms and theorems:[25]

• $EQ_s(=)$, $s \in S$:

$\forall x_s (x = x)$,

$\forall x_s y_s (x = y \rightarrow y = x)$,

$\forall x_s y_s z_s (x = y \wedge y = z .\rightarrow. y = x)$,

• for all $f \in \Gamma$-FUN_s:

$$\forall x_{s_1} y_{s_1} \ldots x_{s_n} y_{s_n} (x_1 = y_1 \wedge \ldots \wedge x_n = y_n \rightarrow f(x_1,\ldots,x_n) = f(y_1,\ldots,y_n)),$$

• for all $R \in \Gamma$-REL_s:

$\forall x_{s_1} y_{s_1} \ldots x_{s_n} y_{s_n} (x_1 = y_1 \wedge \ldots \wedge x_n = y_n \wedge R(x_1,\ldots,x_n) \rightarrow$

24 The use of the subscripts of these constants, will be explained below.

25 The general reasons for adding the axioms and theorems can be found in the proof of 2.4.4.

$\rightarrow R(y_1,\ldots,y_n))$,

- for all basic subformulas $\alpha(x_1,\ldots,x_n,t_1,\ldots,t_m)$ of a sentence in H in which the closed terms $t_1,\ldots,t_m$ occur [not necessarily in that order, and possibly embedded in one another]:
  $\forall x_1\ldots x_n\,[\alpha(x_1,\ldots,x_n,t_1,\ldots,t_m) \rightarrow \exists y\,(t_1 = y) \wedge\ldots\wedge \exists z\,(t_m = z)]$.

Adding axioms and theorems to Γ cannot cause inconsistency, so Γ' is consistent too. Our objective is to turn Γ' into an equalized Hintikka set. To achieve this goal, we proceed in stages each consisting of a number of steps. Each successive stage in this process provides a closer approximation of the set we are after.

In our proof we restrict ourselves to dpnf-sentences, so that negation only occurs in basic sentences. As a consequence we have to treat all the other connectives and quantifiers separately. As in the familiar Henkin argument, we introduce 'fresh' witnessing constants for the existential sentences. This causes a slight problem for the universally quantified sentences. When we encounter them, we add all possible substitutions using all witnessing constants for previous stages. But in the course of events new constants are added. So if a universally quantified sentence is introduced at a certain stage, its substitution instances have to be updated at all later stages. To this end we introduce doubly indexed constants $c_{i\,j}$ for each sort. The right-hand index tells us at which stage we are, the left-hand index keeps track of the steps in that stage. So if we keep the left-hand index constant, say j, we get an enumeration of all constants $c_{i\,j}$ used at stage j.

We first fix an enumeration of constants:

$$c^{0}_{0\,0},\ c^{0}_{1\,0},\ c^{1}_{0\,0},\ c^{0}_{0\,1},\ldots.$$

In this enumeration the superscript indicates the sort relative to an enumeration of S. Notice that from this enumeration we can extract an enumeration of constants for each sort s and each stage n: $c^{s}_{0\,n},\ldots,c^{s}_{k+1\,n},\ldots.$ Let us style the Hintikka set we are after Γ^+. We define the approximations of Γ^+ as follows:

STAGE 0 Set $\Gamma^0 := \Gamma'$

STAGE K+1 Let Γ^k be defined and let $\gamma_1,\ldots,\gamma_n,\ldots$ be an enumeration of $\Gamma^k \backslash \{\varphi \in \Gamma^{k-1} \mid \varphi$ is a non-universal sentence$\}$ if $n > 0$, an enumeration of Γ^0 otherwise.[26] This makes sure that universal sentences already introduced at a previous stage are processed again at all later stages. Now define:
$\Gamma^{k+1}_0 := \Gamma^k$, and:

$$\Gamma^{k+1}_{n+1} := \begin{cases} \Gamma^{k+1}_n \cup \{\varphi, \psi\} & \text{if } \gamma_n \equiv \varphi \wedge \psi \\ \Gamma^{k+1}_n \cup \{\varphi(c_{n+1}{}^{s}{}_{k+1})\} & \text{if } \gamma_n \equiv \exists x_s\, \varphi \\ \Gamma^{k+1}_n \cup \{\varphi(c^s_{i\,j}) \mid i \in \omega, j \leq k\} & \text{if } \gamma_n \equiv \forall x_s\, \varphi \\ \Gamma^{k+1}_n \cup \{\varphi\} & \text{if } \gamma_n \equiv \varphi \vee \psi \text{ and } \Gamma^{k+1}_n, \varphi \nvdash \bot \\ \Gamma^{k+1}_n \cup \{\psi\} & \text{if } \gamma_n \equiv \varphi \vee \psi \text{ and } \Gamma^{k+1}_n, \varphi \vdash \bot \end{cases}$$

Finally: $\Gamma^{k+1} := \bigcup_n \Gamma^{k+1}_n$ and
$\Gamma^+ := \bigcup_k \Gamma^k$

CLAIMS: (i) Γ^k is consistent, for all $k \in \omega$
(ii) Γ^+ is an equalized Hintikka set.

PROOF OF CLAIM (i). We use induction on k. The consistency of Γ^0 is given, so let's proceed to Γ^{k+1}. Subinduction: Γ^{k+1}_0 is consistent by induction hypothesis. Assume therefore that Γ^{k+1}_n is consistent. First observe that $\gamma_n \in \Gamma^k \subseteq \Gamma^{k+1}_n$. So it is enough to show that Γ^{k+1}_{n+1}'s inconsistency implies $\Gamma^{k+1}_n, \gamma_n \vdash \bot$. For then $\Gamma^{k+1}_n \vdash \bot$, contrary to the consistency of Γ^{k+1}_n. Regarding Γ^{k+1}_{n+1} there are five cases to consider:

(a) $\Gamma^{k+1}_{n+1} = \Gamma^{k+1}_n \cup \{\varphi, \psi\}$. I.e. $\gamma_n \equiv \varphi \wedge \psi$. Suppose Γ^{k+1}_{n+1} is inconsistent. Then $\Gamma^{k+1}_n, \varphi, \psi \vdash \bot$, and thus: $\Gamma^{k+1}_n, \varphi \wedge \psi \vdash \bot$.

(b) $\Gamma^{k+1}_{n+1} = \Gamma^{k+1}_n \cup \{\varphi(c_{n+1}{}^{s}{}_{k+1})\}$. I.e. $\gamma_n \equiv \exists x_s\, \varphi$. If Γ^{k+1}_{n+1} is inconsistent, then $\Gamma^{k+1}_n, \varphi(c_{n+1}{}^{s}{}_{k+1}) \vdash \bot$. And, since $c_{n+1}{}^{s}{}_{k+1}$ does not occur in Γ^{k+1}_n by the lemma of constants: $\Gamma^{k+1}_n, \exists x_s \varphi \vdash \bot$.

26 Of course, when Γ is finite, this enumeration is of finite length.

(c) $\Gamma^{k+1}_{n+1} = \Gamma^{k+1}_{n} \cup \{\varphi(c^{s}_{ij}) \mid i \in \omega, j \leq k\}$. I.e. $\gamma_n \equiv \forall x_s\, \varphi$. Note that $\gamma_n \vdash \varphi(c^{s}_{ij})$ $[i \in \omega, j \leq k]$. And thus $\Gamma^{k+1}_{n} \vdash \varphi(c^{s}_{ij})$, since $\gamma_n \in \Gamma^{k+1}_{n}$. Hence, if Γ^{k+1}_{n+1} is inconsistent, so is Γ^{k+1}_{n}.

(d) $\Gamma^{k+1}_{n+1} = \Gamma^{k+1}_{n} \cup \{\varphi\}$. I.e. $\gamma_n \equiv \varphi \vee \psi$, and Γ^{k+1}_{n+1} is consistent by definition.

(e) $\Gamma^{k+1}_{n+1} = \Gamma^{k+1}_{n} \cup \{\psi\}$. I.e. $\gamma_n \equiv \varphi \vee \psi$ and $\Gamma^{k+1}_{n}, \varphi \vdash \bot$. If $\Gamma^{k+1}_{n}, \psi \vdash \bot$ too, then $\Gamma^{k+1}_{n}, \varphi \vee \psi \vdash \bot$.

PROOF OF CLAIM (ii). Γ^+ is an equalized Hintikka set by construction. That $\bot \in \Gamma^+$ and that for no atomic sentence α both α and its negation are in Γ^+, follows from (i). The only other case worth considering is:

$$\begin{aligned}
\forall x_s.\varphi \in \Gamma^+ \quad &\Rightarrow \quad \exists k \in \omega: \forall m \geq k: \forall x_s.\varphi \in \Gamma^m \\
&\Rightarrow \quad \exists k \in \omega: \forall m \geq k: \forall j < m: \forall i \in \omega: \varphi(c^{s}_{ij}) \in \Gamma^m \\
&\Rightarrow \quad \forall i \in \omega: \forall j \in \omega: \varphi(c^{s}_{ij}) \in \Gamma^m \\
&\Rightarrow \quad \varphi(c) \in \Gamma^+ \text{ for all } c \in C_s
\end{aligned}$$

That Γ^+ is equalized is immediate from downward closedness and the fact that we added the relevant axioms beforehand. For instance, for 3.3.3 (i) we use a relevant instance of

$$\forall x_1 \ldots x_n\, [\alpha(x_1,\ldots,x_n,t_1,\ldots,t_m) \rightarrow \exists y\,(t_1 = y) \wedge \ldots \wedge \exists z\,(t_m = z)] \qquad \square$$

The following observations make it clear that we can use 3.3.4 and 3.3.5 to obtain a completeness result.

3.3.6 OBSERVATIONS. Let φ^{pn} denote a prenex normal form of φ and set $\Gamma^{pn} := \{\psi^{pn} \mid \psi \in \Gamma\}$

(i) $\Gamma \vdash \varphi \Leftrightarrow \Gamma^{pn} \vdash \varphi^{pn}$

(ii) $\Gamma \models \varphi \Leftrightarrow \Gamma^{pn} \models \varphi^{pn}$

PROOF. Observation (ii), for instance, is an immediate consequence of a many sorted variant of the Coincidence Lemma (see §1). $\square$

3.3.7 COMPLETENESS FOR MANY SORTED PARTIAL PREDICATE LOGIC.
PROOF. Suppose $\Gamma \nvDash \varphi$. By observation (i): $\Gamma^{pn} \nvDash \varphi^{pn}$. So $\Gamma^{pn} \cup \{\neg\varphi^{pn}\}$ is consistent. Downward Closure Lemma: $\Gamma^{pn} \cup \{\varphi^{pn}\}$ is contained in an equalized Hintikka set H. Model Lemma: H has a partial model, say **M**. Hence, $\mathbf{M} \vDash^{+} \Gamma^{pn}$ and $\mathbf{M} \vDash^{-} \varphi^{pn}$ From observation (ii) we conclude that $\mathbf{M} \vDash^{+} \Gamma$ and $\mathbf{M} \vDash^{-} \varphi$. □

It is straightforward to find contingent sentences for which the produced countermodel is indeed partial. The following example shows that this can also be true for derivations with denumerably many premisses. For each $n \in \omega$ let P_n be a predicate letter of sort $<s_n>$. Now look at:

$$\{\exists x_{s_n} \exists y_{s_n} (P_n x \wedge \neg P_n y) \mid n \geq 1\} \nvDash \exists x_{s_0} \exists y_{s_0} (P_0 x \wedge \neg P_0 y).$$

Assuming an enumeration of this set according to the indices of the predicate letters, the construction in the completeness proof gives a model $\mathbf{M} = \langle \mathbf{D},* \rangle$ such that $P_0^* = \langle \emptyset, C_o \rangle$, which is classical, and for $n \geq 1$ the partial interpretations $P_n^* = \langle \{c^{n}_{n+1\,1}\}, \{c^{n}_{n+1\,2}\} \rangle$. The next theorem, a rephrasing of Hintikka's lemma[27], is therefore no empty gesture.

3.3.8 COMPLETENESS FOR MANY SORTED CLASSICAL PREDICATE LOGIC.
PROOF. Suppose $\Gamma \nvDash \varphi$. Theorem 1 gives a partial model **M**, such that $\mathbf{M} \vDash^{+} \Gamma$ and $\mathbf{M} \vDash^{-} \varphi$. From the monotonicity lemma we conclude that every extension of **M** to a classical model will serve as a countermodel for $\Gamma \vDash \varphi$ □

It is worth to observing that the principles used in the proof of 3.3.5 are all available in the deductive systems for the strong consequence relation.[28] (See for example van Benthem (1984)). So if we change the classical systems used in this and the previous section to a strong consequence logic, then we also have correctness and completeness as to this notion of consequence.

---

27 Each downward closed set of sentences has a classical model.

28 φ is a strong consequence of Γ iff if all $\psi \in \Gamma$ are verified then so is φ.

Conclusions

Section 1 shows how a consequence relation that gives rise to classical logic in a partial setting, can be used to link the different variants of IQ with IQ-Prolog. This raises the question of how this partial interpretation of PROLOG is related to other proposals in this direction. A comparison with the work of Fitting (1985) may be especially enlightening.

The soundness and completeness results for the interval based IQ^{int} have as a bonus that they point to yet another way of building temporal databases within the framework of IQ, since all important axioms are Horn clauses. Pursuing this strand of research will facilitate the comparison of temporal databases built on the basis of principles of IQ with other proposals in the field (Kowalski and Sergot (1986), Allen and Hayes (1985)). The different treatments of instantaneous events and the differences in efficiency, will play a crucial rôle in eventually determining which strategy to adopt.

The results in §3 provide in a general way soundness and completeness results for extensions of IQ^{int} similar to those defined in Chapter 7. The completeness proof shows in detail the usefulness of Hintikka sets when working in a partial environment.

9

Indexed Operators and Completeness

JAAP VAN DER DOES

Introduction

IQ's origins lie in the semantics of natural language where rich and expressive formal systems are commonly used. From a logical point of view, however, it is useful to focus on the propositional part of IQ, if only to clarify IQ's essential properties.

This chapter begins with a description of the syntax and semantics of IQ^{π}. Stricly speaking, IQ^{π} is not IQ's propositional fragment but rather a bimodal extension thereof. In this extension we eliminate some asymmetries between the syntax and semantics of the original formulation. The semantics of IQ is based on interval structures which carry two relations, viz. 'is before' and 'is a subinterval of'. In IQ's syntax, however, there are operators which quantify over the former, but none which quantify over the latter. To remove this limitation we add two operators $\uparrow$ and $\downarrow$ which function like the familiar F and P except for the fact that they quantify over the subinterval relation instead of the relation 'is before'.[1] That these operators are not indexed points to another minor deviation from the original approach. As well as the Priorean F and P and the already mentioned $\uparrow$ and $\downarrow$, we use only one indexed

[1] Compare van Benthem (1983: 193).

operator, viz. A_v.[2] We shall show that IQ^{π} is powerful enough to define IQ's original indexed tense operators, and also to define all the 'simple', non-quantificational operators defined in Chapter 1.

In Chapter 7 the relation between IQ and its implementation in PROLOG, viz. IQ-Prolog, is given via an intermediate language IQ^{E}. In Section 2 we argue that in this process the distinctive feature of IQ's operators is lost. This discussion is followed by the definition of a program which directly implements IQ into PROLOG. A procedural completeness result is given stating that the procedures used are correct and complete with respect to their intended meaning.

The final section opens with a discussion of the notion of logical consequence used. Next we note and remove another asymmetry between IQ's syntax and semantics. The original languages only allowed constants, parameters and variables as interval terms. But such structureless terms cannot syntactically capture the fact that intervals in a model are characterized by means of their endpoints. Once we have remedied this limitation, we shall prove a completeness result as regards IQ^{π}-models which are induced by a finite total order.

§1 The Syntax and Semantics of IQ^{π}

We begin with a brief description of the syntax. There is an infinite supply of propositional variables together with an infinite set of interval variables and a possibly empty set of interval constants. The main syntactic novelty of IQ^{π} is the availability of indexed operators A_v where v is an interval variable or a constant.[3] We also have four one-place operators: P, F, $\uparrow$ and $\downarrow$.

---

2 Blackburn was the first to make a similar move in his Nominal Tense Logic. (See Blackburn 1989).

3 The structured interval terms mentioned in the introduction are introduced in §3.

FORMULAS. The set of IQ^π formulas is the smallest set which contains the propositional variables and is closed under:

- if φ is a formula, so is $\neg\varphi$;
- if φ and ψ are formulas, then so is $\varphi\wedge\psi$;
- if v is an interval term and φ is a formula, then $A_v\varphi$ is formula;
- if φ is a formula, then so are $P\varphi$, $F\varphi$, $\uparrow\varphi$ and $\downarrow\varphi$.

What does the semantics of IQ^π look like? From its inception intervals in IQ have been taken to be the convex sets over a point structure, i.e. they are of the form

$$[n,m] = \{k \mid n \leq k \leq m\}.$$[4]

In Chapter 6 the models for IQ are defined on top of such an interval structure. In the environment of IQ^π, we take a more 'radical' approach and define models for this interval logic using *models* over a point structure. More precisely, we proceed as follows:

IQ^π-MODELS. Let $\mathbf{T} = \langle T, <, *\rangle$ be a model for a propositional language over the linearly ordered time structure $\langle T, <\rangle$ such that $p^* \subseteq T$ for all propositional variables p. An IQ^π-model **M** is a pair $\langle I_T, ^\circ\rangle$ with

(i) $I_T = \langle I, \ll, \sqsubseteq\rangle$ an interval structure, such that:
  - I the set of all convex intervals over $\langle T, <\rangle$;
  - $\emptyset \notin I$;
  - $[n,m] \ll [k,l] \quad \Leftrightarrow \quad m < k$;
  - $[n,m] \sqsubseteq [k,l] \quad \Leftrightarrow \quad k \leq n$ and $m \leq l$.

(ii) $^\circ$ an interpretation function such that
  - $i^\circ \in I$, for all interval constants, and
  - $p^\circ = \{i \in I \mid \forall t \in i: t \in p^*\}$, for all propositional variables.

---

4 In the sequel we shall only mention the closed intervals and take the other variants for granted.

In these models we have a 'bottom-up' approach, where the intervals in p° are seen as 'collectors' of sequences of points at which p is true.

There are some important similarities and differences between IQ^{π}-models and the models for IQ's propositional fragment which we now discuss.

An important feature of IQ-models is *homogeneity*, and it can be proved that IQ^{π}-models have this property too:

$$[n,m] \in p^{\circ}$$
$$\Rightarrow \quad \forall t \in [n,m]: t \in p^*$$
$$\Rightarrow \quad \text{For all } [k,l] \sqsubseteq [n,m]: \forall t \in [k,l]: t \in p^* \quad (\text{since } n \leq k \text{ and } l \leq m)$$
$$\Rightarrow \quad \text{For all } [k,l] \sqsubseteq [n,m]: [k,l] \in p^{\circ}.$$

In other words, p° is closed under subintervals.

A second feature of IQ-models is the *partial* character of the interpretation function on intervals, with the exception of point intervals at which it is *total* and *consistent*. Note that in connection with points the interpretation function ° defined above inherits *totality* and *consistency* from the function *. For any point interval [k,k] = {k} we have:

$$[k,k] \in p^{\circ} \Leftrightarrow \forall t \in [k,k]: t \in p^* \Leftrightarrow k \in p^*.$$

And k either is or is not, but certainly not both, an element of p*. This leads to the main departure from the original definition: IQ^{π}-models are total throughout. So, in the propositional fragment homogeneity does *not* force the interpretation function to be partial.[5]

Another difference between IQ^{π}-models and the original ones is that in the latter a sentence can be true at all 'point' subintervals of an interval while not being true at that interval itself, a situation which is excluded in the models defined above.

---

[5] The situation is different for the predicate logical variant of IQ. See Chapter 6 and the discussion on strong homogeneity in Chapter 8.

Before defining satisfaction of a formula in a model, we must first define the interpretation of interval terms. We do so in the standard way.

INTERPRETATION OF INTERVAL TERMS. Let $\mathbf{M} = \langle\langle I, \ll, \sqsubseteq\rangle, {}^\circ\rangle$ be an IQ^π-model and g an assignment of interval variables into I. The interpretation of terms, denoted by $[\![t]\!]$, is defined by:

$[\![t]\!] = t^\circ$ for constants,

$[\![t]\!] = g(t)$ for variables.[6]

The definition of satisfaction now becomes:

SATISFACTION. Let i be an interval, φ a sentence and g an assignment. Satisfaction of φ at i under g, notation $i \models \varphi\ [g]$, is defined by:

$i \models p\ [g] \Leftrightarrow i \in p^\circ$

$i \models \neg\varphi\ [g] \Leftrightarrow$ not: $i \models \varphi\ [g]$

$i \models \varphi\wedge\psi\ [g] \Leftrightarrow i \models \varphi\ [g]$ and $i \models \psi\ [g]$

$i \models A_v\varphi\ [g] \Leftrightarrow [\![v]\!]^g = i$ and $i \models \varphi\ [g]$

$i \models P\varphi\ [g] \Leftrightarrow \exists i' \ll i: i' \models \varphi\ [g]$

$i \models F\varphi\ [g] \Leftrightarrow \exists i' \gg i: i' \models \varphi\ [g]$

$i \models \downarrow\varphi\ [g] \Leftrightarrow \exists i' \sqsubseteq i: i' \models \varphi\ [g]$

$i \models \uparrow\varphi\ [g] \Leftrightarrow \exists i' \sqsupseteq i: i' \models \varphi\ [g]$

This covers all cases.

From the satisfaction definition it is plain that the introduction of the operators $\uparrow$ and $\downarrow$ remedies the limitation existing in the formalization of IQ in Chapter 6, where the subinterval relation is only mentioned in the homogeneity condition.

6 In general we do not indicate the dependency of $[\![t]\!]$ on $\mathbf{M}$ and g. The context will take care of that.

Comparison with the propositional fragment of IQ

As it stands, IQ^{π} does not have operators which are similar to IQ's indexed tense operators. But they can be introduced as abbreviations:

$$P_v\varphi :=_{def} A_vP\varphi$$
$$F_v\varphi :=_{def} A_vF\varphi$$

Where $H\varphi$ and $G\varphi$ respectively abbreviate $\neg P\neg\varphi$ and $\neg F\neg\varphi$, we similarly have:

$$H_v\varphi :=_{def} A_vH\varphi$$
$$G_v\varphi :=_{def} A_vG\varphi$$

We leave it to the reader to verify that these operators have the desired meaning, for example:

$$i \models P_v\varphi\,[g] \quad \Leftrightarrow \quad [\![v]\!] = i \text{ and } \exists i' \ll i\text{: } i' \models \varphi\,[g];$$
$$i \models G_v\varphi\,[g] \quad \Leftrightarrow \quad [\![v]\!] = i \text{ and } \forall i' \gg i\text{: } i' \models \varphi\,[g].$$

It is instructive to note that, due to the 'hidden' conjunction in the meaning of P_v and F_v, we cannot define, say, $H_v\varphi := \neg P_v\neg\varphi$, for then:

$$i \models H_v\varphi\,[g]$$
$$\Leftrightarrow \quad i \models \neg P_v\neg\varphi\,[g]$$
$$\Leftrightarrow \quad \text{not: } i \models P_v\neg\varphi\,[g]$$
$$\Leftrightarrow \quad \text{not } (\,[\![v]\!] = i \text{ and } \exists i' \ll i\text{: } i' \models \neg\varphi\,[g]\,)$$
$$\Leftrightarrow \quad [\![v]\!] \neq i \text{ or } \forall i' \ll i\text{: } i' \models \varphi\,[g]$$

And surely we do not want $H_v\varphi$ to be true at an interval only because the index v fails to refer to that specific interval.

In fact the definition of the syntax and semantics of IQ^{π} would be closer to the original format if one were to use indexed operators P_v, F_v, $\uparrow_v$ and $\downarrow_v$

instead of their unindexed 'counterparts'. All formulas of the form $O_v\varphi$ with $O \in \{P, F, \uparrow, \downarrow\}$ would then have an interval specific character which could be removed by applying the G-operator to them:

THE G OPERATOR. *(Syntax)* If v is an interval variable and φ is a formula, then $Gv\varphi$ is a formula. *(Semantics)* $i \models Gv\varphi\ [g] \Leftrightarrow i \models \varphi\ [g^v_i]$

Then one could define, say, $P\varphi := GvP_v\varphi$. Assuming that v does not occur free in φ, it can be shown that $P\varphi$ has the same Priorean truth conditions as the operator P which is taken to be primitive in IQ^π:

$$
\begin{array}{ll}
 & i \models P\varphi\ [g] \\
\Leftrightarrow & i \models GvP_v\varphi\ [g] \\
\Leftrightarrow & i \models P_v\varphi\ [g^v_i] \\
\Leftrightarrow & g^v_i(v) = i \text{ and } \exists i' \ll i\text{: } i' \models \varphi\ [g] \\
\Leftrightarrow & \exists\, i' \ll i\text{: } i' \models \varphi\ [g]
\end{array}
$$

The last equivalence holds, since v is not free in φ, so g^v_i can be replaced by g. Similar proofs exists for the other indexed operators.

Here one might ask: does the language with the operators A_v, P, F, $\uparrow$ and $\downarrow$ differ in expressive power from the language consisting of their indexed variants together with the G-operator? To answer this question, we have to look at the application of the G-operator to the 'referential' operator A_v. Again assuming that v does not occur free in φ, it turns out that in this case the vacuous operator results:

$$i \models GvA_v\varphi\ [g] \Leftrightarrow i \models \varphi\ [g]$$

This is immediate from the truth clause of the operator involved and the fact that $g^v_i(v) = i$ is always fulfilled. So if we limit ourselves to the class of admissible sentences[7] the answer to the above question must be that both

[7] For a precise definition of *admissible formula* see Chapter 6. As usual, a sentence is a formula without free variables.

languages do not differ in expressive power. Or, to put it in another way, the expressive power of the system IQ mainly resides in the referential feature of the operator A_v.

Other quantificational and non-quantificational operators

When reading some of the chapters in Part I, one might get the feeling that it would be desirable if the many quantificational and non-quantificational operators introduced there could be defined within a simple, more basic logical system. We shall show that IQ^π is a step in that direction.

To begin with we consider the quantificational operators ALWAYS_r and NEVER_r. We first observe that $\text{NEVER}_r\varphi$ can be defined by $\text{ALWAYS}_r\neg\varphi$, so it suffices to find a definition of ALWAYS_r. It is not difficult to check that the 'coverless'

$$\text{ALWAYS}_r\psi :=_{def} A_r\Downarrow\psi$$

where $\Downarrow\psi$ is defined by $\neg\downarrow\neg\psi$, will do.[8] Here $A_r\Downarrow\psi$ gets the intuitive meaning that all r's subintervals verify ψ. The quantifier $\text{EXACTLY TWICE}_r\varphi$ is also introduced in Chapter 1, but we have not been able to find a definition of this quantifier in IQ^π.

In Chapter 1 non-quantificational operators are introduced like On_v and $Before_v$ with truth-conditions:

$$i \models On_v\varphi \quad \Leftrightarrow \quad i \sqsubseteq [\![v]\!] \text{ and } i \models \varphi$$
$$i \models Before_v\varphi \quad \Leftrightarrow \quad i \ll [\![v]\!] \text{ and } i \models \varphi$$

That the expressive power of the system IQ mainly resides in the referential feature of the operator A_v is forcefully shown in Blackburn (1989). But there is a subtle shift in perspective. His *nominals,* which belong to the category of formulas, function like our indices, which do not so belong. The IQ^π-formulas which come closest to Blackburn's nominals are those of the form A_vp with p a propositional variable. But A_vp is true at at most one interval whereas an (interval) nominal is true at exactly one interval.

8 Similarly $\Uparrow\varphi :=_{def} \neg\uparrow\neg\varphi$. For the notion of cover, see Chapter 1.

For each interval relation there are in fact four such operators with truth-conditions of this form. For completeness sake, we list the four subinterval operators below:

$$i \models \mathrm{SUB}_v\varphi \quad \Leftrightarrow \quad i \sqsubseteq [\![v]\!] \text{ and } i \models \varphi$$
$$i \models \mathbf{SUB}_v\varphi \quad \Leftrightarrow \quad i \sqsubseteq [\![v]\!] \text{ and } [\![v]\!] \models \varphi$$
$$i \models {}_v\mathrm{SUB}\varphi \quad \Leftrightarrow \quad [\![v]\!] \sqsubseteq i \text{ and } i \models \varphi$$
$$i \models {}_v\mathbf{SUB}\varphi \quad \Leftrightarrow \quad [\![v]\!] \sqsubseteq i \text{ and } [\![v]\!] \models \varphi$$

Similarly we have $\mathrm{BEF}_v\varphi$, $\mathbf{BEF}_v\varphi$, ${}_v\mathrm{BEF}\varphi$ and ${}_v\mathbf{BEF}\varphi$ using the 'is before' relation. It is not difficult to show that these non-quantificational operators can be defined in IQ^π by means of the following abbreviations:

$$\mathrm{SUB}_v\varphi :=_{\mathrm{def}} \uparrow A_vT \wedge \varphi$$ [9]
$$\mathbf{SUB}_v\varphi :=_{\mathrm{def}} \uparrow A_v\varphi$$

Dually we have ${}_v\mathrm{SUB}\varphi$ and ${}_v\mathbf{SUB}\varphi$ using $\downarrow$ instead of $\uparrow$. Much in the same manner we have:

$$\mathrm{BEF}_v\varphi :=_{\mathrm{def}} FA_vT \wedge \varphi$$
$$\mathbf{BEF}_v\varphi :=_{\mathrm{def}} FA_v\varphi$$

Again we dually get ${}_v\mathrm{BEF}\varphi$ and ${}_v\mathbf{BEF}\varphi$, now using P instead of F. We only show that $\mathrm{SUB}_v\varphi$ and $\mathbf{SUB}_v\varphi$ have the meaning desired, the other cases are shown *mutatis mutandis* in the same way. First note that:

$$\begin{aligned} & i \models \uparrow A_vT\,[g] \\ \Leftrightarrow\quad & \exists i' \sqsupseteq i\ (\, i' \models A_vT\,[g]\,) \\ \Leftrightarrow\quad & \exists i' \sqsupseteq i\ (\, i' = [\![v]\!]^g \text{ and } i' \models T\,[g]\,) \\ \Leftrightarrow\quad & i \sqsubseteq [\![v]\!]^g \end{aligned}$$

Using this we get:

---

9 'T' denotes *verum*.

$$\begin{aligned} & i \models SUB_v\varphi\ [g] \\ \Leftrightarrow\ & i \models \uparrow A_v T \wedge \varphi\ [g] \\ \Leftrightarrow\ & i \sqsubseteq [\![v]\!]^g \text{ and } i \models \varphi\ [g]. \end{aligned}$$

Furthermore it is true that:

$$\begin{aligned} & i \models \mathbf{SUB}_v\varphi\ [g] \\ \Leftrightarrow\ & i \models \uparrow A_v\varphi\ [g] \\ \Leftrightarrow\ & \exists i' \sqsupseteq i\ (\ i' \models A_v\varphi\ [g]\ ) \\ \Leftrightarrow\ & \exists i' \sqsupseteq i\ (\ i' = [\![v]\!] \text{ and } i' \models \varphi\ [g]\ ) \\ \Leftrightarrow\ & i \sqsubseteq [\![v]\!]^g \text{ and } [\![v]\!]^g \models \varphi\ [g] \end{aligned}$$

as required.

At the beginning of this subsection we remarked that we have not been able to define the quantifier EXACTLY TWICE$_r$ in IQ^π. The same holds for the operator HAVE and the connective WHEN.[10] Given the more complicated first-order character of their definitions, this may indicate that IQ^π does not coincide with a 'full-blown' first-order interval logic. On the other hand it may exhibit a lack of imagination on our part.

We end this discussion with a list of the non-quantificational operators defined in Chapter 1 and the form these operators get within IQ^π.

AT 9.0	$A_{9.0}$
AT then	A_{then}
BEFORE 1492	BEF_{1492}
ON 4/1/1989	$SUB_{4/1/1989}$
AFTER 3/1988	$_{3/1988}BEF$
DURING 1990	$_{1990}SUB$

[10] See Chapter 1.

§2 A Procedural Approach.

In Chapter 7 IQ and IQ-Prolog are related by means of an intermediate language IQ^E. After it is shown that a subset of the IQ formulas can be translated into IQ^E, the Horn clause fragment of the latter is exploited to find a strategy for constructing temporal databases in PROLOG.

The main 'obstacle' to translating IQ into IQ^E concerns the interval specificity of IQ's operators: if an IQ formula of the form $\Pi_v\varphi$ is true in a model, it is true at exactly one interval, the one referred to by the index v. The indexed tense operators in IQ^E lack this specificity.[11] The $Pres_v$-operator in IQ^E, for instance, which shifts the interval of evaluation to the interval referred to by v, is different from the $PRES_v$-operator in IQ. In IQ^E $Pres_v\varphi$ is true at *all* intervals in a model, if φ is true at v.[12] To translate IQ tenses into IQ^E something extra is needed. The specificity of the IQ formula

$PAST_i\varphi$,

is captured in IQ^E by the translation

$now(i) \wedge past_i\ \tau(\varphi)$,

where $\tau(\varphi)$ is the translation of φ. In this translation the referential aspect of $PAST_i\varphi$ is taken care of by the conjunct *now(i)*.

---

[11] The quantificational resources of IQ^E together with the special character of its tenses allow the elimination of tenses, other then the present tense, in favour of explicit quantification over intervals. (See e.g. (78) in Chapter 7) This format facilitates the implemention of IQ into PROLOG.

[12] At this point the reader may wonder about the relation of the A_v operator in IQ^π and the $Pres_v$ operator in IQ. Formally they function the same, but in fact there is a conceptual difference. The A_v-operator in IQ^π is a purely referential operator, whereas the $PRES_V$ in IQ is a tense operator which has referential features. That this difference cannot be discerned formally results from the fact that in Priorean languages the present tense is modeled by the empty operator Ø. Strictly speaking, we must say that IQ's $PRES_V$ is modeled by A_vØ in IQ^π.

In IQ-Prolog one finds the procedure

past(X,A) :- at(Y,A), Y « X.[13]

which defines the past tense along the lines of IQ^E. This raises the question whether the differentiating character of IQ's operators is preserved in IQ-Prolog. The answer is plainly 'no', since there is no restriction which fixes the value of X to *now*. This is just to say that past(X,A) does not correspond to the past tense of IQ; in IQ-Prolog the interval specificity of IQ's operators is lost.

There are several ways to retain IQ's main features within a procedural framework. The above translation already indicated one: use a predicate *now* which goes to true for exactly one interval and take the procedure

past(X,A) :- now(X), Y « X, at(Y,A).

Then it is immediate from the translation results obtained in Chapter 7 that the essentials of IQ's past operator are preserved.

In this section we shall use a different technique. Instead of employing an indexical operator like *now*, we implement part of the semantics of IQ^π.[14] We do so by making a distinction between the index of an operator and the index of evaluation. This enables us to directly use IQ^π for writing programs akin to IQ-Prolog, in particular we can circumvent a translation of IQ^π into an intermediate language like IQ^E. We also obtain simple proofs of soundness and completeness in regard to the intended models by applying techniques discussed in Fitting (1987).

---

13 In Chapter 7 two procedures are defined, the one used here and one using 'at_hom(Y,A)' instead of 'at(Y,A)'. Eventually the last one is chosen, but for our purposes nothing essential is lost if we discuss the simpler version.

14 This language must *not* be seen as having an intermediate status like that of IQ^E. As is argued in section 1, IQ^π is devised to fulfill the same rôle as IQ.

We begin our exercise by showing how each IQ^{π}-model induces a (many sorted) *workspace* **W** in the sense of Fitting (1987):

WORKSPACE. Let $\mathbf{M} = \langle I_T, ^\circ \rangle$ be an IQ^{π}-model over the time structure $\langle T, < \rangle$. We associate with **M** the workspace

$$\mathbf{W} = \langle I, \text{Form}, \text{PROP}, \text{BEFORE}, \text{SUB}, \text{AT} \rangle,$$

with domains I, the set of intervals induced by $\langle T, < \rangle$, and Form, the set of IQ^{π}-formulas. PROP, BEFORE, SUB and AT are *reserved* identifiers whose interpretations may not be altered. As a consequence a reserved identifier may not occur in the head of a procedure. PROP represents the set of propositional variables, and BEFORE and SUB respectively represent the relations $\ll$ and $\sqsubseteq$. AT represents the relation $\{\langle i, p \rangle \in I \times \text{PROP} \mid i \in p^\circ\}$. So, AT(i, p) holds if and only if $i \models p$ in **M**. □

For the workspace **W** associated with the model **M** one can find an expansion $\langle \mathbf{W}$, ex_form, at_int$\rangle$ in which the relation *at_int* expresses the sufficient truth conditions of the set of existential formulas—generated by *ex_form*—as regards **M**.[15] Existential formulas are negationless formulas which, apart from $\wedge$, $\vee$ and A_v, only contain the 'existential' operators P, F, $\uparrow$ and $\downarrow$:

EXISTENTIAL FORMULAS. The set EF of existential formulas is the smallest set which contains the propositional variables and is closed under the rule: if φ and ψ are in EF then so are $\varphi \wedge \psi$, $\varphi \vee \psi$, $A_v\varphi$, $P\varphi$, $F\varphi$, $\uparrow\varphi$ and $\downarrow\varphi$.

The following expansion of **W** will do:

---

15 An *expansion* of a workspace consists of procedures which generate new relations on the domains of the workspace. In the body of the procedure definitions one may use the relations given in the initial workspace or procedures added earlier to the workspace.

/* First a procedure for the syntactical relation *ex_form* that generates the existential formulas from the propositional variables. Here 'down' corresponds to '↓' and 'up' to '↑'.*/

- ex_form(P) :- PROP(P).
- ex_form(and(F1, F2)) :- ex_form(F1), ex_form(F2).
- ex_form(or(F1, F2)) :- ex_form(F1), ex_form(F2).
- ex_form(at_int(I, F)) :- ex_form(F).[16]
- ex_form(past(F)) :- ex_form(F).
- ex_form(fut(F)) :- ex_form(F).
- ex_form(up(F)) :- ex_form(F).
- ex_form(down(F)) :- ex_form(F).

/* Finally a procedure for the semantical relation *at_int(I, Form)* stating that the existential formula *Form* is true at interval I.*/

- at_int(I, P) :- PROP(P), AT(I, P).
- at_int(I, and(Form1, Form2)) :-
  ex_form(Form1), ex_form(Form2),
  at_int(I, Form1), at_int(I, Form2).[17]
- at_int(I, or(Form1, Form2)) :- at_int(I, Form1).
  at_int(I, or(Form1, Form2)) :- at_int(I, Form2).
- at_int(I, at_int(I, Form)) :- at_int(I, Form).
- at_int(I, past(Form)) :- BEFORE(J, I), at_int(J, Form).
- at_int(I, fut(Form)) :- BEFORE(I, J), at_int(J, Form).
- at_int(I, up(Form)) :- SUB(I, J), at_int(J, Form).
- at_int(I, down(Form)) :- SUB(J, I), at_int(J, Form).

/* This completes the definition. */

---

16 Variables of the form *I* and *J* are taken to range over the domain of intervals.

17 In the sequel we suppress clauses of the form *ex_form(Form)*; all variables commencing with 'Form' are taken to range over existential formulas.

Now we shall show how the *at_int* relation captures the interval specific character of IQ's indexed tense operators. As stated earlier, in IQ^{π} a tense operator Π_i is defined by $A_i\Pi$ with Π the corresponding Priorean operator. Note that formulas of the form $F_i\varphi$ and $P_i\varphi$ are existential if φ is. As a result a query using IQ's past operator gets the form:

```
? at_int(I, at_int(J, past(Form))).
```

In evaluating this query the relevant clause is:

```
at_int(I, at_int(I, Form)) :- at_int(I, Form).
```

If $I \neq J$, we will get the answer 'no'. So, making use of the fact that the intervals occuring in its head respectively model the interval of evaluation and the index of the A_i-operator, it is this procedure which embodies the referential character of IQ's operators. In the case where $I = J$ this clause reduces the above query to:

```
? at_int(I, past(Form)).
```

Here the relevant rule is

```
at_int(I, past(Form)) :- BEFORE(Z, I), at_int(Z, Form),
```

which leads to the required reduction

```
BEFORE(Z, I), at_int(Z, Form).
```

Similar derivations can be made for the other indexed operators, including those having nested occurrences in a query. So, the strategy embodied in the expansion clearly shows that IQ's 'computable part' can be directly translated into PROLOG without the use of an intermediate stage.

Let $(\varphi)^+$ be the obvious translation of a existential formula φ into its counterpart within the range of the procedure *ex_form*, and let $\mathbf{M} \models A_v\varphi$ mean: $[\![v]\!] \models \varphi$.[18] We now prove that queries of the form ?at_int(i, $(\varphi)^+$) which get an affirmative answer are true in the intended model, and *vice versa*.

SOUNDNESS AND COMPLETENESS. Let **W** be the workspace related to the model **M**. If we expand **W** as described above, then for all existential formulas φ: 'at_int(i, $(\varphi)^+$)' is derivable from the expansion if and only if $\mathbf{M} \models A_i\varphi$.[19]

PROOF. In fact we have to prove a completeness and soundness result for both relations involved and not only for the *at_int* relation. But we assume the result to be given for *ex_form*.

[$\Rightarrow$:] The soundness part of the argument is proved by means of an induction on the complexity of the proof of at_int(i, $(\varphi)^+$). We therefore have to prove that all reserved relations are true in the underlying point structure—which is true by definition—and that all substitution instances of the procedures are true—which is straightforward—and that heads are true if all the clauses in the body are true—which is obvious. So soundness is no problem.

[$\Leftarrow$:] The completeness part is proved by induction on the complexity of φ. The proof is a bit tedious, so we shall only provide a sample case:
$(\varphi \equiv A_j\psi)$
Assume $\mathbf{M} \models A_iA_j\psi$. Then $i = j$ and $\mathbf{M} \models A_j\psi$. By the induction hypothesis at_int(j,$(\psi)^+$) is derivable from the expansion. And thus, using Modus Ponens and the procedure instance

---

18 The rationale behind the latter is discussed in depth in §3's subsection 'Logical consequence'.

19 To be precise, we show that the relation $\{\langle i, \varphi\rangle \mid \varphi$ is existential and $\mathbf{M} \models A_i\varphi\}$ can be generated in the workspace. Here and in the proof we identify interval terms and their interpretations.

$$\text{at\_int}(i, \text{at\_int}(j, (\psi)^+)) \text{ :- } \text{at\_int}(i, (\psi)^+),$$

$\text{at\_int}(i, \text{at\_int}(j, (\psi)^+)) \equiv \text{at\_int}(i, (A_j\psi)^+)$ is derivable from the expansion as well. □

Implementing intensional logics

Although the previous result is theoretical in spirit, it does capture a useful idea concerning the implementation of intensional logics. One of the main insights gained from Kripke's semantics for these logics is that syntactical principles correspond to structural properties of the ontology. When it comes to implementing intensional forms of reasoning, it is therefore natural to attempt to incorporate within the implementation the set of axioms corresponding to the appropriate ontological structure. In this process, however, one is likely to discover that the required axioms do not have a proper formulation within the programming language used. This will be the case, for instance, if one implements a tense logic in PROLOG via a translation into a first-order language. It is not obvious that a particular set of axioms can be meaningfully translated into the Horn clause fragment.

The procedures above circumvented the need to use characterizing axioms by defining part of the *semantics* of IQ^{π} in PROLOG rather than providing a theorem prover for one of its complete deduction systems. Instead of implementing syntactical principles and leaving the intended models unspecified, we implement a specific intended model. Quering the database now mimics the evaluation of a sentence in the implemented model.

Using this strategy, the properties of the accessibility relation have to have a definition within the programming language. In the case of PROLOG, for instance, these properties must have a formulation within the Horn clause fragment. So in some cases one may encounter problems akin to those for the syntactical approach of writing a theorem prover, where—as remarked earlier—the axioms required may not have a formulation within the language used. When implementing tense logic, however, we can in fact use structures like the integers and reals, since they will be provided by each reasonable computer system. And if we use the trick of having sequences of natural numbers as worlds, then the same holds for intensional logics in general.

§3 A General Completeness Result

In IQ's original syntax and semantics only constants, parameters and variables are allowed as interval terms. They are structureless terms which cannot reflect the fact that the intervals in a model are characterized by means of their endpoints. Once we have remedied this limitation, we shall prove a completeness result as regards IQ^{π}-models—for the newly introduced languages—which are induced by a finite total order. But we begin this section with a discussion of the notion of logical consequence.

Logical consequence

Are there any sentences of the form $A_V\varphi$ which are intuitively valid? A prime example seems to be the sentence

$$A_V(\varphi \vee \neg\varphi).$$

But observe that the notion of universal validity as it is commonly used in intensional logic, does not capture this intuition. To see this, recall that this notion is defined by:

$\models A_V\varphi$ if and only if:

for all $\mathbf{M}$ (= $\langle\langle I, «, \sqsubseteq\rangle, °\rangle$) and all assignments g for $\mathbf{M}$ and all $i \in I$: $i \models A_V\varphi$ [g]

But for all $i \in I$: $i \models A_v\varphi$ [g] can only hold—relative to a particular model **M** and an assignment g—in case **M**'s domain is the singleton $\{[\![v]\!]^g\}$. So using this definition of validity, one does not have $\models A_v(\varphi \vee \neg\varphi)$.

There are many ways to achieve $\models A_v(\varphi \vee \neg\varphi)$. The one we opt for is to let $\mathbf{M} \models A_v\varphi$ [g] mean $[\![v]\!]^g \models \varphi$, and to define the notion of validity by:

> $A_v\varphi$ is valid—notation $\models A_v\varphi$—if and only if:
> for all **M** and all assignments g for **M**: $\mathbf{M} \models A_v\varphi$ [g].

That it is possible to define $\mathbf{M} \models A_v\varphi$ as above, is due to the fact that the index of $A_v\varphi$ can be taken to provide an interval of evaluation. No such possibility exists for propositional variables and sentences of the form $O\varphi$ where $O \in \{P, F, \uparrow, \downarrow\}$. In regard to models—as opposed to intervals—we shall, therefore, restrict ourselves to the class of contextual formulas:

CONTEXTUAL FORMULAS. The set CF of contextual formulas is the smallest class which contains all IQ^π formulas of the form $A_v\varphi$ and which is closed under:

- if φ is in CF, so is $\neg\varphi$;
- if φ and ψ are in CF, then so is $\varphi\wedge\psi$.[20]

Truth with respect to a model for CF formulas of the form $\neg\varphi$ and $\varphi\wedge\psi$ is defined in the familiar manner. We now define:

LOGICAL CONSEQUENCE. Let $\Gamma \cup \{\varphi\}$ be a class of *contextual formulas*.

> $\Gamma \models \varphi$ iff for all IQ^π-models **M** and all assignments g for **M**:
> $\mathbf{M} \models \psi$ [g] for all $\psi \in \Gamma \Rightarrow \mathbf{M} \models \varphi$ [g].

With respect to this consequence relation $A_v(\varphi \vee \neg\varphi)$ is indeed universally valid, since for all **M** and all assignments g $[\![v]\!]^g \models (\varphi \vee \neg\varphi)$ holds.

---

20 The restriction to contextual formulas is reminiscent of Fitting's use of prefixes (See Fitting (1983: Chapter 8).

Using the above consequence relation seems to be a move towards a first-order interval logic, as will also be plain from the techniques used below to prove completeness. In this connection we note that redefining $\mathbf{M} \models A_v\varphi$ [g] to mean $[\![v]\!]^g \models \varphi$, introduces the meta notion $[\![v]\!]^g \models \varphi$ into the object language. This enables us to state the truth conditions of IQ^π sentences as regards a finite model within the object language, a fact on which the completeness result proved is based.

We leave it for subsequent study to determine whether IQ^π is a notational variant of a first-order interval logic. We conjecture that it is not.[21]

Structured interval terms

In Chapter 7 one finds procedures like:

past(X, A) :- Y « X, at(Y, A).

In this procedure the variables X and Y range over interval terms of the form $[t_1, t_2]$, but these interval terms were not allowed in the original definition of IQ. At first it may seem that allowing structured interval terms is but a minor move. In the following subsections we shall suggest that this is not so.

Let *con* = $\{c_1,\ldots,c_k\}$ be a particular finite set of point constants. We define:

INTERVAL TERMS. If c and c' are point constants, then [c, c'] is an interval term.

This syntactic definition requires a restriction on the interpretation of interval terms. As in Section 1 interval models are induced by point models. And if in a particular point model the point constants c and c' get the interpretations c* and c'*, the interpretation of the the interval term [c, c'] is defined by:

---

21 Compare Van Benthem (1983: 133). For an approach within the tense logical tradition, see Blackburn (1989).

$[c, c']^\circ = [c^*, c'^*]$.

So in a point model where one has $c'^* < c^*$, the interpretation of the term $[c, c']$ does not denote an interval. We eliminate this inconvenience by introducing the empty set within our interval domain together with the stipulation this set is the denotation of all interval terms $[c, c']$ with $c'^* < c^*$.

Gathering together all changes we arrive at the following definition of an IQ^π-model:

IQ^π-MODELS. Let $\mathbf{T} = \langle T, <, * \rangle$ be a model for a propositional language over the linearly ordered time structure $\langle T, < \rangle$ with $p^* \subseteq T$ for all propositional variables and $c^* \in T$ for all $c \in$ *con*. An IQ^π-model $\mathbf{M}$ is a pair $\langle I_T, ^\circ \rangle$ with

(i) $I_T = \langle I, \ll, \sqsubseteq \rangle$ an interval structure, such that:
- I the set of all convex intervals over $\langle T, < \rangle$;
- $\emptyset \in I$;
- $[n,m] \ll [k,l] \quad \Leftrightarrow \quad m < k$;
- $[n,m] \sqsubseteq [k,l] \quad \Leftrightarrow \quad k \leq n$ and $m \leq l$.

(ii) $^\circ$ an interpretation function such that
- for all interval terms:
  $[c, c']^\circ = [c^*, c'^*]$ if $c^* \leq c'^*$, $[c, c']^\circ = \emptyset$ otherwise, and
- $p^\circ = \{i \in I \mid \forall t \in i: t \in p^*\}$ for all propositional variables.

The definition of satisfaction is as before except for the addition of the clause:

not: $\emptyset \models \varphi$ for all formulas φ.

Towards a deduction system

We shall now identify relations among interval terms which correspond with the relations pertaining among intervals themselves. We will then be able to show that the language used is powerfull enough to correctly state the satisfaction conditions of formulas with respect to a particular finite structure. Completeness will be immediate with the help of Henkin's method.

The solution given below is based on the fact that each partition of the constants induces an interpretation in a point model and conversely that each interpretation * of the constants in a point model invokes a partition of the constants. It also holds that there are only finitely many different partitions and that the equivalence classes of these partitions can be linearly ordered. We shall show that for each partition we can find a sentence which 'encodes' all the crucial information. Relativizing the axioms to such sentences will then enable us to precisely mirror the satisfaction definition within the axiom set.

Partitions

Since partitions figure prominently in our solution, we introduce a syntactic device with which they can be conveniently described.

Let $C_1 = \{c_1,\ldots,c_n\}$ be a subset of *con* $= \{c_1,\ldots,c_k\}$, the set of point constants fixed previously. To state that all constants of C_1 receive the same interpretation one can do so by means of the sentence $A_{c_1}A_{c_2}\ldots A_{c_n}T$. But note that this sentence is far from unique: all possible orders on the A-operators yield equivalent sentences. These syntactical peculiarities complicate the proofs, so we shall dispose of them by introducing a new kind of operator:

(Syntax) If φ is a formula and $t = \{t_1,\ldots,t_n\}$ is a set of interval terms, then $A_t\varphi$ is a formula.

(Semantics) For all assignments g:

$$i \models A_t\varphi\,[g] \Leftrightarrow i \models \varphi\,[g] \text{ and } \forall t_i \in t\colon i = [\![t_i]\!]$$

With the help of this 'generalized' A_v-operator we can define indexed tense operators as in §1; for instance $F_t\varphi := A_tF\varphi$. Checking the satisfaction definition shows that the sentence $F_{con}\varphi$—with *con* $= \{c_1,\ldots,c_k\}$—is equivalent to, among others, $A_{c_1}A_{c_2}\ldots A_{c_k}F\varphi$. This clearly indicates that with each sentence in the new language we can associate a sentence in the 'old' language which has the same meaning, and *vice versa*.

Using this syntactic device one can find sentences which describe finite partitions and the possible linear orders on their equivalence classes. To show this, we have to develop some theory.

FROM PARTITIONS ON CONSTANTS TO POINT MODELS

The set *con* gives rise to a finite number of partitions which we denote by bold **p**'s. All **p**'s induce an equivalence relation $\sim_p$, and we refer to each equivalence class $\{c' \mid c \sim_p c'\}$ in **p**—which has c as its witness—by **c**. *con* is finite, so all **p**'s of *con* are finite, and each **p** allows $|\mathbf{p}|!$ possible linear orders on **p**. We have:

PROPOSITION 1. For all **p** and all linear orders $<_p$ on **p** and all sets T of cardinality at least $|\mathbf{p}|$ there is a model $\mathbf{T_p} = \langle T, <, * \rangle$ that preserves the relations $\sim_p$ and $<_p$ in the following way:

(i) $c_1 \sim_p c_2 \Leftrightarrow c_1^* = c_2^*$

(ii) $\mathbf{c}_1 <_p \mathbf{c}_2 \Leftrightarrow c_1^* < c_2^*$

PROOF. Let **p** be $\{\mathbf{c}_0,\ldots,\mathbf{c}_{n-1}\}$. Without loss of generality we may assume that the linear order $<_p$ on **p** is $\mathbf{c}_0 <\ldots< \mathbf{c}_{n-1}$. Let T be a set of cardinality at least $|\mathbf{p}| = n$. So we can choose n distinct elements $t_0,\ldots,t_{n-1}$ from T. Define for all $c \in \mathbf{c}_i$ $(i < n)$: $c^* = t_i$. Also define < to be such that $t_0 <\ldots< t_{n-1}$ and extend < arbitrarily to a linear order which covers all the elements of T. Now (i) and (ii) are true by construction. □

This fact can be captured within the language in the folowing way. Let **p** be $\{\mathbf{c}_0,\ldots,\mathbf{c}_{n-1}\}$, and let the linear order $<_p$ on **p** be $\mathbf{c}_0 <\ldots< \mathbf{c}_{n-1}$. With **p** and $<_p$ we associate the sentence

$$\Lambda_{\mathbf{p},<} :=_{\text{def}} A_{\mathbf{c}_0}T \qquad \text{if } |\mathbf{p}| = 1,$$
$$\Lambda_{\mathbf{p},<} :=_{\text{def}} F_{\mathbf{c}_0}F_{\mathbf{c}_1}\ldots F_{\mathbf{c}_{n-1}}T \qquad \text{otherwise.}$$

$\Lambda_{\mathbf{p},<}$ has the following property:

PROPOSITION 2. $\mathbf{T} = \langle T, <, ° \rangle \models \Lambda_{\mathbf{p},<}$ if and only if $\mathbf{T}$ is a model $\mathbf{T_p}$ as defined in Proposition 1.

PROOF. [$\Rightarrow$:] We only consider the case where $|\mathbf{p}| > 1$. Note that $\mathbf{T}$ must contain at least $|\mathbf{p}| = n$ elements, otherwise $F_{\mathbf{c}_0}F_{\mathbf{c}_1}\ldots F_{\mathbf{c}_{n-1}}T$ could not be true. It is immediate from the truth conditions of $F_{\mathbf{c}_0}F_{\mathbf{c}_1}\ldots F_{\mathbf{c}_{n-1}}T$ that $\mathbf{c}_0<\ldots<\mathbf{c}_{n-1}$. We also have that $\sim_p$ is preserved in T. That $c_1 \sim_p c_2 \Rightarrow c_1^* = c_2^*$ is plain. And if $c_1^* = c_2^*$ then c_1 and c_2 cannot be members of different indices in $F_{\mathbf{c}_0}F_{\mathbf{c}_1}\ldots F_{\mathbf{c}_{n-1}}T$. Hence $c_1 \sim_p c_2$ by definition. We conclude that $\mathbf{T}$ must be a $\mathbf{T_p}$.

[$\Leftarrow$:] It is immediate that for each $\mathbf{T_p}$ we have $\mathbf{T_p} \models \Lambda_{\mathbf{p},<}$. □

COROLLARY. All models of $\Lambda_{\mathbf{p},<}$ are the same except for the 'unnamed' elements in their domains. □

FROM POINT MODELS TO PARTITIONS ON CONSTANTS

Conversely each model $\mathbf{T} = \langle T, <, * \rangle$ induces an equivalence relation among the constants defined by:

$$c \sim c' \Leftrightarrow_{def} c^* = c'^*.$$

Let $\mathbf{p}$ be the partition given by $\sim$, i.e. the elements of $\mathbf{p}$ are of the form $\mathbf{c} = \{c' \mid c \sim c'\}$. The linear order on $\mathbf{p}$ is now defined by:

$$\mathbf{c}_1 < \mathbf{c}_2 \Leftrightarrow c_1^* < c_2^*.$$

It is immediate that this definition is independent of representatives, i.e. that

$$\text{if } c_1 \sim c_1', c_2 \sim c_2' \text{ and } \mathbf{c}_1 < \mathbf{c}_2, \text{ then } \mathbf{c}_1' < \mathbf{c}_2'.$$

Using Proposition 2, we see that $\mathbf{T}$ is a $\mathbf{T_p}$ and hence that $\mathbf{T} \models \Lambda_{\mathbf{p},<}$. In fact we have something stronger:

PROPOSITION 3. Each model satisfies exactly one $\Lambda_{\mathbf{p},<}$.

PROOF. Let $\mathbf{T} = \langle T, <, *\rangle$ be a model for the different $\Lambda_{\mathbf{p},<}$ and $\Lambda_{\mathbf{p}',<'}$. Propositions 1 and 2 give that $\mathbf{T}$ preserves the relations $\sim_p$ and $<$ as well as the relations $\sim_{p'}$ and $<'$. But $\mathbf{T}$ induces a unique partition on the constants and a unique linear order among its equivalence classes, so $\sim_p$ is identical with $\sim_{p'}$ and $<$ is identical with $<'$. But this contradicts the assumption that $\Lambda_{\mathbf{p},<}$ and $\Lambda_{\mathbf{p}',<'}$ are different. □

Summarizing we have that *con* allows finitely many partitions and that for each partition there are finitely many linear orders. As a consequence there are finitely many different sentences of the form $\Lambda_{\mathbf{p},<}$; one for each particular **p** and linear order $<_p$. We have shown that each $\Lambda_{\mathbf{p},<}$ has a model, and that all these models are unique modulo the 'unnamed' elements in the domain. Conversely we proved that each model satisfies exactly one $\Lambda_{\mathbf{p},<}$.

The deduction system FS_n

Now we shall show how to describe the relations among intervals relative to a sentence $\lambda \equiv \Lambda_{\mathbf{p},<}$.

Syntactic conditions.

- $c_1 =_\lambda c_2$ iff c_1 and c_2 occur in the same index set of an A_t-operator in λ.
- $c_1 <_\lambda c_2$ iff c_1 and c_2 respectively occur in the set indices **c** and **c**', and **c** occurs to the left of **c**' in λ.
- $c_1 \leq_\lambda c_2$ iff $c_1 =_\lambda c_2$ or $c_1 <_\lambda c_2$.
- $\mathrm{INT}_\lambda([c_1,c_2])$ iff $c_1 \leq_\lambda c_2$.
- $[c_1,c_2] \sqsubseteq_\lambda [c_3,c_4]$ iff $\mathrm{INT}_\lambda([c_1,c_2])$ and $\mathrm{INT}_\lambda([c_3,c_4])$ and $c_3 \leq_\lambda c_1$ and $c_2 \leq_\lambda c_4$.
- $[c_1,c_2] \ll_\lambda [c_3,c_4]$ iff $\mathrm{INT}_\lambda([c_1,c_2])$ and $\mathrm{INT}_\lambda([c_3,c_4])$ and $c_2 <_\lambda c_3$
- $c_1 <_\lambda \ldots <_\lambda c_n$ is a gapless sequence iff for all $c_i <_\lambda c_{i+1}$ in this sequence c_{i+1} is the immediate $<_\lambda$-successor of c_i.

In each model **M** of λ the *syntactic* relations defined above coincide with the corresponding *semantic* relations in **M**. For instance, $[c_1,c_2] \sqsubseteq_\lambda [c_3,c_4]$ holds syntactically iff for all IQ^π-models for λ we have: $[c_1^*,c_2^*] \sqsubseteq [c_3^*,c_4^*]$. And *mutatis mutandis* the same for the other relations.

For all interval terms i define $IB_\lambda(i) = \{i' \mid i' \ll_\lambda i\}$. Since the set of constants we use is finite, $IB_\lambda(i)$ is finite too. Similarly we define:

$$IA_\lambda(i) = \{i' \mid i \ll_\lambda i'\}$$
$$ISUB_\lambda(i) = \{i' \mid i' \sqsubseteq_\lambda i\}$$
$$ISUP_\lambda(i) = \{i' \mid i' \sqsupseteq_\lambda i\}$$

Using these definitions, we can have conjunctions and disjunctions like $\wedge_{i' \in IB(i)} A_{i'}\varphi$ and $\vee_{i' \in IB(i)} A_{i'}\varphi$. As regards a finite model these conjunctions and disjunctions respectively model restricted universal and existential quantifiers. So we can introduce these quantifiers as abbreviations.

ABBREVIATIONS. The following are understood to be relative to a given λ, although we suppress λ as an index.
We define:

$$\forall i' \ll_\lambda i\ A_{i'}\varphi := \wedge_{i' \in IB(i)} A_{i'}\varphi$$
$$\exists i' \ll_\lambda i\ A_{i'}\varphi := \vee_{i' \in IB(i)} A_{i'}\varphi$$

And *mutatis mutandis* the same for the other sets. Here $\vee_{i' \in IB(i)}\varphi$ denotes a disjunction, if $IB(i) \neq \emptyset$; $\perp$ (falsum) otherwise. $\wedge_{i' \in IB}(i)\varphi$ denotes a conjunction, if $IB(i) \neq \emptyset$; T (verum) otherwise. Similarly for IA(i), ISUB(I) and ISUP(i).

Above we fixed *con* = $\{c_1,\ldots,c_k\}$ as the set of point constants. Let $n \leq k$ and let $\lambda_1,\ldots,\lambda_r$ enumerate all sentences $\Lambda_{\mathbf{p},<}$ which are associated with a partition **p** of cardinality n. We abbreviate the conjunction $\lambda_1 \wedge \neg\lambda_2 \wedge \ldots \wedge \neg\lambda_r$, stating that only λ_1 is true, by $\lambda_1!$ and similarly for all other lambdas.

The sentence $\lambda_1! \vee \lambda_2! \vee \ldots \vee \lambda_r!$, which is one of the axioms, captures the content of Proposition 3 restricted to models of cardinality n. The full set of axioms is:

AXIOMS OF FS_n. Let $\lambda_1,\ldots,\lambda_r$ be as in the previous paragraph. Where $\lambda \equiv \lambda_j$ $(1 \leq j \leq r)$, we write $[\alpha]_\lambda$ instead of $\lambda \rightarrow \alpha$. From axiom (iii) onwards it is assumed that all subscripts i satisfy $\mathrm{INT}_\lambda(i)$. In A_c c denotes the point interval $[c,c]$.

() All tautologies formed from contextual formulas are axioms.

(i) $\lambda_1! \vee \lambda_2! \vee \ldots \vee \lambda_r!$

(ii) $[\neg A_{[c_m,c_n]}\varphi]_\lambda$ if not $\mathrm{INT}_\lambda([c_m,c_n])$

(iii) For gapless sequences $c_1 <_\lambda \ldots <_\lambda c_n$:
$[(A_{c_1}p \wedge \ldots \wedge A_{c_m}p) \leftrightarrow A_{[c_1,c_m]}p]_\lambda$

(iv) $[A_i\neg\varphi \leftrightarrow \neg A_i\varphi]_\lambda$

(v) $[A_i(\varphi\wedge\psi) \leftrightarrow (A_i\varphi \wedge A_i\psi)]_\lambda$

(vi)^a $[A_iA_i\varphi \leftrightarrow A_i\varphi]_\lambda$

(vi)^b $[\neg A_iA_j\varphi]_\lambda$ if $i \neq_\lambda j$

(vii) $[A_iP\varphi \leftrightarrow \exists i' \ll_\lambda i\ A_{i'}\varphi]_\lambda$

(viii) $[A_iF\varphi \leftrightarrow \exists i' \gg_\lambda i\ A_{i'}\varphi]_\lambda$

(ix) $[A_i\uparrow\varphi \leftrightarrow \exists i' \sqsupseteq_\lambda i\ A_{i'}\varphi]_\lambda$

(x) $[A_i\downarrow\varphi \leftrightarrow \exists i' \sqsubseteq_\lambda i\ A_{i'}\varphi]_\lambda$

DERIVATION RULE. Modus ponens: from φ and $\varphi \rightarrow \psi$ derive ψ.

We want to comment briefly on the treatment of iterated tenses within FS_n. In Chapter 6 it is shown that not all sequences of IQ tense operators lead to satisfiable formulas; $A_iA_j\varphi$ with $i \neq_\lambda j$, for example, is not. In principle a phenomenon like this can be handled in two ways. One could place syntactical restrictions on the set of formulas to be considered, e.g. by invoking the G-operator to eliminate all the problematic cases. This, however, has a somewhat *ad hoc* flavour about it. Is there an independent justification for admitting the selected formulas and not the others? On the other hand, one could view a formula $A_iA_j\varphi$ ($i \neq_\lambda j$) as being a 'referential contradiction'. It is impossible for the finger in Figure 1 to point to both points at the same time.

Figure 1

In a similar vein it is impossible for a sentence to simultaneously refer to two times of utterance by means of an iteration of A-operators. But being contradictory, we only have to make sure that sentences like $A_iA_j\varphi$ ($i \neq_\lambda j$) are not provable within FS_n. And this is how we treat them. (Compare Theorem (iii) below.)

Although we do not need them for the completeness proof, we want to give an impression of the kinds of theorem provable within FS_n. We shall show that the sentences stating the truth-conditions of indexed operators are provable within the system. The proofs for the non-indexed operators are even simpler.

Some theorems

Let $\lambda \equiv \lambda_i$ $(1 \leq i \leq r)$

(i) $[A_i\Downarrow_i\varphi \leftrightarrow \forall i' \sqsubseteq_\lambda i\ A_{i'}\varphi]_\lambda$

(ii)[22] $[\neg A_i\Downarrow_j\varphi]_\lambda$ if $i \neq_\lambda j$

(iii)[23] $[\neg A_iP_kP_k\varphi]_\lambda$

PROOF OF (i). Assume λ. Then:

$A_i\Downarrow_i\varphi$	$\leftrightarrow A_iA_i\Downarrow\varphi$	(definition of $\Downarrow_i$)
	$\leftrightarrow A_i\Downarrow\varphi$	(axiom (vi)^a)
	$\leftrightarrow A_i\neg\downarrow\neg\varphi$	(definition of $\Downarrow$)
	$\leftrightarrow \neg A_i\downarrow\neg\varphi$	(axiom (iv))

22 Similar theorems hold for the remaining indexed and unindexed operators.

23 Similarly for other inconsistent strings of operator, including those having a nested occurrence in a formula.

$\leftrightarrow \neg\exists i' \sqsubseteq_\lambda i\ A_{i'}\neg\varphi$ (axiom (x))

$\leftrightarrow \forall i' \sqsubseteq_\lambda i\ A_{i'}\varphi$ (propositional logic, axiom (iv))

Hence $[A_i \Downarrow_i \varphi \leftrightarrow \forall i' \sqsubseteq_\lambda i\ A_{i'}\varphi]_\lambda$.

PROOF OF (ii). Assume λ. Then we have $A_i \Downarrow_j \varphi \leftrightarrow A_i A_j \Downarrow \varphi$ as above. But since $i \neq_\lambda j$ axiom (vi)[b] gives $\neg A_i A_j \Downarrow \varphi$. So $\neg A_i \Downarrow_j \varphi$ and hence $[\neg A_i \Downarrow_j \varphi]_\lambda$.

PROOF OF (iii). Assume λ. If $i \neq_\lambda k$, then the theorem $\neg A_i P_k \psi$—proved as theorem (ii)—gives $\neg A_i P_k P_k \varphi$. If $i =_\lambda k$ then we discern two cases. Firstly: $IB_\lambda(i) = IB_\lambda(k) = \emptyset$. According to our convention in this case $\exists i' \ll_\lambda k\ A_{i'} P_k \varphi \equiv \bot$. Using axiom (vii) we get $\neg A_i P_k P_k \varphi$. If $IB_\lambda(i) = IB_\lambda(k) \neq \emptyset$, then reason as follows. First observe that for all $i' \in IB_\lambda(k)$ $i' \neq_\lambda k$. Given this, it can be proved that $A_{i'} \neg P_k \varphi$ and $\neg\exists i' \ll k\ A_{i'} P_k \varphi$. Axiom (vii) gives $\neg A_i P_k P_k \varphi$ as required. □

Soundness and completeness

Now we are in a position to prove the lemmas needed for the completeness theorem pursued.

LINDENBAUM'S LEMMA. Every FS_n-consistent set Γ of contextual sentences is contained in a maximal FS_n-consistent set Δ of contextual sentences.

PROOF. As usual. □

CONSISTENCY LEMMA. Every maximal FS_n-consistent set of contextual sentences has an IQ^π-model over a total order of cardinality n.

PROOF. Let Γ be such a set. Due to maximality and the axiom $\lambda_1! \vee \lambda_2! \vee \ldots \vee \lambda_r!$ Γ contains exactly one $\lambda_i \equiv \Lambda_{\mathbf{p},<}$ $(1 \leq i \leq r)$. We only consider the case where $|\mathbf{p}| > 1$, the other case is similar. In this case $\Lambda_{\mathbf{p},<}$ is of the form $F_{c_0}F_{c_1}\ldots F_{c_{n-1}}T$. The total order on which we base the IQ^π-model is therefore $\mathbf{D} := \langle\{c_0,\ldots,c_{n-1}\}, <\rangle$ with $c_i < c_j$ iff $i < j$. The 'point' model over $\mathbf{D}$ is defined to be $\langle \mathbf{D}, * \rangle$ with $*$ an interpretation function such that:

$c^* := \mathbf{c}_i$ for all $c \in \mathbf{c}_i$ [24]
$p^* := \{\mathbf{c} \in \mathbf{D} \mid A_{[c,c]}p \in \Gamma\}$.

$\langle \mathbf{D},^* \rangle$ induces an IQ^π-model $\mathbf{M} = \langle I_D, «, \sqsubseteq, ^\circ \rangle$ as defined at the beginning of this section and we have to check that **M** coincides with Γ in the familiar way. First we prove

(*) $A_i\varphi \in \Gamma \Leftrightarrow i^\circ \models \varphi$.

We have to discern the cases $\text{INT}_\lambda(i)$ and not $\text{INT}_\lambda(i)$. If not $\text{INT}_\lambda(i)$ then, using axiom (ii) and the consistency of Γ, $A_i\varphi \notin \Gamma$. But since in this case $i^\circ = \emptyset$ we also have $i^\circ \not\models \varphi$. If $\text{INT}_\lambda(i)$, we use induction on the complexity of φ. A sample case is:

(φ is a propositional variable)

$i^\circ \models p$
$\Leftrightarrow$ $i^\circ \in p^\circ$
$\Leftrightarrow$ $\forall k \in i^\circ: k \in p^*$
$\Leftrightarrow$ $\forall k \in i: A_{[k,k]}p \in \Gamma$ by definition
$\Leftrightarrow$ $A_ip \in \Gamma$ axiom (iii), i° is finite

The other cases follow easily from the induction hypothesis. Finally we prove:

$\mathbf{M} \models \varphi \Leftrightarrow \varphi \in \Gamma$

Using (*) this is immediate, for Γ is a maximal consistent set of contextual sentences and hence closed under composition and decomposition of Boolean combinations. □

SOUNDNESS AND COMPLETENESS. The system FS_n is sound and complete as regards IQ^π-models over total orders of cardinality n.

---

24 Remember that the operators used have a *set* of point constants as their index.

PROOF OF SOUNDNESS. An easy but cumbersome check shows that all axioms are sound with respect to models of cardinality n.

PROOF OF COMPLETENESS. If $\Gamma \nvdash \varphi$, then $\Gamma \cup \{\neg\varphi\}$ is FS_n-consistent. Lindenbaum: $\Gamma \cup \{\neg\varphi\}$ is contained in a maximal FS_n-consistent set, say Δ. Consistency lemma: Δ has an IQ^π-model **M** over a total order of cardinality n. Clearly $\mathbf{M} \models \psi$, for all $\psi \in \Gamma$ and $\mathbf{M} \models \neg\varphi$. So $\Gamma \nvDash \varphi$. □

References

Allen, J. F. and Hayes, P. J. (1985) A Common-sense Theory of Time. In *Proceedings of the Ninth International Joint Conference on Artificial Intelligence*, University of California at Los Angeles, Los Angeles, Ca., August 18–23, 1985, pp528–531.

Allen, J. F. and Hayes, P. J. (1987) Moments and Points in an Interval-Based Temporal Logic. Technical Report No. 180, Departments of Computer Science and Philosophy, University of Rochester, Rochester.

Benthem, J. van (1983) *The Logic of Time*. Dordrecht: D. Reidel.

Benthem, J. van (1984) Partiality and Nonmonotonicity in Classical Logic. Report No. CSLI–84–12, Center for the Study of Language and Information, Stanford.

Blackburn, P. (1989) Reasoning in and about Time. PhD Thesis, Centre for Cognitive Science, University of Edinburgh.

Blamey, S. (1986) Partial Logic. Chapter 1 in Gabbay, D. and Guenthner, F. (eds.) *Handbook of Philosophical Logic*, Volume 3, pp1–70. Dordrecht: D. Reidel.

Clocksin, W. F. and Mellish, C. S. (1981) *Programming in PROLOG*. Berlin: Springer-Verlag.

Costa, R. (1972) Sequence of Tenses in That-Clauses. In Peranteau, P. M., Levi, J. N. and Phares, G. C. (eds.) *Papers from the Eighth Regional Meeting of the Chicago Linguistics Society*, Chicago, April 14–16, 1972, pp41–51.

Cresswell, M. J. (1977) Interval Semantics and Logical Words. In Rohrer, C. (ed.) *On the Logical Analysis of Tense and Aspect*, pp7–29. Tubingen: Gunter Narr Verlag.

Davidson, D. (1968) On Saying That. *Synthese*, **19**, 130–146. Reprinted in Davidson, D. *Inquiries into Truth and Interpretation*, pp93–108. Oxford: Clarendon, 1984.

Dowty, D. (1981) *Word Meaning and Montague Grammar*. Dordrecht: D. Reidel.

Dowty, D. R., Wall, R. E. and Peters, S. (1981) *Introduction to Montague Semantics*. Dordrecht: D. Reidel.

Dry, H. (1979) Four Temporal Effects of Narrative 'Now'. *Texas Linguistic Forum*, **15**, 60–69.

Enç, M. (1986) Towards a Referential Analysis of Temporal Expressions. *Linguistics and Philosophy*, **9**, 405–427.

Feferman, S. (1984) Towards Useful Type-Free Theories I. In Martin, R. L. (ed.) *Truth and the Liar Paradox*, pp237–287. Oxford: Oxford University Press.

Fitting, M. (1985) A Kripke-Kleene Semantics for Logic Programs. *Journal of Logic Programming*, **4**, 295–312.

Fitting, M. (1987) *Computability Theory, Semantics and Logic Programming*. New York: Oxford University Press.

Gabbay, D. (1987) Executable Temporal Logic for Interactive Systems. 2nd draft, xerox, Imperial College, London.

Heny, F. (1982) Tense, Aspect and Time Adverbials II. *Linguistics and Philosophy*, **5**, 109–154.

Humberstone, I. L. (1979) Interval Semantics for Tense Logic: Some Remarks. *Journal of Philosophical Logic*, **8**, 172-196.

Kamp, J. A. W. (1971) Formal properties of 'Now'. *Theoria*, **37**, 227–273.

Kamp, H. and Rohrer, C. (1983) Tense in Texts. In Bauerle, R., Schwarze, C. and von Stechow, A. (eds.) *Meaning, Use and Interpretation of Language*, pp250–269. Berlin: de Gruyter.

Kaplan, D. (1977) Demonstratives: An Essay on the Semantics, Logic, Metaphysics and Epistemology of Demonstratives and Other Indexicals. Draft No2, UCLA xerox.

Kaplan, D. (1979) On the Logic of Demonstratives. In French, P. A., Uehling, Jr., T. E. and Wettstein, H. K. (eds.) *Contemporary Perspectives in the Philosophy of Language*, pp401–412. Minneapolis: University of Minnesota Press.

Kleene, S. C. (1952) *Introduction to Metamathematics*. New York: North Holland.

Kowalski, R. and Sergot, M. (1986) A Logic-based Calculus of Events. *New Generation Computing*, **4**, 67–95.

Kowalski, R. (1986) Database Updates in the Event Calculus. Technical Report No. DOC 86/12, Department of Computing, Imperial College, London.

Kripke, S. (1975) Outline of a Theory of Truth. *Journal of Philosophy*, **72**, 690–716.

Lascarides, A. (1988) A Formal Semantic Analysis of the Progressive. PhD Thesis, Centre for Cognitive Science, University of Edinburgh.

Lewis, D. (1975) Adverbs of Quantification. In Keenan, E. L. (ed.) *Formal Semantics of Natural Language: Papers from a colloquium sponsored by King's College Research Centre, Cambridge*, pp3–15. Cambridge: Cambridge University Press.

Lloyd, J.W. (1984) *Foundations of Logic Programming* Berlin: Springer Verlag.

Moens, M. and Steedman, M. (1988) Temporal Ontology and Temporal Reference. *Journal of Computational Linguistics*, **14**.

Montague, R. (1963) Syntactical Treatments of Modality, with Corollaries on Reflexion Principles and Finite Axiomatizability. *Acta Philosophica Fennica*, **16**, 153–167.

Montague, R. (1968) Pragmatics. In Klibansky, R. (ed.) *Contemporary Philosophy: A Survey*, pp102–122. Florence: La Nuova Italia Editrice. Reprinted in R. H. Thomason (ed.) 1974, pp95–118.

Oberlander, J. (1987) The Semantics of Temporal Indexicals. PhD Thesis, Centre for Cognitive Science, University of Edinburgh.

Prior, A. N. (1967) *Past, Present and Future*. Oxford: Clarendon Press.

Reichenbach, H. (1947) *Elements of Symbolic Logic*. London: Macmillan.

Richards, B. (1982) Tense, Aspect and Time Adverbials I. *Linguistics and Philosophy*, **5**, 59–107.

Richards, B. (1986) Tenses, Temporal Quantifiers and Semantic Innocence. In Lepore, E. (ed.) *The Philosophy of Donald Davidson: A Perspective on Inquiries into Truth and Interpretation*. Oxford: Basil Blackwell.

Russell, B. (1903) *The Principles of Mathematics*, 2nd edition, 1937. London: George Allen and Unwin.

Smullyan, R. M. (1968) *First-Order Logic*. Berlin: Springer-Verlag.

Steedman, M. J. (1982) Reference to Past Time. In Jarvella, R. and Klein, W. (eds.) *Speech, Place and Action*, pp125–157. New York: John Wiley and Sons.

Sterling, L. and Shapiro E. (1986) *The Art of PROLOG* Massachusetts: MIT Press.

Taylor, B. (1977) Tense and Continuity. *Linguistics and Philosophy*, **1**, 199–220.

Thomason, R. H. (ed.) (1974) *Formal Philosophy: Selected Papers of Richard Montague*. New Haven, Conn.: Yale University Press.

Tichy, P. (1980) The Logic of Temporal Discourse. *Linguistics and Philosophy*, **3**, 343–369.

Tichy, P. (1985) Do we need Interval Semantics? *Linguistics and Philosophy*, **8**, 263–282.

Vendler, Z. (1967) Verbs and Times. Chapter 4 in *Linguistics in Philosophy*, pp97–121. Ithaca, N.Y.: Cornell University Press.

Subject Index

Author Index